MGB Electrical Systems

YOUR colour-illustrated guide to understanding, repairing & improving the MGB's electrical systems & components
Now covers all models, including MGB, MGC and MGB-V8

Publisher's acknowledgement
We are indebted to Justin Banks who kindly supplied the MGB pictures for the cover of this book. Justin often has MGBs for sale at
www.justinbanks.com

Other great books from Veloce –

Speedpro Series
4-Cylinder Engine Short Block High-Performance Manual – New Updated & Revised Edition (Hammill)
Alfa Romeo DOHC High-performance Manual (Kartalamakis)
Alfa Romeo V6 Engine High-performance Manual (Kartalamakis)
BMC 998cc A-series Engine, How to Power Tune (Hammill)
1275cc A-series High-performance Manual (Hammill)
Camshafts – How to Choose & Time Them For Maximum Power (Hammill)
Competition Car Datalogging Manual, The (Templeman)
Cylinder Heads, How to Build, Modify & Power Tune – Updated & Revised Edition (Burgess & Gollan)
Distributor-type Ignition Systems, How to Build & Power Tune – New 3rd Edition (Hammill)
Fast Road Car, How to Plan and Build – Revised & Updated Colour New Edition (Stapleton)
Ford SOHC 'Pinto' & Sierra Cosworth DOHC Engines, How to Power Tune – Updated & Enlarged Edition (Hammill)
Ford V8, How to Power Tune Small Block Engines (Hammill)
Harley-Davidson Evolution Engines, How to Build & Power Tune (Hammill)
Holley Carburetors, How to Build & Power Tune – Revised & Updated Edition (Hammill)
Honda Civic Type R High-Performance Manual, The (Cowland & Clifford)
Jaguar XK Engines, How to Power Tune – Revised & Updated Colour Edition (Hammill)
Land Rover Discovery, Defender & Range Rover – How to Modify Coil Sprung Models for High Performance & Off-Road Action (Hosier)
MG Midget & Austin-Healey Sprite, How to Power Tune – New 3rd Edition (Stapleton)
MGB 4-cylinder Engine, How to Power Tune (Burgess)
MGB V8 Power, How to Give Your – Third Colour Edition (Williams)
MGB, MGC & MGB V8, How to Improve – New 2nd Edition (Williams)
Mini Engines, How to Power Tune On a Small Budget – Colour Edition (Hammill)
Motorcycle-engined Racing Car, How to Build (Pashley)
Motorsport, Getting Started in (Collins)
Nissan GT-R High-performance Manual, The (Gorodji)
Nitrous Oxide High-performance Manual, The (Langfield)
Race & Trackday Driving Techniques (Hornsey)
Retro or classic car for high performance, How to modify your (Stapleton)
Rover V8 Engines, How to Power Tune (Hammill)
Secrets of Speed – Today's techniques for 4-stroke engine blueprinting & tuning (Swager)
Sportscar & Kitcar Suspension & Brakes, How to Build & Modify – Revised 3rd Edition (Hammill)
SU Carburettor High-performance Manual (Hammill)
Successful Low-Cost Rally Car, How to Build a (Young)
Suzuki 4x4, How to Modify For Serious Off-road Action (Richardson)
Tiger Avon Sportscar, How to Build Your Own – Updated & Revised 2nd Edition (Dudley)
TR2, 3 & TR4, How to Improve (Williams)
TR5, 250 & TR6, How to Improve (Williams)
TR7 & TR8, How to Improve (Williams)
V8 Engine, How to Build a Short Block For High Performance (Hammill)
Volkswagen Beetle Suspension, Brakes & Chassis, How to Modify For High Performance (Hale)
Volkswagen Bus Suspension, Brakes & Chassis for High Performance, How to Modify – Updated & Enlarged New Edition (Hale)
Weber DCOE, & Dellorto DHLA Carburetors, How to Build & Power Tune – 3rd Edition (Hammill)

RAC handbooks
Caring for your car – How to maintain & service your car (Fry)
Caring for your car's bodywork and interior (Nixon)
Caring for your bicycle – How to maintain & repair your bicycle (Henshaw)
Caring for your scooter – How to maintain & service your 49cc to 125cc twist & go scooter (Fry)
Efficient Driver's Handbook, The (Moss)
Electric Cars – The Future is Now! (Linde)
First aid for your car – Your expert guide to common problems & how to fix them (Collins)
How your car works (Linde)
How your motorcycle works – Your guide to the components & systems of modern motorcycles (Henshaw)
Motorcycles – A first-time-buyer's guide (Henshaw)
Motorhomes – A first-time-buyer's guide (Fry)
Pass the MoT test! – How to check & prepare your car for the annual MoT test (Paxton)
Selling your car – How to make your car look great and how to sell it fast (Knight)
Simple fixes for your car – How to do small jobs for yourself and save money (Collins)

Enthusiast's Restoration Manual Series
Beginner's Guide to Classic Motorcycle Restoration YOUR step-by-step guide to setting up a workshop, choosing a project, dismantling, sourcing parts, renovating & rebuilding classic motorcycles from the 1970s & 1980s, The (Burns)
Citroën 2CV, How to Restore (Porter)
Classic Large Frame Vespa Scooters, How to Restore (Paxton)
Classic Car Bodywork, How to Restore (Thaddeus)
Classic British Car Electrical Systems (Astley)
Classic Car Electrics (Thaddeus)
Classic Cars, How to Paint (Thaddeus)
Ducati Bevel Twins 1971 to 1986 (Falloon)
How to restore Honda CX500 & CX650 – YOUR step-by-step colour illustrated guide to complete restoration (Burns)
How to restore Honda Fours – YOUR step-by-step colour illustrated guide to complete restoration (Burns)
Jaguar E-type (Crespin)
Reliant Regal, How to Restore (Payne)
Triumph TR2, 3, 3A, 4 & 4A, How to Restore (Williams)
Triumph TR5/250 & 6, How to Restore (Williams)
Triumph TR7/8, How to Restore (Williams)
Triumph Trident T150/T160 & BSA Rocket III, How to Restore (Rooke)
Ultimate Mini Restoration Manual, The (Ayre & Webber)
Volkswagen Beetle, How to Restore (Tyler)
VW Bay Window Bus (Paxton)
Yamaha FS1-E, How to Restore (Watts)

Expert Guides
Land Rover Series I-III – Your expert guide to common problems & how to fix them (Thurman)
MG Midget & A-H Sprite – Your expert guide to common problems & how to fix them (Horler)

Essential Buyer's Guide Series
Triumph Herald & Vitesse (Davies)
Triumph Spitfire & GT6 (Baugues)
Triumph Stag (Mort)
Triumph Thunderbird, Trophy & Tiger (Henshaw)
Triumph TR6 (Williams)
Triumph TR7 & TR8 (Williams)

Great Cars
Austin-Healey – A celebration of the fabulous 'Big' Healey (Piggott)
Triumph TR - TR2 to 6: The last of the traditional sports cars (Piggott)

General
11/2-litre GP Racing 1961-1965 (Whitelock)
AC Two-litre Saloons & Buckland Sportscars (Archibald)
Alfa Romeo 155/156/147 Competition Touring Cars (Collins)
Alfa Romeo Giulia Coupé GT & GTA (Tipler)
Alfa Romeo Montreal – The dream car that came true (Taylor)
Alfa Romeo Montreal – The Essential Companion (Classic Reprint of 500 copies) (Taylor)
Alfa Tipo 33 (McDonough & Collins)
Alpine & Renault – The Development of the Revolutionary Turbo F1 Car 1968 to 1979 (Smith)
Alpine & Renault – The Sports Prototypes 1963 to 1969 (Smith)
Alpine & Renault – The Sports Prototypes 1973 to 1978 (Smith)
Anatomy of the Classic Mini (Huthert & Ely)
Anatomy of the Works Minis (Moylan)
Armstrong-Siddeley (Smith)
Art Deco and British Car Design (Down)
Autodrome (Collins & Ireland)
Autodrome 2 (Collins & Ireland)
Automotive A-Z, Lane's Dictionary of Automotive Terms (Lane)
Automotive Mascots (Kay & Springate)
Bahamas Speed Weeks, The (O'Neil)
Bentley Continental, Corniche and Azure (Bennett)
Bentley MkVI, Rolls-Royce Silver Wraith, Dawn & Cloud/Bentley R & S-Series (Nutland)
Bluebird CN7 (Stevens)
BMC Competitions Department Secrets (Turner, Chambers & Browning)
BMW 5-Series (Cranswick)
BMW Z-Cars (Taylor)
BMW Boxer Twins 1970-1995 Bible, The (Falloon)
BMW Cafe Racers (Cloesen)
BMW Custom Motorcycles – Choppers, Cruisers, Bobbers, Trikes & Quads (Cloesen)
BMW – The Power of M (Vivian)
Bonjour – Is this Italy? (Turner)
British 250cc Racing Motorcycles (Pereira)
British at Indianapolis, The (Wagstaff)
British Café Racers (Cloesen)
British Cars, The Complete Catalogue of, 1895-1975 (Culshaw & Horrobin)
British Custom Motorcycles – The Brit Chop – choppers, cruisers, bobbers & trikes (Cloesen)
BRM – A Mechanic's Tale (Salmon)
BRM V16 (Ludvigsen)
BSA Bantam Bible, The (Henshaw)
BSA Motorcycles – the final evolution (Jones)
Bugatti Type 40 (Price)
Bugatti 46/50 Updated Edition (Price & Arbey)
Bugatti T44 & T49 (Price & Arbey)
Bugatti 57 2nd Edition (Price)
Bugatti Type 57 Grand Prix – A Celebration (Tomlinson)
Caravan, Improve & Modify Your (Porter)
Caravans, The Illustrated History 1919-1959 (Jenkinson)
Caravans, The Illustrated History From 1960 (Jenkinson)
Carrera Panamericana, La (Tipler)
Chrysler 300 – America's Most Powerful Car 2nd Edition (Ackerson)
Chrysler PT Cruiser (Ackerson)
Citroën DS (Bobbitt)
Classic British Car Electrical Systems (Astley)
Cobra – The Real Thing! (Legate)
Competition Car Aerodynamics 3rd Edition (McBeath)
Competition Car Composites A Practical Handbook (Revised 2nd Edition) (McBeath)
Concept Cars, How to illustrate and design (Dewey)
Cortina – Ford's Bestseller (Robson)
Coventry Climax Racing Engines (Hammill)
Daily Mirror 1970 World Cup Rally 40, The (Robson)
Daimler SP250 New Edition (Long)
Datsun Fairlady Roadster to 280ZX – The Z-Car Story (Long)
Dino – The V6 Ferrari (Long)
Dodge Challenger & Plymouth Barracuda (Grist)
Dodge Charger – Enduring Thunder (Ackerson)
Dodge Dynamite! (Grist)
Dorset from the Sea – The Jurassic Coast from Lyme Regis to Old Harry Rocks photographed from its best viewpoint (Belasco)
Dorset from the Sea – The Jurassic Coast from Lyme Regis to Old Harry Rocks photographed from its best viewpoint (souvenir edition) (Belasco)
Draw & Paint Cars – How to (Gardiner)
Drive on the Wild Side, A – 20 Extreme Driving Adventures From Around the World (Weaver)
Ducati 750 Bible, The (Falloon)
Ducati 750 SS 'round-case' 1974, The Book of the (Falloon)
Ducati 860, 900 and Mille Bible, The (Falloon)
Ducati Monster Bible (New Updated & Revised Edition), The (Falloon)
Ducati 916 (updated edition) (Falloon)
Dune Buggy, Building A – The Essential Manual (Shakespeare)
Dune Buggy Files (Hale)
Dune Buggy Handbook (Hale)
East German Motor Vehicles in Pictures (Suhr/Weinreich)
Fast Ladies – Female Racing Drivers 1888 to 1970 (Bouzanquet)
Fate of the Sleeping Beauties, The (op de Weegh/Hottendorff/op de Weegh)
Ferrari 288 GTO, The Book of the (Sackey)
Ferrari 333 SP (O'Neil)
Fiat & Abarth 124 Spider & Coupé (Tipler)
Fiat & Abarth 500 & 600 – 2nd Edition (Bobbitt)
Fiats, Great Small (Ward)
Fine Art of the Motorcycle Engine, The (Peirce)
Ford Cleveland 335-Series V8 engine 1970 to 1982 – The Essential Source Book (Hammill)
Ford F100/F150 Pick-up 1948-1996 (Ackerson)
Ford F150 Pick-up 1997-2005 (Ackerson)
Ford GT – Then, and Now (Streather)
Ford GT40 (Legate)
Ford Midsize Muscle – Fairlane, Torino & Ranchero (Cranswick)
Ford Model Y (Roberts)
Ford Small Block V8 Racing Engines 1962-1970 – The Essential Source Book (Hammill)
Ford Thunderbird From 1954, The Book of the (Long)
Formula 5000 Motor Racing, Back then ... and back now (Lawson)
Forza Minardi! (Vigar)
France: the essential guide for car enthusiasts – 200 things for the car enthusiast to see and do (Parish)
From Crystal Palace to Red Square – A Hapless Biker's Road to Russia (Turner)
Funky Mopeds (Skelton)
Grand Prix Ferrari – The Years of Enzo Ferrari's Power, 1948-1980 (Pritchard)
Grand Prix Ford – DFV-powered Formula 1 Cars (Robson)
GT – The World's Best GT Cars 1953-73 (Dawson)
Hillclimbing & Sprinting – The Essential Manual (Short & Wilkinson)
Honda NSX (Long)
Inside the Rolls-Royce & Bentley Styling Department – 1971 to 2001 (Hull)
Intermeccanica – The Story of the Prancing Bull (McCredie & Reisner)
Italian Cafe Racers (Cloesen)
Italian Custom Motorcycles (Cloesen)
Jaguar, The Rise of (Price)
Jaguar XJ 220 – The Inside Story (Moreton)
Jaguar XJ-S, The Book of the (Long)
Jeep CJ (Ackerson)
Jeep Wrangler (Ackerson)
The Jowett Jupiter - The car that leaped to fame (Nankivell)
Karmann-Ghia Coupé & Convertible (Bobbitt)
Kawasaki Triples Bible, The (Walker)
Kawasaki Z1 Story, The (Sheehan)
Kris Meeke – Intercontinental Rally Challenge Champion (McBride)
Lamborghini Miura Bible, The (Sackey)
Lamborghini Urraco, The Book of the (Landsem)
Lambretta Bible, The (Davies)
Lancia 037 (Collins)
Lancia Delta HF Integrale (Blaettel & Wagner)
Land Rover Series III Reborn (Porter)
Land Rover, The Half-ton Military (Cook)
Laverda Twins & Triples Bible 1968-1986 (Falloon)
Lea-Francis Story, The (Price)
Le Mans Panoramic (Ireland)
Lexus Story, The (Long)
Little book of microcars, the (Quellin)
Little book of smart, the – New Edition (Jackson)
Little book of trikes, the (Quellin)
Lola – The Illustrated History (1957-1977) (Starkey)
Lola – All the Sports Racing & Single-seater Racing Cars 1978-1997 (Starkey)
Lola T70 – The Racing History & Individual Chassis Record – 4th Edition (Starkey)
Lotus 18 Colin Chapman's U-turn (Whitelock)
Lotus 49 (Oliver)
Marketingmobiles, The Wonderful Wacky World of (Hale)
Maserati 250F In Focus (Pritchard)
Mazda MX-5/Miata 1.6 Enthusiast's Workshop Manual (Grainger & Shoemark)
Mazda MX-5/Miata 1.8 Enthusiast's Workshop Manual (Grainger & Shoemark)
Mazda MX-5 Miata, The book of the – The 'Mk1' NA-series 1988 to 1997 (Long)
Mazda MX-5 Miata Roadster (Long)
Mazda Rotary-engined Cars (Cranshaw)
Maximum Mini (Booij)
Meet the English (Bowie)
Mercedes-Benz SL – R230 series 2001 to 2011 (Long)
Mercedes-Benz SL – W113-series 1963-1971 (Long)
Mercedes-Benz SL & SLC – 107-series 1971-1989 (Long)
Mercedes-Benz SLK – R170 series 1996-2004 (Long)
Mercedes-Benz SLK – R171 series 2004-2011 (Long)
Mercedes-Benz W123-series – All models 1976 to 1986 (Long)
Mercedes G-Wagen (Long)
MGA (Price Williams)
MGB & MGB GT– Expert Guide (Auto-doc Series) (Williams)
MGB Electrical Systems Updated & Revised Edition (Astley)
Micro Caravans (Jenkinson)
Micro Trucks (Mort)
Microcars at Large! (Quellin)
Mini Cooper – The Real Thing! (Tipler)
Mini Minor to Asia Minor (West)
Mitsubishi Lancer Evo, The Road Car & WRC Story (Long)
Montlhéry, The Story of the Paris Autodrome (Boddy)
Morgan Maverick (Lawrence)
Morgan 3 Wheeler – back to the future!, The (Dron)
Morris Minor, 60 Years on the Road (Newell)
Moto Guzzi Sport & Le Mans Bible, The (Falloon)
Motor Movies – The Posters! (Veysey)
Motor Racing – Reflections of a Lost Era (Carter)
Motor Racing – The Pursuit of Victory 1930-1962 (Carter)
Motor Racing – The Pursuit of Victory 1963-1972 (Wyatt/Sears)
Motor Racing Heroes – The Stories of 100 Greats (Newman)
Motorcycle Apprentice (Cakebread)
Motorcycle GP Racing in the 1960s (Pereira)
Motorcycle Road & Racing Chassis Designs (Noakes)
Motorhomes, The Illustrated History (Jenkinson)
Motorsport In colour, 1950s (Wainwright)
MV Agusta Fours, The book of the classic (Falloon)
N.A.R.T. – A concise history of the North American Racing Team 1957 to 1983 (O'Neil)
Nissan 300ZX & 350Z – The Z-Car Story (Long)
Nissan GT-R Supercar: Born to race (Gorodji)
Northeast American Sports Car Races 1950-1959 (O'Neil)
Nothing Runs – Misadventures in the Classic, Collectable & Exotic Car Biz (Slutsky)
Off-Road Giants! (Volume 1) – Heroes of 1960s Motorcycle Sport (Westlake)
Off-Road Giants! (Volume 2) – Heroes of 1960s Motorcycle Sport (Westlake)
Off-Road Giants! (volume 3) – Heroes of 1960s Motorcycle Sport (Westlake)
Pass the Theory and Practical Driving Tests (Gibson & Hoole)
Peking to Paris 2007 (Young)
Pontiac Firebird (Cranswick)
Porsche Boxster (Long)
Porsche 356 (2nd Edition) (Long)
Porsche 908 (Födisch, Neßhöver, Roßbach, Schwarz & Roßbach)
Porsche 911 Carrera – The Last of the Evolution (Corlett)
Porsche 911R, RS & RSR, 4th Edition (Starkey)
Porsche 911, The Book of the (Long)
Porsche 911 – The Definitive History 2004-2012 (Long)
Porsche – The Racing 914s (Smith)
Porsche 911SC 'Super Carrera' – The Essential Companion (Streather)
Porsche 914 & 914-6: The Definitive History of the Road & Competition Cars (Long)
Porsche 924 (Long)
The Porsche 924 Carreras – evolution to excellence (Smith)
Porsche 928 (Long)
Porsche 944 (Long)
Porsche 964, 993 & 996 Data Plate Code Breaker (Streather)
Porsche 993 'King Of Porsche' – The Essential Companion (Streather)
Porsche 996 'Supreme Porsche' – The Essential Companion (Streather)
Porsche 997 2004-2012 – Porsche Excellence (Streather)
Porsche Racing Cars – 1953 to 1975 (Long)
Porsche Racing Cars – 1976 to 2005 (Long)
Porsche – The Rally Story (Meredith)
Porsche: Three Generations of Genius (Meredith)
Preston Tucker & Others (Linde)
RAC Rally Action! (Gardiner)
RACING COLOURS – MOTOR RACING COMPOSITIONS 1908-2009 (Newman)
Racing Line – British motorcycle racing in the golden age of the big single (Guntrip)
Rallye Sport Fords: The Inside Story (Moreton)
Renewable Energy Home Handbook, The (Porter)
Roads with a View – England's greatest views and how to find them by road (Corfield)
Rolls-Royce Silver Shadow/Bentley T Series Corniche & Camargue – Revised & Enlarged Edition (Bobbitt)
Rolls-Royce Silver Spirit, Silver Spur & Bentley Mulsanne 2nd Edition (Bobbitt)
Rover P4 (Bobbitt)
Runways & Racers (O'Neil)
Russian Motor Vehicles – Soviet Limousines 1930-2003 (Kelly)
Russian Motor Vehicles – The Czarist Period 1784 to 1917 (Kelly)
RX-7 – Mazda's Rotary Engine Sportscar (Updated & Revised New Edition) (Long)
Scooters & Microcars, The A-Z of Popular (Dan)
Scooter Lifestyle (Grainger)
SCOOTER MANIA! – Recollections of the Isle of Man International Scooter Rally (Jackson)
Singer Story: Cars, Commercial Vehicles, Bicycles & Motorcycle (Atkinson)
Sleeping Beauties USA – abandoned classic cars & trucks (Marek)
SM – Citroën's Maserati-engined Supercar (Long & Claverol)
Speedway – Auto racing's ghost tracks (Collins & Ireland)
Sprite Caravans, The Story of (Jenkinson)
Standard Motor Company, The Book of the (Robson)
Steve Hole's Kit Car Cornucopia – Cars, Companies, Stories, Facts & Figures: the UK's kit car scene since 1949 (Hole)
Subaru Impreza: The Road Car And WRC Story (Long)
Supercar, How to Build your own (Thompson)
Tales from the Toolbox (Oliver)
Tatra – The Legacy of Hans Ledwinka, Updated & Enlarged Collector's Edition of 1500 copies (Margolius & Henry)
Taxi! The Story of the 'London' Taxicab (Bobbitt)
Toleman Story, The (Hilton)
Toyota Celica & Supra, The Book of Toyota's Sports Coupés (Long)
Toyota MR2 Coupés & Spyders (Long)
Triumph Bonneville Bible (59-83) (Henshaw)
Triumph Bonneville!, Save the – The inside story of the Meriden Workers' Co-op (Rosamond)
Triumph Motorcycles & the Meriden Factory (Hancox)
Triumph Speed Twin & Thunderbird Bible (Woolridge)
Triumph Tiger Cub Bible (Estall)
Triumph Trophy Bible (Woolridge)
Triumph TR6 (Kimberley)
TT Talking – The TT's most exciting era – As seen by Manx Radio TT's lead commentator 2004-2012 (Lambert)
Two Summers – The Mercedes-Benz W196R Racing Car (Ackerson)
TWR Story, The – Group A (Hughes & Scott)
Unraced (Collins)
Velocette Motorcycles – MSS to Thruxton – New Third Edition (Burris)
Vespa – The Story of a Cult Classic in Pictures (Uhlig)
Vincent Motorcycles: The Untold Story since 1946 (Guyony & Parker)
Volkswagen Bus Book, The (Bobbitt)
Volkswagen Bus or Van to Camper, How to Convert (Porter)
Volkswagens of the World (Glen)
VW Beetle Cabriolet – The full story of the convertible Beetle (Bobbitt)
VW Beetle – The Car of the 20th Century (Copping)
VW Bus – 40 Years of Splitties, Bays & Wedges (Copping)
VW Bus Book, The (Bobbitt)
VW Golf: Five Generations of Fun (Copping & Cservenka)
VW – The Air-cooled Era (Copping)
VW T5 Camper Conversion Manual (Porter)
VW Campers (Copping)
You & Your Jaguar XK8/XKR – Buying, Enjoying, Maintaining, Modifying – New Edition (Thorley)
Which Oil? – Choosing the right oils & greases for your antique, vintage, veteran, classic or collector car (Michell)
Works Minis, The Last (Purves & Brenchley)
Works Rally Mechanic (Moylan)

BATTLE CRY!

Hubble & Hattie

www.veloce.co.uk

First published in March 2011 by Veloce Publishing Limited, Veloce House, Parkway Farm Business Park, Middle Farm Way, Poundbury, Dorchester, Dorset, DT1 3AR, England.
Reprinted July 2013, April 2014, October 2016 & December 2017.
Fax 01305 250479/e-mail info@veloce.co.uk/web www.veloce.co.uk or www.velocebooks.com.
ISBN: 978-1-787110-52-6 UPC: 6-36847-01052-2
© Rick Astley and Veloce Publishing 2011, 2013, 2014 & 2016. All rights reserved. With the exception of quoting brief passages for the purpose of review, no part of this publication may be recorded, reproduced or transmitted by any means, including photocopying, without the written permission of Veloce Publishing Ltd. Throughout this book logos, model names and designations, etc, have been used for the purposes of identification, illustration and decoration. Such names are the property of the trademark holder as this is not an official publication.
Readers with ideas for automotive books, or books on other transport or related hobby subjects, are invited to write to the editorial director of Veloce Publishing at the above address.
British Library Cataloguing in Publication Data – A catalogue record for this book is available from the British Library.
Typesetting, design and page make-up all by Veloce Publishing Ltd on Apple Mac. Printed and bound by CPI Group (UK) Ltd, Croydon, CR0 4YY.

THE ESSENTIAL MANUAL™

MGB Electrical Systems

YOUR colour-illustrated guide to understanding, repairing & improving the MGB's electrical systems & components
Now covers all models, including MGB, MGC and MGB-V8

Rick Astley

UPDATED & REVISED NEW EDITION

VELOCE PUBLISHING
THE PUBLISHER OF FINE AUTOMOTIVE BOOKS

Contents

Acknowledgements & about the author 7
Foreword 8

Chapter 1. Safety first 9
General 9
Electric shock 9
Heat burns 9
Acid burns 9
Fire 10
Toxic gas 10
Vehicle integrity 10

Chapter 2. Tools, wire handling & connectors 11
Tools 11
Screwdrivers 11
   Safety 11
   Blade drivers 11
   Phillips (crosspoint) 11
   Pozidrive® 11
   Precision screwdrivers 11
Circuit tester 11
Multimeter 12
Wire handling 12
   Automotive wire 12
   Jumper wires 13
Connectors 13
   Connector terminals 13
   Bullet connectors 13
   Soldering bullet connectors 13
   Blade connectors 13
   Crimping blade connectors 14
   Piggyback connectors 15
   Earthing connectors 15
   Splicing connectors 15
   IDC taps 16
Wire protection 16
   Harness tape 16
   Heat-shrinkable and self-amalgamating tape 16
   PVC tape 16
   Convoluted tubing 16
   Heat-shrink tubing 17
   Cable clamps 17
   Adding circuits 17

Chapter 3. Basic electrical theory 18
Electrical units 18
   Volt 18
   Amp 18
   Watt 18
   Ohm 18
   Other electrical units 18
Some useful formulae 19
A practical exercise 19
Corrosion 20
   Atmospheric corrosion 20
   Galvanic corrosion 20

Chapter 4. Emergency repairs 22
General 22
What to carry 22
   Mobile phone 22
   Jump start cables 22
   Fan belt 22
   Fuses 22
   Sparkplugs 22
   Bulbs 22
   Wire 23
   PVC adhesive electrical tape 23
   Torch (flashlight) and plug-in light 23
   Water repellent 23
   Rain-X® 23
Tools 23
Running repairs 23
   Battery/generator problems 23
   Ignition problems 23
   High-tension wires 24
   Checking for a spark 24
Poor connections 24
   Blade and bullet connectors 24
   Switch contacts 24
Ignition switch 25
Fuel pump 25
Sealed beam units 25
Poor earths 25
Joining wires 25

Chapter 5. Sneak currents 26
What are sneak currents? 26
Sneak example 26
MGB/C sneak currents 27
   Stop/tail lamps 27
   Stop/tail circuit 27
   Engine run-on 27
   Unintended engine starting 28
   Engine earth/ground strap 28

Chapter 6. Wire harness 29
Wires & components 29
   Wire colours 29
   Component codes 29
Major harnesses 30

MGB ELECTRICAL SYSTEMS – THE ESSENTIAL MANUAL

MGB wire function finder 31
Component codes................................38
Wire sizes 40

Chapter 7. Fusing & fuses 41
Fuse technology...................................41
Fusing architecture...............................41
Fuse rating 41
MGB/C fuses.......................................42
    Fuse block......................................42
    Fuse values 43
    Line fuses 43
    Blown fuses 43
Adding additional fuses........................44
    Selecting a fuse value and
    wire size 44
Fuse types 45
Fuse-holders 45
    Circuit-breakers 46
    PolySwitch® polymer PTCs.............47

Chapter 8. Battery...............................48
Battery ratings 48
    Ampere hours (Ah) 48
    Reserve capacity (RC) 48
    Cold cranking amps (CCA) 48
    Cranking amps (CA) 48
    Battery size 49
    Group size......................................49
Battery charging...................................49
    Charging methods 49
Battery discharge 50
Battery problems..................................50
    Temperature effects........................50
Battery testing & maintenance 51
    Battery connections 51
    Electrolyte 51
    No load voltage 51
    Load testing 51
Jump starting 52
    Connections for cars
    of like polarity................................52
    Connections for cars
    of unlike polarity............................52
    Starting the car 52
Dual to single battery conversion.........52
    Battery selection 52
    Battery choice................................53
    Fitting the battery...........................53
Under-bonnet battery location..............54
    Left hand drive cars 54
    Battery clamp.................................54
Why batteries fail.................................54
Adding a battery disconnect
switch 54
    Why add a disconnect switch?........54
    Switch selection.............................54
    Earth switching 55
    Schematic 55
    Earth connection 55
    Installing the switch 55
    Attaching the cables 56
Adding a radio memory & clock
    maintainer 56

Battery system fault-finding 56

Chapter 9. Charging system 57
Motor & generators 57
Isolate the problem 58
System Iterations.................................58
Dynamo...59
    Checking the system 59
    Dynamo service 60
    Disassembly...................................60
    Armature 61
    Field coils 61
    Commutator 61
    Brushes 61
    Re-assembly 62
    Body and end plates.......................62
Dynamo control box.............................62
    Description 62
    Service 63
    Identification 63
    Maintenance 64
    Adjustment 64
    Checking the ignition warning
    lamp 64
    Dynamo charging circuit 64
Dynamo circuit fault-finding 65
Alternator...65
    Description 65
    Checking the ignition
    warning lamp 67
    Testing the alternator......................67
    Alternator service 67
    Checking the rectifier 69
    Voltage regulator............................69
    Zener diode...................................69
    Capacitor 69
ACR-series alternator wiring 70
    5-terminal alternator wiring 70
    3-terminal alternator wiring 70
    Replacement alternators.................70
Alternator with external regulator 71
5-terminal alternator 71
3-terminal alternator............................72
Conversion from positive to
negative earth......................................72
    Preparation 73
    Procedure 73
Dynamo to alternator conversion 73
    Preparation 73
    Procedure 74
Conversion from a 5-terminal to
    3-terminal alternator......................74
    Why change? 75
    Procedure 75
Alternator circuit fault-finding..............75

Chapter 10. Starting system 77
General 77
Starter circuit 1962-1967 77
    Circuit description..........................77
Starter circuit 1967-1969 77
    Circuit description..........................77
Starter circuit 1970-1974½ 78
    Circuit description..........................78

Starter circuit 1974½-1980 78
    Circuit description...........................78
Starter Solenoid...................................79
    Solenoid 1962-1967 79
    Solenoid 1968-1980........................80
    Solenoid diagnostics.......................81
Starter relay 82
    1970-1974½ 82
    1974½-1980 relay 82
    Alternative relay 82
    Checking the relay 83
Starter motor 83
    Schematic 83
    Early motor 83
    Later motor 83
    Why starter motors fail....................84
Upgrading from an inertia to a
pre-engaged starter 84
Adding a remote cranking switch..........85
Starter circuit fault-finding 86

Chapter 11. Ignition system 87
Conventional ignition...........................87
Electronic ignition 88
    Variable reluctance pick-ups 89
    Constant energy ignition 89
    Magnetic pick-up coils....................89
    Hall effect sensors 89
    Optical ignition switching................89
    Capacitive discharge ignition...........90
    Electronic ignition sparkplug
    gap 90
Ignition circuit 1962-1964.....................91
    Circuit description..........................91
Ignition circuit 1964-1974½..................91
    Circuit description..........................91
Ignition circuit 1974½-1977..................91
    Circuit description..........................91
Ignition circuit 1977-1980
(excluding North America)....................92
    Circuit description..........................92
Ignition circuit 1977-1980
(North America) 92
    Circuit description 92
Ignition components............................93
    Ignition relay..................................93
    Alternative relay 94
Ignition coil 94
    Why ignition coils fail 94
Ballast resistor and low resistance
coil 95
    Coil selection 96
    Adding a ballast resistor 96
    Ballast resistor 96
    Diode ballast isolation 96
    Relay ballast isolation 96
Distributor...97
    Description 97
    Rotor arm 98
    Capacitor 98
    Distributor variants.........................98
Distributor advance mechanisms.........99
    Centrifugal advance........................99
    Vacuum advance 101

MGB ELECTRICAL SYSTEMS – THE ESSENTIAL MANUAL

Electrical vacuum advance 101
Distributor drive orientation 102
Distributor clamp 102
Dwell angle and contact-breaker gap 102
Setting the dwell angle.................. 104
Drive gear position 105
Firing order 106
Ignition timing................................... 106
Approximate timing 107
Static timing 107
Dynamic timing 108
Anti run-on valve 109
Sparkplugs....................................... 109
Heat range 109
Standard plugs............................. 110
Projected nose plugs 110
Plug gap 110
Recommended plugs.................... 111
Spark polarity 111
Ignition wires 111
Ignition switch 112
Dash mounted switches 112
Column mounted ignition switch... 112
Ignition system fault-finding 113

Chapter 12. Lighting 115
Filament lamps 115
Voltage effect on brightness 116
Brightness perception................... 116
Voltage effect on lamp life 116
Light emitting diodes........................ 117
Lighting circuits 118
Early car lighting circuit................. 118
Late car lighting circuit.................. 118
Lighting switches.............................. 119
Dip switch 120
Parking lamps 120
Instrument lamps 120
Side marker lamps 120
Halogen bulbs 120
Fitting halogen headlamps 121
Beam alignment 121
Headlamp relays............................... 122
Installing headlamp relays............. 122
Daytime running lamps.................... 122
Installing DRLs 123
Linking lighting relays 124
Turn signals and hazard flashers........ 125
Flasher module 125
Electronic flasher modules............ 126
Early car turn signal circuit 127
Late car turn signal circuit 127
Using an electronic flasher module 128
Making turn signals more audible 129
Brake lamps 129
Early brake circuit 130
Later brake circuit 131
Brake lamp circuit with handbrake warning lamp 131
Improving lamp earthing 132
Improving stop and turn signals 133

Courtesy lamps 133
Reversing lamps................................. 135
Light bulb chart.................................. 136
Lighting fault-finding 136

Chapter 13. Overdrive & gearbox 137
Overdrive 137
Pre-1968 overdrive circuit 137
Post 1968 overdrive circuit................ 138
Post 1977 North American overdrive circuit.. 139
Overdrive problems 139
Gear and reversing switches 140
Inhibitor switch 141
Automatic transmission inhibitor and reverse switch 141
Making a start-while-in-gear prevention circuit 141
Using the inhibitor switch to initiate DRLs 142
Flip-on, flip-off, overdrive circuit.... 142
Night dimming a overdrive warning lamp 143

Chapter 14. Instrumentation 144
Instrumentation 144
Gauges 144
Moving iron gauge 144
Thermal gauges 145
Voltage regulator 145
Making a semiconductor regulator...................................... 146
Senders 147
Fuel sender 147
Temperature sender...................... 148
Oil pressure sender....................... 148
Adding an oil pressure warning lamp 149
Instrumentation circuit....................... 149
Instrumentation fault-finding 150
Tachometer 151
Principle of operation.................... 151
Current driven tachometers 151
RV1 1419/00 tachometer 152
RV1 1433/00 tachometer 153
RVC tachometers 154
Tachometer calibration 155
Comparison calibration 155
Road testing 155
Calibrating with a signal generator...................................... 155
Tachometer fault-finding................ 156
Speedometer.................................... 156
Speedometer operation 156
Speedometer calibration............... 156
Clock 157
Adding an ammeter 157
Adding a voltmeter 157

Chapter 15. Wipers & washers 158
1962 to 1967 wiper circuit 158
Auto-park operation 159
Early wiper motor 159
Auto-park mechanism................... 160

Regenerative braking 160
Adding regenerative braking.......... 160
1968 and later wiper circuit........... 161
Later auto-park mechanism........... 162
Later wiper motor 162
Windscreen washer........................... 164
Wiper and washer fault-finding 165

Chapter 16. Fuel pump 166
Location.. 166
Fuel pump electrical circuit 167
Fuel pump identification 167
Fuel pump operation 167
Capacitor snubbed pump 168
TVS diode snubbed pumps 168
Fuel pump service......................... 169
Fuel pump polarity reversal........... 170
Breather pipes.............................. 171
Installing an aftermarket fuel pump.... 171
Fuel pump fault-finding...................... 172

Chapter 17. Horn................................ 173
Horn construction.............................. 173
Horn identification......................... 173
Horn circuit – pre-1977 174
Horn circuit from 1975 175
Horn volume 175
Improving the horn circuit 176
Using a relay in the early horn circuit 176
Using a relay in the late horn circuit 176
Horn fault-finding 177

Chapter 18. Cooling & heating fans 178
Electric cooling fan............................ 178
Thermostat................................... 178
Radiator fan circuits 179
Adding relays to the fan circuit 179
After-market cooling fans.................. 180
Heater fan... 181
Carburettor cooling fan 181
Air-conditioning (a/c)......................... 181
Electrical circuit............................ 182

Chapter 19. Miscellaneous systems 183
The sequential seat belt system......... 183
Fitting a radio 183
Heated backlight............................... 184
Manifold heater 184

Appendix 1. Relays 185
Relay operation 185
Automotive relays 185
Coil resistance 186

Appendix 2. Diodes............................ 187
Rectifier diodes 187
Over-voltage diodes 188
Selecting and using diodes 188

Index... 191

Acknowledgements & about the author

ACKNOWLEDGEMENTS
This book could not have been written in a vacuum and I owe thanks to the following for their generous contributions.

Jeff Zorn of Farmington Hills, Michigan, owner of Little British Car Co. who loaned me many of the parts that appear in the photographs.

Kim Rutherford of Sarnia, Ontario for data on the air-conditioning system.

Rich Wagner of Walled Lake, Michigan for letting me use his idea of a low annoyance audible turn signal reminder.

Nic Housilp, of Solihull, Warwickshire, for his help on the subject of battery technology.

Dave Sharp, of Letchlade, Gloucestershire for his help regarding very early RHD MGBs.

Wray Lemke and Jim Tahler via e-mail who suggested the best semiconductors for the updated voltage stabilizer.

Bob Muenchausen of Boise, Idaho for his wisdom on various topics.

Anthony Pearson, owner of Classic and Vintage Bulbs of Blackwood, S. Australia for advice regarding lamps and lighting.

Dave Barton of Melbourne, Australia for information on his under-bonnet battery installation.

My friends Tony Cilluffo and Mo Zeidan for their advice.

My late father Sidney Astley, an electrical engineer who gave me the enthusiasm to want to become one too.

My brother Pete, who encouraged me to get an education and my brother John who restored a TD and an MGA in the 1960s and sparked my interest in the marque.

Mike Plumstead of Farnborough, Kent who kindly hosted the web site that preceded this book.

The members of the Windsor-Detroit MG Club, especially Guy St John, Andrew and Scott Turner, Bill Weakley and Philip Wiltshire, who offered advice, photographs and access to whatever I found to be unique among the club's over 300 MGBs.

The literally hundreds of MGB owners who visited the web site that preceded this book and whose questions and suggestions helped me make improvements, additions and corrections. Special thanks to those who encouraged me to turn the web site into this book.

ABOUT THE AUTHOR
Rick Astley is a dual British-Canadian citizen living in the USA. He has owned at least one MG in all three countries.

An electrical engineer, he was educated in Britain and worked mostly in, or with, the avionics and marine electronics industries before moving close to the motor city of Detroit.

He currently works as the Automotive Applications Manager for a Silicon Valley company. This has entailed his being embedded with the electrical architecture group of one of the big-3 car makers where he was able observe first hand the process behind the design of vehicle electrical systems.

His wife, Anne, his 1970 MGB roadster and 1970 MGB-GT V8 conversion, were all raised in Abingdon, England. He has two grown sons, Oliver and Tom.

Foreword

I'm a really bad cook. I have no natural ability in the art, but I'm intelligent enough to follow a recipe. Unfortunately, when I'm in charge of the kitchen it always seems that the Yorkshire pudding won't rise or the cream won't whip or the cake has the consistency of glue. I'm sure I followed the instructions correctly, so what should I do differently next time? What effects do acids like vinegar or lemon juice have, and why cook at this temperature for that time rather than some other combination?

It struck me that the MGB or MGC books I read were like recipe books too; telling the reader to do this or that but not saying why. No two are alike any more, each car has seen different service in various climates and has been repaired and modified to different degrees with very varied levels of expertise. It's not surprising then that things don't always go as they should. What is the average owner who is not an engineer to do other than repeat the same instructions and arrive at the same bad result?

I thought I could do something about the situation – at least as far as the electrical system is concerned. The result was a website that grew in size and complexity. With it came correspondence from all over the world, scores of e-mails each week, and I found myself running an on-line clinic for MGB electrical problems. That provided an understanding of the needs of the average user and a constant improvement to the website content.

Websites are viewed using a 'browser' but, paradoxically, they are very difficult to actually browse. There's nothing like a book for the ease with which its pages that can be flicked through, its instant access, and you can consult it virtually anywhere. At least that's what many correspondents were telling me; they couldn't drag their computers into the garage, they said, so why didn't I put it on paper?

This book is the result. In many ways it is as if it had been through several different issues even at its first printing, produced as it is with the benefit of so much user feedback.

If you find it didactic then I don't apologize; it is meant to be just that. There is no simple recipe for fixing many of the problems that arise in MGBs or Cs, the cars' apparent simplicity seems to have made everyone who has touched them think that they can fix the wiring system, often with horrible results.

You won't find disparaging remarks about Joseph Lucas Ltd. here. I think I have heard every joke there is about Lucas electrics but sincerely believe the criticism to be unfair and misplaced. Many people would write to me starting with words like, "The curse of Lucas has struck my car ...", only to describe a problem with their fuel pump made by SU, their fuel gauge made by Smiths Industries or, most frequently of all, an earthing problem, which is down to the MG designers in Abingdon and the rigours of time, moisture, and often salt. Lucas products were not always perfect, but they were no worse in my experience than contemporary products from Delco, Ducellier or Bosch.

The circuit diagrams are broken down by system so that they are much less complex to read than the birds' nests of wires published elsewhere. Moreover, each wire is coloured for easier recognition. For those who are, like the author, colour blind, each wire is labelled with its colour code too.

In an effort to help locate components, the circuit diagrams also place each part in its approximate position in the car. Owners of RHD cars must forgive the fact that LHD cars are represented. That's not the result of jingoism on the part of the US resident author, but it happens to be the most practical way to present the data. If RHD cars were shown everything would be cramped on the right.

Rick Astley

Chapter 1
Safety first

GENERAL
This chapter deals wholly with safety as it pertains to the vehicle's electrical distribution system.

Working on the electrical system will inevitably require carrying out operations that are no different from many mechanical jobs. Don't forget, therefore, to follow the safety rules that are not specific to the electrical system especially when:
- working under the vehicle
- the car is on a jack or ramps
- the engine is running
- working close to any fuel
- working near hot surfaces

ELECTRIC SHOCK
The standard 12 volt battery has a maximum voltage across it when charging of about 14.5 volts. Electric shock is not normally considered a hazard for voltages below 60 volts, and so is not a concern for the low voltage circuits of the vehicle.

By contrast, the high-tension circuit – everything from the centre terminal of the coil, to the distributor and from there to the sparkplugs – may have voltages in excess of 30,000 volts present. This voltage level is very capable of giving an electric shock, but the amount of current available is so low that it does not even come close to the 8 thousandths of an Ampere considered necessary to stop the human heart. The greatest hazard is from the body's automatic reaction to the electric shock that may cause the hand and arm to retract quickly, forcibly and somewhat uncontrollably, from the source of the shock.
- Take great care when handling the plug leads on a running engine, especially that for #1 cylinder which is very close to the alternator, the fan and their drive belt. An uncontrolled reflex toward these components can cause very serious injury.

Many sources suggest testing for the presence of a spark by pulling off a plug lead. With no place else to go, the spark can find its way through even thin rubber gloves, the insulation on the handles of pliers and your clothing if you are leaning against the vehicle. A plastic clothes peg snapped over the plug connector and insulated pliers applied over that will help a lot in avoiding shock. In any event, pulling plug leads off is not the ideal way to check for a spark because the energy, looking for some place to go, can cause damage to the coil and absolutely ruin an electronic ignition system.

HEAT BURNS
Even if not capable of inflicting electric shock, nominal 12 volt vehicle battery systems can produce hundreds of amperes of current, which will heat any small cross-section of metal it happens to pass through. That may include jewellery, tools or any metal object that could come in contact with a live part of the system and chassis. This is not a trivial issue; a watchband or ring that turns to molten metal has obvious consequences for the wearer.
- Remove or cover any rings, metal watchbands or other jewellery.
- Disconnect the system from the battery where possible.

MGB/C batteries are difficult to access and so there is always a temptation to leave them connected when working on the car, especially when, in order to test the effectiveness of the work done, it is necessary to reconnect them immediately afterward. Take the trouble to fit a battery disconnect switch, and add safety, convenience and security in one fell swoop. See page 54.

ACID BURNS
It is extremely unlikely that any MGB/Cs are running today with the original batteries, although very similar units are still being made for those who want to keep their vehicles as original as possible and can pay the asking price.

MGB ELECTRICAL SYSTEMS – THE ESSENTIAL MANUAL

Modern batteries still contain a strong dilution of sulphuric acid but are much better sealed than before. The exposed position of the batteries in MGB/Cs does, however, make them vulnerable to impact damage that could cause acid leakage.
• Do not invert batteries
• Wear rubber gloves and proper eye protection if you have to handle a suspected damaged battery.

FIRE

This is the unmentionable four-letter 'F' word in the automotive industry, so do what the industry does and use the euphemism 'thermal event'. Seriously, the MGB /C is not as well protected as a modern car; some direct-from-battery circuits not being fused at all.

The PVC wire used in MGs, and in almost all post 1960s cars, is naturally fire retarded; the 'C' in PVC, or Polyvinyl Chloride, is a halogen that helps extinguish any combustion. However, anything will burn when exposed to sufficient levels of heat and/or oxygen and a car battery is very capable of causing components like the wiring to become very hot. PVC is also a thermoplastic, which means it can melt off the wire. Even a momentary short circuit can cause adjacent wires in a harness bundle to short together permanently, resulting in progressive failure likely to result in fire. With fuel around too, it is not possible to be too alarmist, a car fire can burn down your garage, your home and may have lethal consequences.
• Disconnect the battery when working on the car's electrical system.

The MGB/C under-dash area is particularly difficult to work on; even changing an instrument bulb is a painful experience. While some mid-production MGBs, the MGC and MGB-GT V8 had an electric oil gauge, others had a direct reading type in which the oil pressure line comes right into the dash area and connects to the back of it. One owner reported that without his knowledge, it had been leaking very slightly and spraying a fine oil mist under the dash. A small spark, caused when he connected a powered circuit, resulted in the under-dash area catching fire. Fortunately, he had a fire extinguisher handy. He has now fitted a battery disconnect switch and vows to use it, knowing he was lucky not to have lost his home in this incident.

Another source of fire is from hydrogen, a by-product of the battery charging process. MGB batteries are located under the car in a well-ventilated area. Moreover, modern batteries do not vent much hydrogen into the atmosphere. Nevertheless, some risk remains so do not do anything that could cause a spark in close proximity to the battery soon after fast charging.
• Have a fire extinguisher at hand in the work area.

TOXIC GAS

As noted above, PVC when burning, or even close to burning, gives off chlorine gas that combines with water in the atmosphere to create hydrochloric acid, a poisonous and an aggressive corrosive substance. Observe the fire precautions listed above.

Some tuning operations require the car to be running while it is worked upon. There is a real risk of poisoning from carbon monoxide that is a component of the exhaust gases. This is an insidious poison that is a frequent cause of death
• Never operate a car in a closed garage and take care even in a garage with the door open.
• Work outside or with the back of the car well into the driveway.

VEHICLE INTEGRITY

By the standards of its day, the MGB was a very safe car. Many of the projects in this book are intended to improve further on what MG did by, for example, upgrading the lighting so the car is more visible and the driver can see better at night. However, badly planned or executed work can also compromise safety so please always have that in mind when using this book to maintain or modify your car. In particular:
• It is pointless making a modification meant to improve safety using a standard of workmanship that reduces reliability and possibly your security.
• Do not add accessories, such as bracket-mounted instruments or a cigarette-lighter/power outlet in positions that could harm you or your passenger in an accident. See Figure 1.1
• If you choose to move the battery or fuel pump from their original and very safe mid-car location to the boot or under-bonnet area, make sure they are fixed and connected securely and think about what might happen to them should the car impact something.

Figure 1.1. Rather than use sharp-edged brackets, this voltmeter and clock were installed in a pod between the gear lever and centre console.

Chapter 2
Tools, wire handling & connectors

TOOLS
In order to service or enhance the MGB/C electrical distribution system and its components, many of the same tools used for general servicing: spanners (wrenches), sockets, screwdrivers, jacks, axle stands, a shop light and the like, are needed. However, some additional tools are desirable, if not essential, and some traditional tools need special consideration when intended for electrical work.

SCREWDRIVERS
Safety
Try to get screwdrivers with plastic insulated shafts. If you cannot, then heat shrink tubing or tape can be used over them to prevent accidental electrical contact that could cause a fire hazard. Having different lengths available is also an advantage, some screws requiring long reach, but some spaces allowing only short screwdriver access.

Blade drivers
For most electrical work, ⅛in (3mm) and ³⁄₁₆in (5mm) screwdrivers will suffice. Electrical screws often seem to have very narrow drive slots and it may be necessary to grind some screwdriver blades down to fit them.

Philips   Pozidrive

Figure 2.1. Pozidrive® screws can be distinguished from Phillips by the additional X embossed in the head.

Phillips (crosspoint)
There are not that many, if any, true Phillips screws on MGBs. If you don't have Pozidrivers, then PH#1 and PH#2 Phillips screwdrivers will suffice.

Pozidrive®
Pozidrive screws are found on all mid-60s onward MGBs, and not just on the electrical system. These look like Phillips screws but their slot geometry (Figure 2.1) is different and, whereas a Phillips screwdriver often seems to work well on Pozidrive screws, they can tear up a stubborn head or at least cosmetically spoil it. Pozidrivers are sized similarly to Phillips, so try to obtain sizes PZ#1 and PZ#2. Pozidrive screws can be distinguished from Phillips by an additional X lightly embossed in the head.

Precision screwdrivers
Sometimes described as watchmakers' or instrument screwdrivers, precision screwdrivers are normally sold in sets and will often include blades and perhaps other head geometries. They are all metal, but since they should only be used on equipment already removed from the vehicle, there is no danger of them shorting and they do not need any insulation.

CIRCUIT TESTER
A circuit tester is an extremely useful tool for fault-finding disabled electrical circuits. Placing the probe end on any point where power is expected will result in an immediate indication as to whether or not it is a live circuit. In construction, it is simply a bulb that is connected on one side to an

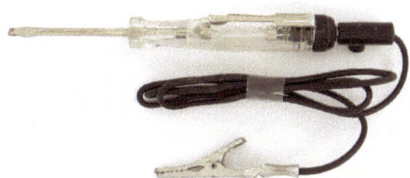

Figure 2.2. A typical circuit tester used to check if power is present at a particular point.

MGB ELECTRICAL SYSTEMS – THE ESSENTIAL MANUAL

alligator clip that can be attached to an earth point and on the other side to a probe that, when touched on a 'hot' terminal, will illuminate the bulb. Such an arrangement would be easy to construct but, because they are inexpensive and readily available in convenient packages that protect the lamp, it is hardly worth the trouble.

The tester shown in Figure 2.2 is typical of those that can be found in stores and catalogues. It doubles as a small screwdriver. Note that the cable to the alligator clip plugs into the top of the tool. The bulb can be seen inside the handle.

Unfortunately, many circuit testers are very poorly constructed and are next to useless. If the tester cannot be relied on to give the correct indication then a lot of time can be wasted.

Automotive testers are usually marked 6V – 12V, but their shape and general appearance is not unlike those used to test power outlets in the home. Great care should be taken not to put both types of tester in the same toolbox. Confusing a mains voltage tester with an automotive tester can result in nuisance, because it will not operate at low voltages. By contrast, confusing an automotive tester for a mains voltage tester can be lethal, because if used in the home, the tester will apply high voltage with potentially high current, directly to the body.

MULTIMETER

The multimeter is so called because it is multi functional; at least being able to measure volts, amps and ohms, but many can do much more. They are not essential tools but can, nonetheless, be useful. The price of these instruments has dropped dramatically in the last few years and while it is one of those products where you get what you pay for. For occasional work a low cost digital device like that in Figure 2.3 is usually adequate. Digital multimeters are sometimes described as LCD meters; this simply describes the type of dial, which is a liquid crystal display, just like that in a digital watch. The older analogue meters, those that have an indicating needle, are still very useful especially when monitoring rapidly changing parameters. If the meter is primarily to be used only for car work then look for:
1. An audible continuity tester. This tells you if two points on a circuit are connected together, even if there are never 12 volts present (such as when

Figure 2.3. A multimeter with a digital liquid crystal display.

testing earth continuity) and even when the battery is not connected; for both these conditions the circuit tester is unsuitable.
2. If you think you may work on alternators and/or dynamos, look for a multimeter with a resistance accuracy of 0.1Ω. In addition, for testing alternators, a diode test facility is almost essential.
3. Many inexpensive meters cannot measure sufficiently high currents for automotive use. A dc current of 10A minimum should be sought, and more if possible.

WIRE HANDLING
Automotive wire
The wire used in MGBs has insulation made from PVC. PVC is a thermoplastic; that is, it will melt when heated. The maximum continuous operating temperature for the grade of PVC used in automotive applications is 185°F (85°C) with short excursions allowed to about 221°F (105°C). It is important not to pass too much current down a wire, otherwise it will overheat and the insulation will exceed

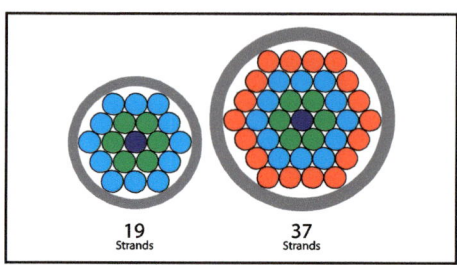

Figure 2.4. For easy handling, wires are multi-stranded and laid-up in concentric bundles that make a rounder construction.

its melt temperature. See page 40 for recommendations. Wire should also be kept away from hot surfaces, especially the exhaust system.

PVC wire contains plasticizers, which tend to evaporate from the material to the extent where the nose can sense them. Anyone who has opened a new large area PVC product, such as an air-bed, will be familiar with its odour. Over the years since the MGB has been built, the plasticizers have been evaporating from its wires and indeed other items such as the dash and seats, causing them to become brittle. This is generally not a problem but the very act of disturbing the wires in order to service the electrical harness can result in cracking of the insulation. This in turn can damage the internal copper wire as it allows a point of entry for moisture and a region of high flexibility that can result in the conductor work-hardening and breaking.

The electrical conductor used in automotive wires and cables is always made from copper, it is usually bare but you may find some after-market wire with tinned plating that helps prevent the wire surface from oxidizing. Copper is a very good electrical conductor, is malleable, making it easy to crimp and, when it is clean, easy to solder too.

Even though an automotive wire may sometimes only be required to carry a very low current, gauge sizes less than 20AWG (0.5mm^2) are seldom used because smaller wires do not have sufficient mechanical strength. The wires are also stranded, that is to say made up of a number of smaller gauge conductors laid together to form a more flexible construction than would be possible with a single copper conductor. If you purchase new wire it will probably be concentrically laid-up like that in Figure 2.4. This involves an expensive manufacturing process.

TOOLS, WIRE HANDLING & CONNECTORS

By contrast the original wiring is of an inherently less flexible, but inexpensive-to-produce bunched construction that requires more strands to compensate for its stiffness. As a result, some of the original wire in the car is made up of 44 smaller strands.

Jumper wires

These can be built using the terminals described below. They are useful for diagnostic work, where for example you want to jump between a known good circuit with power present, and a suspect one.

CONNECTORS

Connector terminals

The MGB uses two main types of connector terminals: the bullet type, for in-line connections, and the blade, Lucar™ or Faston™ connector for making connections to fixed components.

Bullet connectors

The bullet connectors shown in Figure 2.5 take their name from the male connector that is soldered to the wire ends. However, there are several versions of the female available that can accept various numbers of male contacts. In order to spur off to an additional wire it is simply necessary to fix a male contact to the end and either push it into a spare cavity in the female, or exchange the female for one with additional cavities.

Since the steel female contact corrodes more than the copper male connector and also loses its spring tension over time, it is a good fault prevention measure to buy new ones and replace as many as possible on the car. Take care when replacing them; old and corroded female connectors can break when trying to remove the male and the broken spring steel can cause nasty cuts.

The bullet connector has the disadvantage that a supply side disconnected male contact has no insulation and can be live, causing a safety hazard and/or nuisance fuse blowing.

In most cases, bullet connectors have to be soldered to the wire, a process that needs some skill. Note that you may find crimp style bullet connectors available in automotive accessory stores but these are not usually the same size as those used by MG. The MGB device is 3/16in (4.76mm) diameter, whereas the crimp connectors are smaller having a 5/32in (4mm) diameter. It may be necessary to acquire new male and female bullet connectors from a classic British car parts company, as they are not generally available elsewhere.

Soldering bullet connectors

You will need a soldering iron. For small jobs, whether you choose a 12V soldering iron that is powered from the cigar lighter or a mains voltage type is a matter of choice depending on your access to power. The latter power source is preferred, especially as it is recommended that electrical work be done on the car only with the battery disconnected. For soldering heavy wire, and for bullet connectors, which rapidly conduct heat away, a pistol style soldering iron will be needed.

Figure 2.6 shows the process of installing a bullet connector.
1. Strip the wire such that when it is inserted in the connector it just pokes through the end. The strip length necessary varies depending on the wire size as an internal stop in the connector allows thinner insulation to penetrate further.
2. 'Tin' the wire, that is, heat the exposed wire with a soldering iron and apply solder to it until it wicks into the wire strands. Note: always heat what is being soldered, not the solder wire itself.
3. Insert the wire into the connector
4. Solder the wire to the connector, again apply the soldering iron to the wire end and connector and then bring the solder to the job. A 'third hand' such as a small vice or alligator clip is useful here. Try not to apply too much solder, otherwise it will run down the side of the connector and interfere with its insertion into the female connector. The wire end will grow out a little because the PVC wire in the bullet shrinks back under the heat, but it can always be snipped off with small wire cutters.

Blade connectors

The blade style of contact shown in Figure 2.7 is available on the after-market in many forms.
- Style 1 is probably the most common but the least preferred. Always try to use contacts with insulation over the whole length so as not to expose a large potentially live surface that is susceptible to short-circuit.
- Style 2 has a heat shrink tube with a hot-melt adhesive lining that not only

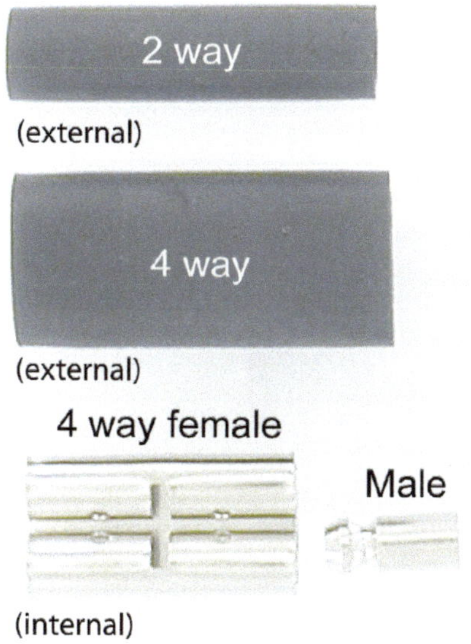

Figure 2.5. Bullet connectors are used for joining wires together. Several different female connectors are available which can accept various numbers of wires that are terminated with male bullet connectors.

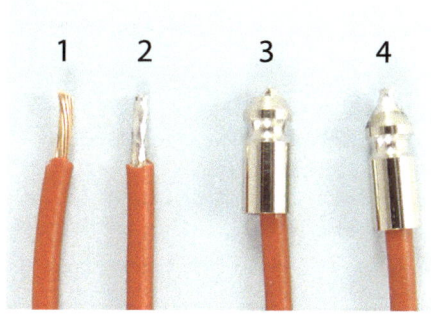

Figure 2.6. Terminating a wire in a bullet connector.

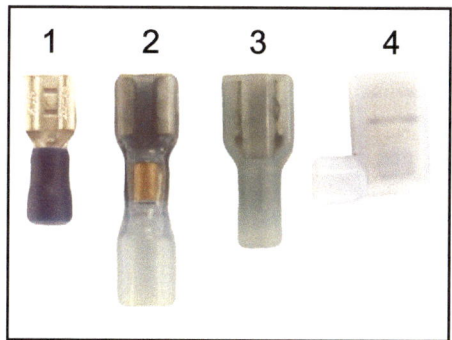

Figure 2.7. Spade or bladed connectors come in a variety of styles; some have superior attributes.

MGB ELECTRICAL SYSTEMS – THE ESSENTIAL MANUAL

insulates the connector end but that when heated, also seals and strain-relieves the wire connection. It is most often used where the connection is exposed to the elements.

- Style 3 is the more common insulated type. It has a tough nylon cover that extends over the whole contact length and beyond the crimp barrel so that it supports the wire insulation too.
- Style 4, a right-angle connector, is often useful but may be difficult to access with some models of crimp tool.

As an alternative to bullet connectors, blade style contacts can also be used for in-line connections as shown in Figure 2.8. If you choose to use this form of connection then make sure of two things:

1. The female connector is always on the supply or 'hot' side of the circuit, otherwise a situation could occur where a disconnected contact pair has a live, exposed male contact that could easily be inadvertently short-circuited to earth.
2. The female is always fully insulated over its whole length preferably with some overhang on the front edge, again to prevent accidental contact with earth.

Tight connections are very important. Every time a female blade connector is disconnected it loses some spring force and surface plating. This both increases resistance and allows moisture ingress into the connection point, promoting corrosion. It is possible to re-tighten the connection by slightly squeezing the female contact with pliers. Try to do this just behind the front opening so that the connectors can still be easily mated.

Crimping blade connectors

Crimp tools usually have colour coded crimp jaws that are matched with those on the contacts. The correct contact and crimp position should be selected for the wire size as shown in Table 2.1.

Even very inexpensive crimping pliers, like type 1 shown in Figure 2.9, seem to do a good job of crimping terminals onto wires. Type 2 is a little more costly and makes a more sophisticated crimp. The jaws of the crimp tools in Figure 2.9, are shown in close-up in Figure 2.10.

Type 1 forms an oval and type 2 a dimple crimp. The dimple crimp is more secure than the oval because it more effectively reduces the volume of the crimp barrel — that part of the contact into which the wire is inserted — and thus compresses the wire rather than simply distorting it. However, the resulting crimp connection can be worse than that of an oval crimp if the crimp barrel of the contact is not correctly inserted into the jaws. Most crimp terminal barrels are made, not from solid tube, but from folded metal, so that they have a slit down them where the edges join. The dimple of the crimp jaw must always compress the barrel as shown by the arrows in Figure 2.11, never on the slit side.

Crimping is less skill sensitive than soldering so can provide a better connection so long as certain rules are observed.

1. Make sure that the wire, connector and crimp tool jaw cavity all equate in AWG or mm² size.
2. Strip the wire to the correct length for the crimp barrel. The wire insulation should abut the back of the barrel and the wire itself should just emerge from the front end.
3. Crimp in the centre of the crimp barrel. This can be hard to determine because of the overhang of the plastic

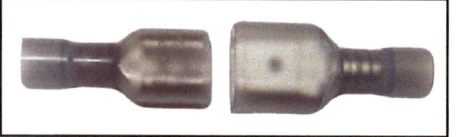

Figure 2.8. With both the male and female contacts insulated, this style of bladed connector is an ideal alternative to bullet connectors for in-line connections.

Colour	AWG Range	mm² Range
Red	22-18	0.35-1
Blue	16-14	1.25-2.5
Yellow	12-10	3-6

Table 2.1. Crimp tool and contact colour codes.

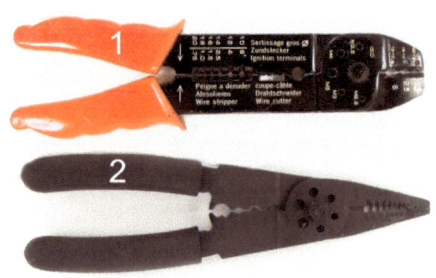

Figure 2.9. Two of the many kinds of crimping tools available.

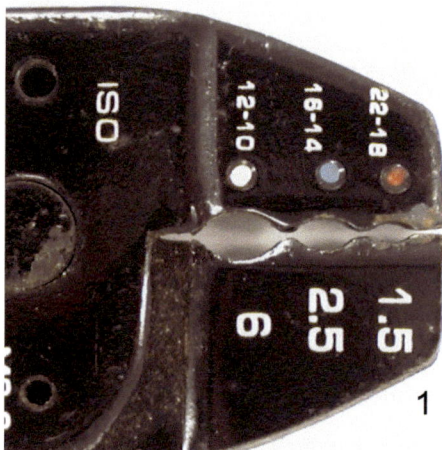

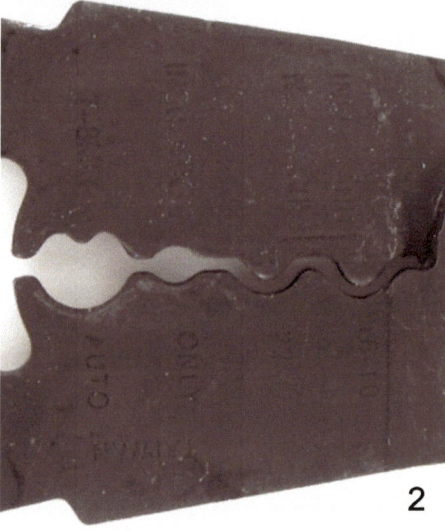

Figure 2.10. Crimp tool style 1 makes an oval crimp whereas type 2 produces a more secure dimpled crimp.

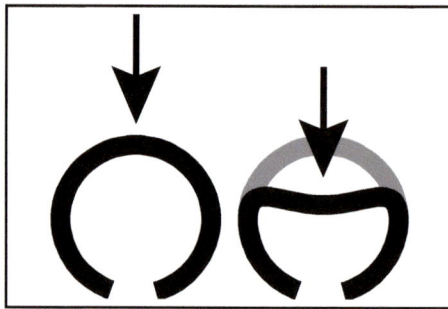

Figure 2.11. A dimple crimp must be applied to the side of the crimp barrel that is opposite to the split section.

TOOLS, WIRE HANDLING & CONNECTORS

insulation. Most crimp barrels are 0.120in (3mm) long and most crimp tool jaws are 0.040in (1mm) wide. The front of the crimp barrel is usually visible so that a centralized crimp can be made by placing the jaws 0.040in (1mm) back from the front edge of the barrel, an easy distance to judge if you make yourself familiar with a metric ruler.

4. Squeeze the crimp tool closed as far as possible. Most crimp tools have stops that prevent over-crimping.

5. Tug on the finished crimp. A good crimp should be able to withstand a 15lb (7kg) pull.

Piggyback connectors

There are occasions when it is necessary to join two female blade terminals to a single male. There are a variety of styles of piggyback devices that can achieve this objective, some of which are shown in Figure 2.12.

It is also possible to crimp two wires into a single connector as shown in Figure 2.13. Strip the wires, twist them together and slide them into the connector crimp barrel. If it is a tight fit, you will need to use the next largest size of contact as listed in Table 2.1.

Earthing connectors

When making connections to body metal, it is useful to have a selection of ring terminals available like those shown in Figure 2.14. Besides having different crimp barrel sizes, colour coded for the correct wire gauges, a number of different hole sizes are also required in order to fit under existing bolts, and avoid the necessity to drill yet one more hole in the vehicle's sheet metal. Serrated washers (Figure 2.15), are recommended on ring terminals in order cut through any paint or superficial rust on the metal surfaces. Use the type on the left above the terminal, or the style in the middle below it. The anti-rotation type of washer, like those on the right, are not nearly as good at providing electrical continuity.

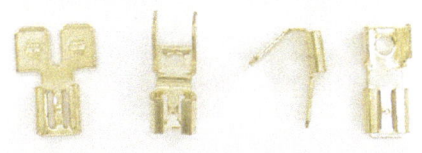

Figure 2.12. There are a number of different piggyback contacts which allow two female contacts to join to a single male. The choice of which to use is determined by the application.

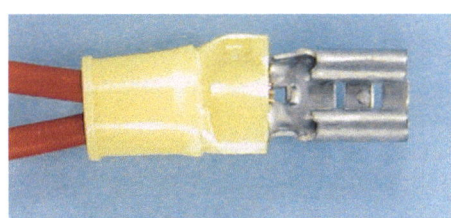

Figure 2.13. So long as the crimp barrel is not overloaded, splicing can also be achieved by crimping more than one wire into a single connector.

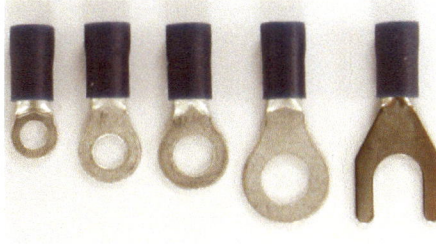

Figure 2.14. A selection of ring terminals for making earth connections.

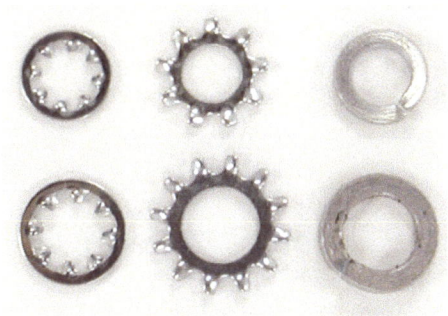

Figure 2.15. Serrated washers, left and centre, are preferred for making electrical connections to the split anti rotation washers shown on the right.

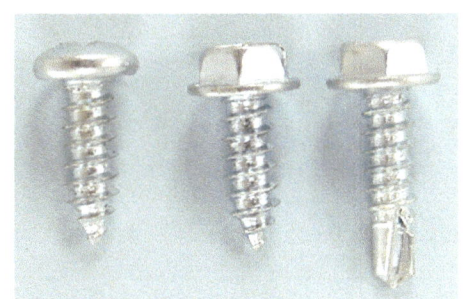

Figure 2.16. Panel and self-tapping screws cut into the vehicle's body metal and are far superior to nut & bolt fasteners for earthing.

Panel screws like those in Figure 2.16 cut into the metal and are far better than nut and bolt fasteners as far in ensuring good electrical connection to body metal, but see page 20.

Splicing connectors

Temporary wire splicing is discussed in Emergency Equipment page 22.

There are basically two types of splices, butt splices in which both wires enter the connector from the same side and in-line splices in which one wire enters from one side of the connector and the other wire from the other end.

Referring to Figure 2.17, the top device is simply a double ended crimp barrel. The bottom device is a large crimp barrel that can take more than one wire. Both of these devices can be used to join more than two wires as long as the combined wires fit with little interference into the crimp barrel.

The centre in-line device is manufactured by Swenco® and called a Posi-Lock™. There is also a similar butt splice called a Posi-Twist™. They are useful for a couple of reasons.

1. Apart from a wire stripper no other tools are required. It is simply necessary to strip each wire ½in (13mm) and insert it into the device and tighten the end nut by hand.

2. The wire acceptance range is very wide. There are a number of colour coded sizes but the blue device, for example, can accept 18AWG to 12AWG (1mm² to 6mm²) and so can be used with a large number of wire combinations.

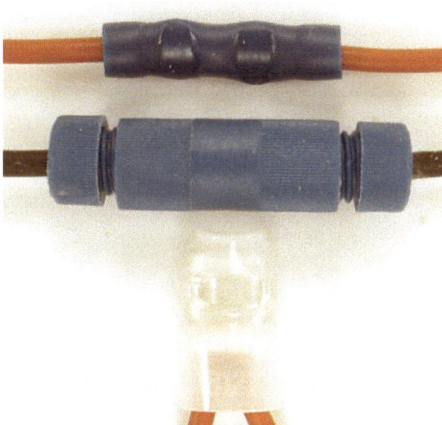

Figure 2.17. Splice connectors are designed to join two or more wires that are not normally intended to be disconnected.

MGB ELECTRICAL SYSTEMS – THE ESSENTIAL MANUAL

IDC taps

IDC or insulation displacement connectors are often supplied along with car accessory equipment as they provide a quick and easy way to splice a tap or spur circuit to an existing wire.

The connectors contain a blade that has two slots in it as shown in Figure 2.18. The wire is forced into a slot, cutting (or displacing) the insulation so that the blade can make electrical connection to the copper conductor. Obviously, if a wire is inserted into each slot then there will be an electrical connection made between the wires via the blade.

Figure 2.19 shows two views of a typical automotive IDC tap. The existing wire is pushed into the bottom hole through the slot provided. A spur wire, usually routed to an added accessory, is pushed into the blind hole. Pliers are used to squeeze the blade into the connector and over the wires. The cover is then snapped over the top in order to prevent the blade from pushing back out.

IDCs are used extensively in the telecommunications industry for joining the thin 24AWG (0.2mm²) solid wire that is required to carry the 20 thousandths of an amp or so of telephone loop current. They are carefully designed to work with one type of solid wire only and as such are very reliable. Wire that small is not practical for use in vehicles and solid wire would be too stiff to use in the larger gauges required for cars. Unfortunately, stranded wire does not work well in IDCs because its conductor is not as structurally stable as that of a solid conductor. Rather than grip the conductor tightly, the blade tends to cut the strands or just reshape the bundle. The fact that the IDC cuts the wire insulation and often damages the wire strands weakens the wire from which the tap is made and makes it vulnerable to degradation due to moisture ingress. While IDCs make quick and convenient automotive connections, they are generally unreliable and not recommended.

WIRE PROTECTION

The insulation around a copper wire is primarily there for electrical reasons. Although it does afford some mechanical protection, wire bundles need additional covering to prevent wire insulation abrasion resulting from vibration that can cause open and short-circuits.

Harness tape

This material, shown in Figure 2.20, was used as original wire bundle covering and, like all tapes, while not easy to apply, can be used over in-situ cables. It has the advantage that it can be used to cover the crotch where a harness divides.

It is perhaps truly self-adhesive since it tends to stick to itself and nothing else without the use of an adhesive layer. It also has a high coefficient of friction so that, especially when wrapped over itself, it does not tend to slip.

Various colours are available but the tape used in MGB/Cs was generally blue.

Heat-shrinkable and self-amalgamating tape

These tapes, which look very similar to one another and while, like other tapes, are applied by wrapping are very different in other respects.

Unrestricted, polyolefin heat-shrink tape (Figure 2.21) can reduce in length by about 30% when heated above about 275°F (135°C). If applied around a wire bundle it tightens in is attempt to shrink and holds the assembly together very firmly. While hot, its surface becomes a little tacky, so that it sticks to itself to a degree but cannot be relied upon not to unravel unless held with a tie or threaded under itself.

Self-amalgamating butyl-rubber tape needs no heat. Instead a protective layer is pealed off and the tape wound over the cable much like any other tape. However, being based on a form of rubber, it can elongate some 700% allowing a very tight wrap. So long as it is dry, after about an hour the tape will fully amalgamate into a solid mass. It does not stick to the wires beneath it but cannot be unwrapped, a knife being required to remove it.

This product is often used where protection from water is required It does make a very stiff assembly, which some regard as a disadvantage,

PVC tape

PVC tape is every electrician's friend, and a selection of colours is useful. Unfortunately, even the best brands don't seem to hold up very long, especially in the high temperatures found in the engine bay or where oil, grease or fuel may be present. Most of us are familiar with the tacky mess that this tape leaves at the end of its useful life. As a result, it is not a good material for the permanent protection of the vehicle wiring.

Convoluted tubing

This excellent material, illustrated in Figure 2.22, is frequently used in modern cars. It is usually supplied slit down its length so that it can be slipped over the wire bundle. A wide range of sizes and colours are available, including even a chrome effect.

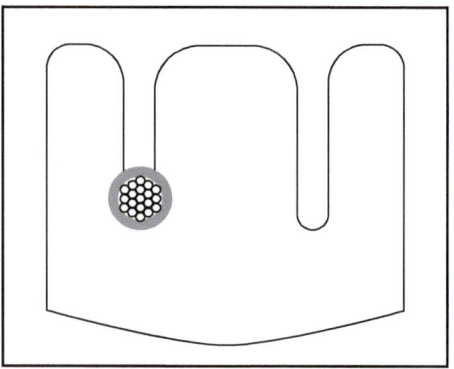

Figure 2.18. The blade of IDC connectors cuts through the insulation of the wire and connectors to the copper conductor inside.

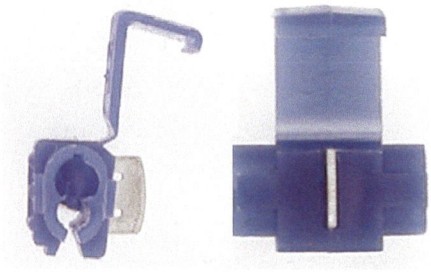

Figure 2.19. Two views of a typical IDC connector.

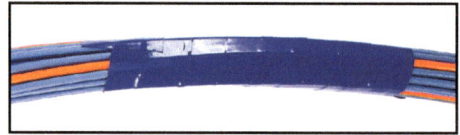

Figure 2.20. Harness tape.

Figure 2.21. Heat shrink-tape. When applied, self-amalgamating tape looks very similar.

TOOLS, WIRE HANDLING & CONNECTORS

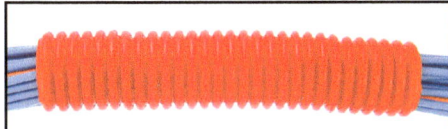

Figure 2.22. Convoluted tubing

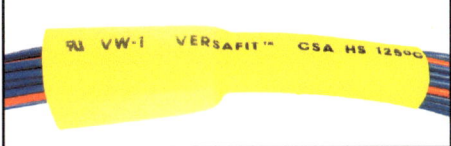

Figure 2.23. Heat-shrink tubing

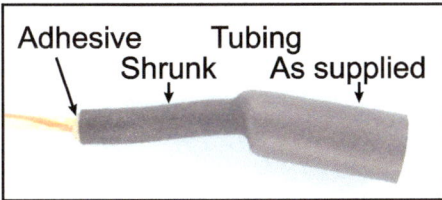

Figure 2.24. Adhesive-lined shrink tubing.

Figure 2.25. Even without an adhesive lining, shrink tubing can be used to cap-off wires.

Heat-shrink tubing

Heat-shrink tubing, Figure 2.23, is a very good product for protecting wires, although it has its limitations too, especially the fact that it has to slide over the section of wire or cable being protected, which requires end access.

Heat-shrink is really a misnomer; the product is correctly described as heat-recoverable, since it starts out as a tube that is extruded at the smaller diameter. After extrusion, it is radiation cross-linked, a process that renders it no-longer thermoplastic and improves many of the material's functional characteristics including its temperature withstand and resistance to cut-through and abrasion. The process also results in giving it shape memory, meaning that it can be heated, distorted and then cooled, after which the distortion remains in the product. On re-heating, the cross-linked polymer 'remembers' its original shape and tries to recover to it. The distortion most often imparted is to expand the material above its original diameter so that the subsequent application of heat causes it, if unrestricted, to return to its original diameter. Don't therefore think that applying more and more heat to the tubing will make it shrink smaller and smaller. Once it has recovered its original size or tightened over whatever is restricting it, then it will shrink no further and additional heat may only scorch it and perhaps melt the wiring underneath.

Heat-shrink ratios, that's the supplied diameter compared to the fully shrunk diameter, of 2:1 or 3:1 are available but these are not always sufficient to allow the tubing to be passed over whatever might be on the end of the wire; a connector for example. Furthermore, heat shrink tubing requires a 'hot air gun' to shrink it down at temperatures around 275°F (135°C); that's above the service temperature for PVC of 185°F (85°C), and so shrinking has to be done very quickly so as not to permanently damage the wire insulation. Hot air guns are available from hardware stores and double as household paint strippers.

The heat shrink tubing in Figure 2.24 has adhesive lining which melts when the tubing is shrunk and can be seen emerging slightly from the tube end. This property is not really of much advantage for simply covering wire but it does provide very good protection for splice repairs. The wire cores can be soldered or crimped together and covered in the heat shrink tubing which, with its hot-melt glue lining, provides insulation, sealing and strain relief all in one operation. Even tubing without adhesive is tacky enough when hot that it can be used to cap-off unused wires by shrinking it over the end and squeezing the overhang with pliers, as shown in Figure 2.25

Cable clamps

Bundles of wires can become quite heavy so most manufacturers supported the cable along its length using metal clips (Figure 2.26) with rubber protection between the clip and the cable. After many years of service, the rubber often deteriorates and falls away, leaving the cable loose and at risk of damage from the sharp edges of the clip. It is prudent to check and replace them where necessary.

Adding circuits

There are several projects in this book that will require that new circuits are

Figure 2.26. Cable support clamps.

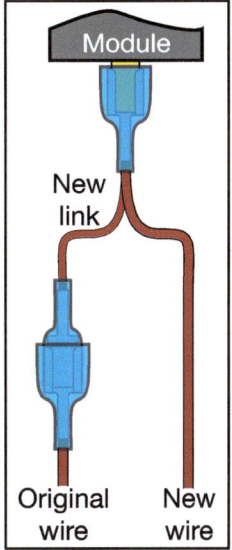

Figure 2.27. A link wire facilitates adding a new circuit to an existing one.

linked into an existing system in which there is no spare connector on a module, such as the fuse block, a relay or flasher. Piggyback connectors, like those in Figure 2.12, will sometimes suffice but are often unreliable when carrying the weight and stiffness of the extra wire. When adding a new circuit that has to join into an existing one, consider adding a link wire as in Figure 2.27

Fragile components, like diodes and resistors, are best mounted on some kind of circuit board, like the example shown in Figure 2.28.

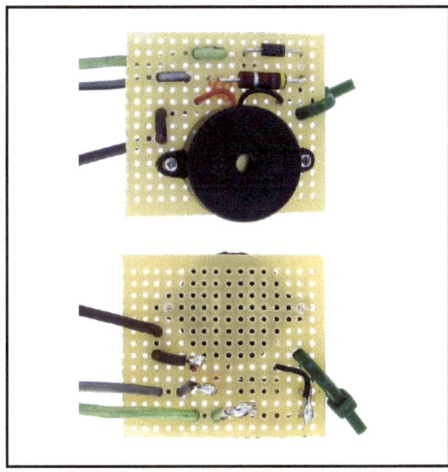

Figure 2.28. Perforated board used to build the circuit in Figure 12.34 (page 129).

17

Chapter 3
Basic electrical theory

ELECTRICAL UNITS

In trying to explain electricity to the layman, it is usual to use physical analogies, which is what we shall do here.

Volt

Voltage can be compared to pressure. Just as high pressure allows water to be pushed through narrow pipes and jump over wide distances, so high voltage can push electrical current down the thin electrical conductors and jump over gaps like those on sparkplugs.

When expressing a quantity, the volt is usually written as 'V' as in 12V meaning 12 volts.

Amp

The amp, which is short for Ampere, is a measure of the rate at which electrical current flows. Just as a current of water flow can be expressed as a certain volume per unit time – such as gallons per minute or litres per second – so an amp is a measure of the quantity of electrical current that flows through an electrical circuit each second. In fact, an amp is equal to 1 coulomb per second, the coulomb being a quantity of electricity.

When expressing a quantity, the amp is usually written as A as in 100A meaning 100 amps.

Watt

A watt is the measure of electrical power, or rate of energy use. The watt is calculated by multiplying the voltage (pressure) across a load, by the Amperage (rate of current flow) through it. The high voltage (high pressure) circuits in a home, of about 110V to 240V depending on the country, can power all sorts of appliances using relatively low current flowing through quite thin wires. At the same time, a low voltage, like that of a car battery, which is 10 or 20 times less pressure than that of home wall outlets can crank an engine via the starter motor by pushing a high current, perhaps hundreds of amps, through thick wires.

When expressing a quantity the watt is usually written as W as in 60W meaning 60 watts.

Ohm

The ohm is the measure of electrical resistance. It is an indicator of how much an electrical conductor restricts current flow. Wide conductors – that is those with a large cross-section like a thick wire – conduct electricity with less restriction than thin wires because they offer lower resistance to flow. Similarly, a large bore pipe restricts water flow much less than a narrow one and is said to offer low resistance. The material that a conductor is made from also affects its resistance; copper has a relatively low resistance, aluminium somewhat higher and carbon higher still. When a material is extremely poor at conducting electricity it is called an insulator. (A material that is somewhere between a conductor and an insulator is called a semiconductor, but that's another subject altogether).

When expressing a quantity, the ohm is usually written as the Greek letter omega as in 10Ω meaning 10 ohms.

Other electrical units

There are many other electrical units, which have relevance to automotive applications, but which would not be appropriate to delve into in a chapter called 'Basic electrical theory'. The list in Table 3.1, although not exhaustive, is given to complete the picture somewhat. When a unit is named after a person, as are most electrical units, it is standard practice to capitalize its abbreviation.

In front of some of the abbreviations, there may be other modifying letters that indicate quantity and that save adding lots of decimal places or zeros. These are shown in Table 3.2. Using the table, it can be seen that writing 1mΩ, meaning

BASIC ELECTRICAL THEORY

Name	Description	Abbreviation	Symbol
Ampere	Electrical current	A	I
Coulomb	Electrical qty or charge	C	Q
Farad	Electrical capacitance	F	C
Henry	Electrical inductance	H	L
Hertz	Frequency	Hz	f
Joule (Watt second)	Energy	J	W
Mho	Electrical conductance	mho or 1/Ω	G
Ohm	Electrical resistance	ohm or Ω	R
Volt	Potential difference	V	V
Watt	Electrical power	W	P

Table 3.1. Electrical units.

Name	Abbreviation	Power of 10	Meaning
Giga	g	10^{12}	1 million million
Mega or Meg	m	10^{6}	1 million
Kilo	k	10^{3}	1 thousand
Deci	d	10^{-1}	1 tenth
Centi	c	10^{-2}	1 hundredth
Milli	m	10^{-3}	1 thousandth
Micro	μ	10^{-6}	1 millionth
Nano	n	10^{-9}	1 billionth
Pico	p	10^{-12}	1 millionth of a millionth

Table 3.2. Electrical unit modifiers.

one thousandth of an ohm, is often preferable to writing 0.001Ω.

SOME USEFUL FORMULAE

volts = amps × resistance
volts = watts ÷ amps
volts = √(watts × resistance)
amps = volts ÷ resistance
amps = watts ÷ volts
amps = √(watts ÷ resistance)
resistance = volts ÷ amps
resistance = volts × volts ÷ watts
resistance = watts ÷ (amps × amps)
watts = volts × amps
watts = amps × amps × resistance
watts = volts × volts ÷ resistance

A PRACTICAL EXERCISE

Figure 3.1 is an electrical circuit, sometimes called a schematic. The 12V power supply could be, for example, a car battery. The 60W load could be any of a number of loads found in a vehicle, a headlamp bulb or the heater blower-motor perhaps. The load has a resistance 'R' and draws a current 'I'. The capital letter 'I' may not seem a very logical symbol for a unit measured in Amperes and called current, but in some languages the word for current starts with I and is similar to the English word 'Intensity' so that is what, in 1950, the International Electromechanical Commission chose to use, and we won't argue with them.

Using the formulae above we can find the resistance 'R' and the current 'I' as follows:

I (amps) = watts ÷ volts = 60 ÷ 12 = 5A
Further:
resistance (Ω) = volts ÷ amps = 12 ÷ 5 = 2.4Ω
or
resistance (Ω) = volts × volts ÷ watts = 12 × 12 ÷ 60 = 2.4Ω
or
resistance (Ω) = watts ÷ (amps × amps) = 60 ÷ (5 × 5) = 2.4Ω

In Figure 3.1, the negative side of the battery, marked '-' is connected to a symbol like that in Figure 3.2. This symbol will become quite familiar; it is called earth or ground; neither of which terms is a good description for a platform like a vehicle that sits on rubber tyres. It indicates that a wire or component is connected to the vehicle's chassis or frame. Chassis or frame would therefore be more appropriate terms but 'earth' is used throughout this book because that it the standard terminology in the MGB/C's native land. Since this frame is a large mass of continuous metal, any two things attached to it will effectively be connected together and earthed. One side of the battery is always connected to earth, and in most cars, including MGCs and all MGBs from 1967, the negative side is earthed. Earlier MGs had positive connected to earth. What is the advantage of one method over the other? In cars with electronic systems there is a clear benefit to negative earth, which best suits the electrical conduction direction of most transistors. Various claims are made concerning which method is better for offsetting corrosion, or making sparkplugs operate more efficiently, but if you have a positive earth vehicle there is no real need to attempt to switch it over, unless you want to use a modern radio, alternator or electronic ignition.

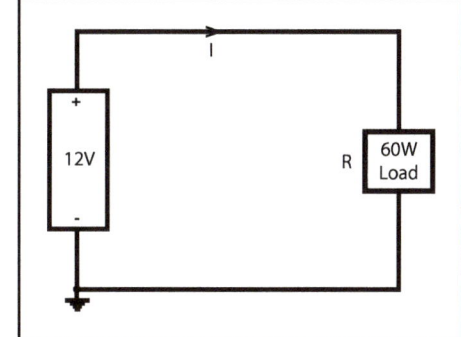

Figure 3.1. A very basic electrical circuit.

Figure 3.2. The earth or ground symbol will become very familiar.

MGB ELECTRICAL SYSTEMS – THE ESSENTIAL MANUAL

CORROSION
The issue of corrosion is, of course, not solely an electrical one, but deserves consideration in this chapter because so many of the problems that occur in MGB electrical systems are directly or indirectly caused by the phenomenon.

Corrosion is a complex chemical process, much of which is beyond the scope of this book, but some basic understanding may help enhance MGB reliability when making repairs or modifications.

Atmospheric corrosion
Atmospheric corrosion, which occurs, for iron and steel, at a humidity greater than about 60%, is largely a problem for the body of the vehicle and not one that needs to be considered alone for the electrical system.

Galvanic corrosion
Galvanic corrosion, sometimes called dissimilar metal corrosion, occurs when two different metals are joined in the presence of an electrolyte. An electrolyte is effectively water mixed with impurities that may be, in the case of a vehicle, road salt, the by-products of combustion such as sulphur-dioxide or airborne chlorides often called acid rain.

The two different metals and intervening electrolyte actually form a small battery. The word galvanic comes from the name of the Italian physician and anatomist Luigi Galvani (1737-1798) who first discovered that dissimilar metals in an aqueous solution caused an electrical potential to be set up. He accidentally found this phenomenon when dissecting frogs; his scalpel was a different metal from the clamp he was using to hold the frog and this caused its muscles to contract.

In an electrical circuit there are many metal-to-metal contacts as indeed there are in a mechanical one. If there is a difference in the surface metals and there is any danger of moisture coming between them then corrosion may occur. The mechanical engineer has the luxury of being able to coat metals with a material such as paint in order to both seal the moisture out and to insulate to prevent any electrochemical action. The electrical engineer, by contrast, has to allow full metal to metal contact because he absolutely needs to allow electric currents to flow.

It is well known that certain metals are highly resistant to corrosion. These are called the noble metals; gold, platinum and to a lesser extent silver being among them. Another name for these metals is 'cathodic'. When two metals and an electrolyte set up a battery effect, one metal will become the anode or positive pole, and the other will be the cathode or negative pole.

In a galvanic cell, only one of the two metals will corrode and that is always the metal that is the more anodic or least noble.

Table 3.3 show the relative nobleness of various common metals that may be found in vehicles. By using the matrix, it is possible to determine which combinations of metals will best resist corrosion in an electrical circuit. To use the table, look at the horizontal and vertical intersection of the two metals that will be in contact and check the shading against the key. For example, if the vehicle has, as most cars do, a mild steel frame and we are considering installing one of a number of screws – a zinc-plated, a tin-plated or a stainless steel screw – into it, we can use the table to make a choice. Mild steel and zinc intersect at a red square, so galvanic action, that is corrosion, will occur. Mild steel and tin intersect at a white square, so there will be no significant galvanic action. Surprisingly, this is a better choice than a stainless steel screw because mild steel and stainless steel intersect at a grey square, so galvanic action may occur.

To take a more complex example: say we wish to make a new earth connection. A hole is drilled into the panel to accept a stainless steel self-tapping or panel screw. This will retain a tin-plated ring terminal and we have chosen to use a zinc-plated serrated washer on both sides of it to make a good connection by cutting into the terminal, the body sheet metal and the screw. In this case we have also decided to crimp two wires into the ring terminal and it turns out that one has a tinned-copper and the other a bare-copper conductor.

Starting with the stainless steel screw, which is tapped into the mild steel sheet metal, the intersection of stainless steel and mild steel is a grey box that indicates corrosion 'may occur'. Since the mild steel panel is less noble than stainless steel, it will corrode and not the screw.

The screw head will also be in contact with the zinc-plated serrated washer. Looking at the intersection of stainless steel and zinc we see that corrosion 'will occur'. Again, the screw is the nobler, so it will not corrode, whereas the washer will do so. Similarly, the zinc-plated washers will also corrode in contact with the mild steel panel, the screw and the tin-plated ring terminal.

The tin-plated terminal will obviously not galvanically react with the tin-plated wire but corrosion 'may occur' between the bare-copper wire conductor and the terminal.

Should we and can do anything about this situation? The table is really a worst case scenario for a 2% saline electrolyte solution If the ring terminal is to be located in an absolutely dry area of the vehicle or if the car resides in a hot dry desert region, then any corrosion may be so slow as to be worth ignoring.

Otherwise we would turn our attention to the worst problems first, and they are the zinc-plated washers that are key to making good connections to the panel and terminal. A few years ago, these washers would have almost certainly have been cadmium-plated. From Table 3.3 it can be seen that a cadmium-plated washer would perform well in contact with both the mild steel panel and the tin-plated terminal. It would be a problem in contact with the stainless steel screw, but that could be solved by also using a cheaper, and at the time more readily available, cadmium-plated screw. In most countries, toxicity issues have lead to severe restrictions in the use of cadmium because of the fear of it getting into land-fills and so into the water supply. A tin-plated screw and washers would solve the problem. If the bare-copper wire can be substituted for a tin-plated wire then another weakness of the assembly will be eliminated.

Sealing may also be an option. The sharp end of the screw should certainly be painted or under-sealed. Painting of the electrical side may not be very desirable or even effective. Electrical grease will certainly keep out moisture but is messy and attracts dirt.

Some anti-corrosion systems on ships and oil rigs use sacrificial anodes and impressed currents to force the structural members to be cathodes and thus prevent them from corroding preferentially. You may also have a sacrificial anode in your home water heater or to protect the propeller of your boat's outboard motor. It could

BASIC ELECTRICAL THEORY

be argued that in a running car, current flow is such that it also impresses a current that may reinforce or reverse the galvanic cell that is causing corrosion. There is some truth to this so that in an operating negative earth car the steel body becomes the more cathodic and will corrode last, while the opposite is true in a positive earth car. Remember however that a vehicle – and hence also its electrical system – runs for relatively brief periods: a car designed for a 10 year, 100,000 mile (160,000km) life that runs at an average of 50mph (80km/h) will actually only be in use, with electrical current flowing, for a total of 2000 hours (about 12 weeks) or 2.3% of the time.

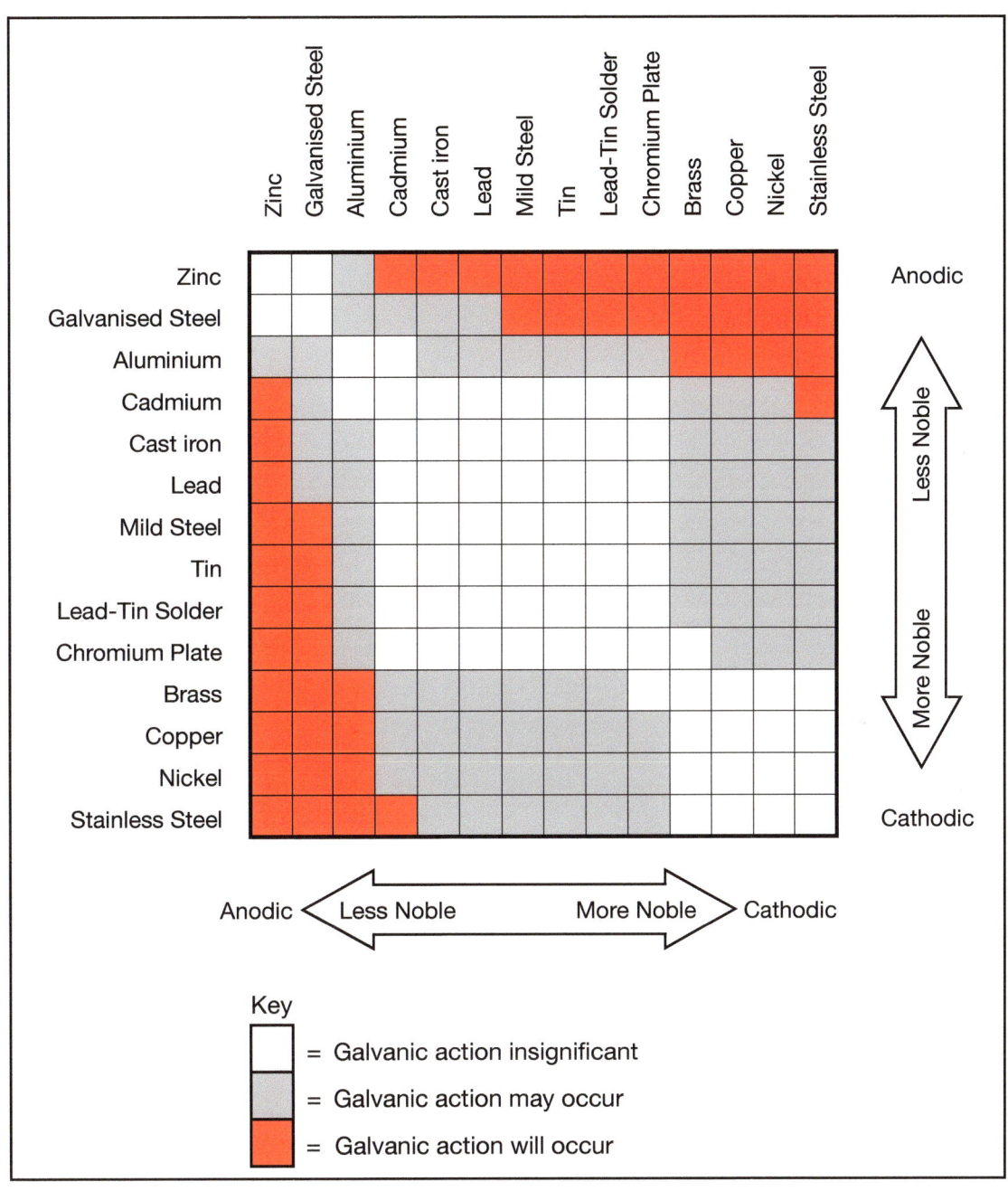

Table 3.3. Galvanic corrosion table.

Chapter 4
Emergency repairs

GENERAL
Although prevention is the best policy, it makes sense with a car like the MGB/C, any example of which is decades old, to be prepared in the event of an unexpected electrical problem.

This chapter provides some suggestions on what 'being prepared' means and what to do if, unfortunately, electrical things go wrong. What you choose to carry will depend on how far you travel from home and how inclined you are to make repairs on the road.

WHAT TO CARRY
Mobile phone
If you have a cell phone it is real reassurance but useless unless you know whom to call. Make sure you have listed or stored all the numbers of any organizations and individuals who would be willing to come to your help.

If you don't smoke, you may never have tested the cigar lighter socket. If you are going to use it as a phone charging source, make sure it works before you leave.

Jump start cables
It goes almost without saying that jump (booster) cables are a necessary accessory, not just in your ancient MGB/C, but for your modern car, too. (See page 52 for tips on using jump cables). Inexpensive, lightweight cables are almost useless, 4AWG (the smaller the number the larger the cable size), 135A, 12ft (3.5m) being the minimum needed.

Fan belt
The ignition light will be the first indication of the fan belt failing and the generator not turning. It is also, of course, a good warning before the effects of the inoperative fan and water pump exacerbate the situation.

Fuses
In theory, fuses always fail for a reason and replacing them without fixing the overload or short circuit causing the failure should be futile; the new fuse failing immediately. In fact, we all know of fuses that have failed for no apparent reason, so having the correct fuse available, (rather than risking a fire by bridging with foil, nails, etc.), makes some sense. An intermittent fault may not repeat itself for a while and an overload can take 30 minutes to blow a fuse.

Sparkplugs
A set of sparkplugs is inexpensive and will never be wasted, even if you never need them in an emergency. Actual failures with modern plugs are rare. Flooding an engine during starting is all too easy, and a new set of plugs will get you on the road sooner than it would take to dry out the original set.

Bulbs
Make sure you have spare bulbs for the safety-related functions: stop/tail, turn signals and front side lights. Sealed beam units may not be practical to carry as a spare, but see Sealed Beam Units on page 25.

www.velocebooks.com/www.veloce.co.uk
All books in print • New books • Special offers • Gift Vouchers

EMERGENCY REPAIRS

Wire
A few feet of wire, perhaps 16AWG (1.5mm^2) or 14AWG (2.5mm^2) can often be used to band-aid a bad circuit that cannot be properly diagnosed on the road.

Special jumper wires as described below can also by-pass electrical trouble spots.

PVC adhesive electrical tape
This is so ubiquitous, useful and inexpensive that we all must already own some.

Torch (flashlight) and plug-in light
Although a lamp that plugs into the cigar lighter socket will give more light for longer, and so is a good investment, remember a battery powered flashlight will work even if there is no power available from the car (provided of course that the batteries are fresh).

Water repellent
There are many brands of products designed to assuage the effects of water on electrical systems, WD40® being the most well know. Note that many people use WD40 and its kin for cleaning electrical contacts. This is a mistake, the makers do recommend it for cleaning purposes but they also claim it leaves a protective film. Any such film could work as an electrical insulator, which is exactly what is not wanted on a connector or relay contact.

There is an old joke about WD40, and like most jokes, there is a hint of truth in it. If it doesn't move but should, use WD40; if it does move but shouldn't, use duct tape.

Rain-X®
A fresh application of this product, and presumably its competitors' too, really does allow the vehicle to be driven, with caution, without windscreen wipers. You probably have a bottle in the garage; it's so small that it makes sense to carry it just in case those wipers fail.

TOOLS
Make sure you have the necessary spanners required to remove battery terminals and to replace a fan belt. Inch sizes of ¼, ⅜, ⁷⁄₁₆, ½, ⁹⁄₁₆ and ⅝ across flats (A/F) will usually suffice.
- A sparkplug spanner is also a necessary adjunct to the tool kit.
- A set of screwdrivers that including a least a flat blade and a cross-head will be necessary to access lamp bulbs. See also Tools and Components.
- A tool to cut and strip wires such as a pocket knife or proper wire strippers.
- A small piece of Emery cloth or sandpaper for cleaning contacts.

RUNNING REPAIRS
Battery/generator problems
Batteries do have a finite life and sometimes the failure to start the car is indeed the signal to buy a new one. However, before spending out on one prematurely, check for other problems too.

Starting problems are very often due to a poor connection at the battery, which can exhibit itself as a warm-to-the-touch battery terminal after an attempt to start the car. Check that the battery connections are tight and clean. Remove the earth clamp, then the other one (this sequence prevents the spanner from causing sparks and possible burns if it touches earth while removing the 'hot' clamp). Clean the clamps and battery posts. Twist them when reinstalling them on the battery posts to further wipe any oxides away, attaching the hot (positive on a negative earth car) connection first and then the earth.

Get a jump start. A battery that cannot start the car will usually get you home after it has been started from another car; even at night if you have a good generator. Unfortunately, the output from the earlier generators or dynamos is often not sufficient to handle running the ignition, lights and other accessories such as windscreen wipers, so turn off anything not absolutely essential, such as the heater fan and the radio. Once started, keep the engine running if possible until you get home.

Check that the fan belt is present and tight.

If the ignition light doesn't come on when the key is turned then the problem could be the generator (usually the brushes), be it a dynamo or an alternator, or could just be the ignition bulb itself. The bulb provides the initial magnetizing current for the generator; but once generating, the generator provides its own current. Check the bulb by removing the small yellow/brown wire from the generator. Have an assistant switch the ignition on and verify that the bulb illuminates when the wire is touched to earth. If it doesn't, then the problem is the bulb, if it does, unfortunately, the problem is in the generator.

If the problem is the bulb, then start (or jump start) the car and pull the choke no more than half way so that the engine is revving without a rich mixture. Then take your circuit tester and connect it between the generator small terminal, which carries the yellow/brown wire, and the engine block. This should provide sufficient magnetizing current to the generator field winding or rotor to kick it into action.

If you suspect the alternator or dynamo then you will have to persuade the Samaritan who gave you a jump start to keep his/her engine running with jump cables connected for as long as possible. That way you may get enough charge to get you home. Again, don't stop the engine, keep it running and revving (half choke) and be miserly about using any electrical power.

Ignition problems
If you are certain a fault diagnosis points to the ignition, (and such problems can be hard to differentiate from fuel and mixture issues), then do the simple checks first.

Look:
- Is the white wire to the coil attached?
- Is the white/black wire from the coil to the distributor attached at each end?
- Is the high-tension wire from the coil to the centre of the distributor attached?
- Is each of the wires from the distributor to the sparkplugs attached?
- If it is night time, do attempts to start the car, or the badly running engine, result in sparks? Look around the high-tension wires, coil and distributor.
- Are there signs of water or coolant deposits on the coil, distributor or high-tension cables?

Listen:
- Even if sparks cannot be seen, their tell tale tick can often be heard.

Touch:
- Besides looking at all the wires listed above, check for firm wire and cable attachment by lightly tugging on each.

Check that the distributor is firmly clamped and could not have rotated, thus throwing the ignition timing way off. Most 4-cylinder MGBs will run if the vacuum advance diaphragm on the distributor is pointing straight up.

Most of any problems seen, heard or felt can be easily rectified. Others

MGB ELECTRICAL SYSTEMS – THE ESSENTIAL MANUAL

may take a little more investigation.

Should connections to the low tension wires, white and white/black, seem suspect, see 'Joining wires' page 25.

High-tension wires

High-tension wires to and from the distributor are notoriously problematic. Most have brittle carbon cores that can separate under the insulation. Initially, the spark can jump the small gap, but the internal arcing causes further erosion of the carbon until the gap becomes too wide to jump. They often fail at the extremities. If the sparkplug caps are removable – not all are – then a knife may be used to cut an inch (25mm) or so off the suspect wire before re-termination. Similarly, the high-tension wires in the early MGB with the side-entry distributor are retained by a pointed screw accessed from inside the distributor cap. The suspect wire ends can be cut back about ½in (13mm) and re-secured.

High-tension wire replacement is a real case of prevention being the best policy. Old wires will have deteriorated over time, both as far as the inside conductors and the outside insulation are concerned. New wires will be of better technology than those they replace and last at least another decade.

Uneven running, particularly after the engine has warmed up, is sometimes due to #4 sparkplug wire having worn thin as it passes close to, and vibrates against, the heater valve, hose or cable. Check for sparking around that point. Polythene (polyethylene), the material supermarket plastic bags are made from, is an excellent electrical insulator, and a few wraps of that around the offending cable should get you home.

The heater valve itself can leak and spray water onto the distributor, as can a leak from the head gasket. Polythene can again be used, this time to shield the distributor cap from any spray. Once again, it should get you home if the coolant level is also carefully monitored.

Checking for a spark

In order to check for a spark it's helpful to either have an assistant available to turn the ignition key or to have a remote start switch under the bonnet. The cylindrical starter solenoid, (see page 80) used until 1966 has a rubber button on one end that can be pressed

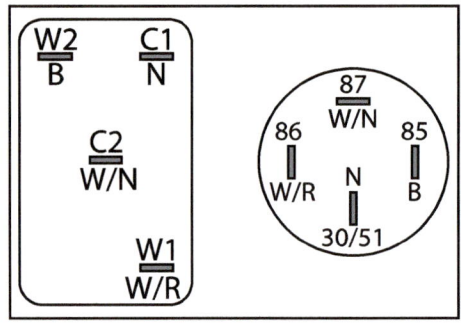

Figure 4.1. Starter relays may be of two forms, rectangular or cylindrical. They are located to the rear of the fuse block.

to turn the starter motor. For later cars, a remote starter switch is required as described on page 85.

If a rectangular solenoid is installed, like that used in cars in 1966 and 1967 (Figure 10.7), then a remote starter switch can be used to jump from the brown wire at the fuse block to the small terminal on the side of the solenoid that carries a white/red wire.

Cars from 1968 have a starter relay to which any remote start switch can be connected. Figure 4.1 shows the starter relays, which were fitted from about 1969, viewed from the contact side. The starter relay, which may be rectangular or cylindrical, is mounted under the bonnet on the right-hand side, close to the bulkhead and just to the rear of the car from the fuse block.

The connections from any remote start switch should be attached: one to the contact with a brown wire and the other to the contact with a white/red wire. If the clip size does not allow attachment without removing wires from the relay, remove the white/red wire and join one clip to its vacated relay terminal and then attach the other wire to where a brown or a white wire connects to the fuse terminals.

Whether you use an assistant or a remote start switch, pull off one plug wire at a time and attach one of your spare sparkplugs. While holding the spare sparkplug by the metal part of the body, pressing it against the engine block, run the starter (with ignition on, of course). Sparks should be seen at the sparkplug gap.

POOR CONNECTIONS
Blade and bullet connectors

Poor connections due to oxidization or low spring pressure are a common cause of problems. They can sometimes be pinpointed because they will run a little warm. Just the wiping

Figure 4.2. A jumper wire with a male connector each side can be carried in the car to connect between the wires that terminate to a bad switch.

action of breaking and remaking a suspect contact will often be enough to temporarily clean it sufficiently to carry current. Loose contacts can be repaired by prudently squeezing the female using pliers. Male contacts can be cleaned with judicious use of emery cloth or sandpaper, remembering that tin plating on a contact is there to protect it; over-abrading it, exposing base metal, will cause the problem to return in future unless that contact is replaced soon afterward.

Switch contacts

MGB switches contain springs that seem to weaken over time. This lowers contact pressure, increases contact resistance, causes heating and possible arcing and an overall worsening of the situation.

In an emergency, a small wire like that shown in Figure 4.2 with a male contact at each end can serve as an extremely useful jumper around switches that might be performing badly. Pull the female contacts from the switches and plug the jumper wire in to each.

The lighting switch is somewhat more of a challenge, having one power input and two output wires, one for side lamps and one for headlamps. In this case, desperate situations require desperate measures. Cut off the contact from whichever is the longer of the red or red/green (side lamps) or blue (headlamps) wire, strip it back ½in (13mm) and jam it under one of the male terminals as you plug the jumper wire into the remaining two female contacts. Wrap some PVC adhesive tape around the connection in case there is a wayward wire strand poking out. Always connect the brown wire last, it is live and unfused, and make sure it is the first to be removed when you get home.

EMERGENCY REPAIRS

IGNITION SWITCH
It will be necessary to 'hot wire' the car to start it without an effective ignition switch. This is not practical if the key is lost and the vehicle is other than an early car without a steering lock.

Just take a long enough length of your spare piece of wire, strip off about ½in (13mm) of insulation, and jam the end under the white wire to the coil, and the other end under the brown wire at the fuse block. If the ignition switch is damaged so as not to also run the starter motor, again take a length of wire and momentarily join it between the brown wire on the fuse block and the white/red wire on the relay (or solenoid if the car has no relay).

FUEL PUMP
Hard to actually fix on the road, the fuel pump can often be persuaded to jump into life with a few smart blows around its periphery. The correct advice is to use a rubber hammer, but anything that can be wielded should do the job. However, take care not to hit fuel lines.

SEALED BEAM UNITS
You may not wish to carry a spare sealed beam unit but if the outside one fails, driving on the kerb side headlamp can be dangerous, approaching vehicles mistaking the car's width for that of a motorcycle.

Switching them over is quick and easy. Don't lose the chrome rims; toss them in the boot until you get home. If you do not know how to change the unit, refer to page 121.

POOR EARTHS
If tightening and cleaning fails to cure poor and intermittent earth connections, try to use a piece of wire which you can strip at one end and clamp under a good chassis bolt and then improvise some way to clamp the stripped end of the other to the bulb holder or whatever. It is hard to be specific in this case as there are too many possible scenarios.

JOINING WIRES
Twist-on connectors, like those shown

Figure 4.3. Wire nuts offer a quick and easy way to temporarily join and insulate wires.

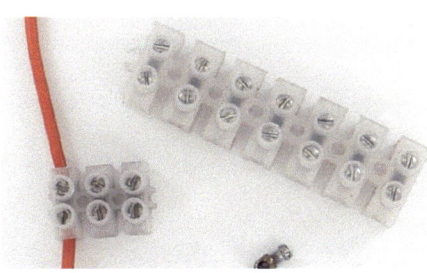

Figure 4.4. Terminal strips can be cut to length with a knife. The wires are pushed into a metal sleeve contained within the insulator block, and secured with screws.

in Figure 4.3, are so familiar to North Americans as to require no description; house wiring there is spliced together with them. However, in Europe, most electrical codes forbid them so they are virtually unheard of. Whether or not safe on 220V-240V house wiring, they do make good, inexpensive, easy and quick wire splices for use in cars. They should probably be considered temporary, but once used for an emergency they seldom seem to get replaced.

Formerly of porcelain, these now plastic tapered caps contain a spiral thread both in the plastic and the internal metal ferrule at the tip. They are available in a number of sizes indicated by colours and can accept from one (as a cap) to almost any number of wires, depending on the size selected. Wires are simply stripped to a length about ⅔rds as long as the connector, twisted together and inserted into the connector. The connector is then twisted on until it is tight. Whether in house or car, PVC tape should then be wrapped around the interface of the cap and wires. The purpose of this is three-fold: (1) the tape will contain and tame any errant strands, (2) particularly in a car, it will discourage the connector from vibrating off and (3) wire insulation, which is stretched during stripping, tends to shrink back, exposing conductor below the connector base.

Europeans are more familiar with the terminal strip (Figure 4.4) that also makes a good semi permanent wire repair. In these blocks, a metal ferrule with clamp screws is used to secure the wire(s). The ferrules are contained and recessed in a plastic housing so that no electrical conductor is exposed. Several such splices may be joined together in a row, the webs linking each having holes in them for fixing down the strip. The webs can easily be cut across the holes with a knife and so adjust the number of terminals in a strip. Again, while rated for house wiring, they make good sense to have around in the car, too. PVC tape around the splice is a prudent measure with these connectors.

Other splicing methods are discussed in 'Wire handling' page 12.

Wires often fail just behind blade and bullet connectors. Crimping and soldering work-hardens the copper conductor and the sudden flex point, where the wire exits the contact, results in a weak section. The insulation often stays intact so the wire looks OK. If the conductor is broken then tugging on the wire usually reveals the problem as the insulation stretches abnormally. The temporary fix is to cut off the contact, strip the wire and reconnect the contact with the stripped conductor secured under it.

www.velocebooks.com/www.veloce.co.uk
All books in print • New books • Special offers • Gift Vouchers

Chapter 5
Sneak currents

WHAT ARE SNEAK CURRENTS?
Sneak is an unexpected path within a system, which under certain conditions can initiate an undesired function or inhibit a desired function. It is a common phenomenon in vehicles in which the electrical earths may have deteriorated due to corrosion.

Sneak is not confined to cars, some famous examples which Boeing research reported as resulting from unanticipated sneak paths are:
• Missile accidentally launched from B-52 bomber while on the runway.
• Bombs accidentally released from a B-52.
• Nuclear bomb inadvertently armed.
• Business jet lost electrical power and drained its batteries without any indication to the crew while in flight.
• Electrical utility worker electrocuted while working on a power line to which the power was "off."
• School fire alarms triggered by flushing toilets.

MGB/Cs and most other vehicles can exhibit strange operational phenomena that occur when a current sneaks through an unexpected path. This could be caused, for example, by the normal path being unavailable because of a poor earth connection or the loss of a fuse.

SNEAK EXAMPLE
Figure 5.1 shows a rather famous example of a sneak current that occurred in an American vehicle, not due to a failure, but due to an original design flaw. Many US vehicles have turn signals, which unlike those used elsewhere, flash the brake lights during a turn.

In this circuit, the hazard switch powers a hazard module that flashes the brake/turn lights. This circuit is connected directly to battery so it can be used even when the ignition is off.

The ignition switch supplies several circuits, in this case only the radio is shown for simplicity.

The brake lights only operate when

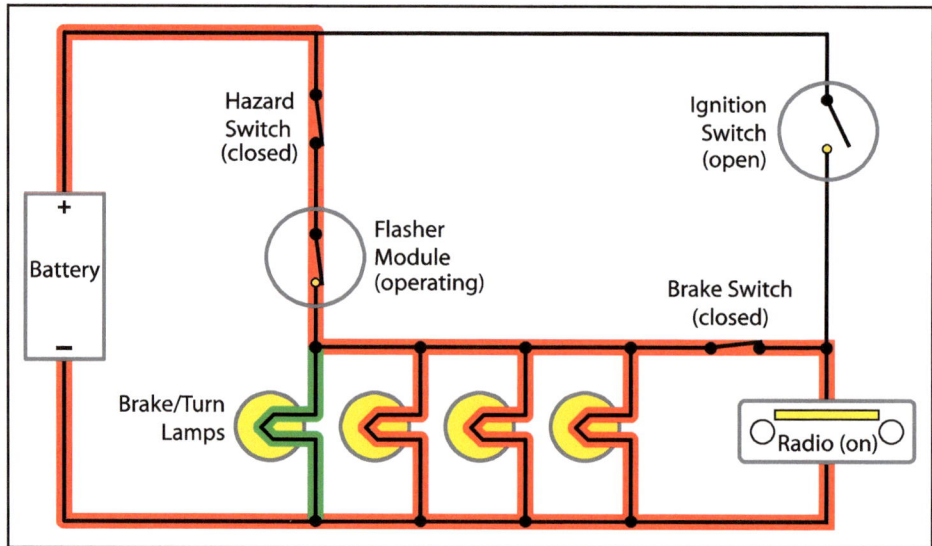

Figure 5.1. A sneak current example in which the radio operates in sequence with the hazard flashers.

SNEAK CURRENTS

the ignition is on, and they do so via a switch from ignition to the brake/turn lamps.

These three circuits all work well independently, but can interact with one another with strange results. In Figure 5.1 the situation is shown where the hazard flashers are on, the radio is switched on (but not operating because the ignition is off), and the driver happens to depress the brake pedal and, in doing so, closes the brake switch. Note how the shaded line shows the current path. Not only do the brake/turn lights flash but in concert with them, the radio pulses on and off too!

MGB/C SNEAK CURRENTS

Strange lamp behaviour is often due to sneak currents resulting from poor earths. The sneak currents described here can occur on MGBs but may also be evident on almost every other vehicle.

Stop/tail lamps

Figure 5.2. Stop/tail lamps almost universally use double filament bulbs, that is to say that the two separate lamp filaments are contained in the same glass envelope and share a common earth path in the form of the outer sleeve of the bulb cap.

Stop/tail circuit

In the stop/tail lamp circuit the right and left hand bulbs are connected together, each filament being connected to its respective circuit – brake or lighting switch. The common stop and tail light terminal, which is the bulb cap, is taken to an earth point physically close to each bulb location on the right and left of the car.

Figures 5.3 through 5.6 show how a double filament bulb with a common earthing cap can result in a sneak current that causes strange behaviour in a stop/tail lamp. The same thing occurs when other lamps share the

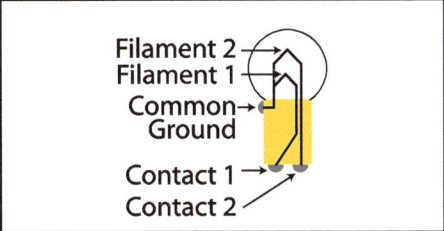

Figure 5.2. The dual filament lamp is a frequent conduit for sneak currents.

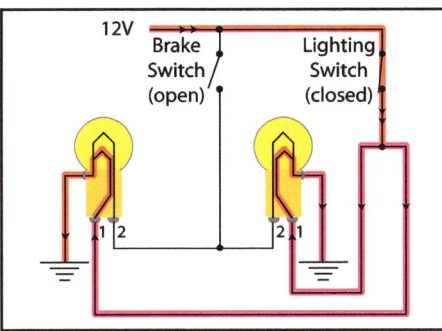

Figure 5.3. The lighting switch has been closed and current, indicated by the shaded line, can flow to the tail lamp filaments via the bulb terminals (1).

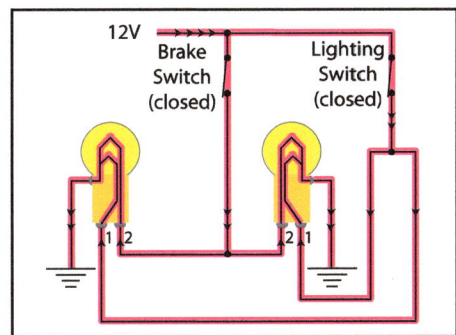

Figure 5.4. The brake switch has been closed, so current can now flow to the stop lamp via the bulb terminals (2).

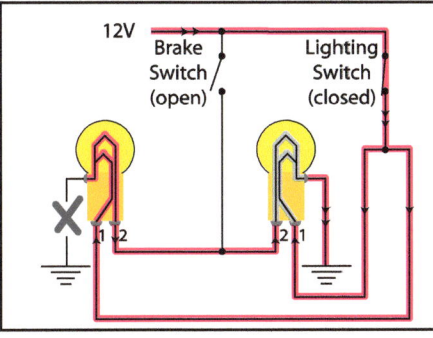

Figure 5.5 is similar to Figure 5.3 but the earth connection at point X has been broken to the left-hand bulb. Note, however, that the current which would normally go to earth through the left-hand tail light now "sneaks" up through the filament for the left-hand stop light, through the stop light wire connecting both lamps, and to earth via the right-hand stop light filament. The effect is that the left-hand lamp is somewhat dimmer than usual (two filaments running at reduced voltage on each), and the right-hand lamp a little brighter (one filament at full voltage, the other at reduced voltage).

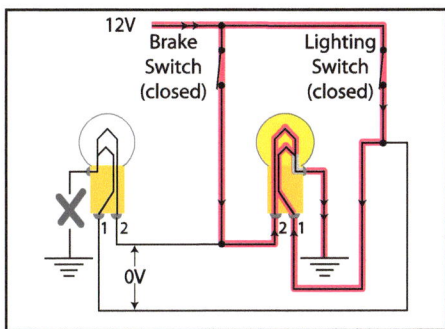

Figure 5.6. When the brake is operated the sneak current flowing between the left and right-hand lamps is opposed by the current flowing to the left-hand stop lamp, and the left tail light goes out. Remember that voltage is electrical pressure and with the earth open to the left-hand bulb and equal voltage being applied to both its filaments, there is zero voltage, or no pressure, differential between contacts 1 and 2 that can push any current through the bulb. The overall effect here is that the left tail light, which appeared to work nearly normally goes out when the brake is applied.

same earth path even though they may not be combined in the same light bulb. For example, the MGB rear turn signal bulb is earthed to the same metal lamp plate as the stop/tail lamps, and if the earth from it is rusted out, or otherwise poor, the turn signal lamp will also use a sneak path back through the stop/tail lamp on the other side. Here, the brake lights can often be seen to be flashing on the wrong side of the car and the rear turn signal fails to work at all when the brake pedal is pressed.

Engine run-on

In a real fault condition found on an MGB, the engine would continue running at night until the driver switched the lights off. Although he didn't notice it at first, the driver was in the habit of keeping his foot firmly on the brake until the engine stopped. The problem was tracked down to a faulty earth on the stop/tail assembly as described above. With the lights on, current would flow into the filament of a tail light, and with no earth to go to, would then sneak its way back through the brake light filament, through the brake switch (because his foot was on the pedal) and so to the hot side of the ignition switch, which also feeds current to the ignition, keeping it alive.

Late cars with ignition relays need very little sneak current to keep the

MGB ELECTRICAL SYSTEMS – THE ESSENTIAL MANUAL

relay coil (and thus also the ignition system) energized, so are especially vulnerable to engine run-on. See page 94.

Unintended engine starting
Another real life example. Whenever the headlights were switched on, the engine would start. Late MGBs earth the front lights and some other systems through a single machine screw which goes into a captive nut, (welded from inside the wheel housing and situated in the engine bay at the right side inner wing (fender) right below the ignition relay and across from the distributor. (The same screw also carries a harness clamp). This earth had become rusted and detached and so the headlamp current was finding a path back through the starter and ignition relay coils which are also earthed – or rather not earthed in this case – via the same screw. They became activated and started the engine.

Engine earth/ground strap
Almost every vehicle engine and the rest of the powertrain, clutch, gearbox, back axle and exhaust are attached to the body by rubber mountings. These not only insulate the vehicle from noise, vibration and harshness (NVH) but electrically insulate it too. However, the engine, or rather the equipment bolted to it – the starter motor, alternator or dynamo and ignition – need to find very low resistance earth paths back to battery. To achieve this, an earthing strap, a wide flexible strap made of several thin copper laminations or many strands of tinned copper wire braided together, is taken from the engine block or transmission to the body metal. On chrome bumper MGBs this can usually be found bridging the left front engine mount, whereas on rubber bumper models it is situated on the gearbox. When an engine and/or transmission have been removed from the vehicle it is very easy to forget to reinstall the earth strap and there are cases recorded when an earth strap was never fitted to the vehicle during build. The problem is that the vehicle can appear to start and run quite well without an earth strap and the consequential problems are never associated with the true cause.

The starter motor requires a current of some hundreds of amps for a short time and the generator may be driving currents of the order of tens of amps for long periods. If these currents are not carried by an earthing strap they will find some sneak paths to get to and from the battery. Such paths include:
- Cables to the choke, heater, speedometer and handbrake
- The gearbox, drive shaft, differential and rear axle.

The problem is that these components were never designed to carry high current via the moving parts.

A Rover SD1 was reported to have had three back axle failures due to crown wheel and pinion pitting before the root cause was found – no earth strap.

Check you have earthing straps on your vehicle, you may find out just why you have always had short-lived cables, poor starting performance and mediocre charging efficiency.

www.velocebooks.com/www.veloce.co.uk
All books in print • New books • Special offers • Gift Vouchers

Chapter 6
Wire harness

WIRES & COMPONENTS
Wire colours

MGB wiring, unlike that of earlier vehicles, is all PVC insulated, a material that allows colour coding of each individual circuit for easier identification. Identification and colour differentiation can nevertheless be difficult. Over the years, many cars will have been painted inside and out, often with little effort to mask-off wiring. Grime and aging will also have taken their toll on wire colouring.

Some wires have single base colours. These are largely confined to the main vehicle functions. Those used in the MGB follow British Standard AU7 as listed below.

Brown	Battery fed (no fuse)
Purple	Battery fed (fused)
White	Ignition fed (no fuse)
Green	Ignition fed (fused)
Blue	Headlamps
Red	Side lamps
Yellow	Overdrive
Black	Earth

Subordinate circuits have tracer stripe colours added to the base colours. For example, the panel lamps operate only when the side lamps (parking) lamps are on and so the wiring can be said to be subordinate to the side lamp circuit. The panel lamps wires have an added white tracer stripe. Similarly, the map lamp is also subordinate to the red circuit and its wires also have a tracer stripe, in this case a purple stripe. Unfortunately there are a lot of anomalies to the base colour rule. A red wire with a light green tracer is, inexplicably, used as part of the two-speed wiper circuit.

Shorthand colour codes are necessary in circuit diagrams and are not always immediately obvious. Having three colours, black, brown and blue all starting with 'b' does not help. The following letter codes are generally accepted.

B	Black
G	Green
K	Pink
LG	Light Green
N	Brown
O	Orange
P	Purple
R	Red
S	Slate or grey
U	Blue
Y	Yellow

Colour codes are written as base-colour/tracer-colour when space allows

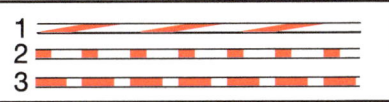

Figure 6.1. How a white/red wire may look in the car (1), its representation in circuit diagrams (2) and a red/white wire (3) for comparison.

or simply as the letter code for the base colour followed directly by that for the tracer if applicable. Thus a red wire with a light-green tracer would be written as red/light-green or simply as RLG.

For graphic production reasons, wires in this book do not look exactly like a those in your car. For example, the white/red wire, (1) in Figure 6.1, is represented in circuit diagrams as per (2). Note that the white segments are wider, unlike the red/white wire (3) in which the red segments are wider.

Component codes

MG used certain numbers to identify components in circuit diagrams where there was not room to fully label each one. Unfortunately, they were not very consistent over the years. This book follows the MG original coding where possible. Table 6.2 provides the full listing.

MGB ELECTRICAL SYSTEMS – THE ESSENTIAL MANUAL

MAJOR HARNESSES

Figure 6.2 is an aid to locating the major harnesses and the most common equipment attached to them. It is not wholly comprehensive, the component fit varying so much from model to model and year to year. For space reasons, it has been necessary to show a left-hand drive vehicle; obviously the cluster and brake switches are located on the right on right hand drive models.

The numbers at each node refer to those found in the circuit diagrams and listed in the 'Component codes chart' Table 6.2.

If you find a wire and do not know its purpose, note its colour and go to the 'Wire function finder' Table 6.1 to identify it.

An oval shape on a harness indicates where it penetrates the body metal.

Smaller harnesses exist at each front corner and to the steering column switches from the cluster node.

The instrument cluster and centre console nodes go to components too numerous to list on the chart, these are:-

Cluster:
6, 7, 10, 13, 14, 24, 26, 27, 34, 36, 38, 43, 44, 46, 64, 72, 76, 82, 95, 118, 159, 211

Console:
20, 32, 53, 57, 58, 60, 67b, 101, 115, 150, 152, 153, 168, 208, 240

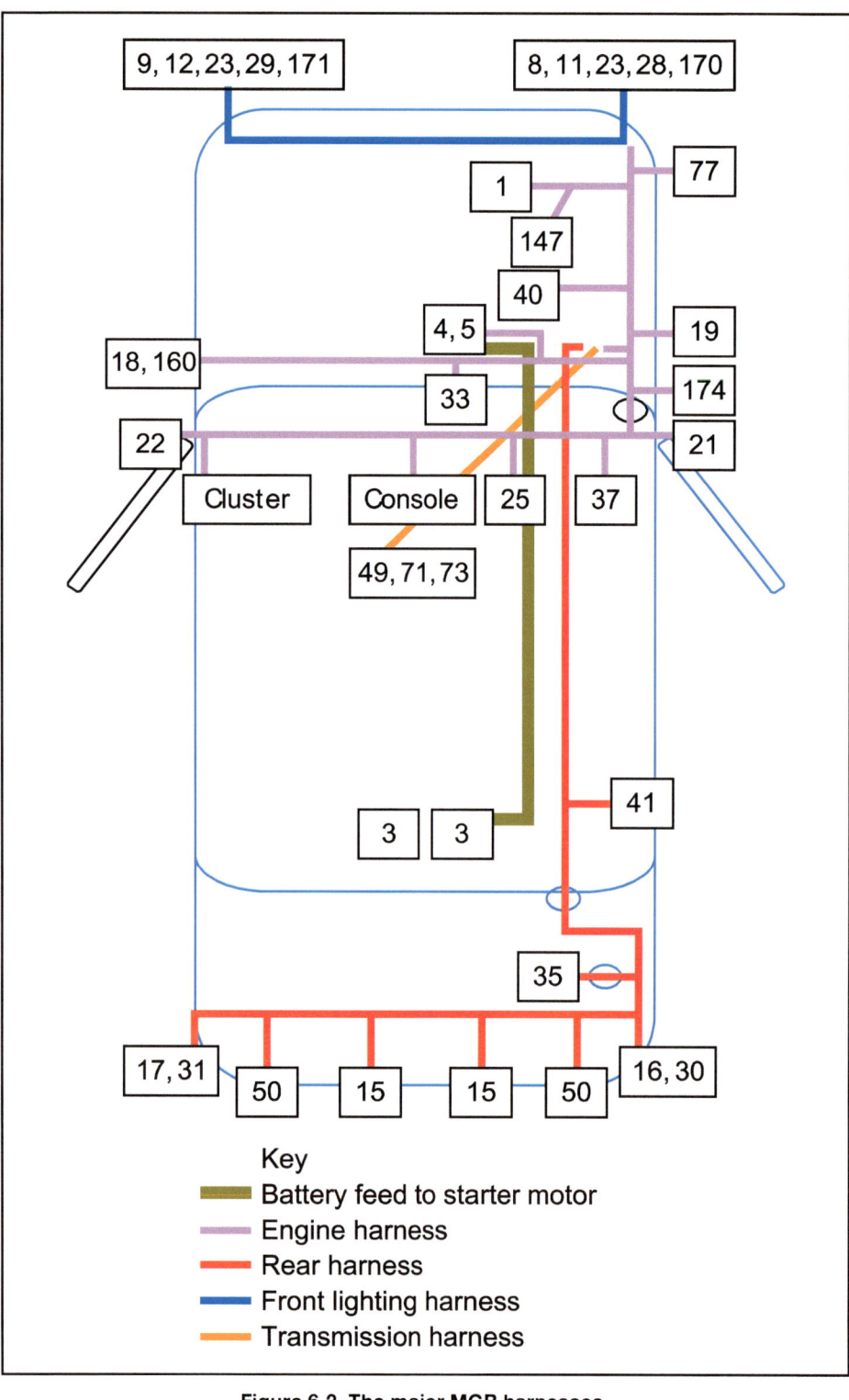

Figure 6.2. The major MGB harnesses.

WIRE HARNESS

MGB WIRE FUNCTION FINDER

Table 6.1 is an aid to identifying the purpose of wires found in the MGB. The function, start and end point of each wire are given for each wire colour.

Some colours are not unique. Where colour duplications occur, a number has been used to discriminate one from another, e.g. G(1), G(2), G(3).

MGB colour codes generally follow the guidelines of British Standard BS-AU7. The base colours indicate the prime function:-

B   Black   Earth
G   Green   Ignition fed (fused)
N   Brown   Battery fed (no fuse)
P   Purple   Battery fed (fused)
R   Red   Side lamps
U   Blue   Headlamps
W   White   Ignition fed (no fuse)
Y   Yellow   Overdrive

A stripe or tracer is used to indicate subordinate circuits.

The component codes refer to those listed in Table 6.2

Table 6.1. Wire function identification by colour

Colour code	Colour base/tracer	Wire Function	From Description	Code	To Description	Code
B	Black	Earth	Any component	NA	Earth	NA
BG (1)	Black/Green	Single speed wiper	Wiper switch	36	Single speed wiper	37
BG (3)	Black/Green	Radiator fan power	Radiator fan 'stat †	246	Radiator fan(s) †	247
BW	Black/White	Brake pressure failure	Brake pressure failure switch †	160	Brake pressure warning switch/lamp †	159
G(1)	Green (1)	Ignition + accessory	Fuse	19	Stop lamp switch	18
					Direction flasher unit	25
					Blower motor switch	32
					Reversing lamp switch	49
					Instrument panel voltage regulator †	64
					Windscreen washer pump †	77
					Reversing lamp switch (auto transmission) †	131
					Hazard flasher switch †	153
					Seat belt control unit †	245
G(2)	Green (2)	Flasher lamp*	RH front flasher lamp	28	Bullet connector to wires GR & GW	NA
			LH front flasher lamp	29		
			RH rear flasher lamp	30		
			LH rear flasher lamp	31		

31

MGB ELECTRICAL SYSTEMS – THE ESSENTIAL MANUAL

Colour code	Colour base/tracer	Wire Function	From Description	Code	To Description	Code
G(3)	Green (3)	Hazard flasher	Hazard flasher switch †	153	Direction flasher unit	25
G (4)	Green (3)	Fan fuse	Radiator fan fuse †	67f	Radiator fan thermostat	246
GB (1)	Green/Black	Fuel gauging	Fuel level sender	35	Fuel gauge	34
GB (2)	Green/Black	Heated backlight	Heated backlight switch (GT only)	115	Heated backlight (GT only)	116
GK	Green/Pink	Accessory & ignition functions	Line fuse †	67a	Blower motor switch	32
					Windscreen wiper motor switch	36
					Windscreen wiper motor parking switch	36
					Wiper motor	37
					Cigar lighter	57
					Radio line fuse ('70 on)	67b
GN (1)	Green/Brown	Reversing lamps	Reversing lamp switch	49	Reversing lamps	50
GN (2)	Green/Brown	Blower motor (pre '68)	Blower motor switch	32	Blower motor	33
GO	Green/Orange	H'brake warning lamp	Hand/parking brake switch †	204	Hand/parking brake warning light †	205
GP	Green/Purple	Stop lamps	Stop lamp switch	18	RH Stop lamp	16
					LH Stop lamp	17
GR	Green/Red	Left hand flasher lamps	Flasher switch LH	26	Bullet connector to wires g(2)	NA
					LH flasher indicator lamp	27
					Hazard flasher switch †	153
GU	Green/Blue	Coolant temperature	Coolant temperature sender	47	Coolant temperature gauge	46
GW	Green/White	Right hand flasher lamps	Flasher switch RH	26	Bullet connector to wires g(2)	NA
					RH flasher indicator lamp	27
					Hazard flasher switch †	153
LGB	Light Green/Black	Windscreen washer	Windscreen wash-wipe switch †	118	Windscreen washer pump †	77
LGG	Light Green/Green	Instrument supply	Instrument panel voltage regulator †	64	Fuel gauge	34
					Temperature gauge	46

WIRE HARNESS

Colour code	Colour base/tracer	Wire Function	From Description	Code	To Description	Code
LGN (1)	Light Green/ Brown	Direction flasher	Flasher switch	26	Direction flasher unit	25
LGN (2)	Light Green/ Brown	Hazard flasher	Hazard flasher switch †	153	Hazard flasher unit †	154
LGP	Light Green/ Purple	Hazard flasher	Hazard flasher switch †	153	Hazard warning lamp †	152
LGW	Light Green/White	Seat belt detect	Inhibitor switch †	201	Driver seat switch (NC) †	198
					Passenger seat Switch † (NC)	199
N	Brown	Battery unfused	Fuse block	19	Alternator †	1
					Control box †	2
					Starter solenoid	4
					Lighting switch	6
					Ignition/start switch	38
					Ignition switch relay †	58
					Radio (pre '70) †	60
					Hazard flasher unit †	154
					Starter solenoid relay ('69 on)	174
NB	Brown/Black	Ignition lamp ('67-'68)	Alternator control box (+) †	2	Ignition warning lamp	45
NG	Brown/Green	Field control	Alternator or Dynamo	1	Alternator control box (f) †	2
					Dynamo control box (f) †	2
					Fasten seat belt lamp †	202
NLG	Brown/Light Green	2 Speed wiper (common)	2 Speed wiper motor †	37	Wiper switch (pre '67)	36
					Windscreen wash-wipe switch ('67 on)	118
NP	Brown/Purple	Seat belt detect	Seat belt control unit Fuse (0.5 A) †	67e	Warning buzzer †	168
					Fasten seat belt lamp †	202
					Blocking diode †	203
					Seat belt control unit †	245
NY	Brown/Yellow	Ignition lamp	Alternator † (ind) or Dynamo † (d)	1	Alternator/dynamo control box †	2
					Ignition warning lamp	44

MGB ELECTRICAL SYSTEMS – THE ESSENTIAL MANUAL

Colour code	Colour base/tracer	Wire Function	From Description	Code	To Description	Code
P	Purple	Battery ± fused	Fuse	19	Courtesy or map Lamp †	20
					Horn(s)	23
					Headlamp flash Switch †	26
					Boot lamp †	66
					Courtesy or map Lamp †	102
					Brake pressure warning switch/ Lamp †	159
					Ignition key warning door switch †	169
PB	Purple/Black	Horn	Horn switch	24	Horn(s)	23
PG	Purple/Green	Ignition key warning buzzer	Ignition key warning door switch †	169	Ignition key warning buzzer †	168
					Blocking diode †	203
					Seat belt control unit †	245
PK	Purple/Pink	Key-in warning switch	Ignition switch key-in sense †	38	Ignition key warning buzzer †	168
PU	Purple.blue	Carburettor cooling	Carburettor fan	162	Carburettor thermostat	163
PW	Purple/White	Boot & courtesy lamps	Courtesy/map lamp	102	RH door switch	21
					LH door switch	22
					Boot lamp switch †	65
					Boot lamp †	66
PW	Purple/White	Boot & courtesy lamps	Boot lamp	66	Boot lamp switch	65
R	Red**	Parking lamps	Lighting switch (pre '68) or Fuse ('68 on)	6 or 19	RH Parking lamp	11
					LH Parking lamp	12
					Panel lamp switch or dimmer	13
					Number plate lamps	15
					RH Tail lamp	16
					LH Tail lamp	17
					Fog & driving lamp switch †	53
RG	Red/Green	Parking lamps	Lighting switch ('68 on)	6	Panel lamp switch or dimmer ('68 on)	13
					Fuse ('68 on)	19
					Courtesy or map lamp switch (pre '68)	101

WIRE HARNESS

Colour code	Colour base/tracer	Wire Function	From Description	Code	To Description	Code
RLG	Red/Light Green	2 Speed wiper (fast)	2 Speed wiper motor †	37	Wiper switch (pre '67)	36
					Windscreen wash-wipe switch ('67 on)	118
RN	Red/Brown	Heated backlight (post '70) (GT only)	Heated backlight line fuse †	67c	Heated backlight switch (GT only)	115
					Heated backlight lamp (GT only)	150
RP	Red/Purple	Courtesy or map lamp	Courtesy or map lamp switch †	101	Courtesy or map lamp †	102
RW (1)	Red/White	Panel lamps	Panel lamp switch or dimmer	13	Panel lamps	14
					Cigar lighter illumination †	57
RY	Red/Yellow	Fog lamp	Fog lamp switch †	53	Fog lamp †	55
S	Slate (Grey)	Running-on valve supply	Ignition switch	38	Line fuse	67d
SP	Slate/Purple	Running-on valve switch	Line fuse	67d	Running on control valve switch †	196
SY	Slate/Yellow	Running-on valve	Running on control valve switch †	196	Running on control valve †	197
U	Blue	Headlamps	Lighting switch	6	Dip switch (pre '67)	7
					or	or
					Column dip beam switch ('67 on)	26
					RH front side marker †	170
					LH front side marker †	171
					RH rear side marker †	172
					LH rear side marker †	173
ULG	Blue/Light Green	2 Speed wiper (slow)	2 Speed wiper motor †	37	Wiper switch (pre '67)	36
					Windscreen wash-wipe switch ('67 on)	118
UR	Blue/Red	Dip beam	Dip switch (pre '67) or Column dip beam switch ('67 on)	7 or 26	RH headlamp	8
					LH headlamp	9
					Full beam warning lamp	10
UW	Blue/White	Full beam	Dip switch (pre '67) or Column dip beam switch ('67 on)	7 or 26	RH headlamp	8
					LH headlamp	9
					Full beam warning lamp	10
UY	Brown/Yellow	Driving lamp	Driving lamp switch †	53	Driving lamp †	54

MGB ELECTRICAL SYSTEMS – THE ESSENTIAL MANUAL

Colour code	Colour base/tracer	Wire Function	From Description	Code	To Description	Code
W	White	Ignition + powertrain	Ignition switch	38	Fuse	19
					Ignition coil	39
					Fuel pump	41
					Ignition warning lamp	44
					Ignition relay †	58
					Heated backlight line fuse (GT only)	67c
					Overdrive manual switch †	72
					Electrical tachometer †	95
WB (1)	White/Black	Contact-breaker	Ignition coil	39	Distributor contact-breaker	40
WB (2)	White/Black (2)	Heated backlight ('70 on)	Heated backlight switch (GT only)	115	Heated backlight (GT only)	116
WG	White/Green	Accessory & ignition ±	Ignition switch run and accessory	38	Line fuse †	67a
WN (1)	White/Brown	Starter solenoid drive ('68 on)	Starter solenoid Relay †	174	Starter solenoid	4
WN (2)	White/Brown	Ignition relay power	Ignition relay †	42	Fuel pump	4
					Fuse block	19
					Ignition warning lamp	44
					Ballast resistor †	56
					Radiator fan fuse †	67f
WN (3)	White/Brown	Electrical oil pressure sense	Electrical oil pressure sender †	147	Electrical oil pressure gauge †	43
WR	White/Red	Starter solenoid relay drive	Ignition switch starter contact	38	Starter solenoid (pre '69)	4
					Automatic transmission safety switch †	131
					Starter solenoid relay† ('69 on)	174
					Seat belt control unit †	245
WU	White/Blue	Electronic ignition pwr.	Ignition resistor †	61	Electronic distributor †	40
Y	Yellow	Overdrive control	Overdrive gear switch †	73	Overdrive solenoid †	71
		Vacuum advance †			Vacuum advance micro switch †	249
YB	Yellow/Black	Vacuum advance control	Vacuum advance micro switch †	249	Vacuum advance valve †	250

WIRE HARNESS

Colour code	Colour base/tracer	Wire Function	From Description	Code	To Description	Code
YG	Yellow/Green	Seat belt control	Seat belt control unit †	245	Passenger seat belt switch (NO) †	200
YK	Yellow/Pink	Seat belt control	Seat belt control unit †	245	Starter motor relay	174
YN	Yellow/Brown	Seat belt control	Seat belt control unit †	245	Driver seat switch (NC) †	198
YO	Yellow/Orange	Seat belt control	Seat belt control unit †	245	Inhibitor switch †	201
YP (1)	Yellow/Purple	Overdrive solenoid	Overdrive gear switch †	73	Overdrive solenoid †	71
YP	Yellow/Purple	Seat belt control	Seat belt control unit †	245	Fasten seat belt lamp †	202
YR	Yellow/Red	Overdrive gear switch	Overdrive manual switch †	72	Overdrive gear switch †	73
YU	Yellow/Blue	Seat belt control	Seat belt control unit †	245	Driver seat switch (NO) †	244
YW	Yellow/White	Seat belt control	Seat belt control unit †	245	Driver seat switch (NC) †	199

* These wires use Lucas colour codes but they change to British Standard colour codes at the first bullet connector.

**Most '68-on vehicles have separate left and right hand parking light circuits each on its own fuse. The red wire on the left side may have a black marker sleeve where it connectors to the fuse block.

† Where fitted

www.velocebooks.com/www.veloce.co.uk
All books in print • New books • Special offers • Gift Vouchers

MGB ELECTRICAL SYSTEMS – THE ESSENTIAL MANUAL

COMPONENT CODES

Table 6.2. Component code identification and the colour of the wires attached to each component.
Items in parenthesis will not be found on all vehicles.

Code	Component	Wire colours
1	Alternator or generator	(B), N, (NG), NY
2	(Alternator or generator control box)	(B, N, NG, NY)
3	Batteries	B, N
4	Starter solenoid	N, (WR), (WY)
5	Starter	B
6	Lighting switch	N, (R), (RG), U
7	(Dip switch pre '67)	U, UR, UW
8	RH headlamp	B, UR, UW
9	LH headlamp	B, UR, UW
10	Full beam warning lamp	B, UW
11	RH front parking lamp	B, R
12	LH front parking lamp	B, R
13	(Panel lamp switch or dimmer '68 on)	(R, RW)
14	Panel lamps	B, RW
15	Number plate lamps	B, R
16	RH stop/tail lamp	B, G, GP, R
17	LH stop/tail lamp	B, G, GP, R
18	Stop lamp switch	G, GP
19	Fuse block	N, G, P, (R), (RG), W, WN
20	Courtesy or map lamp	(B), P, PW
21	RH door switch	B, PW
22	LH door switch	B, PW
23	Horn(s)	P, PB
24	Horn switch	B, PB
25	Direction flasher unit	G, LGN
26	Column flasher/dip/horn switch	B, GR, GW, LG, N, P, U, UR, UW
27	Flasher indicator lamp	G, GR or GW
28	RH front flasher lamp	B, GW
29	LH front flasher lamp	B, GR
30	RH rear flasher lamp	B, GW
31	LH rear flasher lamp	B, GR
32	Blower motor switch	G, GY
33	Blower motor	B, GY
34	Fuel gauge	GB, LGG
35	Fuel level sender	B, GB
36	(Windscreen wiper motor switch)	(B, BG), (G, NLG, RLG, ULG)
37	Wiper motor	(NLG, RLG, ULG)
38	Ignition switch	N, (PK), W, WG, WR
39	Ignition coil	W, WB
40	Distributor contact-breaker	WB
41	Fuel pump	B, W, (WN)
42	Ignition relay	B, N, W, WN
43	Oil pressure gauge	B, WN
44	Ignition warning lamp	NB, NY, W, (WN)
45	Speedometer	B, RW
46	Coolant temperature gauge	(B, GU)
47	(Coolant temperature sender)	(GU)
49	Reversing lamp switch	G, GN
50	Reversing lamps	GN
53	(Driving/fog lamp switch)	(R, RY)
54	(Driving lamp)	(B, UY)
55	(Fog lamp)	(B, RY)
56	(Ballast resistor)	(WLG, WN)
57	Cigar lighter /(illumination)	GK, (RW)

WIRE HARNESS

Code	Component	Wire colours
58	Driving lamp switch	G, R, RY
59	(Ignition relay)	B, N, W, WN
60	(Radio)	(G, N)
61	Electronic distributor resistor	(WU)
64	Instrument panel voltage regulator	G, LGG
65	Boot lamp switch	B, PW
66	Boot lamp	P, PW
67a	(Line fuse to 32,36,37,57,67b)	(GK, WG)
67b	(Line fuse to 60)	(GK, RW)
67c	(Line fuse to 116 pre 67)	(W, WB)
67d	(Line fuse to 196)	(S, SP)
67e	(Line fuse to 154)	(N, N)
67f	Line fuse or circuit-breaker to 246)	(WN,G)
70	(Fuel cut-off switch	(W,W)
71	(Overdrive solenoid)	(YP)
72	(Overdrive manual switch)	(W, Y)
73	(Overdrive gear switch)	(YP, YR)
74	(Overdrive vacuum switch)	(Y, YR)
75	(Overdrive vacuum relay)	(W, Y, YR)
77	(Windscreen washer pump)	(G, LGB)
95	Tachometer	W, W
101	(Courtesy or map lamp switch)	(RG, RP)
102	(Courtesy or map lamp)	(P, RP)
115	(Heated backlight switch) (GT)	(GB, WB)
116	(Heated backlight) (GT)	(GB, WB)
118	(Windscreen wash-wipe switch)	(LGB, NLG, RLG, ULG)
131	(Automatic transmission safety switch)	(G, WR)
147	(Electrical oil pressure sender)	(WN)
150	(Heated backlight lamp) (GT only)	(BG)
152	Hazard warning lamp	LGP
153	Hazard flasher switch	G, GR, GW, LGG, LGP
154	Hazard flasher module	LGN, N
159	(Brake pressure switch/lamp)	(BW, P)
160	(Brake pressure failure switch)	(BW, BW)
162	(Carburettor cooling fan)	(G, PU)
163	(Carburettor thermostat)	(PU, B)
168	(Ignition key warning buzzer)	(NP, PG,PK)
169	(Ignition key warning switch)	(PK, PG)
170	(RH front side marker)	(B, U)
171	(LH front side marker)	(B, U)
172	(RH rear side marker)	(B, U)
173	(LH rear side marker)	(B, U)
174	(Starter solenoid relay)	(N, WN, WR) (YK)
196	(Running on control valve)	(SP, SY)
197	(Running on control valve switch)	(SY)
198	(Driver seat switch (NC))	(LGW, NR), (B, YN)
199	(Passenger seat switch (NC))	(B, LGW, YW)
200	(Passenger seat switch (NO))	(NP, YG)
201	(Inhibitor switch)	G, (LGW, YO)
202	(Fasten seat belt lamp)	(NP, YP)
203	(Blocking diode)	(NR, PG)
204	(Hand/parking brake switch)	(GO)
205	(Hand/parking brake warning light)	(GO)
208	(Cigar lighter illumination)	(RW)
211	(Heater control illumination)	(B, RW)
240	(Heated rear window relay)	(B, G, P) WB)
244	(Driver's seat switch)	(NP, YU)
245	(Seat belt control unit)	(B, G, NP, PG, YG, YK, YN, YO, YP, U,(YW)
246	(Radiator cooling fan thermostat)	(BG, G)
247	(Radiator cooling fan motor)	(B, BG)
248	(Radiator cooling fan relay)	(BG, BO, G)
249	(Vacuum advance micro switch)	(Y, YB)
250	(Vacuum advance valve)	(YB, B)

MGB ELECTRICAL SYSTEMS – THE ESSENTIAL MANUAL

WIRE SIZES

American wire gauge (AWG)	Cross section (Inch²)	Cross section (cmil)	Resistance (Ω /1000ft @ 77°F)	Nearest standard metric size (mm²)	Resistance (Ω /1000 metres) @ 25°C)	*Maximum recommended current (Amps)
22	0.0005	642	16.5	0.35	50	7
20	0.0008	1,020	10.4	0.5	36	11
-	-	-	-	0.75	21	12
18	0.00127	1,620	6.51	1	18	13
16	0.00203	2,580	4.09	1.5	12.3	15
14	0.00323	4,110	2.58	2.5	7.3	20
12	0.00512	6,530	1.62	4	4.4	24
10	0.00817	10,400	1.02	6	3.2	32
8	0.01296	16,500	0.64	10	1.75	59
6	0.02060	26,300	0.4	16	1.1	87

*Based on 36 °F (20 °C) maximum temperature rise above ambient.
Note: Treat PVC insulated wire as a 185°F (85°C) product. Table 6.3 therefore assumes a maximum ambient temperature of 149°F (65°C).
Most wires purchased will have 19 strands per conductor.

Table 6.3. Current standard copper wire sizes.

Gauge (AWG)	Gauge (SWG)	Stranding (inch)	Stranding (mm)	Cross section (Inch²)	Cross section (cmil)	Cross section (mm²)	Overall dia. (Inch)	Overall dia. (mm)
16	18	28 X 0.01	28 X 0.254	0.0022	2,800	1.42	0.142	3.60
14	16	44 X 0.01	44 X 0.254	0.0035	4,455	2.23	0.165	4.21

Table 6.4. Most common MGB wire sizes. Overall diameter has been measured over the PVC insulation.

Chapter 7
Fusing & fuses

FUSE TECHNOLOGY
The fuse is a seemingly simple device and indeed some are. In practice it is a purposely introduced weak point in the electrical circuit made by reducing the cross-section area of the conductor at a particular point. Its mechanical equivalent is a shear bolt.

The simplest fuses are necked-down sections of printed circuit board trace or fusible links – sections of relatively thin cable covered in high temperature insulating sleeve that are spliced into the harness wires of many cars.

Like a light bulb, an automotive fuse has a thin filament that heats when current flows through it. Filaments can be constructed of simple wires or metal strips with or without a necked down section like that shown in Figure 7.1. So long as the current is insufficient to heat the filament above its melting point, then current flows uninterrupted. If the current exceeds a certain threshold, where the electrical heating (plus the heat of the surroundings), exceeds the heat it loses to its environment – that is: the air around it, the clips, contacts and wires attached to it – then the filament temperature will rise until it melts; the fuse thus opens and the circuit is interrupted. Around the threshold current the fuse may take a long time to open. At 135% of its rated value, a fuse is not guaranteed to open in less than ¼ hour. Raise the current to 600% of the fuse rating and it opens in less than ½ second. Modern fuses use a shaped wire with a special eutectic metal alloy at the centre that melts at a very low and precise temperature and thus at a better-defined fault current.

The entire vehicle's wiring can be considered as a number of filaments. Each wire heats somewhat as current passes through it, but being thicker than the filament in a fuse, the wire's temperature rises less for any given current. Fuses are normally selected to ensure that they blow before the vehicle wires can reach 185°F (85°C), the temperature at which the PVC insulation around the wires softens.

FUSING ARCHITECTURE
Ideally, the fusing architecture and the wiring it protects should be of a hierarchical structure resembling a tree. As such it would have a main trunk that feeds smaller and smaller branches of wires with appropriately sized fuses at each node. In such a scheme, each function on the vehicle would be fed from the right sized wire with the right sized fuse, saving weight and adding to safety. In such a system, a fault in one system or branch that might blow a fuse would not affect any other system.

FUSE RATING
Fuse rating is a fairly complex subject and the methodology has changed somewhat over the years. It is for this latter reason that the fuse rating given in the driver's manual for the MGB/C is no longer applicable today.
- The old system, used by MG, was to rate the fuse at the current that would blow it in about 1 second.
- Today, the system is to rate the fuse at the current it can reliably carry without nuisance blowing.

As there is about a 2 to 1 ratio between these values, it is not surprising that confusion can occur. Figure 7.2 shows the Time – Current relationship of a typical 15A fast blow fuse, the nearest modern value to the recommended 17A fuse used in the MGB/C fuse block. If you are not familiar with log–log scales, this graph may take a little study. Note that even at 20A the fuse will take between 10 and 100 seconds to blow – this is called the

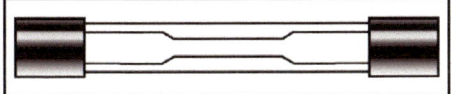

Figure 7.1. The familiar glass fuse like that originally fitted to the MGB.

MGB ELECTRICAL SYSTEMS – THE ESSENTIAL MANUAL

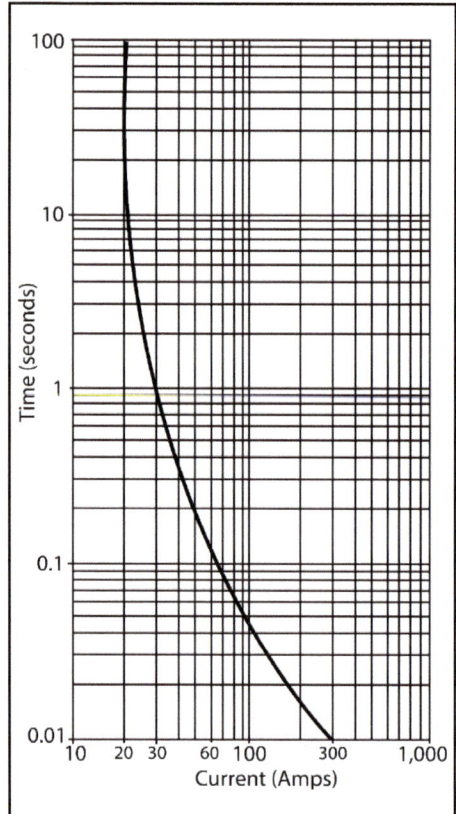

Figure 7.2. The typical time required to blow a 15 amp fuse at different currents.

% of amp rating	Time to blow
100%	Never
110%	4 hours min
135%	1 hour max
200%	10 seconds max

Table 7.1. Thermal devices, like fuses, are not especially accurate, and so minimum and maximum ratings may differ substantially from the manufacturer's 'typical' data.

non-adiabatic region, where the device is losing heat just as fast as it is gaining it and, as a result, it may never blow if the ambient temperature is low. At 30A the fuse takes 1 second to blow; note that is twice the carry current of 15A.

As the current increases the time to blow reduces very rapidly; at 60A the fuse takes only a little over 0.1 or one-tenth of a second to blow, and at 300A the time taken to blow is 0.01, or 1 hundredth of a second.

This explains some of the reasons why the reasonably constant 'carry-current' fuse rating method is preferred today over the old 'blow-current' system. Although MG rated the fuses at 35A blow current, it was not explained that this is a 1 second rating. If whatever is being protected fails in less than a second under an over-current condition of 35A, then this fuse value is of no real use.

Data will vary from fuse type to fuse type but a typical glass fuse will have a characteristic like that in Table 7.1.

Note that the minimum and maximum values given in Table 7.1 are quite different from those you will find in the 'typical' graph Figure 7.2; this is because the thermal nature of a fuse makes its tolerances quite large.

Although the fuse is supposed 'never' to blow at 100% of its nominal carry current rating, fuse manufacturers recommend that you derate this number by 25%. This is because while it will certainly hold the nominal carry current when new, the fuse will fatigue over time, particularly if it feeds a load that takes a high initial or in-rush current, which is to say almost any load on a vehicle.

MGB/C FUSES
Unfortunately, the MGB/C fusing architecture is poor in that there are a number of unprotected circuits, which results in fire hazard. Moreover, most of the electrical system accessories share a single fuse, which means that just one problem circuit can cause all the others to become inoperable.

Fuse block
Figure 7.3 shows a pre 1970 fuse block with only two operating fuses, those standing on end being spares. It is easy to pull off the connectors and replace them incorrectly so it is worth checking that the correct coloured wires are connected to the right fuse block terminals. Referring to Figure 7.3, the letters indicate the correct wire colours that should be connected to the fuse ends.
Fuse 1. Systems that operate only with the ignition on.
Fuse 2. Systems that operate independently of the ignition.
  The colours of the wires connecting to the fuses are:
  N = brown
  P = purple
  W = white
  G = green
From 1970 the fuse block with 4 fuses, illustrated in Figure 7.4, was introduced, the bottom two fuses having similar functions (but note their reversal of position) to those in the early car. The top two fuses supply the side lamps.
Fuse 1. Systems that operate independently of the ignition.
Fuse 2. Systems that operate only with the ignition on.
Fuse 3. Front and rear right side lamps.
Fuse 4. Front and rear left side lamps.
  The colours of the wires connecting to the fuses are:
  N = brown
  P = purple
  W = white
  G = green
  R = red
  Rm = red with black marker sleeve

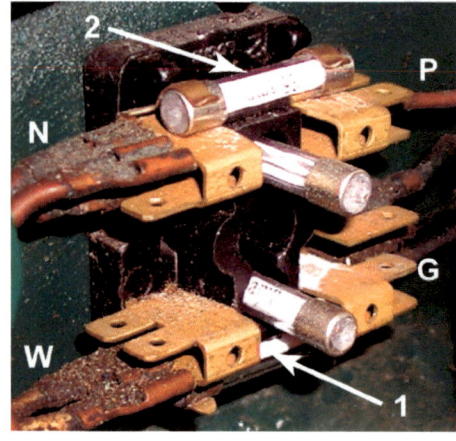

Figure 7.3. The fuse block in cars made prior to 1970 carried only two fuses.

Figure 7.4. In post 1970 cars, the fuse block carried four fuses.

FUSING & FUSES

Function	Base colours of wires	Fuse 2-way block	Fuse 4-way block
Headlamps	Blue	None	None
Ignition Fuel pump	White	None	None
Horn Interior lamps	Purple	Fuse # 2	Fuse # 1
Turn signals Reversing lamps Stop lamps Instruments	Green	Fuse # 1	Fuse # 2
Side lamps	Red	Line fuse	Fuses # 3 & 4

Table 7.2. The primary electrical functions can be represented by the base colours of the wires that power them. The table indicates how those functions are protected, if at all, by the fuses.

Model	Function	Location	Rating (amps)*	Wire colours (each end)
Any	Radio	Behind console	5	White/green Green/pink
GT	Rear window	Below fuse block	10	White White/black
1968-1969	Rear side lamps	To rear of fuse block	5	Red Red
1968-1969	Front side lamps	To rear of fuse block	5	Red Red
~ 1970 onward	Wipers, washer, heater blower, hazard flashers	Below fuse block	10	White/green Green/pink
~ 1977 onward	Anti run-on valve	Below fuse block	5	Slate Slate/purple

Table 7.3. In addition to fuses located in the fuse block, some functions are protected by line fuses located in the harness.

R and Rm may be reversed.

Spare fuses are retained in the fuse block cover.

Table 7.2 is a guide to the major functions and wire colours protected by the main fuses.

Fuse values

All the fuses in the fuse block are rated at 17A carry current, *not* 35A as shown in some manuals and the driver's handbook. See 'Fuse Rating' page 41.

All fuses are 1¼in x ¼in (31.75mm x 6.35mm) fast blow.

Littelfuse® Type 3AG
Bussmann® Type AGC
The nearest modern value is 15A.

Line fuses

Line fuses like that illustrated in Figure 7.5 are additional fuses that are placed in-line with a wire. The line fuses that will be found in some vehicles are listed in Table 7.3. Identification may be assisted by noting the colours of the wires entering and exiting the fuse.

* The current rating shown in Table 7.3 is different from that specified in

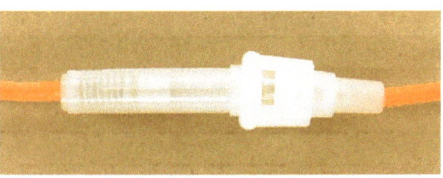

Figure 7.5. Line fuses are located in the harness and supplement those sited in the main fuse block.

the owner's manual. See 'Fuse Rating,' page 41.

Blown fuses

When an electrical system in the vehicle is inoperative, providing there is no other obvious cause, it is reasonable to first verify that a fuse has not blown. Before lifting the bonnet to check, first ascertain if other functions that share the same fuse are also not working.

Using Tables 7.2 and 7.3, it is usually possible to determine if a fuse is the cause of an inoperative function. First the tables indicate which circuits are not fused. Obviously a cause other than a blown fuse must be found for failures of these functions.

Secondly, the tables show which major functions share a fuse. If the turn signals do not work but all other accessories that share the same fuse are operating, then evidently the fuse cannot be at fault. Conversely, if all the functions attached to a single fuse fail, it is reasonable to suspect that fuse.

Why not just look at the fuses to check if one has blown? The fuse block in the MGB/C is notorious for the bad connection it makes to the fuses. As a result, while all symptoms point to fuse failure, a check might reveal that the fuses are good and there is no apparent reason why the power is not getting to the loads. Verification with a circuit tester will often reveal that power is getting to the front side of the fuse block but is not present on the other side – as it should be if the fuse was conducting.

The culprit is usually a combination of failing spring tension of the fuse clips and oxidation of the inside surface of the clip, the first problem actually being the cause of the second, but both making for poor electrical connection to the fuse.

To get the system working, take some fine sandpaper and wrap it – abrasive side out – around the end of a fuse. Insert the assembly into each fuse clip in turn, turning and sliding it so that it cleans the inside of the clip as shown

MGB ELECTRICAL SYSTEMS – THE ESSENTIAL MANUAL

Figure 7.6. Abrasive paper wrapped around a fuse end, with the abrasive side outward, is an effective tool with which to clean the inside surface of the fuse clip.

Figure 7.7. If the fuse block connector blades can be easily rocked from side to side they will not make good electrical connection to the fuse clip. They can be tightened by supporting the top side of the rivet and tapping the bottom side with a nail punch.

in Figure 7.6. Then take some pliers and gently squeeze the clips together so as to increase each one's grip on the fuse cap. Unfortunately, if the spring tension remains poor, the connection will not be gas tight and it will oxidize again over time. In fact failure is progressive. Bad spring tension causes both high resistance connections and allows in corrosive gas and moisture, which in the presence of an electric current, causes a galvanic reaction that further corrodes the connection. If that were not enough, the resulting high resistance connection results in local heating at the connection that accelerates chemical reaction and further decreases the clip spring tension.

The only long-term fix may be a new fuse block, but some respite might be gained by the use of bulb grease. This silicone based material will help keep out moisture but is itself an insulator. When used with light bulbs, the high spring tension and sliding action when inserting the bulb removes the grease at the electrical contact points. When used in a fuse block in which clip spring tension is already light, then using this material requires some more deliberate twisting and sliding action to ensure that the grease does not prevent electrical conduction.

Other fuse connection problems might stem from the fact that the fuse block terminals are riveted to the fuse clip as can be seen in the underside view, Figure 7.7. If it is easy to 'wiggle' the terminal relative to the fuse block plastic housing, then it may be necessary to tighten the rivet. Care must be taken in doing this as the plastic used is not as resilient as that found today and it will have become even more brittle over time. Using a rod, such as a nail-set punch, working from the underside, support the top side of the rivet, which can be seen at the bottom of the fuse clip, and gently tap the bottom side, again using a suitable punch. Note the bar joining the left and right side-lamp fuses. Make sure that the block is reinstalled correctly with the link bar toward the front and top of the car.

ADDING ADDITIONAL FUSES

Fuses may be added to the MGB/C in order to protect auxiliary equipment such as driving lights, trailers and high-power entertainment systems or to enhance the meagre fuse protection of the original car. Some knowledge of fuse technology will help selection.

Selecting a fuse value and wire size

Fuses are protection devices and in most automotive applications what they protected is the harness wiring. Whether adding fuses to protect an existing unfused circuit or an add-on accessory, Table 7.4 can be used to determine the maximum fuse size from the wire size. If the wire is carrying less current than its maximum, then the circuit is protected if the fuse selected is sized to the system current.

For example, if a pair of powerful driving lamps were being added, each of which had 85 Watt bulbs the total wattage would be 2 × 85 = 170W. At 13.5V (the normal car system voltage when the battery is charging) we could calculate the current as 170W ÷ 13.5V = 12.6A or simply go to the table and find the applicable row for 170W which in this case is that for 169W – 224W. This row indicates the minimum wire size that can be used is 16AWG (1.5mm2) and that the maximum fuse size that should be used with that wire is 20A. Thus it would be quite safe to run these lamps through that wire and fuse.

However, reference to table 6.3

System current (amps)	System power (Watts)	Minimum wire size AWG	Minimum wire size mm²	Maximum fuse size (amps)
0 – 1	0 – 14	22*	0.5	2
1 – 4	15 – 56	22*	0.5	5
4 – 6	57 – 70	22*	0.5	7.5
6 – 8	71 – 108	20	0.5	10
8 – 12	109 – 168	18	1	15
12 – 16	169 – 224	16	1.5	20
16 – 20	225 – 280	14	2.5	25
20 – 24	281 – 336	12	4	30
24 – 32	337 – 448	10	6	40

Table 7.4. Knowing either the system current or power, the correct minimum wire size and maximum fuse size to protect that wire can be selected. *While smaller than 22AWG (0.35mm²) wire could be used here, it is not recommended because the physical strength of such thin wire is not normally sufficient for automotive use.

FUSING & FUSES

shows that 16AWG (1.5mm²) wire has a resistance of 4.09Ω per 1000ft (12.3Ω per 1000m). If the wiring from the power source, to the switch and then to the lamp totalled 10ft (3m), the resistance of the wire would be about 0.04Ω, which does not seem very much. At 8.9A, however, the voltage dropped would be:

8.9A × 0.04 = 0.36V (approx).

This means that the lamps will only receive 13.14V and reference to the graph on page 116 shows that the lamp will now run at less than 90% of the intended brightness. We might choose to use 14AWG (2.5mm²) wire instead, which if we do the mathematics would allow the lamps to run at over 93% of design brightness. If 12AWG (4mm²) wire is used the brightness is nearly 96% of design value. In those examples, we should continue to use a 15A fuse because we continue to protect the wire; in fact it could be said that the wire is over-protected.

FUSE TYPES

Figure 7.8 shows a selection of common modern fuses placed beside a glass fuse for comparison.

Fuse 1 is a Maxi™ fuse, which is for high current applications between 20 and 80A.

Fuse 2 is an ATC (or ATO®), which is popular in Japan and Europe and has current ratings from 2A to 40A.

Fuse 3 is a Mini® fuse, which is very common in North America and is available in values of 2A to 40A.

Which fuse type you choose will probably depend on local availability of both the fuse and a suitable fuse-holder.

FUSE-HOLDERS

Figure 7.9 shows the side and edge of an ATC fuse-holder that has push-on contact terminals and is designed to be attached to the harness with a nylon cable-tie.

The fuse-holder shown in Figure 7.10 is similar but is provided with wires already attached, has no fixing mechanism and has a cover that provides a degree of environmental protection.

A number of different styles of commercially available fuse-holders can be used to provide protection to those circuits in MGB/Cs that are not normally fused, and to add fusing for some accessories.

The fuse block illustrated in Figure 7.11 was fitted just below the standard fuse block. The wires that come up from the starter solenoid were cut and joined to the power input stud using ring terminals. Each output wire was then separately connected to one of the six output terminals on the side of the fuse block. The power input stud, incidentally, provides a useful place to attach a battery charger.

This particular fuse block uses ATO fuses. Very similar fuse blocks are manufactured and available internationally from the Cooper-Bussmann® company under reference Series 15600. Versions with 6, 8, 10 and 12 fuses are available.

The fuse-holder shown in Figure 7.12 is manufactured by Littelfuse® Inc. It accepts the same type of glass fuses used in the main MGB/C fuse block and can be easily divided by cutting between individual fuse-holders to provide different numbers of fuse circuits. Although inexpensive, they are well made, the terminals being plated and having ribbing that secures the connectors extremely well. Unfortunately, they are not a good

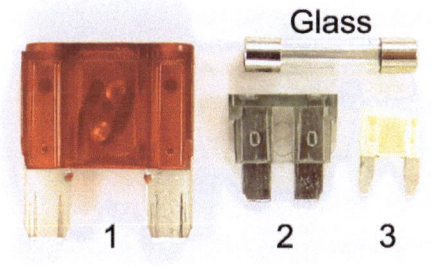

Figure 7.8. Modern cars have blade fuses as an alternative to the glass fuses used in the MGB and its contemporaries. They are worth consideration for protecting added accessories, or for adding protection to circuits that were originally not fused at all.

Figure 7.9. An ATC or ATO fuse-holder can then be connected via blade terminals, and secured to the wire harness with cable ties around the ears on the bottom surface.

Figure 7.10. An alternative form of ATC or ATO fuse-holder that has pre-attached wires which must be spliced into the wiring. The cover helps retain the fuse and provide some protection.

Figure 7.11. Another ATC or ATO fuse-holder. In this case a block with a single power input carrying multiple fuses. The fuse block has been used here to intercept the originally unfused brown power wires routing from the starter motor. They are terminated at the power input stud (arrowed).

Figure 7.12. Here, a fuse-holder that carries glass fuses has been used for an identical purpose to that in Figure 7.11.

MGB ELECTRICAL SYSTEMS – THE ESSENTIAL MANUAL

substitute for the standard fuse block as each fuse end can carry only one connector, unlike the original Lucas fuse block that has two contacts per fuse end.

Here the fuse-holder has been used to achieve the same function as that in 7.11. Again the wrapping around the cable bundle covering the cables coming up from the starter motor has been removed over a short section and the unfused brown wires have been teased out. The fuse-holder was cut down from 4 to 3 ways, installed and the 3 brown wires dressed toward it. They were then cut, terminated with female spade connectors and attached to the fuse-holder. 15A glass fuses were installed, just like those used in the original Lucas fuse block.

Modern cars still rely on the simple, reliable and inexpensive fuse to protect against the effects of over-current, but other methods exists that offer the benefit that they reset and so do not have to be replaced after a temporary fault is cleared or a faulty circuit is repaired.

Circuit-breakers

There are three types of circuit-breakers recognized for use in cars:

Type 1. Cycling devices that open on detection of a fault but that re close automatically. Should the fault still be present the device will open again and then again attempt to re close. The on and off cycle will continue until the fault is cleared or the power is removed. Type 1 circuit breakers are not recommended for protection against short circuits because constantly opening and closing hundreds of amps will quickly damage the contacts. The contacts may become open circuit, requiring the device to be changed, or they may even weld together, leaving the wiring without protection and open to fire hazard.

A Type 1 circuit-breaker is used to protect the motor(s) on those MGBs equipped with electrical operated radiator fan(s), see page 178. Motor protection is a common application for this type of circuit-breaker because its ability to 'retry' the circuit is useful when a fan motor may be temporarily stalled due to some blockage such as snow or road-kill. The current that a stalled motor draws is only two or three times the normal running current so that the circuit-breaker is not required to open and close into a very high magnitude current.

Most windscreen wiper motors, but sadly not those in MGB/Cs, also have Type 1 cycling circuit breakers installed internally. If the wiper blades are blocked by frost, the motor will stall, trip the circuit-breaker and re energize when the circuit-breaker automatically cycles causing the wipers to run as soon as the windscreen is defrosted.

Most circuit-breakers use a bimetal beam in order to open the contacts. The bimetal beam is a strip made from two metals – each with a different coefficient of expansion – laminated together. If the metal that expands the most is on the bottom of the beam, then, when the assembly is heated, it will move more than that on the top and the ends of the beam will bend upward.

Figure 7.13 shows a Type 1 circuit breaker. The blue arrows indicate the current path. Current entering the circuit-breaker via the power-in terminal passes through a pair of contacts, along the bimetal beam and leaves via the power-out terminals. If the current in the beam is sufficient, due to some over-current fault, then the current passing along the beam will heat it such that it will bend upward and the contacts will separate. If the beam is slightly dished across its width, a snap action will occur that will separate or join the contacts very rapidly, minimizing any arcing time.

Once the contacts open, current no longer flows in the beam, it cools, bends downward and re-connects the circuit. If the fault is still there, it will again heat to a point where it will bend sufficiently to open the contacts and so a cycle is established.

Type 2 circuit-breakers have a latching action. They are sometimes called modified reset devices because they are in effect a modified version of a Type 1. Figure 7.14 shows such a device. Note that again, the current passes between two contacts and through a bimetal beam. However, in the Type 2 there is an insulated heater wire wound around the bimetal beam with one end electrically connected to the beam and the other to the fixed contact. When the circuit-breaker is closed and passing current, the heater wire is effectively shorted out by the contacts, so very little current passes through it. However, when a high fault current causes the beam to heat and bend, the contacts open and current can now pass through the heater. The heater wire resistance is such that about 0.5A flows at 12V; not enough current to damage anything in the vehicle wiring but the 6W of heat produced is enough to keep the bimetal beam hot and stop it from closing and cycling on and off. The circuit-breaker thus latches on until the power to the circuit is cut. In practice, the heater does not heat fast enough to latch immediately, so the Type 2 breaker usually acts like a Type 1 and cycles a few times until the heater can raise the beam temperature sufficiently to latch it off.

Type 1 and Type 2 circuit breakers should never be used on circuits that connect directly to the battery because the cycling action of the Type 1 – alternately passing current and then switching off – and the power

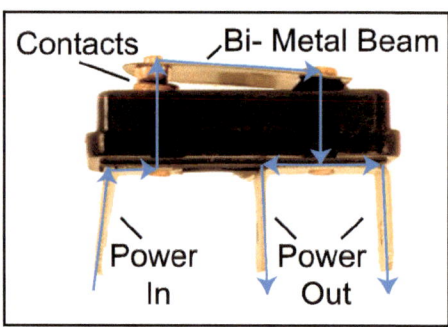

Figure 7.13. A Type 1 cycling circuit-breaker. The blue arrows indicate the current path. When a predetermined amount of current passes through the bimetal beam, it heats to a point where it bends upward sufficiently to open the contacts.

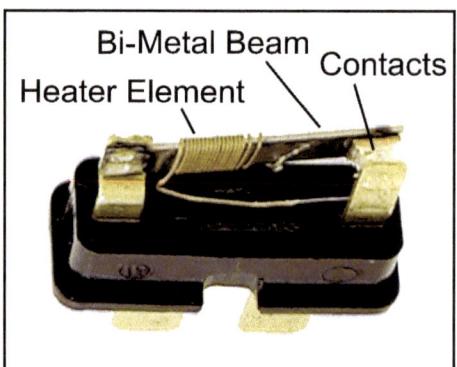

Figure 7.14. A Type 2 latching circuit-breaker. Once the contacts separate, current will flow in the heater element, The heat produced keeps the bimetal beam hot, even though it is not carrying any current itself. The heated beam remains open and the device is said to be latched.

FUSING & FUSES

consumed by the heater of the Type 2, will eventually exhaust the vehicle battery.

Type 3 circuit-breakers are also called manual-reset breakers. Like the Type 1, a bimetal beam bends when more than a certain magnitude of current flows in it. Like the Type 2, the Type 3 has a latching mechanism, but instead of a heater, it has a mechanical latch that holds the bimetal beam in the upward position and which also causes a button, usually mounted on top, to pop up. When the fault is cleared, or the power is removed, the bimetal tries to re close, and exerts a spring force against the latch in trying to do so. Pressing the button allows the bimetal to return to the rest position.

Type 3 circuit-breakers will not drain current once opened and so are suitable for direct-to-battery circuits. That some user intervention is required is often considered a benefit, in that attention has to be drawn to the fact that something caused the device to open. If there are a number of circuit breakers in a fuse block, the raised position of the reset button provides a visual indication as to which circuit experienced a fault current.

PolySwitch® polymer PTCs

In practice, PolySwitch devices can be considered a solid state version of a Type 2 circuit-breaker, but in their operating technology, they are very different. Generically known as polymer PTCs or pPTCs, they are a special form of temperature dependent resistor with a positive temperature coefficient of resistance (PTC) characteristic, which means that as temperature increases, the resistance increases too. They are included here because their use is recommended in conjunction with the battery disconnect switch discussed on page 56. Another temperature dependent resistor, this time an NTC, that goes down in resistance as temperature increases, is used as the sender for the water temperature gauge (see page 148). While temperature increase causes the ceramic element in the temperature sender's NTC resistor to reduce its resistance gradually, the effect of temperature rise on the pPTC device is quite different, causing a sudden and dramatic increase in resistance once a certain temperature threshold is passed.

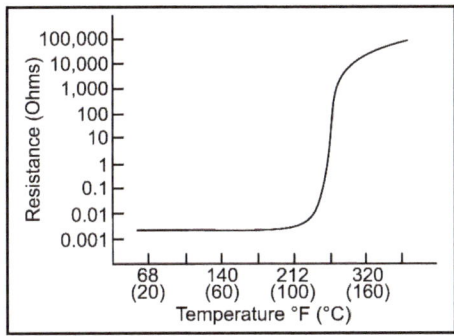

Figure 7.15. The resistance vs temperature curve for a PolySwitch pPTC like that recommended for use with the battery disconnect switch. Note how a small change in temperature at about 265°F (130°C) can result in a very significant change in resistance. The actual amount the resistance increases depends on the magnitude of the voltage driving the device.

Figure 7.15 shows the resistance vs. temperature characteristic of the particular PolySwitch pPTC recommended for use with the battery cut-off switch. Note how, at the switch point, the resistance increases tens of thousands of times in value for just a very small change in temperature. When used in a circuit, in the same position that would normally be occupied by a fuse or circuit-breaker, circuit current will flow through the PolySwitch device and will cause it to heat slightly. As is the case with the fuse, once the current increases to a point where the device is gaining heat faster than it can lose it to its surroundings, it will heat up. When its passes its switching threshold, the PolySwitch device will trip into its high resistance state. Unlike the Type 1 circuit-breaker, once tripped, the PolySwitch device will still pass a small trickle current that will keep it hot and tripped, and in this regard it equates to the Type 2 circuit-breaker in that the power must be shut off, or at least reduced to a very low level, before it will reset.

The PolySwitch pPTC relies on the action of a so-called conductive polymer. In fact, polymers are generally non-conductive so the polymer, usually polyethylene, is loaded with very fine carbon particles. In the solid polyethylene structure, the carbon particles touch one another and allow current to pass. As the polymer

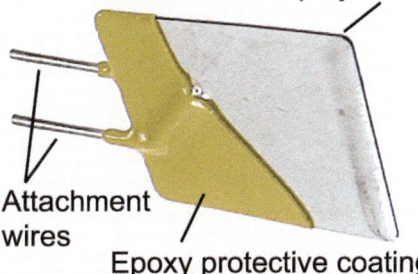

Figure 7.16. A PolySwitch polymer PTC device. Current flows into an attachment wire, which is soldered to one of the foil laminations. It then passes through the black conductive polymer material to the foil on the other side and so out to the other attachment wire. Once a given amount of current causes the polymer to heat past its melt temperature, the resistance increases dramatically, cutting the current to all but a trickle.

heats, it expands and so the particles start to separate – less and less of them touching one another– causing an increase in resistance. A point is reached where the polyethylene actually melts and is no longer a compact crystalline structure but an amorphous liquid. It is the melt point of the polymer that causes the sudden and dramatic change in resistance as the carbon particles are no longer compacted together. So, if it melts, why doesn't the device turn to a blob of molten plastic? The trick is in radiation cross-linking, a manufacturing process in which the device is exposed to radiation that causes the long polymer chains to join together. After cross-linking, the material still melts in the technical sense of the word, but the material can no longer flow. The same process is used to allow heat-shrink tubing to be heated past its melt point, where upon it 'remembers' its original dimensions and shrinks. The rubber in vehicle tyres is also cross-linked, but by chemicals, rather than radiation, that activate during the curing stage. This method of cross-linking is called vulcanization.

Figure 7.16 shows a PolySwitch pPTC with some of its epoxy coat removed. The polymer is extremely thin; in this 16 volt device for automotive applications it is only 0.01in (0.025mm) thick.

Chapter 8
Battery

BATTERY RATINGS

Various parameters are used to distinguish one battery from another. Unfortunately, the definition of those parameters is not the same for all countries.

Ampere hours (Ah)

Still used extensively in Europe and Asia for rating automotive batteries, Ah is little used in North America except for rechargeable batteries in computers, cell phones, cameras and other portable equipment. Ah is an indication of the capacity of the battery. It is the current that the battery can provide without the voltage falling below 1.75V per cell, measured over a 20 hour period. If a fully charged 12V battery could supply a constant 5A for 20 hours, before its voltage fell to 10.5V, then it would be a 100Ah battery (5A X 20 hours). Reference to some older specifications might refer to the 10-hour rate of discharge, which is a more severe test requiring somewhat greater capacity than the 20 hour discharge rate.

Reserve capacity (RC)

Also a measure of capacity, RC is used to indicate the stamina of the battery, and might be used for example to help decide if one battery is better than another in getting you home should the charging system fail. RC is the number of minutes a fully charged battery, at 80°F (27°C), could supply a constant 25A without its terminal voltage falling below 1.75V per cell. You are unlikely to find RC on a battery's rating label, so you may need to consult the manufacturer's published specification.

A battery with a CA of 120 can supply 25A for 120 minutes or 2 hours. Theoretically, it could therefore supply 1A for 25 X 2 hours or 50 hours, so it has an Ampere hour capacity of 50Ah. This example shows that there is a direct relationship between CA and Ah. The approximate rule of thumb is to multiply RC by 0.4 to find Ah or to multiply Ah by 2.5 to find RC.

Cold cranking amps (CCA)

CCA is a measure of the ability of the battery to start the car at low temperature. It is defined differently in various regional specifications so comparisons can be difficult. CCA is defined as the discharge load in amperes that a new, fully charged battery at 0°F (-18°C) can deliver for a given time and maintain a given voltage per cell or higher.

The time and voltage are shown in Table 8.1.

CCA is more relevant than Ah to

Standard	Territory	Time (sec)	End voltage
SAE	North America	30	1.20 V
BS	UK	60	1.40 V
DIN	Germany	30	1.50 V
EN	European Union	10	1.25 V

Table 8.1. Different territories have different standards dictating the times and end voltages for the measurement of CCA.

cars with alternators and for which the battery is usually used only for starting the car. Should local regulations require parking lamps to be used, then Ah or CA may also be useful parameters to know.

Cranking amps (CA)

Used in North America, CA is a less severe version of CCA because it is measured at 32°F (0°C). It is intended to stop people who live in the warmer states from buying more battery capability than they need, but some

BATTERY

regard it as misleading, producing as it does a 30% higher number than CCA. The Battery Council International (BCI) requires that batteries that carry CA ratings must carry CCA ratings too.

Battery size

There appear to be no real internationally recognized standards for automotive battery sizes. Europe has a standard that can tell you something about the battery if you know how to decode it. For example: the 6 volt battery recommended for the MGB/C is a 066 17 036.

- 066 means 66Ah capacity.
- 017 is a special designation for the particular battery.
- 036 indicates 360 cold cranking amps.

Group size

Although defined by the Battery Council International (BCI), group size appears to be used in North America far more than elsewhere. It defines over 50 different battery sizes and terminal configurations. Unfortunately, the numbers don't mean anything obvious. A battery from a group size with a low number might well be bigger than one from a group size with a higher number, or maybe not, you cannot tell.

The dual to single battery conversion section page 52 recommends group size 26/26R to fit one of the cavities behind the seats. According to BCI, the 26 and 26R are:

- 12V
- 8 3/16 in (208mm) long
- 6 13/16 in (173mm) wide
- 7 3/4 in (197mm) high

BATTERY CHARGING
Charging methods

If correctly charged, modern maintenance free batteries should indeed require very little attention. The regulator in a vehicle installed with an alternator uses the voltage limiting method of charging which provides a constant charging current to the battery (limited by the alternator's maximum current output capability) until the gassing voltage of the battery is reached, about 2.4V per cell. The charging voltage is then kept at this level, and as a result, the charging current is reduced significantly and over-charging is prevented. This method of charging, and the reduced antimony chemistry of maintenance free batteries, lessen water decomposition significantly and should mean that the battery never needs topping up with distilled water.

Dynamo chargers, as installed in MGBs prior to 1968, are less efficient at charging than alternators and use an electromechanical control box, rather than a semiconductor regulator, to control the battery charging rate. Dynamo systems will, as standard, produce charge voltages of 2.6V per cell but poor adjustment of the voltage regulator often results in even higher voltages. The higher voltage helps the dynamo charge the battery faster but even so-called maintenance free batteries will suffer electrolyte boil-off at such voltage levels and will require maintenance, see page 51.

When selecting an external charger for vehicle batteries, it is important to ensure that it is of the type that cannot over-charge the battery. These usually cost a little more but are worth the investment. Emulating the charging method of the alternator, a good charger will incorporate a semiconductor based constant voltage regulator that supplies a constant 14.4V, or 2.4V per cell. As the battery reaches this voltage, it opposes the incoming charge current and eventually limits it to a harmless trickle.

Starter/charger devices are often large units installed on a wheeled

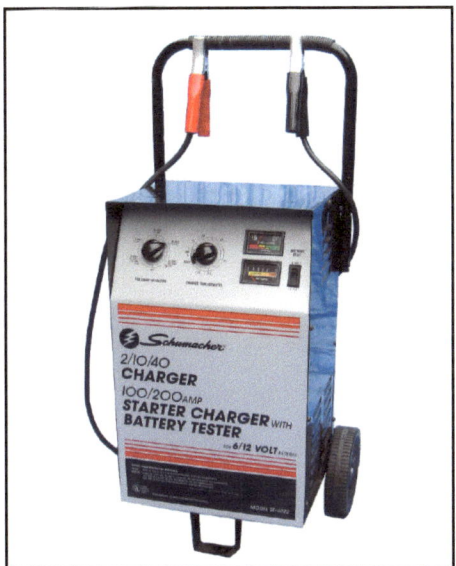

Figure 8.1. This starter-charger is capable of starting a vehicle, fast charging under time-limited conditions and providing a continuous moderate charge.

Figure 8.2. A float charger. This one is designed to be permanently installed in the car and the mains cable plugged in as required.

frame, like that in Figure 8.1. These can produce high charge voltages and currents that can both start the car and charge the battery extremely quickly. Such chargers should have a timer that limits the amount of time a high charge voltage is applied; otherwise damage to the battery will ensue.

At the other end of the spectrum are low cost devices that are described as float chargers, see Figure 8.2. These chargers are ideal for maintaining a battery's state of charge over any prolonged period when the vehicle is not in use. The charge rate from a float charger may only be about 1A, so that a battery with 66Ah capacity would take about 66 hours to charge if it were absolutely discharged. Rather than having to connect directly to the car's difficult to access batteries, an ideal method of applying a float charger, or indeed any battery charger with a charge rate no greater than about 10A, is to use the cigar lighter socket (where fitted) as a charging input connector. Corded lighter outlet plugs are readily available from electrical suppliers.

The two wires making up the cable from the plug should be connected to metal posts, which need only be screws, that are fixed to a terminal board like that shown in Figure 8.3. Space the posts so that the alligator clips of the charger, when attached to them, cannot touch one another. Take great care to ensure that the post on the board, to which the wire from the centre contact of the accessory plug is terminated, is clearly marked '+' and that the red clip from the charger goes to that. Many accessory plugs have a fuse in them and the maximum charge rate will be limited by that and

MGB ELECTRICAL SYSTEMS – THE ESSENTIAL MANUAL

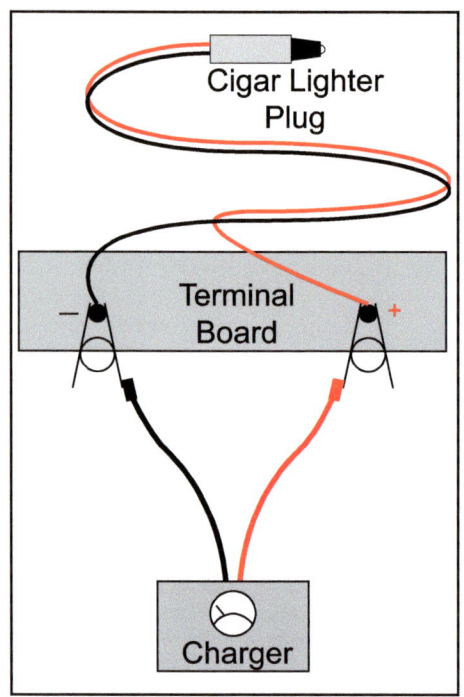

Figure 8.3. It is normal practice to connect a battery charger directly to the vehicle battery, but the MGB's is difficult to access. If the vehicle has a cigar lighter, then a simple board with terminal posts connected to a cigar lighter plug may be used.

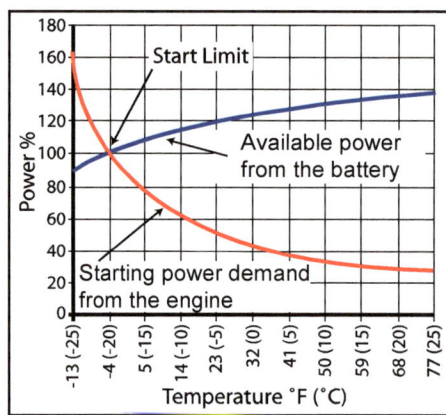

Figure 8.4. Temperature has a profound effect on the ability to start the vehicle. As temperature falls, the power demanded by the engine to turn it increases, while the available power from the battery decreases as it becomes sluggish. Once the power demanded goes above that available power, the car cannot be started.

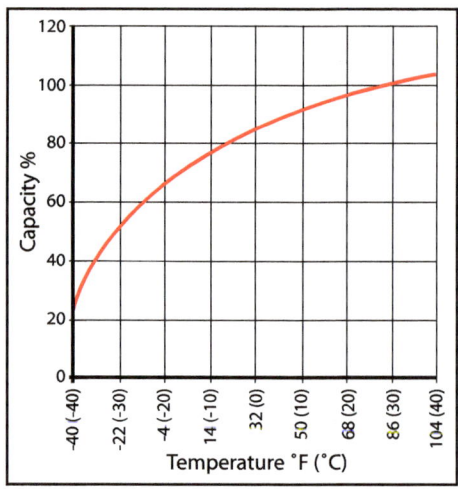

Figure 8.5. The capacity of a battery is also affected by temperature.

the vehicle wiring capacity of about 10A. In any event, normal charging is considered to be at a rate of ¹⁄₁₀ of the Ah of the battery, which is about 5A or 6A for an MGB/C. For fast charging in an emergency, only charge at high rates for sufficient time to get the vehicle running.

BATTERY DISCHARGE

All automotive batteries self-discharge even if they are not supplying any electric current. When new, the loss is small but as the battery ages, self-discharge can increase to about 1% per day and so could completely drain a battery over a vehicle's winter hibernation. Leaving a battery discharged will shorten its life, so if not in service, they should be stored in a dry and cool place. Self-discharge approximately doubles with every 18°F (10°C) increase in temperature. If you have the type of battery charger that cannot overcharge the system, it can be permanently attached and will use very little power as it simply tops up the battery to a maximum of 14.4V although for constant charging,

a lower voltage of about 13.5V is recommended. A discharged battery that is allowed to stand for a long time will be difficult to recharge because of crystallization of lead sulphate. If left too long, sulphation becomes so great as to make the battery unserviceable, but slight sulphation can be reversed. Revitalization will require charging at a very low rate of about 1A or less over 2 or 3 days.

BATTERY PROBLEMS

Battery problems usually exhibit themselves as difficulty in starting the engine. If only a click is heard when turning the key and panel lights dim, or if the starter motor turns extremely slowly in a laboured manner, then the battery is not supplying sufficient power and needs investigation. Lead-acid batteries, the type found in cars, do have a finite life, and so will need changing at some point. However, before making the expensive decision to buy a new one, check the battery's state of charge and its connections.

Temperature effects

Figure 8.4 shows both how the power demand from the engine increases and the available power that can be delivered by the battery decreases as temperature falls. Once the demand for power exceeds that available, the temperature has fallen below the start limit. The power demand increases largely because of the increased viscosity of the engine oil, even when using multigrade oil. The battery power decreases because the electrochemical processes are very sluggish at low temperatures. Not only does the battery deliver less power when cold, it also accepts charge less efficiently. Therefore, in addition to having to work harder to start the car in winter, the battery also does not recharge as quickly. This is exacerbated in an MGB/C because the battery does not benefit from engine heat like those mounted under the bonnet. Indeed, most car batteries get a boost from the self heating that always occurs in an operating battery, but those in MGB/Cs, mounted as they are so that turbulent cold air can pass over them, suffer from wind chill that takes away any self generated heat.

Low temperature not only affects the ability of the battery to supply power, it also decreases the total capacity. As discussed on page 48, the reserve capacity (RC) is measured at 80°F (27°C), which is shown as the 100% value in Figure 8.5. Note that at even 32°F (0°C), the battery has lost about 20% of its capacity.

Low temperatures can also freeze a battery. A fully charged battery may have to drop to below -90°F (-68°C) in order to freeze whereas a discharged battery will freeze at temperatures as high as 18°F (-8°C) because the electrolyte is more dilute. Never attempt to charge a suspected frozen battery, bring it indoors first and let it warm up slowly.

If your car is only used in warm

BATTERY

weather then the data indicates that a smaller capacity and lower CCA battery can be used. However, if the car is stored for long periods at high ambient temperatures, remember that the higher rate of electrochemical process at elevated temperatures can work against you, resulting in the battery self-discharging more quickly.

BATTERY TESTING & MAINTENANCE

Battery connections

Probably the most common cause of starting problems is poor connections to the battery. White lead oxide deposits on the posts and clamps are a sign that there is a probable high resistance connection, as is a warm to the touch terminal immediately after cranking the car. The dirty connections add resistance to the circuit and so limit the current the battery can deliver. There is a double whammy in that when charging at high rates, the additional resistance fools the generator's voltage regulator into interpreting the voltage it sees as battery voltage and it stops charging too early. In fact, some of that voltage is being dropped at the battery connections so the battery is actually at a lower voltage and thus also at a lower state of charge.

Remove the connections. Clean the battery, terminals and carrier compartment with very hot water; this removes all the deposits. Pour the water in copious quantities over the battery connectors and it will leave everything clean. When dry, the terminals can be smeared with one of the available proprietary products, but if none is available, a teaspoon sized portion of Vaseline® with a pinch of baking powder (bicarbonate of soda) mixed in will be equally effective in keeping further deposits at bay.

Electrolyte

Next check the level of the electrolyte, that's the sulphuric acid and water mix

Figure 8.6. This hydrometer uses four beads of different density and, depending on the specific gravity of the battery electrolyte, a certain number will float. All the beads float when in an electrolyte drawn from a charged battery, while none will float in that from a dead battery.

inside the case. Even maintenance free batteries usually have one or two rectangular covers on the top with a pry point for a screwdriver. The electrolyte is very corrosive and common sense precautions should be taken to ensure that no acid can spill or splash from the battery when performing maintenance, that eye protection is worn and that no naked flame, such a cigarette, is present that could ignite any hydrogen gas that may have built up in the battery or its vicinity. Pry off the covers and look inside. The fluid level should be above anything else you can see. If any fin shaped material is visible then the battery needs topping up with distilled water, or at a pinch bottled drinking water. Top up to no higher than ⅛in (3mm) above the separators.

If you have a hydrometer, an inexpensive device for measuring specific gravity, check that of the electrolyte; it should be above 1.23g/ml.

An even easier way is to use an inexpensive hydrometer that contains a set of coloured beads, each with a slightly different density. When the rubber bulb is used to draw electrolyte into the plastic tube, it is simply necessary to check how many beads float and interpret that reading from the scale on the tube.

No load voltage

If no hydrometer is available, use a voltmeter to check the state of charge. Let the battery rest for about 10 minutes after charging, then check the voltage. A reading above 12.4V (6.2V for 6V batteries) indicates a fully charged battery. If necessary, charge the battery as described above, start the car if you can (or get a jump start) and increase the speed to about 2000rpm. If the battery voltage does not rise to 13.1V or above, or if the headlights are dim, the charging circuit needs attention.

Load testing

If a service station tests a battery it will perform a load test. This checks the battery's ability to maintain a reasonable output voltage when under a high load approaching that of cranking the car.

Every voltage source, be it some kind of generator or battery, has some internal resistance. If there were no internal resistance to restrict the amount of current that can be supplied, even an AA size battery could supply 1000s of amps of current, albeit a very short time, until it was exhausted. As a battery drains, or as

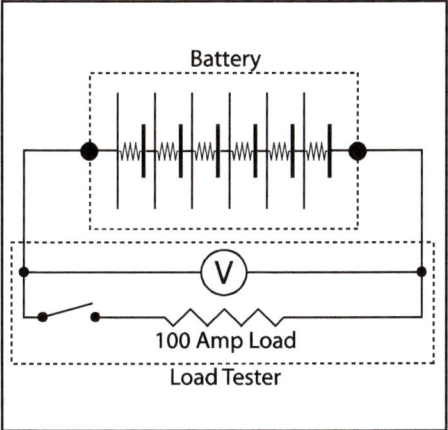

Figure 8.7. The battery depicted above has small resistances (the small zigzag lines) added to each cell, to represent the internal resistance that they (and indeed every other voltage source) have. When a load resistance (the large zigzag line) is switched across the battery, a high current flows. All the internal resistances in the battery then drop some voltage, and that will be indicated on the voltmeter (V) as the measured voltage falls. The amount the voltage drops is indicative of the state of the battery, an ageing battery exhibiting a high internal resistance and hence a higher voltage drop under load.

a rechargeable battery nears end-of-life, its internal resistance increases so that the maximum current it can supply decreases. Applying a load test to a battery is, effectively, an indirect way of measuring the internal resistance, although the technician doing the test will not actually read the resistance. Instead, he will observe how much voltage the internal resistance drops, or he may even just look at a 'Good-Weak-Bad scale'.

The cells of a battery are normally depicted in circuits as a long narrow line, representing the positive pole or anode, and a shorter broader line, representing the negative pole or cathode. In Figure 8.7 the traditional cell representation has been modified to include the internal resistance of each cell. There are six cells in the battery shown, indicating that this is one with a nominal voltage of 12V. The battery is connected to a load tester, a device that has a voltmeter and a switch that can connect and disconnect a 100A load across the battery.

The fully charged, unloaded battery, should have a terminal voltage of about 12.4V. If the 100A load is switched into circuit for about 10

MGB ELECTRICAL SYSTEMS – THE ESSENTIAL MANUAL

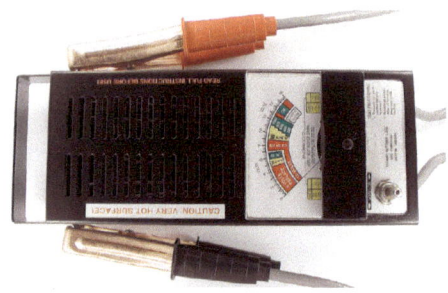

Figure 8.8. The load tester above is very simple to use. The red and black alligator clamps are attached to the positive and negative terminals respectively of the battery under test. The switch at bottom right is actuated for about 5 seconds while the meter is observed. This tester has a scale calibrated both in volts and as 'OK', 'Weak' or 'Bad' to indicate the battery condition. The load used to test the battery is a special resistance wire that becomes very hot during the test. The vents on the instrument must be kept unobstructed so that the device will not overheat.

seconds and the voltage dropped to 11.4V we would know that the internal resistances of the battery had dropped the voltage 12.4V – 11.4V = 1V. As the circuit current is 100A the internal resistance can be calculated as 1 ÷ 100 = 0.01 or 10mΩ. The higher the car battery's CCA rating the lower its internal resistance will be. To account for this, the load tester is calibrated for different CCA ratings or different engine capacity ratings on the assumption that a larger engine car will have a higher CCA rating battery than a smaller one. In general, however, once the internal resistance goes above 30mΩ, indicated by the battery voltage dropping below 8.5V on the 100A load test, then it requires replacement.

Battery load testers are no longer the preserve of professionals, their cost having decreased substantially in recent years. That shown in Figure 8.8 has an analogue meter (one with a needle indicator) but digital versions are also available at reasonable cost.

JUMP STARTING

Never jump start the car without the recipient vehicle's own battery present. The car may start but as soon as the donor vehicle's battery feed is removed the recipient car's generator voltage will rise abruptly for a short period until the regulator can shut it down. This phenomenon, known as load dump, will damage any electronic add-ons you have, such as electronic ignition and modern entertainment systems that are never fully disconnected because they need to keep station memory alive.

Start the donor vehicle and let it warm up a little. Take proper precautions regarding ventilation if working in a closed space.

Connections for cars of like polarity

Always connect the red jumper cable (black cable for positive earth cars) first to the donor vehicle battery's hot terminal and the other end to the recipient vehicle battery's hot terminal.

Next, connect the black jumper cable (red cable for positive earth cars) to the donor vehicles frame and the other end to a known good earth on the recipient vehicle some distance from the battery. This ensures that any spark that occurs when the last connection is made does not ignite any gases in the vicinity of the battery.

Connections for cars of unlike polarity

Make sure the vehicles are not touching one another.

Connect a jumper cable first to the donor vehicle battery's hot terminal and the other end to a known good earth on the recipient vehicle some distance from the battery.

Then connect a jumper cable to the recipient vehicle battery's hot terminal and the other end to a known good earth on the donor vehicle some distance from the battery.

Starting the car

The donor vehicle's engine should already be running. If there is an assistant available, accelerate the donor vehicle's engine to a fast idle. Don't attempt to start the recipient vehicle for at least a minute after the cables are connected, this gives a chance for its battery to accept some charge and assist in the starting operation.

DUAL TO SINGLE BATTERY CONVERSION

Battery selection

MGB/Cs made up to October 1974 are famous for their two 6V batteries, ostensibly fitted for better weight distribution. Unfortunately, although this type of battery is still available, they are very costly, less efficient and require more maintenance than a modern single 12V battery. Unless you are dedicated to having a vehicle as original as possible, and you care about balance so much that you always carry a passenger of equal weight to yourself, converting to a single battery is an easy and worthwhile project.

Selecting the battery needs some care. In Europe batteries are usually rated by Ampere-hours (Ah). Each of the original type 421 batteries had a capacity of 56Ah. This capacity is usually quoted at the 20 hour rate, thus a 56Ah battery can supply 2.8A for 20 hours, but not 56A for 1 hour, at that rate the battery would only last about 50 minutes. Capacity was important when generators, at that time dynamos, could not keep up with the heaviest electrical demands. (For example, driving at night with headlights on full beam, rear lights, number plate lights, wipers, heater blower and rear window de-fog (on the GT only). Under this circumstance the battery would have to fill-in for any deficit the dynamo could not supply and a high capacity was needed in order to keep the vehicle running for a long journey and still start the car again afterward.

When the change was made to a 12V battery for the 1975 model year, a 66Ah Type 074 or 73Ah Type 089 was selected, contrasting with the 56Ah available from the two former 6V batteries. Note that when used in series, two identical batteries still only have the same Ah capacity as single battery, but the available voltage is doubled. If used in parallel, the Ah rating will double but the available voltage remains the same. In addition to the increased battery capacity, remember also that by this time the MGB had a second-generation alternator, with a fully electronic regulator, capable of meeting all possible electrical demands and charging the battery too. As a result, the battery's role changed; its only purpose being to start the car and run the ignition until the alternator spins fast enough to provide the electrical power itself.

The change in the role of the battery has also been accompanied by one concerning the way a battery is rated. With the compression ratio raised from that of original vehicles, and higher mechanical loads on the fan belt – the extra output from an alternator does not come free-of-charge, more mechanical input is required to drive it and US vehicles needed an air pump added, to meet emissions regulations – cranking capability became a more useful parameter by which to rate batteries.

BATTERY

Battery choice

Cold cranking amps (CCA), and cranking amps (CA), are now common measures of the ability of a battery to perform its now primary function of starting the vehicle. A small engine British car like an MGB, and even the MGC and V8, can be adequately cranked by any battery of 300CCA.

In North America, a group size 26 has maximum dimensions of about
- 8³⁄₁₆in (208mm) long
- 6¹³⁄₁₆in (173mm) wide
- 7¾in (197mm) high,

and tapered posts. This fits the MGB/C tray with little room to spare on the sides but plenty of room on top. Some may have flanges that interfere with easy fitting but these soon succumb to a wood rasp. The CCA will vary from brand to brand and within brands by type, but even an inexpensive version has a rating of 450CCA with premium quality offering 650CCA.

In the UK, the 063 size battery rated at 400CCA, available nationally, is ideal.

In other countries, it may be necessary to buy with a tape measure in hand. Make sure that the battery will be fairly secure in the tray because, if it is allowed to vibrate excessively, it will fail early.

Fitting the battery

On the more common negative (-ve) earth two-battery system shown in Figure 8.9 the left-hand battery -ve terminal is earthed. A link wire then goes from the positive (+ve) terminal to the right-hand battery -ve terminal. The right hand battery +ve is then connected to the main power wire running under the car to the starter motor solenoid that is used as an anchor point. In the earlier +ve earth cars, GHN3 roadsters and GHD3 GTs, all the above polarities are reversed as shown in Figure 8.10.

When fitting a single battery, it is much easier to remove the old left-hand battery, which has an earthed terminal. It is then a simple matter to drill a new hole in the battery carrying frame through which to make the new earth connection, making sure, of course, that the earth cable can reach it.

Note that the BCI type batteries in Figures 8.10 and 8.11 have group numbers 26 or 26R respectively, these having been selected to best work with the cable entry and exit points on most cars. With the terminals closest to you, the 26 has + on the left whereas the 26R has + on the right. Because a reverse connected battery might possibly explode and will certainly burn the harness and ruin the alternator diodes, always try to find a battery and arrange cable lengths or tie them back so that the battery connections cannot be accidentally reversed. Avoid the use of the Group 26S battery, which has terminals disposed along the centre line and is therefore easily reverse installed and connected.

Figure 8.11 shows the single battery connections for a negative earth car. Figure 8.12 shows the single battery connections for a positive earth car

Figure 8.13 shows a single 12V battery installation in an MGB with negative earth.

Acid neutralizing mats are widely available and it is recommended that one of these be placed at the bottom of the frame as a cushion on which to sit the battery. The battery frames on many vehicles may be rusted out due to the combined effects of water, salt and battery acid. If this is the case then some strong support for the heavy lead-acid battery needs to be contrived, either by welding up a new frame or using one of the plastic bins available from MGB catalogues and that suspend themselves by a wide tough rim.

For safety reasons, the battery should be strapped down. A woven nylon strap surrounding the battery and threading under the framework of the car's battery cavity works well and is

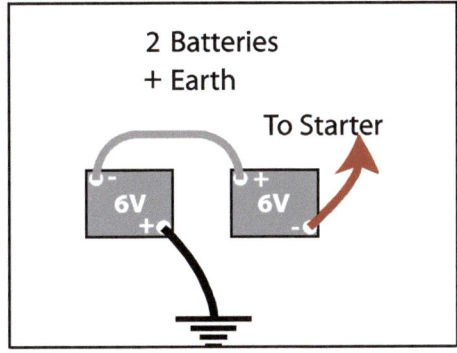

Figure 8.10. Battery arrangement for two battery cars with a positive earthed system.

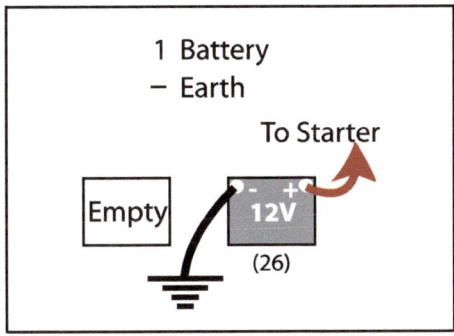

Figure 8.11. Battery arrangement for single battery conversion cars with a negative earthed system.

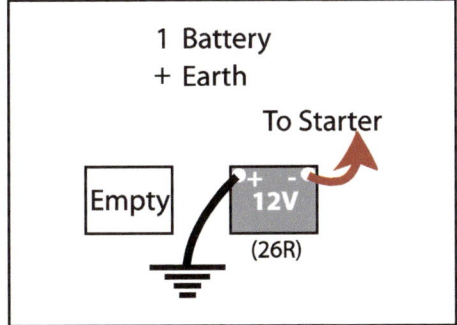

Figure 8.12. Battery arrangement for single battery conversion cars with a positive earthed system.

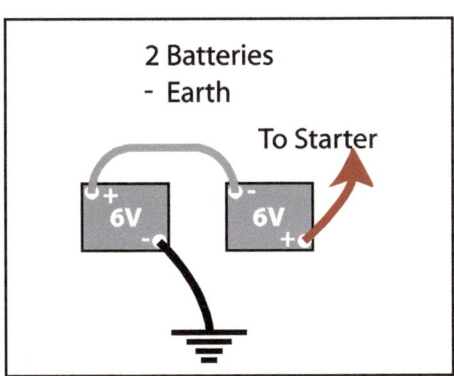

Figure 8.9. Battery arrangement for two battery cars with a negative earthed system.

Figure 8.13. A single 12 volt battery installed in the right-hand bay of an MGB-GT.

MGB ELECTRICAL SYSTEMS – THE ESSENTIAL MANUAL

sufficient to meet British MoT testing. If the battery used does not have a carrying strap then a second strap fitted loosely around the battery helps its removal considerably.

UNDER-BONNET BATTERY LOCATION

It was stated earlier that the rear location of the MGB/C's battery results in a number of disadvantages.
1. The long cable length from the battery to the starter motor introduces a voltage drop that limits the starter's cranking efficiency.
2. Wind chill takes away the effects of the battery's self-heating and it cannot benefit from the elevated under-bonnet temperature. These disadvantages reduce its energy capacity, its ability to accept charge and the available power when supplying energy.
3. Attaching a battery charger is time consuming.

The obvious solution is to put the battery under the bonnet where most would say it belongs, and that's exactly what Australian Dave Barton, has done in his 1972 roadster.

Figure 8.14 shows the installation. Dave used a wooden battery mock-up to determine the best battery type and its position. His RHD, Oz-brewed MGB has plenty of free area for the battery in front of the left-hand bulkhead but the height is somewhat restricted.

The battery finally selected was a Hawker Odyssey PC925T, the 'T' indicating that it has SAE terminals. Depending on the car's polarity, whether it is left or right-hand drive and the preferred battery orientation, the PC925LT, which has the positive terminal on the left, might sometimes be a better choice.

Including the terminal height, the battery is 6.6in (168mm) long, 7.1in (180mm) wide and 5.8in (147mm) high. The 380CCA rating is more than adequate for a 4-cylinder MGB but it is a little light on capacity at 38Ah, especially if it were to be used in a car with a dynamo generator and that also needed repeated cranking to get it started. The battery only appears to be available from Hawker's costly but high-quality, long-life Odyssey range. Dave reports having no problems with this battery in the years since he installed it.

Left hand drive cars
So long as it is not cluttered with such things as an absorption canister, anti-run-on valve or windscreen washer bottle, then a left-hand drive car could be similarly converted. Indeed the cable length to the starter motor would be even shorter than for the right-hand drive installation. Some mechanical interference can be expected from the main harness but that should not be an insurmountable problem.

Battery clamp
Whatever side of the car the battery is installed, a robust hold-down clamp is essential. Remember that the clamp will need to secure the battery in all axes under high shock and vibration conditions (consider what might happen in a front-end crash) and must itself be incapable of shorting across the battery terminals.

A new cable will be needed to connect the hot (non-earthed) battery terminal to the starter motor. When purchasing this, try to get one that has a lift-up plastic cover over the battery connector. This will help protect against accidental short-circuits.

WHY BATTERIES FAIL
- End of life. A properly maintained battery should last at least 4 years.
- Sulphation. Occurs if the battery is left uncharged for long periods. Recharge at no more than 2A for one day or more.
- Electrolyte level low. Top-up with distilled water. Check that the charging system is not delivering more than 14.4V to a 12V battery or two 6V batteries.
- Battery leakage. Mechanical damage or battery allowed to freeze.

ADDING A BATTERY DISCONNECT SWITCH
Why add a disconnect switch?
The MGB/C is rather vulnerable to electrical fires largely because so many circuits run on unfused wires (those with base colours brown, white or blue). There are several such wires under the dash, an area that is a nightmare under which to work, and where accidental fires and burns are all too easy to provoke (see page 9). A battery disconnect (sometimes called a master cut-off) switch can considerably lessen the risk of an accident by providing an easy and convenient way to remove all power from the vehicle before starting any maintenance. In addition, if installed in a hidden position, a battery switch may fool the opportunist thief who tries to start the vehicle.

Switch selection
The simplest and least expensive battery disconnect switch attaches directly to the battery as shown in Figure 8.15. 'Switch', may not be the correct description but the device certainly does disconnect the battery from the power cable. Installation is easy too, a cable is simply removed from a battery post, the switch is installed in its place and the cable is attached to the switch. The problem with this type of device is that it is unlikely to be used as often as it should because the MGB/C's batteries are in such an inaccessible position.

Another inexpensive alternative is illustrated in Figure 8.16. This plastic switch can carry up to 100A and once closed can survive surge currents up to 1000A. They are common in boats and can be bought where boat supplies are sold. The key can be removed, which has mixed advantages; while removing a key may deter theft, it may also be lost, totally disabling the car.

Figure 8.14. An under-the-bonnet battery installation in a RHD car.

Figure 8.15. The simplest battery disconnect device just clamps to a battery post and the cable clamps to it. Disconnection is simply a matter of unscrewing the knob about half a turn.

BATTERY

Figure 8.16. This true switch is inexpensive and can be mounted with the key in an accessible position for easy use. The key can also be removed to deter vehicle theft. This style of switch is often used in boats and can be bought at ships' chandlers.

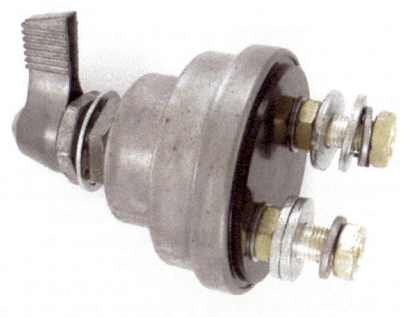

Figure 8.17. A more robust but also more expensive battery disconnect switch. Very good sealing protects the internal mechanism from the effects of moisture; a very real issue for a switch mounted in a MGB where the battery compartment is open to the elements.

The switch illustrated in Figure 8.17 is relatively expensive but is robust and above all, very well sealed. Sealing is an important feature for a switch installed in an MGB because the back of the switch will be in the same open area as the battery and subject to water splash.

Earth switching

The instructions that come with some switches show how to install them in the hot (+ve on negative earth vehicles) side of the battery circuit. However, the safest method is to put the switch in the vehicle's earth circuit. That way, with the switch off, the battery hot terminal can be removed without short-circuiting should the spanner touch any frame metal. It is also easier to install; the earth from the battery being terminated

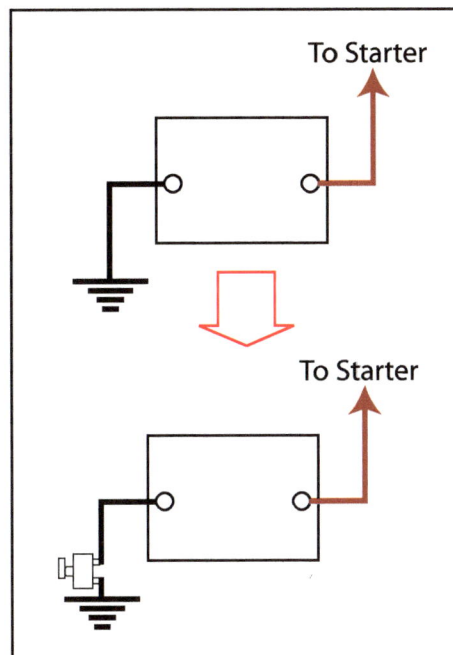

Figure 8.18. Fitting a battery disconnect switch is relatively simple. The normal earth return cable shown in the top diagram has to be disconnected and attached to the disconnect switch. The switch and a new cable then carry the earth current to the car's frame as shown in the bottom diagram.

to the vehicle chassis by an eyelet, which can be joined instead to one of the bolt terminals on the switch.

The exact installation will depend on the vehicle configuration, that is, whether the vehicle is positive or negative earth, if it has 6V or 12V batteries and what brand of switch is selected.

Schematic

The principle is the same whatever the vehicle arrangement; the battery to earth connection has to be broken by the switch as shown in Figure 8.18.

Earth connection

As was stated previously, the battery earth cable has an eyelet that can be removed from the chassis and instead joined to the switch. For the switch to the frame termination a battery strap, like the 14in (355mm) example shown in Figure 8.19 obtained from an auto accessory store, fits the bill very well. It offers (i) very good electrical continuity, (ii) ease of installation due to the two eyelets, one for the switch the other for the earth bolt, and (iii) a very flat profile

Figure 8.19. A braided battery strap offers an advantage over a cable, in that it is very flexible and can be routed around the edge of the battery compartment, where it will not interfere with battery insertion and removal.

Figure 8.20. Already terminated with eyelets at each end, this store-bought cable may also be used to connect from chassis earth to the disconnect switch.

that allows it to route around the edges of the battery box without interfering with the insertion and extraction of the battery itself.

If a braided strap is unavailable, then a standard battery cable with eyelets at both ends, like that in Figure 8.20, will work just as well, so long as it is not so thick as to restrict the installation of the battery. 6AWG (16mm^2) cables, sold as 'switch to starter' cables are readily available, but don't buy one over 18in (450mm) long, the unneeded extra length is hard to manage and the added resistance of a long cable could be detrimental to starter performance.

Installing the switch

First remove the battery. Always remove the earth connection first, that way, when you remove the hot connection, there will be no fireworks if your spanner inadvertently touches chassis metal.

The switch shown in Figure 8.21 and 8.22 has been installed in a vehicle converted to have a single 12V battery in the right hand battery bay. However, the principle remains very similar whatever the battery configuration. The switch has been installed about half way up the vertical panel. When selecting the horizontal position of your

MGB ELECTRICAL SYSTEMS – THE ESSENTIAL MANUAL

Figure 8.21. A view of the disconnect switch from the inside of the battery well.

Figure 8.22. Although discreet, the switch lever is easily accessible from the driver's seat.

you may choose to drill a new hole for the chassis earth. Remember that every hole that exposes bare metal is a potential corrosion point and always be aware of what is behind the panel into which you are drilling; thus avoiding the fuel tank, fuel pump, fuel and hydraulic pipes and electrical wires.

Bolt the now free end of the battery earth cable to the remaining switch contact. Cover the switch terminals, earthing point and the area surrounding any vacated earthing hole with Vaseline® or other brand of petroleum jelly to prevent corrosion.

Reinstall the battery and attach its cables, taking great care to insert it the correct physical orientation and with correct electrical cable polarity.

ADDING A RADIO MEMORY & CLOCK MAINTAINER

Although a battery disconnect switch certainly has its safety benefits, there is a major convenience disadvantage, and that has to do with any clock or electrical entertainment system that might be fitted to the vehicle. All but the latest radios and CD players have volatile memory, that is, they lose their station or track-played memory when power is removed. These devices usually have two power wires, one directly connected to the battery on a purple (always hot but fused) wire to preserve memory, and the other green/white or green/pink (ignition/accessory) wire providing amplifier power when the ignition switch is in the 'run' or 'accessory' position. Of course, a battery disconnect switch removes power from the purple wire, possibly causing equipment amnesia.

There is a way around the memory problem, putting a fuse across the switch terminals allows a limited amount of current to continue to be fed to the clock or radio even when the switch is 'off', yet the vehicle remains protected because, in the event of any attempt to start the car or should a short circuit occur, the fuse will blow. Unfortunately, the MG battery compartment is so inaccessible and, accidental attempts to start the car, or otherwise use several amps, is so easy, the result is a need to constantly change fuses. The solution is to use a PolySwitch; a device that acts like a self-repairing fuse (see page 47).

switch, verify that the particular earth strap or cable you are to use will reach from the switch to the current chassis fixing of the earthed battery cable.

A hole is needed through which to pass the switch shaft. The method of fixing the switch depends on the switch design. Some use a single nut on the shaft while others require that small holes be drilled through which fixing screws can be passed.

Attaching the cables

Attach the earth strap or cable to the switch. Figure 8.21 shows one method but use the most convenient position that allows it to go directly to the bolt currently attaching the battery earth cable to chassis. Remove the battery earthing cable and secure the other end of the braided earth strap in its place. If the length of the earth strap or some other reason makes it preferable,

Figure 8.23. A PolySwitch pPTC can be used to bridge across the switch contacts and bleed enough current to run radios, courtesy lights and a clock, yet will open the circuit in the event that a dangerously high current flows for any reason. Unlike a fuse, the pPTC resets after the switch is turned on, so there is no need to access it.

The PolySwitch pPTC device RGEF500 will pass about 5A but at any current much above that will open the circuit and protect even the thinnest wires in the vehicle. A 5A fuse would work similarly but the PolySwitch device, unlike the fuse, will automatically reset and pass current again after the cut-off switch is switched on for a few seconds, thus removing the voltage from the pPTC.

The PolySwitch device has simply to be attached across the switch terminals as shown in Figure 8.23. Unfortunately, the standard device is designed for use in printed circuit boards and hence has quite short leads, so some additional wire length may have to be soldered on and made into loops that will pass over the switch terminal screws

You can locate a source for this device by visiting the 'where to buy' section of the manufacturer's web site at: www.circuitprotection.com.

BATTERY SYSTEM FAULT-FINDING

Refer to Battery Maintenance page 51 to check the level of the electrolyte, the state of charge and the condition of the electrical connections. Other faults are covered in chapters 9 and 10.

Chapter 9
Charging system

MOTOR & GENERATORS

Michael Faraday (1791-1867) introduced the idea of an imaginary field of lines around a magnet for the purpose of visualising the distribution and intensity of magnetic strength. In 1831, he made a series of discoveries culminating in finding that if a magnet and wire are moved relative to one another, such that the magnetic field crosses the wire, an electric current is generated. Faraday further found that increasing the number of wires that pass through the magnetic field, by winding a coil, and increasing the rate at which the field cuts the wire, increases the voltage generated. Thus the electric generator, also known in its various forms as a dynamo and alternator, was invented. Further, Frans Oersted (1777-1851) had discovered in 1820 that a wire carrying current has a magnetic field around it, which will deflect (move) a magnet. Faraday's generator, effectively exploiting Oersted's discovery, would also work as a motor if operated in reverse mode; that is, passing a current into it and having it move the magnet. Here we have the embryo motor and solenoid.

If a coil of wire is placed in a magnetic field so that it is perpendicular to the field, and it is then rotated, the current would be seen to rise from zero, peak, reduce toward zero, then start to flow in the opposite direction, again reach a (negative) peak, reduce toward zero and begin the cycle all over again (Figure 9.1). If, instead of using a single conductor, a coil is used, many conductors then cross the field and more electricity is generated. This current, which alternates from flowing in one direction to another, is called, not surprisingly, alternating current, or just ac. The battery in a car produces a current that flows from it in one direction only, this being called direct current, or dc. Also, when being charged, the battery needs a current that flows only in one direction, again dc.

A generator of electricity using the principles discovered by Faraday would, therefore, produce ac and some method would have to be found to convert it to dc. The answer,

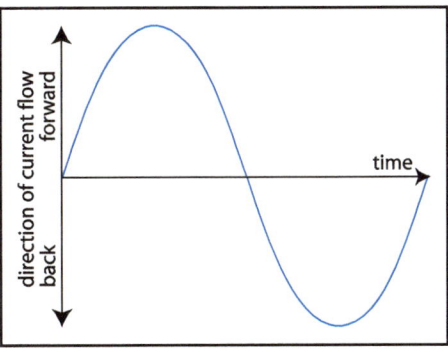

Figure 9.1. When a conductor is rotated between the poles of a magnet, current will at first rise and flow in one direction, then fall and begin to flow in the other, again rising and falling. The cycle is repeated and a rudimentary generator of alternating current is produced.

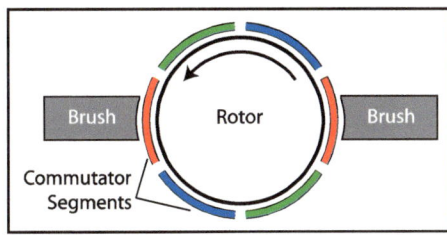

Figure 9.2. In order to produce current flowing in only one direction, a commutator is attached to the rotor with brushes that pick the current from it. The commutator consists of a number of pairs of contacts, arranged opposite one another across the rotor, each pair attached to the ends of a coil. As the current output from one coil starts to diminish, and before its current reverses, the next pair of commutator segments comes around and starts a new current pulse in the same direction as the previous one.

MGB ELECTRICAL SYSTEMS – THE ESSENTIAL MANUAL

until the mid-1960s at least, was the commutator. This is an arrangement of switch contacts on the rotor that turn with it. Stationary contacts, called brushes, pick the current off the commutator (Figure 9.2). As the rotor turns, and the current starts to go in the wrong direction, the next set of contacts comes around and effectively switches the current the right way around. The process of changing ac to dc is called rectification. The dc generator, or dynamo, would not always be powerful enough if it relied on permanent magnets (the type that makes decals stick to your refrigerator door), so on high power machines, permanent magnets are replaced by electromagnets that get their magnetic force by passing current through a coil of wire around an iron alloy core which focuses the magnetic field, due to the low reluctance (magnetic resistance) of the metal.

Later, when efficient power semiconductors based on silicon became available, the automobile generator's commutator became unnecessary, since an arrangement of silicon diodes (Figure 9.4), devices which let current flow in one direction only, was introduced to steer the current in the right direction as it left the ac generator, or what is more properly called the alternator. Brushes would still be required to pick the current off the turning wires, but rather than do that, and have a friction contact carry so much current, modern alternators keep the generator coil stationary and revolve the magnet. For more efficiency still, permanent magnets are replaced by an electromagnet as in the dynamo. Brushes are therefore needed to take the current to the revolving electromagnet, called the field coil, but this current is less than that for the main stationary, or stator, coil. These brushes do not need a commutator, (switching contacts); continuous metal sleeves called slip rings do the job. In all but the smallest alternators, three sets of stator coils and diodes are used to increase the output power.

Having a magnetic field powered by an electromagnet has the benefit that changing its current can vary the field strength. In this manner the output of the dynamo or alternator can be regulated or rapidly switched on and off should current and/or voltage monitoring devices demand that adjustment is necessary.

Electric motors for dc operation are very much like dynamos, however, instead of a rotating mechanical input producing an electrical output, in a motor, electric current enters and results in mechanical rotational output. Small motors can use permanent magnets, but bigger ones need electromagnets to produce sufficient magnetic field strength. The break point between motors that need permanent magnets and those that need electromagnets is found in those about the size of the windscreen wiper motors. Indeed, early MGBs had a field coil in the wiper motor, but improvements in permanent magnets, which are less costly to produce than a coil of copper wire, resulted in a change to a permanent magnet field in later models.

ISOLATE THE PROBLEM

In the event of a power problem, and before doing any work on the charging system, carry out a simple check to ensure the problem is not one related to the battery or its supply cables and connections. Use a battery charger to ensure the battery is as full as it can be. With the car close enough to a wall or board on which you can see the headlamp illumination, switch the headlamps on. Now try to start the car. If the starter will not crank the engine and/or the headlamps dim significantly, there is a battery problem that needs addressing before any in the charging system.

SYSTEM ITERATIONS

There have been essentially four different charging systems used in the MGB/C. Table 9.1 lists them in chronological order of introduction.

The terms generator and dynamo are often used interchangeably and properly describe any machine capable of converting mechanical energy (or indeed any other energy form) into electrical energy. However, in the accepted terminology current in automotive circles, the word dynamo describes a machine that has a generating winding called an armature, that rotates in a fixed magnetic field and that supplies the current to the outside world via a commutator, a kind of rotating switch, and then through

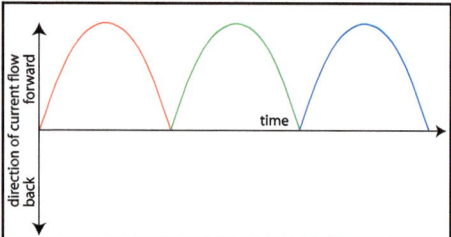

Figure 9.3. If the 6 commutator segments in Figure 9.2 connect to 3 coils, which we will call red, green and blue, then as the rotor and commutator rotate, the brushes will pick current, from each pair in turn, that only flows in one direction. Although not constant, the current is unidirectional and called direct current, or just dc.

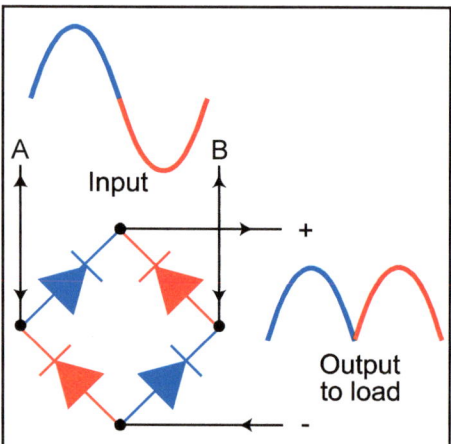

Figure 9.4. In an alternator, semiconductor diodes – devices that only pass current in one direction – replace the commutator. Instead of pairs of contacts, pairs of diodes steer the current. During the positive half cycle, A is positive and B is negative and current flows through the blue diodes. During the negative half cycle, A is negative and B is positive and the red diodes conduct.

1	The positive earth dynamo.	With separate regulator
2	The negative earth dynamo.	With separate regulator
3	The negative earth alternator.	With separate regulator
4	The negative earth alternator.	With integral regulator

Table 9.1. The four major electrical generators used in the MGB, listed in chronological order of introduction.

CHARGING SYSTEM

brushes to the output. The commutator converts, or rectifies, the armature's alternating current (ac) to direct current (dc). The word dynamo will be used here to describe this type of machine.

The term alternator indicates a machine that naturally produces alternating current, but as described above, the dynamo does that also. The main feature of an alternator is that the heavy generating winding is fixed, and so now called a stator, while the magnetic field rotates. The benefit is that the rotor, the name of the component that produces the magnetic field, does not produce power and can be much lighter than the armature in a dynamo. It can therefore be rotated much faster, resulting in higher output at lower engine speeds. Moreover, the rotor only needs to be supplied with a relatively small current in order to produce the magnetic field, and does not have to switched by a commutator and so the brushes run on two smooth annular or concentric rings, called slip-rings, this also contributing to the ability to run at higher speeds.

The alternator's development was made possible by the availability of the power semiconductor that can rectify the ac to dc without the need for a synchronized rotating switch (commutator).

Both the dynamo and the alternator have a natural maximum current output characteristic illustrated by line M in Figure 9.5, that results from the output current itself having a demagnetising effect on the machine. However, whereas the dynamo has a damage current, due to overheating and brush arcing, which is below its maximum current capability, that's not the case with the alternator, so it can employ a much simpler control system without the need for current regulation.

The semiconductor also enhanced regulation of the charging system; the older dynamo being controlled by up to 3 relays:
1. A cut-out that disconnects the dynamo from the battery when the generated voltage drops below that of the battery, as is the case when the engine is not rotating. This prevents the battery discharging back through the dynamo and turning it as if it were a motor.
2. A current regulator that monitors the charge current and adjusts the output accordingly.
3. A voltage regulator that controls the charge at very low output, when the battery is not under load and is almost fully charged.

Although the dynamo regulator evolved into a very sophisticated control system over its some 50 years of use in automobiles, it is nonetheless an electromechanical device that cannot compare in capability to that available from the semiconductor.

Both the dynamo and alternator are relatively simple machines on their own, with very little that can go wrong. Both have brushes that run on rotating surfaces, and these can and do wear. Both also have bearings that can fail.

The most complex parts of the charging system is the regulator and, in the case of the alternator, the rectifier stack and regulator. The regulator is always a separate unit from the dynamo where it is called a control box, but is usually, but not necessarily, an integral part of the alternator alongside the rectifying semiconductors. When this is the case, failure of the alternator cannot always be easily differentiated from failure of the regulator.

DYNAMO

The dynamo itself is fairly robust, although it is possible for the armature or field windings to become damaged. Armature winding failure most often results from the regulator cut-out being forcibly closed or not opening when the engine ceases running, causing the battery to discharge through the armature, burning the windings and insulation. Should this happen the only remedies are rewinding by a specialist shop, replacement or conversion to an alternator.

A more common problem is

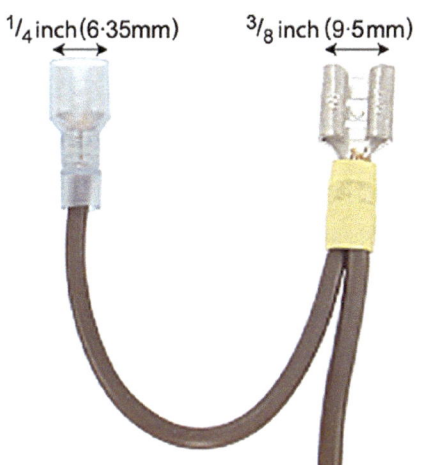

Figure 9.6. A link wire makes a convenient tool for joining the armature and field connections of the dynamo. The free end of the wire disappearing out of the bottom of the picture should be long enough to reach to the fuse block. With the fan belt removed, touch it to a fuse contact that is terminated to a brown harness wire, whereupon a good dynamo should turn as a motor.

bearing failure, which can be caused by lack of lubrication, an over-tight fan belt or just wear and tear. Again a specialist shop should be consulted or the unit changed.

In all probability, any dynamo problem will be confined to the brushes or the commutator on which they run. The brushes, being softer than the commutator, wear at the higher rate, but a time can come in the dynamo's life when commutator wear becomes too great. Mild wear can be dealt with by skimming on a lathe but heavy wear may mean end-of-life for the dynamo unless a replacement armature can be found.

Brush replacement is not difficult and is worthwhile as a service step before they are totally worn out. However, if the dynamo is not working, you may well wish to establish first if the problem resides in the dynamo itself or its regulator.

Erratic behaviour after servicing the regulator or dynamo can be due to the residual magnetic field in the dynamo having been accidentally reversed. Follow the polarity changing procedure shown in section 8, page 73.

Checking the system
If you have no voltmeter, the simplest test of a dynamo is to see if it runs

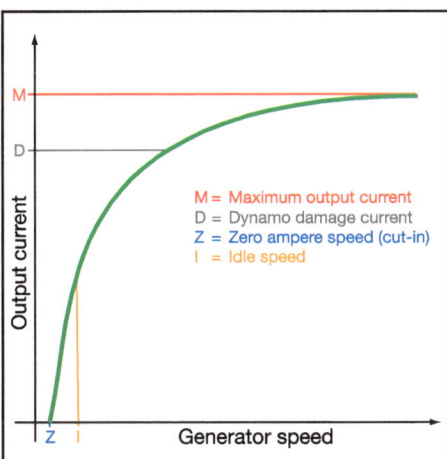

Figure 9.5. Generator output current relative to its rotational speed.

M = Maximum output current
D = Dynamo damage current
Z = Zero ampere speed (cut-in)
I = Idle speed

MGB ELECTRICAL SYSTEMS – THE ESSENTIAL MANUAL

as a motor. First remove the fan belt then remove the wires from its D and F terminals and touch them both to the B terminals on the control box (see Figure 9.16).

Handling the terminals like this can give you a harmless electric shock produced as a result of the same mechanism that allows the ignition system to generate sparks.

An alternative method is to make up a special link cable like that in Figure 9.6 remove the two wires connected to the D and F (see Figure 9.7) contacts at the back of the dynamo. Using the link wire, join the two terminals and bring the free end of wire back toward the fuse block. Holding the insulation of the wire, touch the inner conductor onto where a brown wire connects to a fuse.

Whichever method is used, there will be a harmless spark and the dynamo should turn smoothly. If it does not work as a motor, it won't work as a dynamo either.

To test the dynamo properly requires a voltmeter. With the fan belt in place, remove the wires from the back of the dynamo and connect a link wire between the contacts. If your voltmeter automatically selects the voltage range, then switch to Vdc. If you must also select the range too, switch to one of greater than 20Vdc. Connect the meter between earth and the linked terminals, making sure the red '+' or '–' black leads go to earth depending on whether the car is positive or negative earth respectively. Temporarily tape the ends of the wires that have been removed so that they cannot touch one another, any other wire, or the chassis. Start the car but do not rev it hard. Increase the engine speed to a fast idle of between 750 and 1000rpm. The voltmeter should read at least 14V. Do not increase the speed to a point where the voltage goes above 20V, otherwise permanent damage might occur to the commutator due to heavy arcing.

If there is no reading then the brushes may not be contacting the commutator and need replacing.

If the reading only gets to about 1V then the field is not receiving current. Check that the temporary link wire is properly connected to the field terminal, the smaller of the two. Try again. If an ohm measurement is part of the meter and it has a low resistance range, check the resistance of the field winding; from the small terminal to earth, it should be about 0.5Ω to 0.7Ω.

A low voltage reading of about 5V to 8V indicates that the armature may have a faulty winding.

Before checking the regulator box, use your meter to verify that there is good continuity between the small wire you have removed from the dynamo and the F terminal on the regulator and also between the thicker wire and the D terminal also on the regulator box.

Dynamo service

There are only two real service procedures for the dynamo:
1. Oiling the rear bearing. Oiling is often neglected due to the difficulty in accessing the oil hole, which is horizontally situated and requires some

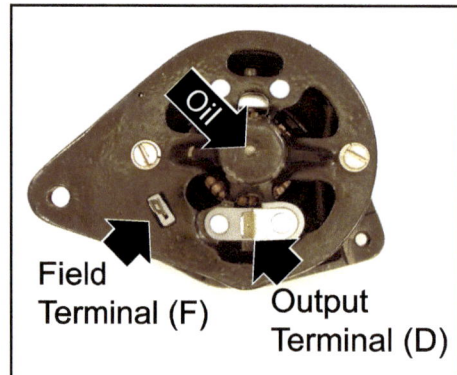

Figure 9.7. The dynamo has only two terminals and they are not easy to confuse, the field terminal (F) being significantly smaller than that of the power output (D). Don't forget to lubricate the rear bearing using the hole at the back of the main shaft. Note the two screws that run the length of the dynamo and hold the assembly together.

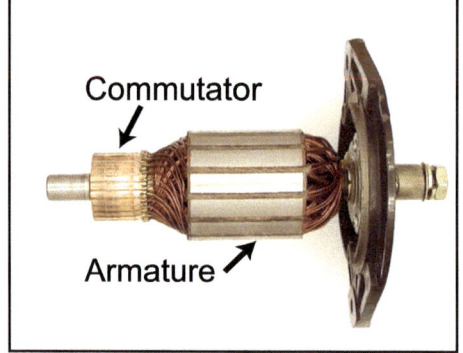

Figure 9.8. The dynamo's rotor consists of the armature and commutator assemblies. Unless there is a front bearing problem, there is no need to separate the front plate (an operation that requires a press).

kind of oil gun to lubricate the plain bearing. See Figure 9.7. Engine oil is a suitable lubricant. There is a felt pad internally which collects the oil and dispenses it to the bearing over time The front bearing, which has a ball race, has no lubrication hole.
2. Changing the brushes. The brushes are wearable items and their demise is the most common cause of dynamo failure. Changing them is easy and inexpensive.

All other service, be it bearing changing or rewinding, requires specialized equipment and it is often less expensive to buy an exchange unit.

Disassembly

The drive pulley does not have to be removed but it is easier to work on the dynamo without the pulley in place. The pulley is retained with a nut and washer. It is sometimes difficult to remove the nut because of the tendency of the dynamo to turn while undoing it. If the nut is slackened while the dynamo is still attached to the engine, the fan belt resistance will assist in preventing rotation. It is also tempting and probably usual to put a screwdriver in the cooling fan vanes in order to also restrict rotation, but it is not recommended because of the fragility of the vanes.

The pulley has a key slot that slides over a half-moon Woodruff key. The pulley should not need a puller to remove it. Once the pulley is off the dynamo shaft the fan may also be removed. Keep the Woodruff key safe or tape it in place to prevent loss.

To remove the dynamo from the car, pull off the cables from the output (D) and field (F) terminals (see Figure 9.7), remove the bottom front bolt that

Figure 9.9. The field coils are saddle-shaped assemblies retained inside the dynamo body. Although they can be replaced, the cost is often greater than that of an exchange unit.

CHARGING SYSTEM

tensions the belt and then remove the 2 bolts that hold the dynamo to the engine block bracket.

Once out of the car, the dynamo can be disassembled. It is held together with 2 long retention screws, see Figure 9.7, which can be very hard to slacken. Clamping the dynamo in a soft-jawed vice will aid their removal. Once the screws are removed, the front and back plates can be separated from the dynamo body.

Armature

Figure 9.8 shows the front plate with the armature still retained in the front bearing. Bearing removal requires drilling out rivets retaining the front bearing and both bearings require a press to remove them. These mechanical processes are outside the scope of this book.

Field coils

The inside of the main body is shown in Figure 9.9. The saddle shape of one of the two field coils can be clearly seen along with the field coil terminal. The black dust inside is a normal deposit derived from brush wear. However, the metallic particulate is not normal and is the result of imminent or actual bearing failure.

If the dynamo has not been operating correctly the field coil resistance should be measured between the dynamo shell and the field terminal. This may be done while the dynamo is still installed in the car. The resistance measured should be between 4Ω and 5Ω. A faulty field coil will need to be replaced or rewound by a specialist shop. Each is retained by a single screw that may need an impact driver to remove it.

Commutator

Inspect the commutator for wear. As shown in Figure 9.10, the commutator is made up of a circular band of metal strips, each of which is terminated to an armature winding.

The profile should be straight with no obvious narrowing due to wear in the bright area where the brushes contact it. If it is not straight, it may require skimming on a lathe.

Figure 9.11 shows an end view of the commutator with the conductor strips standing proud by about 1/32in (0.8mm) of the insulator separators that are located between each of them. Commutator wear can result in the conductors becoming flush with the insulators, in which case the insulators should be recessed by running a halved fine hacksaw blade over their length.

Brushes

Brushes wear and will require replacement at some time. However, they are inexpensive and pre-emptively changing them is worthwhile. Referring to Figure 9.12, the brushes slide in carriers under the force of snail springs. At some point, wear will result in the springs contacting the brush carriers and being unable to push the brushes further to the centre. The resulting low pressure contact between the brushes and the commutator is usually exhibited as flickering of the dash mounted ignition warning light.

Once the brushes are removed, wash the rear assembly as well as the main body and field coils in paraffin (kerosene). Do not wash the armature in any solvent or other degreasing agent because the front bearing is not easy to re-lubricate.

Fit the new brushes and apply the

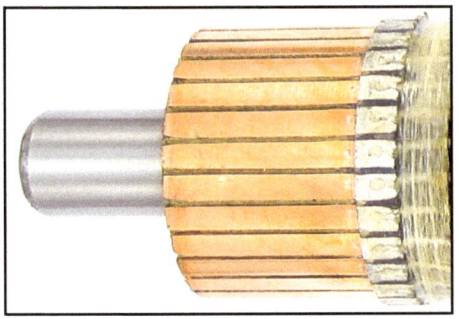

Figure 9.10. The band of metal strips to which the armature windings are attached, and on which the brushes run and pick off power, is called the commutator.

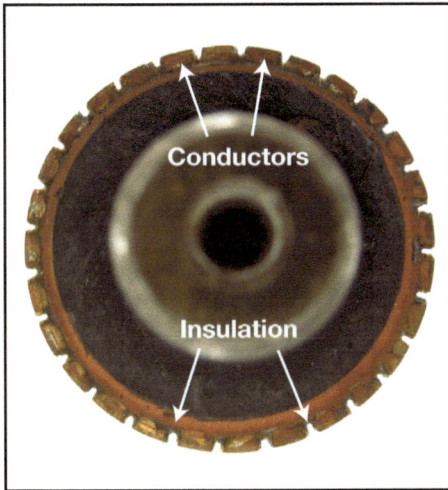

Figure 9.11. An end view of the commutator shows how the metal strips or conductors are separated from one another by recessed insulating strips.

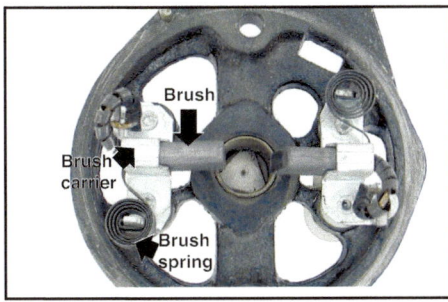

Figure 9.12. The dynamo brushes are pushed toward the commutator by snail springs, and are guided by brush carriers.

Figure 9.13. Small strips of wood, levered outward by the force of a rubber band, can be used to spread the brushes so that they are not damaged by the commutator during re-assembly. Leave the forward part of the brush uncovered by the spreaders so that the commutator can pass through the gap formed, and can push the spreaders out of the way.

Figure 9.14. When assembling the armature and front plate, body and rear plate with the brush assemblies, make sure that the notches in the body align with the keys on the end plates.

MGB ELECTRICAL SYSTEMS – THE ESSENTIAL MANUAL

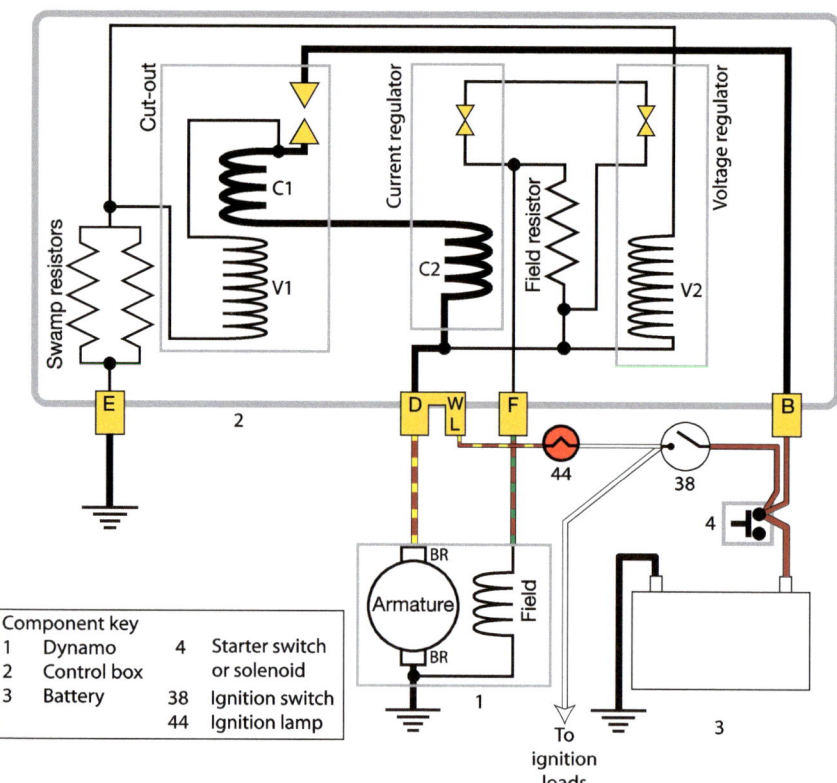

Figure 9.15. The RB340 control box.

brush springs. The brushes need to be held out of the way of the commutator when the dynamo is reassembled so some brush spreaders are required.

Re-assembly
It is often recommended that the brush retention springs not be applied until after the dynamo body is reunited with its end plates. Unfortunately, this does not guarantee that the brushes do not foul the commutator and applying the springs afterward by fishing through the vent holes is fiddly and frustrating. Instead, as shown in Figure 9.13, a makeshift brush spreader can be made from two strips of thin wood and a rubber band. They may be pushed through the vent holes as illustrated in Figures 9.13 (without the body in place).

Body and end plates
Assemble the body over the front plates and armature, making sure that the key and notch align (Figure 9.14). Then place the back plate and brush assembly over the body, taking care that the brush wires are not trapped, again aligning the key and notch and making sure the field coil terminal passes through the special hole provided. In doing so the brush spreaders should eject themselves, if not, they may be pulled out.

Hold the assembly together while re-inserting the long screws through the holes in the back plate and aligning them with the threads tapped in the front plate. This can be tricky if the pulley and fan are not removed because finding the threaded holes without the benefit of sighting them through the front vents is difficult.

DYNAMO CONTROL BOX
Description
Over the many years it was in use, prior to the semiconductor revolution, the control box evolved into a sophisticated and complex piece of equipment. Using temperature compensated relays that vibrated on and off at varying rates to switch the dynamo from full to low output and so arrive at some average depending on the on-to-off ratio (duty-cycle), the control box did a good job of controlling the battery condition under different states of charge and load.

The RB340 control box, used in MGBs until 1968, was the culmination of the device's evolution. It had the advantage over previous designs of providing the maximum charge rate for much longer. Improved temperature compensation is provided in the RB340 by using less turns of wire for the voltage windings resulting in their being less affected by temperature. Their resistance is also less and so resistors are placed in series to compensate. These resistors are much less affected by temperature than is copper wire and so they tend to swamp out the PTC resistance change in the windings to which they join. Not surprisingly these resistors are called swamp resistors. Only one is actually required but to more evenly distribute the heat they produce, two are connected in parallel and are placed under the box, as can be seen under relays C and V in Figures 9.18 and 9.19.

The circuit diagram in Figure 9.15 shows the fundamental principle of operation of the system.

When the engine is at rest, spring action keeps the voltage and current regulator contacts closed and the cut-out contacts open.

When the ignition switch (38) is closed, a small current flows from the battery (3) through the ignition lamp (44) to terminal 'WL' from which point it splits into several routes. Some current can flow through C1, C2, V1 and the swamp resistors to earth. Similarly some can flow through V2 and the swamp resistors to earth. A little of the small bulb current passes to the field via two sets of regulator contacts but most takes the path of least resistance and flows out of the 'D' terminal, into the armature of the dynamo (1) and to earth. These currents illuminate the ignition lamp.

So very little of this already small bulb current passes through the dynamo field coil that, unlike the situation in an alternator described later in this chapter, there is insufficient field current to create a magnetic field that can start the dynamo generating. Instead, the dynamo relies on some residual magnetism that is remains in the iron shoes around which the field is wound from the last time the dynamo operated.

Once the car is started and the fan belt begins to turn the armature, its windings rotate through the weak residual magnetic field, causing it to generate a small current, some of which is fed back to the field winding via 'D', the closed contacts of both regulators and 'F'. The armature, now rotates in a slightly stronger magnetic field causing it to produce yet more current that reinforces that in its own field winding

CHARGING SYSTEM

and so the current and voltage output from the armature grows and grows.

The cut-out voltage winding V1 is connected to the dynamo armature via C1, C2 and terminal 'D' and once the dynamo output voltage reaches about 13V, it produces sufficient magnetizing force to close its contacts. This action connects the dynamo to the battery via C1, C2 and terminal 'B'. Because even a fully charged battery that has been at rest cannot have a terminal voltage greater than 12.6V, the higher voltage (pressure) from the dynamo that now exceeds 13V, will force current into the battery and thus charge it. That charge current, flowing in C1, causes it to close the cut-out contacts even more strongly. With the cut-out contacts closed, terminals 'WL' and 'B' are joined together by the very low combined resistance of C1 and C2, which effectively shunts the ignition bulb out of circuit and so it extinguishes.

That part of the charge current that flows in C2 tends to open the current regulator contacts and will do so if the battery is low and takes a high charge current in the order of 22A, which is the maximum output capability of the dynamo. This action breaks the direct connection to the dynamo's field so that its current now has to pass through the field resistor, reducing its magnitude considerably. The reduction in field current causes both the armature's current and voltage output to reduce. Once this happens C2 can no longer hold the current regulator contacts open and they close again, causing the dynamo field current to once again increase. This cycle, the charge current rising, the current regulator contacts opening, the field current falling, the dynamo output falling and the regulator contacts closing, repeats itself tens of times every second.

Should a large current load, such as headlamps draw a high current from the dynamo, it will pass through C2 and cause the current regulator to open if the total of the charge and load current exceeds some 22A.

When the combined charge and load currents are less than 22A, the battery continues to charge at a lower rate with no danger of damage to the dynamo.

The battery voltage rises as it charges. As was stated in page 49, battery charge voltages above 15V can cause a number of problems. Unfortunately, because of the inferior charge characteristics of earlier control-box designs, it was normal for it to be allowed to charge at up to 16V, which while not truly satisfactory, helps the battery reach full charge. The superior charge control of the RB340 allows it to work efficiently with a maximum charge voltage of about 15V. When this voltage is reached, V2 is able to open the voltage-regulator contacts, which reduces the dynamo field current and output in exactly the same way as does the current regulator described previously. Also like the current regulator, it will cycle on and off tens of times per second as it regulates the dynamo output voltage.

In summary, the current regulator is primarily used when the dynamo is heavily loaded by a flat battery and/or high accessory loads and protects the dynamo from damage that might occur if it were to exceed its maximum rated output for any time. The voltage-regulator comes into operation when a lightly loaded dynamo tends to produce too high a voltage.

When the ignition switch is turned off, the dynamo output voltage reduces, weakening the force in the cut-out voltage coil V1. As the voltage falls below that of the battery, current starts to flow out of the battery and into the dynamo, a situation that would damage its armature if sustained. However, the reverse current in C1 causes a demagnetizing force on the weakening magnetizing force of V1. Before the voltage falls much below that of the battery, the cut-out contacts open under spring tension, disconnecting the dynamo from it. The shunting effect of C1 and C2 across the ignition bulb is now removed but it does not illuminate because the ignition switch is now open.

Service

The best advice that can be given regarding servicing the control box is "Don't." However, since that will not deter most enthusiasts, some things that may and may not be done will be described.

* Do not touch the cut-out regulator relay with the battery connected. If it is operated manually it will latch-in so hard it is almost impossible to release. The battery then becomes directly connected across the dynamo armature and it, and its associated wiring may burn.
* Do not make adjustments unless you have the instruments described.

Identification

There may be differences in the appearance of some of the control boxes, but all those with the same terminal letter codes are interchangeable.

The cover has plastic collet fasteners that require a centre pin to be pushed down to relieve the collet.

The terminals are shown in Figure 9.16.

* E = Earth
* D = Dynamo
* WL = Warning Light
* F = Field
* B = Battery

Any work done on the control box relays should be preceded with cleaning of the contacts, which is most readily done with the control box removed from the car. Again, do not go near the cut-relay with any power applied. At least remove the brown

Figure 9.16. This dynamo control box has push-on terminals. Many early models used screws instead to retain the attachment wires.

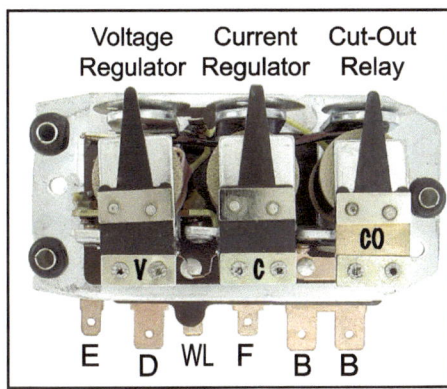

Figure 9.17. The three armatures in the control box identified. It is a good idea to mark the backs, fronts and tops with a felt tip pen so as not to mix them up.

MGB ELECTRICAL SYSTEMS – THE ESSENTIAL MANUAL

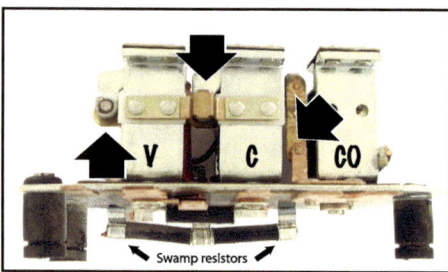

Figure 9.18. The contacts of each armature (arrowed) can be cleaned with fine abrasive paper.

Figure 9.19. The adjustment wheels should be marked with a line through each wheel and frame so that it can be returned to its original position should adjustment prove difficult. This is also the view of the control armatures for which identification letters are both useful and most important.

pull the brown/yellow wire from the WL terminal, and attach the voltmeter between this terminal and earth.

To check and adjust the voltage regulator, get an assistant to start the engine and ensure that no loads are on such as the blower fan, headlamps or stop lamps. Then rev the engine to 3000rpm. The voltage at the WL terminal should be 15V or within 0.5V of that figure. The clockwise movement of cam V will increase the reading and vice versa.

To check and adjust the cut-out, switch on the headlamps and watch the voltmeter as the assistant slowly increases the engine speed from idle. The voltage should rise and then fall slightly. This is sometimes quite difficult to see with a slow sampling digital voltmeter, an analogue type might be preferable if available, or watch the voltmeter and cut-out contacts together to observe at what voltage they close. It should occur at between 12.7V and 13.3V. Again clockwise rotation of the cam increases the voltage reading. Finally, check the voltage at which the cut-out opens by having the assistant reduce the engine speed slowly. Drop-out should be no less than 9.6 volts.

No instructions will be given here for adjusting the current regulator. The required high current ammeter is not likely to be found in the average owner's toolbox either in its own right or as part of a multi-meter. Moreover, connecting it safely in series with the load and with low enough resistance not to produce spurious results is very difficult.

Checking the ignition warning lamp

With ignition on, test the bulb by removing the brown/yellow wire from the WL terminal of the control box and touch it to earth whereupon the bulb should illuminate (it helps to have an assistant to observe the lamp).

Dynamo charging circuit

This circuit, Figure 9.20 is distinguished by use of a dynamo. Understanding of how this circuit operates will be enhanced by reference to the control box description page 62.

Current from the batteries flows on a large cross section area cable to the starter solenoid, which serves as an anchor and terminating point. From

wires from the B terminals. To avoid mistakes, it is a good idea to mark each of the relay armatures with a felt tip pen as shown in Figures 9.17 through 9.19 so that their functions can easily be recognized.

Maintenance

In Figure 9.18, the contact positions are indicated by arrows.

Each contact pair may be cleaned by several passes of a thin piece of folded fine grade sandpaper between them.

Adjustment

You may find that the three adjusting cam wheels are not identical to those shown in Figure 9.19, some versions having toothed centre shafts that are designed for use with a special adjusting tool.

Once again a permanent marker has been used to correctly identify each segment and in addition, each cam has been marked so that it can be returned to the original position if necessary. If you have a good digital voltmeter you can adjust the cut-out and voltage regulator. To adjust both,

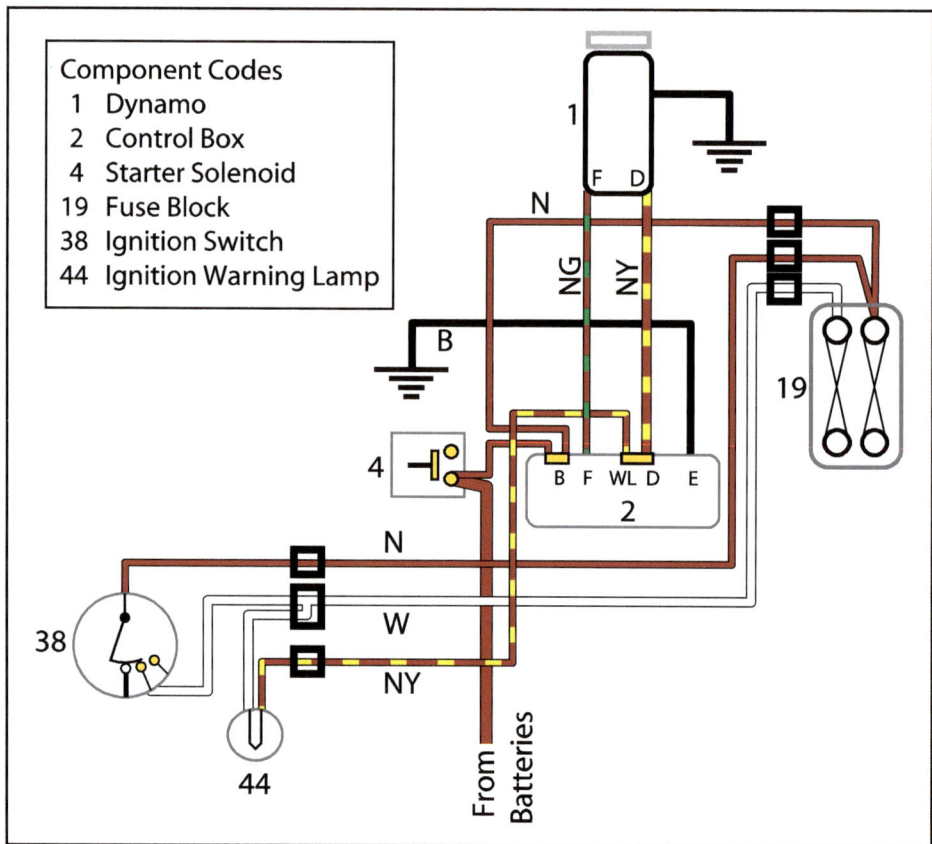

Figure 9.20. The charging circuit for dynamo generator vehicles.

CHARGING SYSTEM

DYNAMO CIRCUIT FAULT-FINDING

Symptom	Possible causes	Action
Ignition (charge) warning lamp does not light.	Bulb blown.	Check the bulb. See page 64. Change the bulb if necessary.
	Armature or field coil open or brushes worn down.	Check that the dynamo works as a motor. See checking the system page 59.
		Check and change the brushes if necessary. See page 61.
Ignition (charge) warning lamp flickers.	Brushes nearly worn down.	Check and change the brushes if necessary. See page 60.
	Brush springs weak or hooked up.	Check the springs and replace or rectify.
	Dynamo field accidentally reversed.	See conversion – positive to negative earth page 72.
Ignition (charge) warning lamp does not extinguish.	Fan belt loose or missing.	Adjust or replace.
	Armature or field coil open or brushes worn down.	Check that the dynamo works as a motor. See checking the system page 59.
	Control box cut-out not closing.	Remove the battery connection then check for free movement of the cut-out. If problem persists, replace control box.
	Cut out contacts need cleaning.	See Maintenance, page 64
Battery does not charge sufficiently.	Voltage regulator needs adjustment.	Check the voltage regulator and adjust if necessary. See page 63.
Battery discharges and dynamo hot.	Control box cut-out sticking closed.	Remove the battery connection then check for free movement of the cut-out. If problem persists, replace control box.

Table 9.2. Dynamo circuit fault-finding.

there a brown wire takes the current to the control box B terminal and fuse block (19), which serves as another anchor point. The current then flows to and through the ignition switch (38) from which it is carried on a white (W) wire to the ignition warning lamp (44). From here the current flows on a brown/yellow (NY) wire to the WL terminal of the control box (2) and via a link to the control box D terminal and so to the dynamo (1) D terminal, which connects to the armature via the brushes. Current can also flow from the control box WL terminal through the internal current sensors to the control box F terminal and from there on a brown/green (NG) wire to the dynamo's F terminal and field coil.

The small current in the field produces a sufficient magnetic force to allow the armature to produce an output that reinforces the field until the system is producing enough voltage to close the cut-out inside the control box. The cut-out connects the B terminal to the armature output and that in turn can then carry the current generated to the batteries and vehicle loads via a brown wire that goes to the starter solenoid (4).

The dynamo is earthed by being bolted to the engine and the control box is earthed by a black (B) wire.

ALTERNATOR
Description

The alternator circuit shown in Figure 9.21 is a typical example of an alternator circuit that uses an internal voltage-regulator and which does not rely on the battery for field excitation. It incorporates the following components.

A. The rotor or field winding, which by means of an electric current fed to it via slip rings, produces a magnetic field. As the rotor rotates, the magnetic field also rotates. In theory, the rotor could be a permanent magnet but such a magnet can neither be controlled nor produce a sufficiently strong field to be practical in a machine of this size.

B1 & B2. Brushes and slip-rings that carry the current to the rotor's field winding.

S. A stator, usually (but not always) consisting of three windings in what is known as a 3-phase star configuration, which means they are all connected at the centre and each is located at an angle 120° from its adjacent counterpart. As the magnetic field produced by the rotor turns, it cuts through each winding of the stator in turn, inducing in it an electric current. Having three windings means that the pulses of current come more regularly and more smoothly, and so the machine is more efficient than it would otherwise be.

D. Power diodes, here configured as part of the rectifier and in 3-phase format to work with the stator windings. The assembly consists

MGB ELECTRICAL SYSTEMS – THE ESSENTIAL MANUAL

of six diodes each of which works like a valve to electric current, letting it pass in one direction but not the other. It basically converts alternating current (ac), the current produced by the stator that alternates from going in one direction to going in the other, to a current that is unidirectional, called direct current (dc) (see Figure 9.4). The power diodes supply the required dc from the stator to the battery and accessories.

F Three field diodes, often called a 'triple' that feed back some of the current generated in the stator to reinforce that in the rotor. As explained in Appendix 2, silicon diodes drop about the same voltage almost irrespective of their size and the current carried. As a result, the voltage at the cathodes of the field diodes is about the same as that at the cathodes of the power diodes and so in some versions of the alternator, their junction is used as a monitoring point for the voltage-regulator.

V The regulator that senses the voltage and in response, opens or closes the current path to the field winding.

Z A zener diode (see Appendix 2) was sometimes incorporated in order to protect the field diodes and regulator from voltage spikes. The zener diode used in Lucas alternators clamps at 30V, a value selected so that it does not conduct when subject to 24V battery voltage sometimes applied by breakdown crews to get an engine started.

C Although often fitted externally, a capacitor was sometimes installed to suppress radio interference that is produced by the slip rings and brushes.

3. The battery, which, via the ignition lamp (44), supplies the initial starting current to the field winding.

The sequence of operation can be considered as per the following

When the ignition switch (38) is closed, current can flow through the ignition lamp (44), the alternator's 'Ind' terminal, the field rotor winding (R) and the voltage-regulator (V) to earth. The resistance of the field winding is relatively small compared to that of the ignition lamp and so it impedes the current very little, allowing the lamp to illuminate at nearly full brightness.

Unlike the dynamo, the alternator does not retain sufficient residual magnetism from last usage to start itself and so needs a source of field current before it can self-initiate. This current is supplied by the ignition bulb. Failure of the bulb may well result in failure of the alternator to start, and so some alternators may have a resistor added in parallel with the bulb so that the field receives a little initial magnetizing current in any case.

Once the engine and alternator begin to turn, the magnetic field produced by the rotor field winding also rotates and cuts through the stator windings (S) and they begin to produces an alternating current. The alternating current passes through the power diodes, (D) which rectify it into dc as described in Figure 9.4.

Some of the current generated is fed back to the field winding via the field diodes (F), reinforcing the weak current supplied via the ignition bulb and increasing the current generated. This further strengthens the field and, as shown in Figure 9.5, as the speed increases, this process, known as self-excitation, causes the alternator to quickly become capable of producing its full output. The current it produces is thus supplied to the battery and the various vehicle loads.

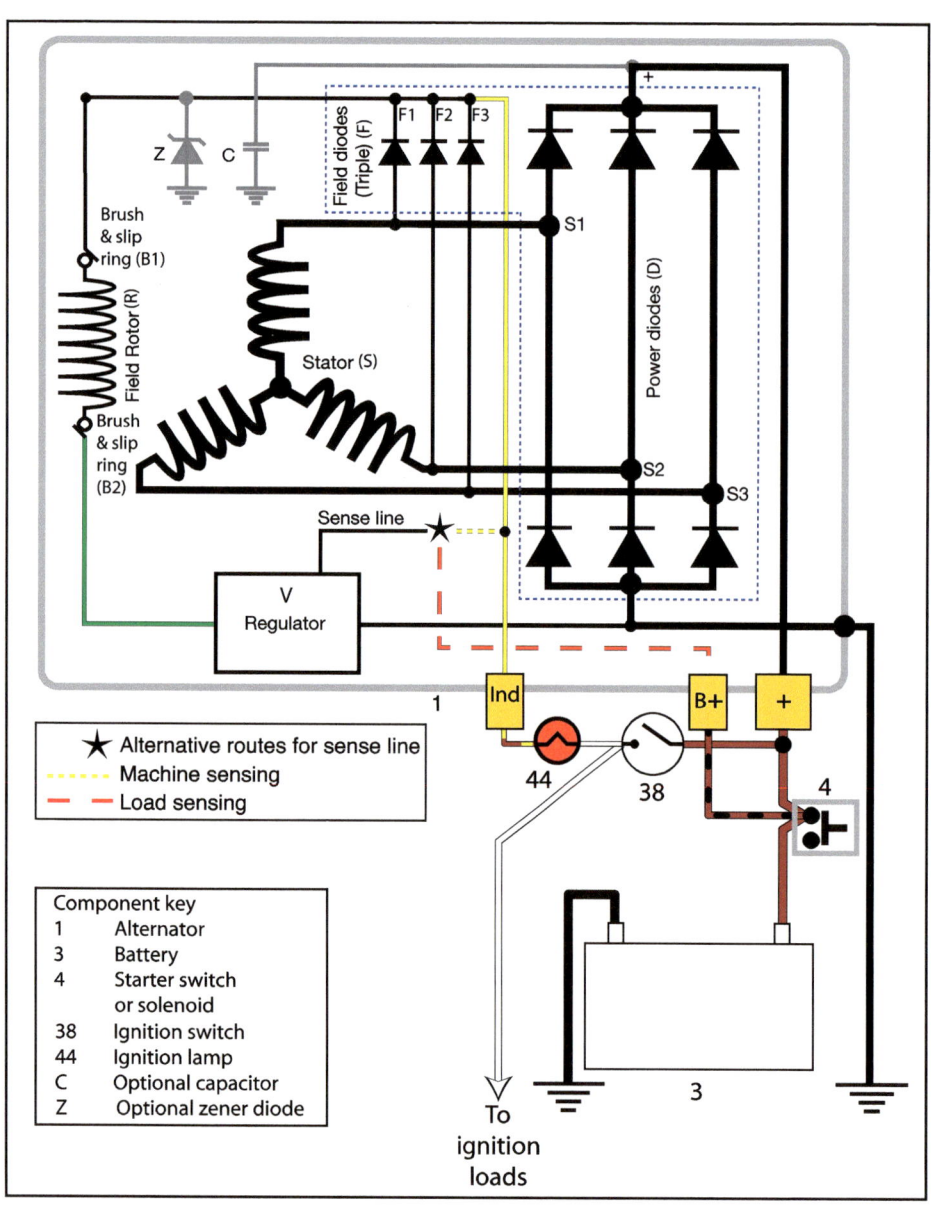

Figure 9.21. The 3 phase alternator circuit.

CHARGING SYSTEM

Once a voltage of about 14.2V is sensed by the regulator, it opens the earth return current path from the rotor's field winding.

Figure 9.21 shows two sensing methods. Load sensing was used in the earliest versions of the circuit. The wire from the large '+' terminal that supplies the battery and vehicle loads can carry high currents, usually 35A or more. That current can result in a voltage drop in the wire and so an additional small '+' terminal was provided that was connected to the voltage-regulator's sense line and to a small gauge wire that was terminated as close to the battery as possible. Via this wire, the regulator could monitor the actual battery voltage rather than the alternator output voltage. The difference, which could be up to 0.5V, is very significant in terms of the resulting battery charging rates.

It was later decided that it was less expensive to use a larger power wire from the alternator, so dropping less voltage and making the separate sensing wire redundant. The sense wire from the regulator was then connected to the output from the field diodes that tend to track that from the power diodes but that are less susceptible to sudden short term changes in voltage due to load variations.

Note also that the ignition lamp is also connected to the output of the field diodes via the 'Ind' terminal. Since the other side of the lamp is connected via the ignition switch to the battery and the output of the power diodes, then once the alternator output reaches the battery voltage, the voltage on both sides of the lamp are the same, and with no voltage difference across it, it extinguishes.

Checking the ignition warning lamp

With ignition on, test the bulb by removing the brown/yellow wire from the alternator or regulator and touching it to earth, whereupon the bulb should illuminate (it helps to have an assistant to observe the lamp).

Testing the alternator

A voltage output test can help determine if the alternator is functioning properly.
1. Ensure the car has not been running for a few minutes, so that the battery can settle.
2. Place a voltmeter between earth and any convenient battery connection such as a brown wire at the fuse block. Start the car and rev the engine hard. The voltmeter should rise from about 12.4V to greater than 13.5V.
3. If this result is satisfactory, switch the engine off and switch the headlights on for about 10 minutes.
4. Restart the car and repeat the test in 2 above. If the voltage doesn't reach 13.5V this indicates the alternator may have an open diode making it incapable of supplying a high charging current.

To test the diodes, see page 69.

Alternator service

Before considering any service of the alternator decide whether a replacement unit is a better bet than changing individual parts. The decision will probably be a matter of:
1. Your budget. Check the cost of parts against that of an exchange unit.
2. The age of the alternator, which might mean that it is nearing the end of its useful life anyway.

In considering a replacement alternator remember that the last type fitted to MGBs, the 18ACR has a higher output than previous models, offering better performance. Look for a supplier who will warranty the replacement part for as long as you own the car.

The alternator shown in Figure 9.22 is the so-called ACR 5-terminal type.
- The '+' contact is the power output.
- The '–' contact is the earth terminal.
- The two 'Ind' contacts are joined by a link wire in the harness connector and also go to the ignition (charge) warning lamp.
- The B+ contact is connected to a wire that goes back to the fuse block, thus allowing the regulator to monitor the voltage that the vehicle systems are receiving.

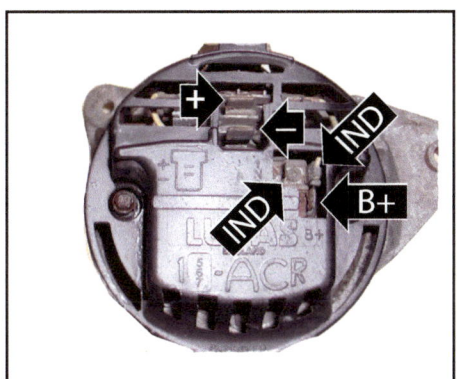

Figure 9.22. A 5-terminal alternator.

Even though the machine shown in Figure 9.23 is described as the ACR 3-terminal alternator, only two wires are usually attached. The two terminals marked '+' are both joined to the middle plate of the rectifier. The main power output is taken on one or two wires from here to the solenoid. No earth terminal is used because the metallic body of the alternator takes current to the engine block. There is only one 'Ind' terminal, the link previously made outside the casing being made inside. As before, 'Ind' goes to the ignition indicator lamp.

With the cover removed, Figure 9.24, the internal components can be seen. As wire colours may vary, before undoing anything, make a sketch of where all the wires in your alternator go. If you lose your way, Figure 9.32 to 9.34 should help.

To access the brushes (A & B), the four screws on top of the plastic brush box must be removed. The brush box itself is retained by two screws.

The regulator is usually piggy-

Figure 9.23. A 3-terminal alternator.

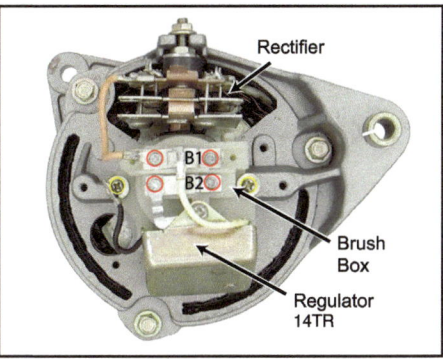

Figure 9.24. A 3-terminal alternator internal view. This is only one of the many types of alternators that were produced for the MGB, so it may look somewhat different from yours.

67

backed onto the brush box by two tines at the bottom and a single screw at the top. Some may be found screwed to the base plate.

The brush box also holds down one end of the rectifier with a rubber bush, shown immediately to the left of the slip rings in Figure 9.27. The other end of the rectifier stack is fixed with a 5/16in A/F nut.

The brushes, Figure 9.25, are not quite identical, before disassembly, note the diagonally cut-off corner on the terminal and its position toward the outside off the brush box.

The wire from the contact to the brush that passes through the middle of the pressure spring restricts the maximum extension of the brush. This prevents unlimited take up of brush wear, which would eventually result in slip-ring damage when the soft brush material gives way to metal.

The brush can extend only about 1/4in (6.4mm) so that when the brush is worn to about half its original 1/2in (13mm) length it will no longer contact the slip ring with any pressure, and will require replacement. Brushes are very inexpensive so are worth changing in any event.

You may find that new brushes you buy have a terminal that is not required on brush A like that shown in Figure 9.26. This is because the brush set was meant for a 5 terminal alternator. It will work fine; just bend the terminal out of the way so that the alternator cover can fit properly. All alternator brush sets come with a new stabilizing spring clip for the centre brush B.

With the brush box removed, Figure 9.27, the concentric slip-rings, on which the brushes run, can be inspected. In this example some scoring can be seen, as well as some metal smear on the insulator between the outer and centre ring. Careful use of fine sand paper followed by wiping off with methylated spirit (denatured alcohol) soaked soft cloth, will clean the slip rings.

If a suitable instrument is available, check the resistance between the centre and outer slip rings. The reading should be 4Ω to 5Ω.

A general view of a typical rectifier is shown in Figure 9.28. Some variations can be expected depending on the particular model of alternator.

A head-on view of the rectifier is shown in Figure 9.29. The connections that go to the stator wires are shown in three groups, S1, S2 & S3. When removing the rectifier the three stator wires have to be removed. Note that one terminal, from each of the groups, will be soldered to one of the wires.

Avoid removing the rectifier unless the intent is to replace it, as it is easy to damage the diodes when unsoldering and removing the wires.

When replacing the rectifier, the three stator wires will have to be re soldered to it. One wire will attach to one terminal in each of the outlined groups indicated in Figure 9.29. It does not matter which wire goes to which group or to which terminal in

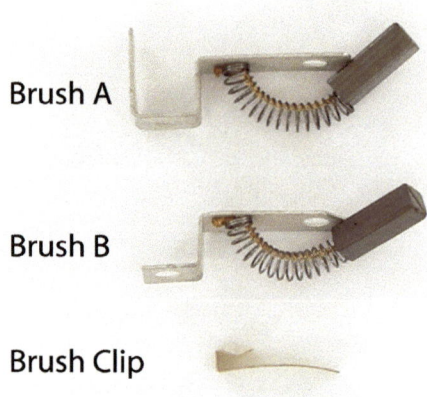

Figure 9.25. A typical brush set.

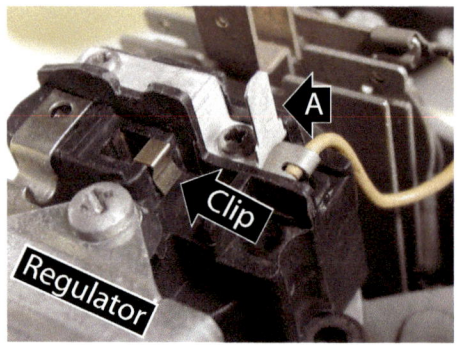

Figure 9.26. When installing new brushes on alternators with concentric slip rings, don't forget to install the stabilizing clip for brush B. If brush A comes with a contact on it that was not on the previous brush set, it may still be used; simply bend it down so that the rear cover will clear it.

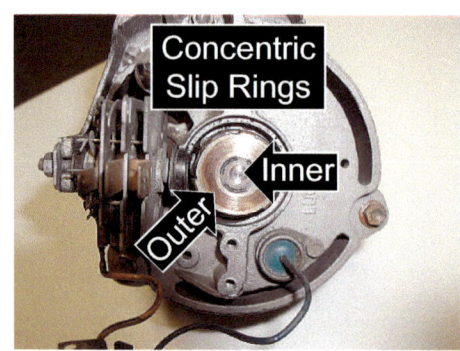

Figure 9.27. On most, but not all MGB alternators, the slip rings are concentric: one at the centre of the shaft, and the other at the periphery.

Figure 9.28. A typical rectifier. Once again, with so many design variations, there may be detail differences compared to that in your alternator.

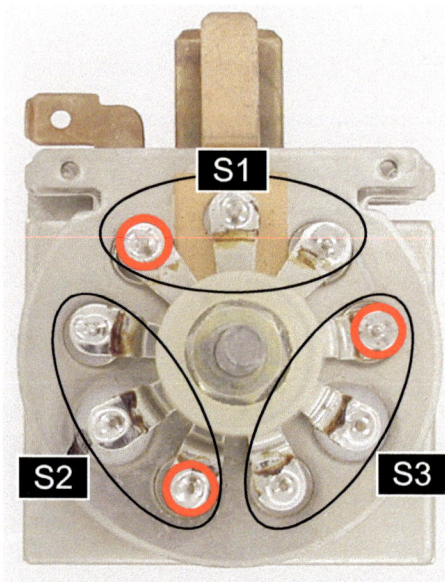

Figure 9.29. The 9 diodes in each rectifier are connected in 3 groups. Each of the 3 stator wires connects to one group.

CHARGING SYSTEM

each group it attaches. However, if the wires will reach, it is best to connect to the terminal that has the longest diode wire, that terminal having been circled in Figure 9.29. This is because the soldering operation can overheat the diodes, and the circled terminals, being connected by the longest wires to the respective diode, will attenuate more of the heat conducted to that diode. Do check that your new rectifier is connected in the groups shown in Figure 9.29 and that the longest diode wire is that indicated; it is quite possible that a replacement device has been connected differently.

Before tightening the rectifier assembly retention nut, check that there is a spacer washer between it and the inside of the alternator body, see Figure 9.24. This earths the rectifier to the body and also helps prevent the connections touching the casing, shorting it out and resulting in a brief life for a new rectifier. Even with a washer fitted, check that there are no solder whiskers or errant wire strands that might touch the casing.

Checking the rectifier

The rectifier can be checked in-situ. A diode test facility on a digital voltmeter (DVM) is preferred but as these are not readily available, for this description a circuit-tester and battery will be used.

Figure 9.30 illustrates how a circuit-tester and jump lead with alligator clips can be used as a continuity and diode tester. In this example the circuit-tester has been initially connected to the '+' terminal of the battery and the jump lead to the negative. The probe of the circuit-tester will be referred to as T and the alligator clip on the free end of the jump lead will be called J. Refer to Figure 9.29 to identify the stator connections S1, S2 & S3. If the alternator has a zener diode (Z), temporarily remove its connection to the alternator.
1. Touch J to T to ensure that the circuit-tester lights.
2. Connect J to the top (W) plate of the rectifier.
3. Touch T to S1 then S2, then S3. Circuit-tester should light.
4. Connect J to the top (+) plate of the rectifier.
5. Touch T to S1 then S2, then S3. Circuit-tester should light.
6. Connect J to the to the alternator case.
7. Touch T to S1 then S2, then S3. Circuit-tester should not light.
8. Reverse the connections to the battery so that the circuit-tester lead is connected to the battery negative and the jump-lead to the positive.
9. Connect J to the top (W) plate of the rectifier.
10. Touch T to S1 then S2, then S3. Circuit-tester should not light.
11. Connect J to the top (+) plate of the rectifier.
12. Touch T to S1 then S2, then S3. Circuit-tester should not light.

Voltage regulator

The most commonly found voltage regulator, the 14TR shown in Figure 9.31, is very reliable. Since its failure is hard to distinguish from failure of the more susceptible rectifier, treat any new newly purchased regulator gently and only buy from a supplier that has a good return policy, as in all probability you will find that it was not at fault. The early regulators that are thinner than those illustrated and those that are bolted to the base of the alternator are less robust. The zener diode (Z) was needed to protect them from over-voltage damage.

Zener diode

The zener diode (Z) can be tested in a similar manner to the rectifier, but as it is only a single diode device, the test is much quicker. Temporarily remove its connecting wire from the rectifier. Use the circuit-tester and jump lead set-up with the circuit tester connected to the '+' terminal of the battery and the jump lead to the negative.
1. Touch J to T to ensure that the circuit-tester lights.
2. Connect J to the to the case of the alternator.
3. Touch T to the (now free) zener diode connector.
   Circuit-tester should not light.
4. Connect J to the to the zener diode connector.
5. Touch T to the case of the alternator.
   Circuit-tester should light.
   Replacements are hard to obtain. If pressed, any 5W, 30V zener diode, available from electronics suppliers can be used, although you may need to use some imagination to get it to wire in and physically fit well. Otherwise, just remove it. The alternator will work fine without it.

Capacitor

The capacitor is also accessible with the alternator still in the car. If it is suspect, remove its wire to the rectifier stack and check the resistance between earth and the capacitor connecting wire. Some DVMs may read short to start with but as a good capacitor charges the meter will read higher and higher resistance. If the capacitor reads short-circuit continuously then remove it or just cut its connecting wire off.

It is only necessary to replace the capacitor if radio interference is heard in the form of a screaming sound that gets higher pitched with engine speed. If this is the case, buy a radio suppression capacitor, like that shown in Figure 16.3, and bolt it down on the rear fixing bolt of the alternator. Attach the flying lead to the B+ terminal of the alternator; to do so may mean that the wire has to be passed through the back of the connector, its end stripped and fixed under the B+ connector.

ACR-SERIES ALTERNATOR WIRING

There are so many variations between

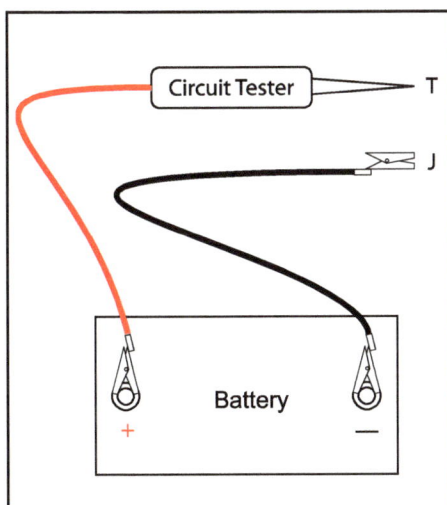

Figure 9.30. A battery, jump lead and circuit-tester can be used to test the rectifier diodes.

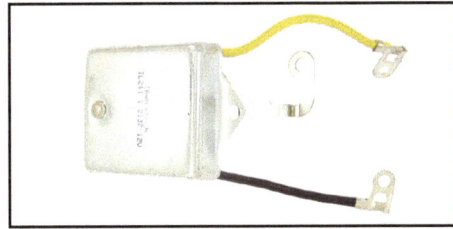

Figure 9.31. The 14TR voltage regulator fitted to ACR-series alternators.

MGB ELECTRICAL SYSTEMS – THE ESSENTIAL MANUAL

the various and very common ACR alternators that some guidance is often required as to their wiring. The three examples below should cover almost all permutations

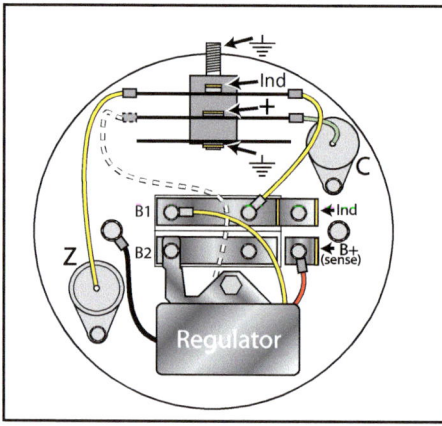

Figure 9.32. ACR 5-terminal alternator wiring

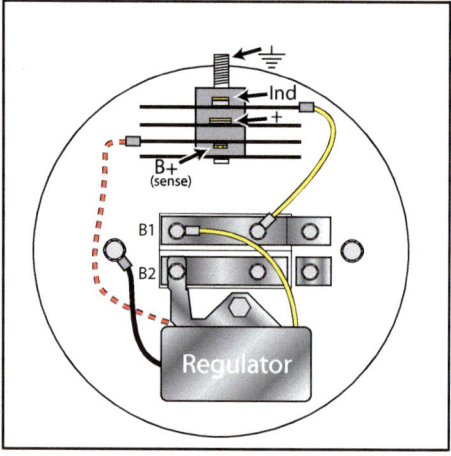

Figure 9.33 ACR 3-terminal alternator wiring type 1.

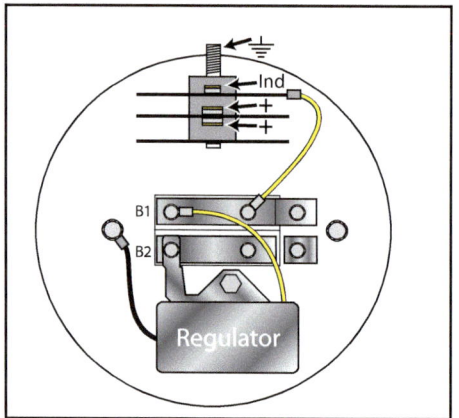

Figure 9.34. ACR 3-terminal alternator wiring type 2.

5-terminal alternator wiring

Figure 9.22 shows an example of a 5-terminal alternator. In almost all installations, not all five are actually connected.

The earth terminal is not necessary because the bolt retaining the rectifier is joined to the rear earth fin and is bolted to the casing of the alternator, which itself is bolted to the engine, and hence earth, of the car.

The two 'Ind' terminals, which go to the brown/yellow ignition lamp wire, are always linked together sometimes inside the alternator, sometimes outside (see Figure 9.21) and sometimes in both locations.

The contact marked 'B+ (sense)' is for monitoring the battery voltage and adjusting the output accordingly. Instead, there may be a white wire that connects to the main alternator '+' terminal that monitors the alternator output (machine sensing). In this case, the red wire may not be present and 'B+' will be left unconnected internally.

In some examples, the metal link between the regulator and brush is not present and a green wire is used instead. Where this is the case, the black wire is not used because the regulator is earthed via its lower fixing screw.

The surge suppressing zener diode 'Z' and/or the radio interference suppression capacitor may not be installed.

3-terminal alternator wiring

There are two different types of 3-terminal alternators commonly found. One has two separate and different size '+' contacts and the other has two identical large '+' contacts that are joined together.

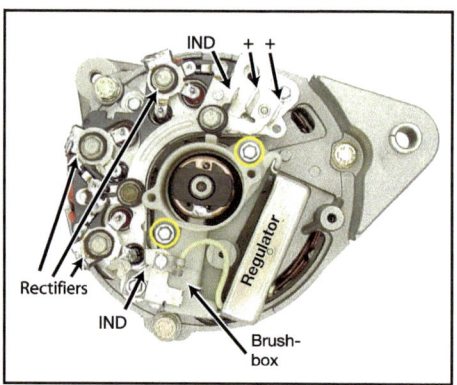

Figure 9.35. This 45 amp alternator was never fitted as original equipment but was supplied as a Lucas replacement part.

In Figure 9.33, the brown/yellow ignition lamp wire is connected to the top terminal.

The main alternator power output terminal to the battery, usually via the starter solenoid, is the middle contact.

The 'B+' contact is for battery sensing but in many examples, the fin to which it is attached is left unconnected and simply becomes a parking spot for the unused harness cable attached to it. Instead, the alternator is machine sensed via the yellow wires.

Figure 9.34 shows an alternator with the so called Euro connector. There appears to be no real European standard for this connection layout, rather it seems to have come about because Bosch needed to clone the Lucas connector in order to win business at Ford UK.

There are only two external connections made, a small brown/yellow wire to the 'Ind' for operation of the ignition lamp and a much larger brown wire to one of the power contacts for connecting back, via the starter solenoid, to the battery. The other '+' contact is redundant.

Replacement alternators

If you find that your alternator is not recognizable from Figure 9.32 to 9.34, then you may have a replacement 45A machine like that shown in Figure 9.35. It has quite a different rectifier and the brushes run on annular rings that sit side-by-side on the rotor shaft and that are accessed by brushes that come from the side.

No suitably sized Lucas alternator being available at the time, the MGB-GT V8 was equipped with a British built 46A AC Delco model, for which the later Lucas 45A machine makes a good substitute.

Almost any alternator can be used to replace the original Lucas machines, the main problems are mechanical fitment and getting the electrical connections spliced into the car harness. If an alternator has a larger pulley than the original, it will not turn as fast and although it may be more modern and larger, it may nevertheless produce disappointing results, particularly at idling speeds (see Figure 9.5).

ALTERNATOR WITH EXTERNAL REGULATOR

The alternator circuit Figure 9.36 is distinguished by its external regulator.

CHARGING SYSTEM

Understanding of how the circuit operates will be enhanced by reference to the internal description of the alternator page 65.

Current from the batteries flows on a large cross section cable to the starter solenoid (4) which serves as an anchor and terminating point for several battery connected wires. From this point a brown (N) wire takes the current to the fuse block (19) that serves as another anchor point. From there it flows to and through the ignition switch (38) from which it is carried on a white wire to the ignition warning lamp (44). From here the current flows on a brown/yellow (NY) wire to the '+' terminal of the regulator (2). A further brown/yellow wire carries field current to the slip-ring via the alternator's 'Ind' terminal (1).

The small current flowing through this circuit and back to earth via the regulator on a brown/green (NG) wire is sufficient to produce a weak magnetic field in the alternator (1) rotor.

Once the engine is started and the alternator turns, the weak rotating magnetic field causes a current to be generated in the stator windings, some of this current flows through the slip rings and reinforces the field strength of the rotor and in turn the output from the stator. The output from the stator increases more and more until the voltage at the '+' terminal is greater than the battery voltage and thus current can flow to it on the brown wires and charge it.

The brown wires can also supply various loads with current from the fuse block (19). A brown wire is connected between the starter solenoid battery terminal and the B+ regulator terminal. The regulator can thus monitor the charge and adjust the field current and with it the output voltage.

When the alternator (1) produces a voltage equal to the battery voltage, the voltages both sides of the ignition warning lamp are also equal. With no potential difference across it, no current flows through the lamp and it extinguishes.

5-TERMINAL ALTERNATOR

This alternator is generally described as having 5-terminals, but requires only four wires. The earth terminal marked '–' is not connected because the casing provides the necessary earth path.

Understanding of how the circuit operates will be enhanced by reference to the internal description of the alternator on page 65.

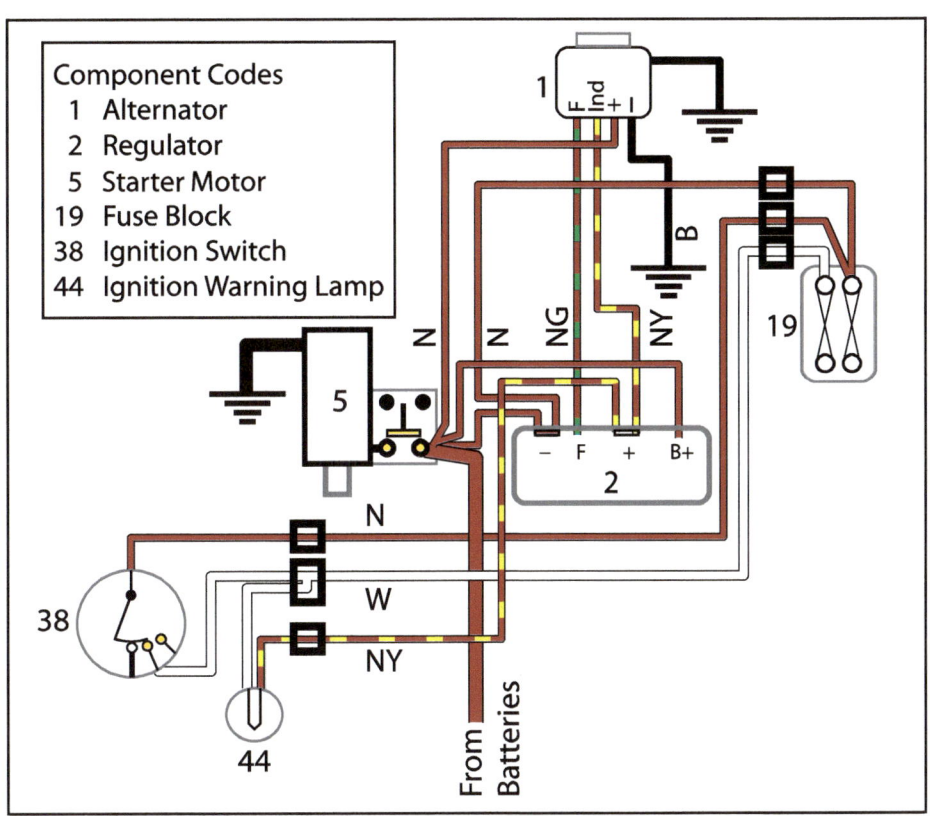

Figure 9.36. Charging circuit for alternators with an external regulator.

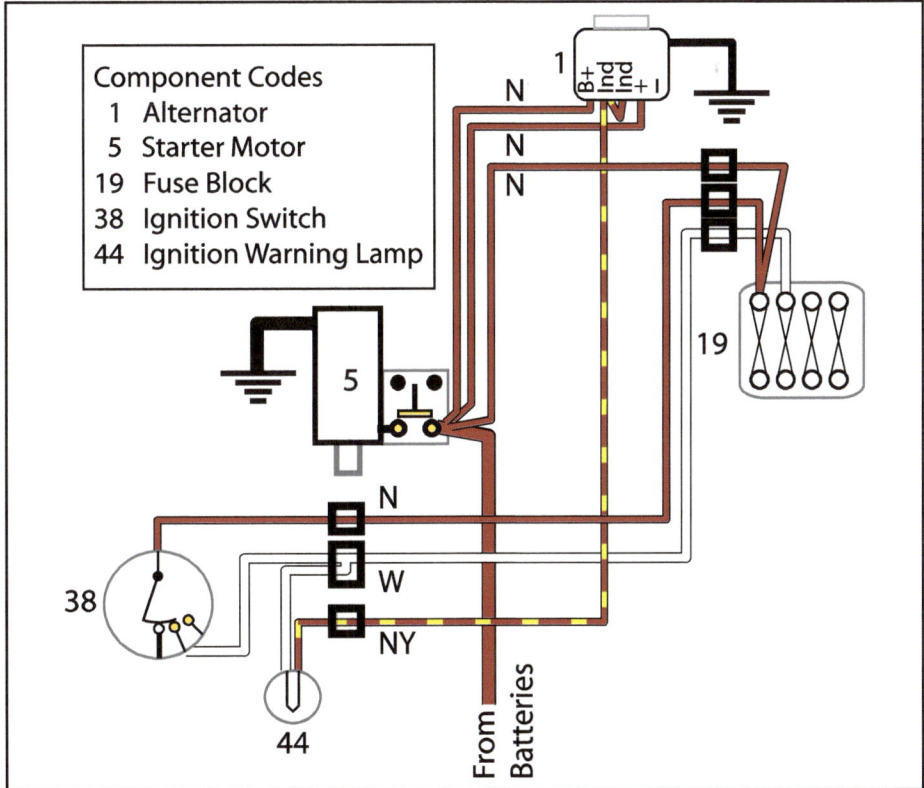

Figure 9.37. Charging circuit for 5-terminal alternators.

MGB ELECTRICAL SYSTEMS – THE ESSENTIAL MANUAL

Referring to Figure 9.37, current from the battery flows on a cable with a large cross section area to the starter solenoid (4) which serves as an anchor and terminating point for several battery connected wires. From this point a brown wire (N) takes the current to the fuse block (19) that serves as another anchor point. From the fuse block it flows to, and through, the ignition switch (38) from where it is carried on a white wire to the ignition warning lamp (44). From there the current flows on a brown/yellow (NY) wire to one of the 'Ind' terminals of the alternator (1). A link wire joins the slip-ring and field diodes, there being no internal connection inside. The 'Ind' terminal is the field connection.

The small current flowing through the ignition warning lamp is sufficient to produce a weak magnetic field in the alternator rotor.

Once the engine is started and the alternator turns, the weak rotating magnetic field causes a current to be generated in the stator windings, some of this current flows through the slip rings and reinforces the field strength of the rotor and in turn the output from the stator. The output from the stator increases more and more until the voltage at the '+' terminal is greater than the battery voltage and thus current can flow to it on the brown wires and charge it.

The brown wires can also supply various loads with current from the fuse block (19). A brown wire is connected between the starter solenoid battery terminal and the B+ regulator terminal on the alternator. The regulator can thus monitor the charge and adjust the field current and with it the output voltage.

When the alternator (1) produces a voltage equal to the battery voltage, the voltages both sides of the ignition warning lamp are also equal. With no potential difference across it, no current flows through the lamp and it extinguishes.

3-TERMINAL ALTERNATOR

This alternator, while generally described as a 3-terminal, requires only two wires. The number of wires can be reduced from the previous 5-terminal type because of an internal link between the slip rings and field diodes and the combination battery-sense and output terminals.

Understanding of how the circuit operates will be enhanced by reference to the internal description of the alternator on page 65.

Referring to Figure 9.38, current from the battery flows on a large cross section area cable to the starter solenoid (4) which serves as an anchor and terminating point for several battery connected wires. From there a brown (N) wire takes the current to the fuse block (19) that serves as another anchor point. From this point it flows to and through the ignition switch (38) from which it is carried on a white wire to the ignition warning lamp (44). From here the current flows on a brown/yellow (NY) wire to the 'Ind' terminal of the alternator (1). The 'Ind' terminal is the field connection.

The small current flowing through the ignition warning lamp is sufficient to produce a weak magnetic field in the alternator rotor. Once the engine is started and the alternator turns, the weak rotating magnetic field causes a current to be generated in the stator windings. Some of this current flows through the slip rings and reinforces the field strength of the rotor and in turn the output from the Stator.

The output from the stator increases until the voltage at the '+' terminal is greater than the battery voltage and thus current can flow to it on the brown wires and charge it. The brown wires can also supply various loads from the fuse block.

When the alternator (1) produces a voltage equal to the battery voltage, the voltages both sides of the ignition warning lamp are also equal. With no potential difference across it, no current flows through the lamp and it extinguishes.

CONVERSION FROM POSITIVE TO NEGATIVE EARTH

Although some ignition system and corrosion benefits are claimed for negative earth systems, they are at best marginal. The only really worthwhile reason for converting a dynamo based vehicle to negative earth is so that electronic equipment, such as semiconductor based entertainment or ignition systems, can be used. Note that positive earth electronic ignition systems are available.

The steps necessary for all vehicles are: battery reversal, dynamo re-polarization and ignition coil reversal.

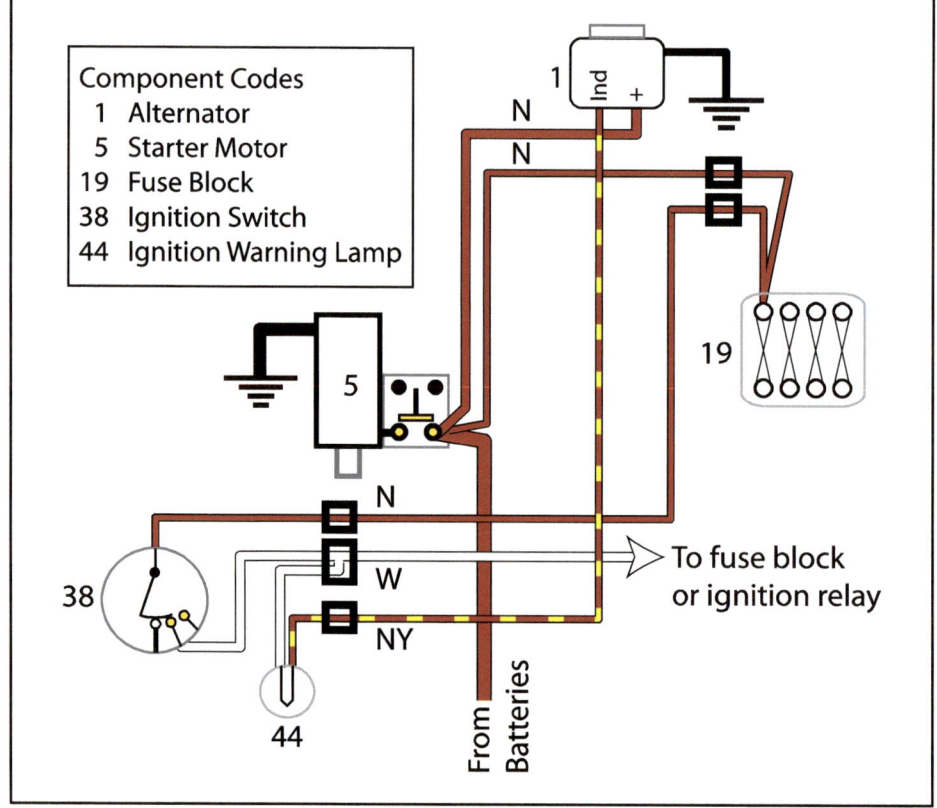

Figure 9.38. Charging circuit for 3-terminal alternators.

CHARGING SYSTEM

Depending on equipment fitted, conversion of other devices may be necessary such as the fuel pump, other motors and the tachometer.

Preparation
1. Disconnect the batteries and remove both from their wells.
2. Remove the brown/green wire from the F terminal and the brown/yellow wire from the D terminal of the control box.

Procedure
1. Swap the wires from the CB to the SW terminal of the ignition coil and vice-versa.
2. If you are sure you have an original fuel pump then no action is required. If the pump has been updated then it may be polarity sensitive. Some pumps have a diode that can be reversed. With the rear cap removed, look for a small cylindrical device with one fork and one ring terminal. You can reverse them or buy an inexpensive negative polarity diode. See fuel pump, page 170, for more details.
3. Original equipment on positive earth vehicles is a manual windscreen washer pump. However, if an electric type has been fitted, the wires to that will have to be reversed.
4. Any ammeter or voltmeter that has been fitted will need the wires reversed.
5. The connections to the heater blower motor must be reversed.
6. If there is an electronic tachometer this will need both the signal and power supply wires swapped. This means opening the device, and doing some fairly delicate soldering. If you do not feel confident about doing such work, a used post 1968 replacement might be the best option, new instruments being either unobtainable or very expensive. In this case you will still have to change the white wire signal connections. A description of the process can be found in the section beginning page 152.
7. Reconnect the batteries. It is probably best to fit a new black coloured earth-to-battery negative cable. It will probably also be necessary to change the now positive battery cable connector for one that better fits the positive battery post. That may require cutting off the old connector and using a clamp-on type. Some red paint on the positive cable connector helps anyone working on the car to recognise that the car has been converted.
8. The field coil of the generator will have a residual magnetic field that is incorrect for the new polarity. It may be reversed by the weak magnetic field induced by the warning light current at switch on, but it's best to make sure by manually hitting it with a really high current. Take the brown/green wire that was removed from the regulator (control box) and touch it for an instant on the B terminal of the regulator. Try not to touch the metal of the terminals yourself because, by the same process that allows the ignition coil to produce a high voltage, the field coil of the generator will produce a voltage that can cause an alarming, but harmless, electric shock. Also be prepared for a spark as the wire touches the terminal. Now reconnect the brown/green wire to the F terminal and the brown/yellow to the 'D' terminal of the regulator.
9. Reconnect the ignition coil with the white wire going to the CB (or +) terminal and the white/black wire to the SW (-) terminal.

Note that certain electrical contacts can cause problems following a change in vehicle polarity, in particular the distributor contact-breaker and the fuel pump, which have contacts that constantly open and close and so may need attention. Electrical contacts operating on direct current tend to exchange metal from one to the other as they operate, so one erodes and the other grows – a phenomenon known as pitting and piling (see page 104), yet they tend to still mate together fairly well. Reversing the polarity of the electrical current starts the metal deposition process in reverse and the contacts often fail to make good contact after a short period. Change them if you can.

DYNAMO TO ALTERNATOR CONVERSION

The alternator is a far superior generating machine than its predecessor the dynamo. Moreover, the semiconductors that made the alternator a practical machine also enabled the charge regulator that comes with an alternator to be much more efficient than the electromechanical type that was used with dynamos. These instructions discuss conversion to the 3-terminal alternator, the only type now readily available new or refurbished.

Preparation
1. Make sure you already have a negative earth car. If the electrical system is still positive earth, then procedures 1, 2, 4, 5, 6, 7, and 8 commencing on page 73, will need to be completed first.
2. Prepare the mechanical hardware.

As Figure 9.39 shows, the length of the alternator is somewhat shorter than the dynamo it is replacing. The brackets on the engine accommodate the span for the dynamo, shown by the red arrow, of 6 3/32 in (154.8mm), whereas that for the alternator is only 3 7/8 in (98.4mm) or 3 5/8 in (92mm), depending on type. The difference is best taken up by making a steel spacer tube equal to the difference in length.

The tube shown in Figure 9.40 was cut from steel gas pipe and covered in heat shrink tubing for aesthetic purposes. Cut as squarely as possible and to a shorter length rather than longer, then use washers to shim up the difference. It is important to get the spacer right because the flanges on the alternator must not be put under strain.

A 5/16 in x 3 3/4 in (M8 X 90mm) bolt will be needed to span the spacer with two appropriately sized flat washers and one anti rotation washer. It is worth

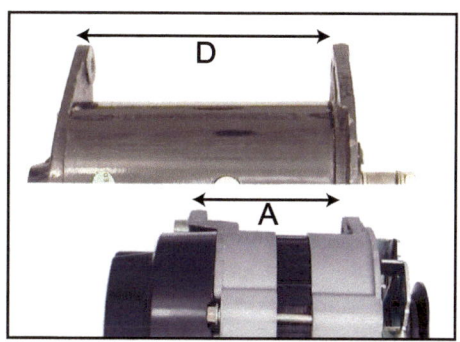

Figure 9.39. Length 'A' of the alternator is shorter than length 'D' of the dynamo, so a spacer tube is necessary to fill the gap between the support bracket.

Figure 9.40. The spacer tube, long bolt and optional new front bolt for fitting an alternator in place of a dynamo.

MGB ELECTRICAL SYSTEMS – THE ESSENTIAL MANUAL

Figure 9.41. A dynamo to alternator installation.

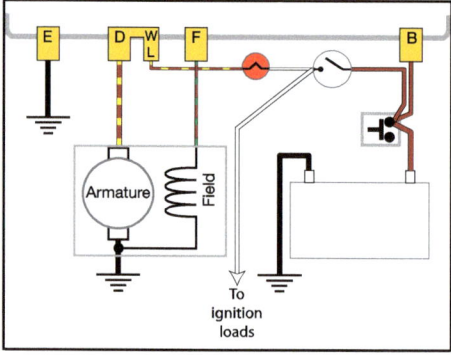

Figure 9.42. The original control box connections to the dynamo.

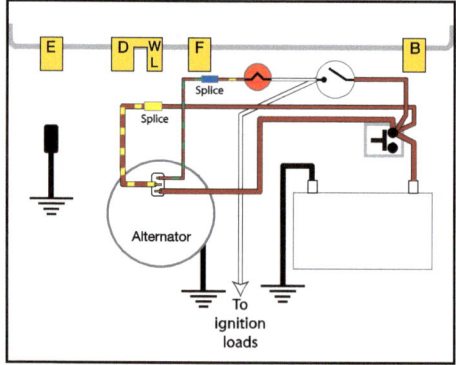

Figure 9.43. After conversion. The original control box is shown for reference, but may be removed if wished.

getting new 5/16in x 2in (M8 x 50mm) fasteners for the other end too.

Procedure

Figures 9.42 illustrate the before and after conversion wiring.
1. Disconnect the battery(ies).
2. Remove the dynamo and install the alternator in its place as shown in Figure 9.41 using the hardware discussed above. Obtain the right fan belt for the alternator and fit that in place of that used with the dynamo.

The alternator pulley is smaller, requiring a shorter belt. Even if the old belt appears to fit it will have bedded into the old dynamo pulley and should not be re-used.
3. Remove the earth connection from the E terminal of the control box (Figure 9.43). Tape it back so there is no danger of it touching any live connections.
4. Remove the small brown/yellow wire from the 'WL' terminal and the brown/green wire from the 'F; terminal. Cut off the spade connectors, strip the wire insulation and splice them together, see Figure 2.17.
5. Remove the larger brown/yellow wire from the 'D' terminal. Remove the brown wire from the 'B' terminal. Cut off the spade connectors, strip the wire insulation and splice these wires together.
6. Connect the alternator. The existing connectors that were used on the dynamo should work fine with the alternator. Attach the small push on connector with the brown/green wire to the small terminal 'F' (field). Then connect the heavy brown/yellow wire with the large connector to either of the wide contacts arrowed '+' (positive).
7. The heavy brown/yellow wire was designed to carry the approximately 22A maximum output from the dynamo, whereas the alternator potential output is probably twice that value. The brown/yellow wire is unlikely to overheat but it will, unless supplemented, limit the alternator's output. It is recommended therefore that a second current path, at least as large as that of the brown/yellow wire, is provided to reduce the resistance between the alternator, the battery and the loads to which it connects. To provide this path, follow the instructions below.
In Figure 9.43, a 12AWG (4mm²) wire has been connected, using a 3/8in (9.5mm) connector like that in Figure 9.45 connected to the spare large '+' terminal of the alternator with the other end connected, using a large ring terminal, to the starter switch or solenoid terminal to which other wires are already connected. It is important that this wire is routed on as short as possible. .
10. Ensure everything is switched off. As the battery is reconnected, check there are no sparks that would indicate that something (that shouldn't) is drawing a high current.
11. Switch the ignition on. Check that the ignition warning light illuminates.
12. Start the car and verify that the ignition warning light extinguishes when the engine is revved.
13. If you have a voltmeter, check the voltage at a brown wire at the fuse block. It should reach at least 13.5V when the engine is revved to about 3000rpm.

CONVERSION FROM A 5-TERMINAL TO 3-TERMINAL ALTERNATOR

Although commonly used to describe the alternator, the terms 3-terminal and 5-terminal really refer to the connector, rather than the alternator itself.

The life of the MGB happened also to span that of the development of

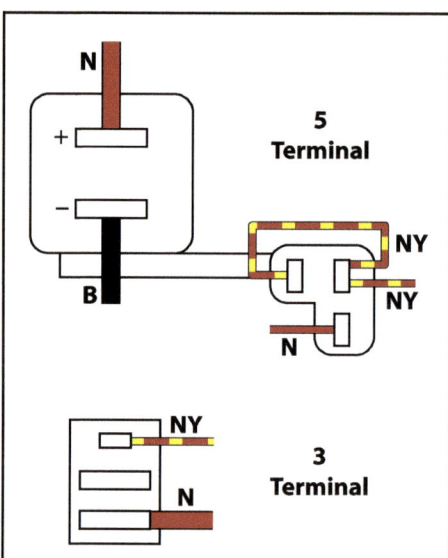

Figure 9.44. The complicated 5-terminal connector is replaced by the simple 3-terminal.

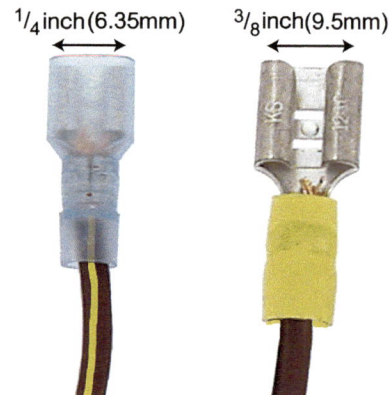

Figure 9.45. If the correct 3-terminal connector is unavailable, standard female blade connectors may be purchased and fitted instead.

CHARGING SYSTEM

the alternator. Originally the car had a dynamo that required only two terminals to connect it. The first alternator fitted had an external regulator and its connector had five terminals, four of which were connected, although only three had to be, a superfluous earth wire being used, see Figure 9.36. The next iteration was to incorporate the regulator inside the alternator. This alternator's connector also had five terminals, four of which were used, two being joined together at the alternator and two being joined together at the battery, so that in fact, only two were required, see Figure 9.37.

Finally, a so-called 3-terminal alternator was used as in Figure 9.38. To confuse the issue it in fact has three or sometimes four terminals, one of which is an unnecessary voltage sensing line from the regulator. Of the three remaining, two are power output terminals, only one being needed. Thus only two terminals are used, just as was the case with the dynamo, one to the warning light and the other to the solenoid, and from there to the battery

Why change?
There are three principal reasons to change from the older 5-terminal alternator to the later 3-terminal.
1. If the 5-terminal is unserviceable, only a 3-terminal type is available a new replacement.
2. Added electrical loads have made the 24% increase in output, from 34A to 45A, worthwhile.
3. Most 45A alternators have a smaller pulley, increasing the rate of charge at idle. See Figure 9.5.

Procedure
1. Disconnect the battery.
2. Cut off all the wires close to the 5-terminal connector, discarding it and the brown/yellow (NY) link wire. See Figure 9.44.
3. Apply PVC tape or heat-shrink tubing to the black (B) wire and to the thin brown (N) wire to insulate the ends as both are no longer required.

If a 3-terminal connector was not supplied with the new alternator, then one may be purchased from an MGB parts catalogue or individual contacts like those in Figure 9.45 may be crimped or soldered to the wires as described below.
4. Connect the brown/yellow (NY) wire to the small terminal.
5. Connect the thicker brown (N) wire to either of the wide terminals. In the interest of safety, the greatest separation and thus the farther of the two wider contacts is preferred

To ensure good electrical connections, make certain that the connectors fit really tightly onto the alternator connector blades. If using individual connectors with exposed metal contacts it is worthwhile putting heat-shrink tubing over the larger connector with a little overhanging the end. This provides a measure of safety should it become disconnected and touch any metal which would otherwise earth and short the battery.
6. Reconnect the battery.

ALTERNATOR CIRCUIT FAULT-FINDING

Symptom	Possible causes	Action
Ignition (charge) warning lamp does not light.	Bulb blown.	Check the bulb. See page 67. Change the bulb if necessary.
	Brushes worn down.	Check and change the brushes if necessary. See page 68.
	Regulator failure.	Change the regulator. See page 66
Ignition (charge) warning lamp flickers or only partially extinguishes. *Note, a very dim warning lamp glow, visible only at night and with headlamps or other high current loads operating, can be considered normal and harmless. The high current consumption causes a voltage drop in the vehicle wiring that produces a small difference voltage across the bulb.*	Fan belt slipping.	Adjust the fan belt tension.
	Brushes nearly worn down.	Check and change the brushes if necessary. See page 68.
	Poor connections in the alternator to the charge warning lamp bulb holder, or from it to either brown/yellow wires to the alternator or the white wiring to the ignition switch.	Check and remake connections as necessary.
	One or more of the diodes is intermittently touching the outer casing.	Check for the presence of a spacer washer between the rectifier and the case as well as the one between the case and the rectifier retention nut. See Figure 10.23. This may also be the cause of failed diodes.
Ignition (charge) warning lamp does not extinguish. *See also above.*	Fan belt loose or missing.	Adjust or replace.
	One or more diodes in the rectifier pack have failed.	Check the rectifier pack as described in page 69 and change if necessary.

MGB ELECTRICAL SYSTEMS – THE ESSENTIAL MANUAL

Symptom	Possible causes	Action
The charge indicator lamp gets brighter as the electrical load is increased.	Fan belt slipping.	Adjust the fan belt tension.
	One or more diodes in the rectifier pack have failed.	Check the rectifier pack as described in page 69 and change if necessary.
	The ignition switch has poor connections or there are other high resistance connections in the white wires of the ignition circuit.	Check all connections in white circuit.
Charge warning lamp fully or partially extinguishes but battery is not charging.	Broken power connection from the alternator to the battery.	Check the voltage at power terminal of the running alternator. If above 14.2V, check also at the use block. If less than 12.4V check the integrity of the power wire from the alternator to the starter solenoid. Failure often occurs invisibly under the wire insulation at one end or the other.
Alternator seems to charge adequately but the voltage never reaches 13.5V	Alternator power wire too small.	Check the voltage at the alternator power contact itself. If 14V or higher, follow procedure 7, page 74.
	Partial rectifier failure	Check rectifier. See page 71.
	Partial stator winding failure	Check stator. See page 71.
The wiring to the alternator gets hot and smokes when the battery is connected.	Disconnect the battery before proceeding further.	
	The battery may have been connected the reverse way around, possibly damaging the rectifier stack or a rectifier diode has spontaneously become short circuit.	Check that the battery is connected properly. Check the rectifier pack as described in page 68 and change it if necessary.
	The capacitor or zener diode may have become short circuit.	Neither component is absolutely necessary. Try removing one at a time to see if that resolves problem.

Table 9.3. Alternator circuit fault-finding.

www.velocebooks.com/www.veloce.co.uk
All books in print • New books • Special offers • Gift Vouchers

Chapter 10
Starting system

GENERAL
The starter circuit is only responsible for getting the engine turning at about 100rpm, which provides sufficient speed for it to build enough compression and momentum such that it can fire and sustain itself.

Problems with starting can be due to a variety of things, including, but not limited to, the fuel and ignition systems. This section deals specifically with electrical issues concerned with the starter system. Before the starter circuit can perform its essential task it needs a powerful electrical source, that being the lead-acid battery (or in the case of MGCs and pre 1974 MGBs: batteries).

Such is the magnitude of the energy required to turn the starter motor that the ignition switch, of which the start switch is a part, cannot itself switch the necessary amount of current. For that reason, an indirect system is used in which a solenoid (a kind of electrically powered actuator) is energized by the start switch and the solenoid then connects the starter motor via very high current carrying contacts.

Later cars use a pre-engaged starter in which the solenoid not only operates the high power electrical switch, but also physically throws the drive pinion into the flywheel ring gear. The additional power required to do this necessitates yet another layer of switching in which the start switch energizes a relay that then operates the solenoid, which in turn operates the starter.

STARTER CIRCUIT 1962-1967
Circuit description
Referring to Figure 10.1, early cars have the batteries' positive terminal connected to earth, so the hot side of the battery is negative polarity. It feeds the system via a large cross section area cable that is terminated at the starter solenoid (4). A smaller brown (N) wire then feeds power to the rest of the vehicle taking current to the fuse block (19) by way of the control box (2). A second brown wire, connected to the first by a bullet connector located close to the fuse block (19), conveys current to the ignition switch (38). When the key is turned to the start position, current can flow via a white/red (WR) wire to the solenoid actuator coil, and through it to earth.

Once current flows in the actuator coil, a magnetic force is created that closes a high current contact allowing current to flow from the batteries to the starter motor (5). The starter motor begins to spin throwing a rotating pinion back toward the motor by means of an inertia drive and in doing so, meshing it with the ring gear on the flywheel and causing the engine to turn.

STARTER CIRCUIT 1967-1969
Circuit description
Referring to Figure 10.2, cars from about 1967 onward have the battery's or batteries' negative terminal connected to earth, so the hot side of the battery is positive polarity. It feeds the system via a large cross section area cable that is terminated at the starter solenoid, which unlike that on earlier cars, is integral with the starter motor (5). A smaller brown (N) wire then feeds power to the rest of the vehicle taking current to the fuse block (19).

A second brown wire, connected to the first by a bullet connector located close to the fuse block, conveys current to the ignition switch (38). When the key is turned to the start position, current can flow via a white/red (WR) wire to the starter solenoid that is now integrated with the starter motor into a pre-engaged starter motor/solenoid assembly (5).

The solenoid coil becomes energized and a strong magnetic force moves a rod, known as an armature, which in turn moves a lever pushing the pinion forward so as to mesh it with the ring gear on the flywheel. At the end of

MGB ELECTRICAL SYSTEMS – THE ESSENTIAL MANUAL

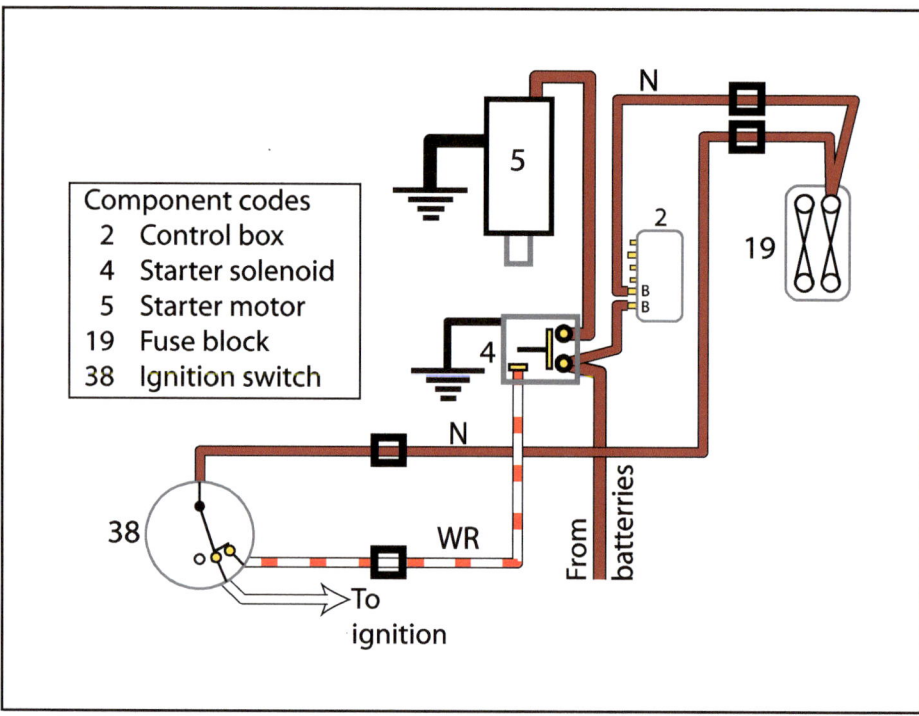

Figure 10.1. The starter circuit for 1962-1967 cars with a separate starter motor solenoid.

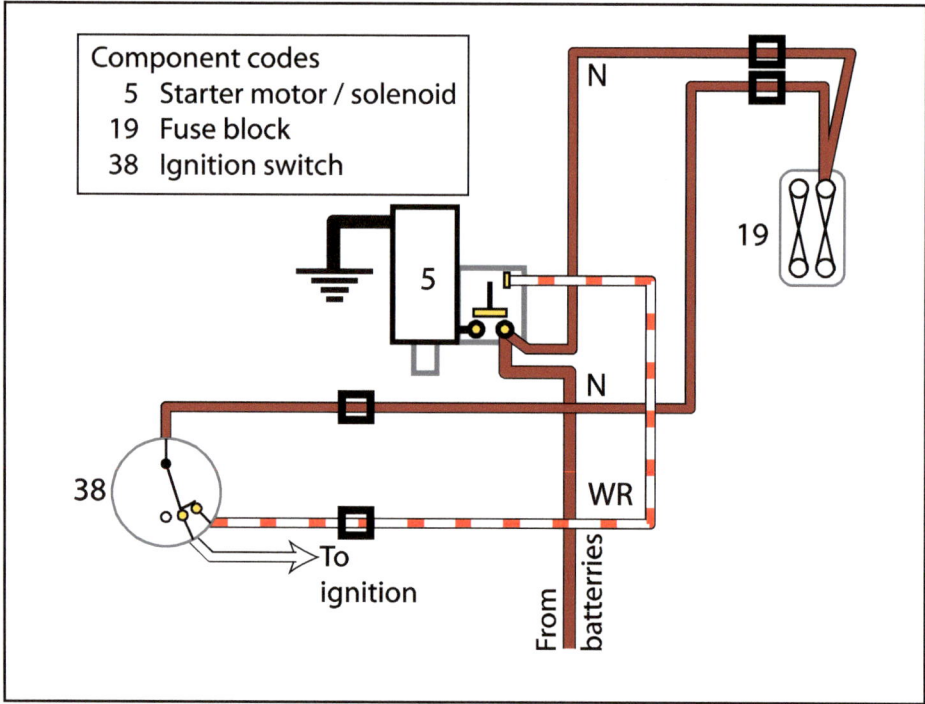

Figure 10.2. The starter circuit for 1967-1969 cars with an integral starter motor and solenoid.

a relay as per that introduced during the 1970 model year.

STARTER CIRCUIT 1970-1974½
Circuit description

Referring to Figure 10.3, cars of this era have the battery's or batteries' negative terminal connected to earth, so the hot side of the battery is positive polarity. It feeds the system via a large cross section cable that is terminated at the starter solenoid, which is integral with the starter motor (5). A smaller brown (N) wire then feeds power to the rest of the vehicle taking current to the fuse block (19).

A second brown wire, connected to the first by a bullet connector located close to the fuse block, conveys current to the ignition switch (38). When the key is turned to the start position, current can flow via a white/red (WR) wire to the starter relay (174) actuator coil winding W1, and through it to winding terminal W2 and to earth on a black wire.

A third brown wire comes from the bullet connector to C1, one of the two main switch contacts of the relay. Once current flows in the relay coil, the contacts close and allow a current to flow from contact C1 to contact C2 and via a white/brown (WN) wire to the starter motor solenoid (5). The solenoid coil becomes energized and a strong magnetic force moves a rod, known as an armature, which in turn moves a lever pushing the pinion forward so as to mesh it with the ring gear on the flywheel. At the end of the rod's travel, a pair of high current contacts closes allowing current to flow from the battery to the starter motor. The pinion rotates and so the engine turns.

STARTER CIRCUIT 1974½-1980
Circuit description

Referring to Figure 10.4, the battery feeds the system via a large cable that is terminated at the starter solenoid, which is integral with the starter motor (5). A smaller brown wire (N) then feeds power to the rest of the vehicle taking current to the fuse block (19).

A second brown wire, connected to the first by a bullet connector located close to the fuse block, conveys current to the ignition switch (38). When the key is turned to the start position, current can flow via a white/red (WR) wire to the starter relay (174) actuator coil winding 86, and through it to winding terminal 85 and to earth on a black wire.

A third brown wire comes from the bullet connector to 87, one of the

the rod's travel, a pair of high current contacts closes allowing current to flow from the battery to the starter motor. The pinion rotates and the engine turns.

The current required to actuate the pre-engaged starter motor/solenoid assembly is substantial and resulted in early failure of the ignition switch. To mitigate the effect on the ignition switch, many cars were retrofitted with

STARTING SYSTEM

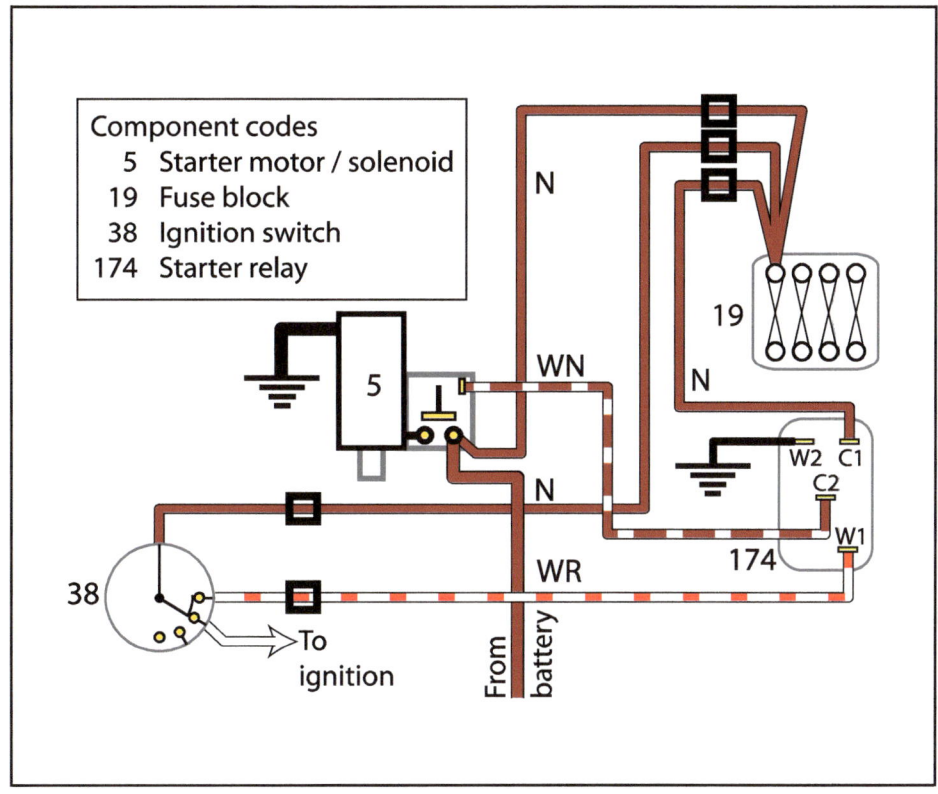

Figure 10.3. The starter circuit for 1970-1974½, cars the first to use a starter motor relay.

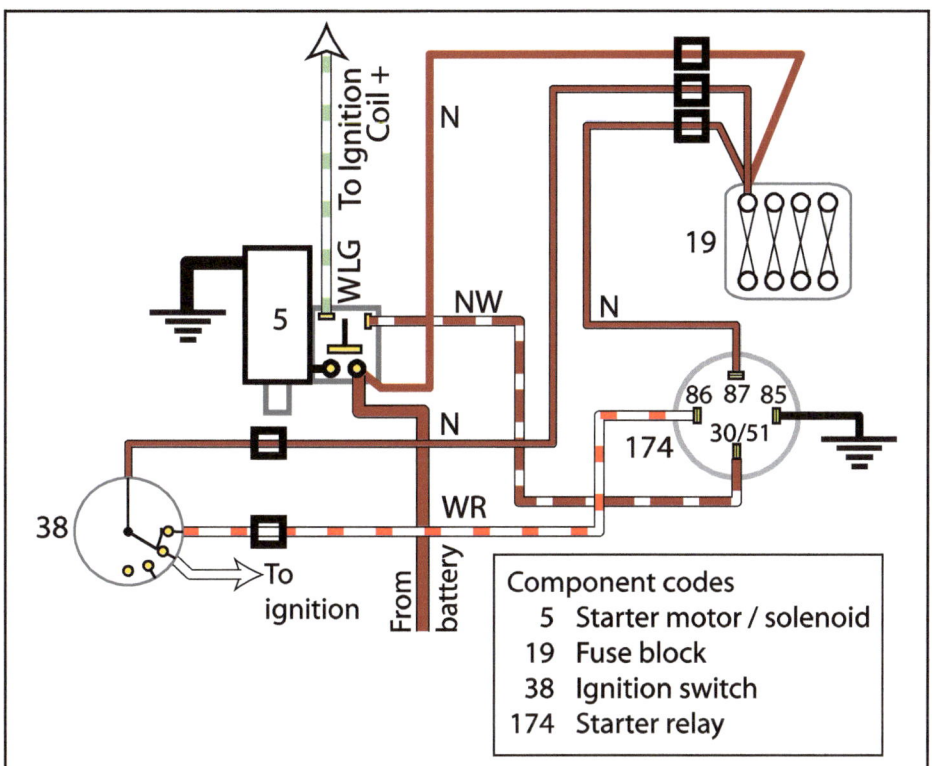

Figure 10.4. The starter circuit for the 1974½ -1980 cars that have a ballast resistor shunt terminal on the starter motor solenoid.

two main switch contacts of the relay. Once current flows in the relay coil, the contacts close and allow a current to flow from contact 87 to contact 30 and via a brown/white (NW) wire (changed from the former white/brown wire) to the starter motor solenoid (5). The solenoid coil becomes energized and a strong magnetic force moves a rod, known as an armature, which in turn moves a lever pushing the pinion forward so as to mesh it with the ring gear on the flywheel. At the end of the rod's travel, a pair of high current contacts closes allowing current to flow from the battery to the starter motor. The pinion rotates and so the engine turns.

A white/light-green (WLG) wire routes from the starter/solenoid to the ignition coil. This is used on rubber bumper cars to aid starting by providing system voltage directly to the coil during starting, thus by-passing the ignition ballast resistor. This subject is discussed further on page 95.

STARTER SOLENOID
Solenoid 1962-1967

In early cars, the solenoid was a separate item from the starter motor, and in fact could very well be called a relay, its only function being, as that of a relay, to use a small magnetizing current to move an armature that closes a high current switch.

The solenoid is located at the rear right of the under-bonnet area, just below the fuse block and generator control box. Figure 10.5 shows the 1962-1966 device. The button is a useful adjunct, allowing operation of the starter from under the bonnet, and saving the need for an assistant when doing jobs such as compression testing or adjusting dwell angle.

Figure 10.5. A 1962-1966 starter solenoid. The rubber button, bottom right, can be pressed to energize the starter motor.

MGB ELECTRICAL SYSTEMS – THE ESSENTIAL MANUAL

The terminals can be better seen in Figure 10.6. The power-input stud connects directly to the battery. It can be easily identified because it carries additional spade terminals for taking battery power to the fuse block and ignition switch.

A later form, installed from 1966-1967, is shown in Figure 10.7.

The output stud connects to the starter motor. The small terminal is sometimes labelled 'actuate' and connects to the red/white wire carrying current from the start switch – part of the ignition switch – to the solenoid coil.

The solenoid schematic, Figure 10.8, is quite simple. Current from the start switch, which again, is part of the ignition switch, goes to the coil. The coil current causes a magnetic force to be created that moves an iron armature toward the main contacts, touching both and allowing current to flow from the battery to the starter motor. The armature works against the force of a spring (not shown) that returns it to its rest position when the magnetizing current is removed by releasing the ignition key.

The solenoid is not serviceable, so failed devices usually require replacement. Unfortunately, the reproduction products available as replacements seem to be of far inferior quality compared to the original Lucas product.

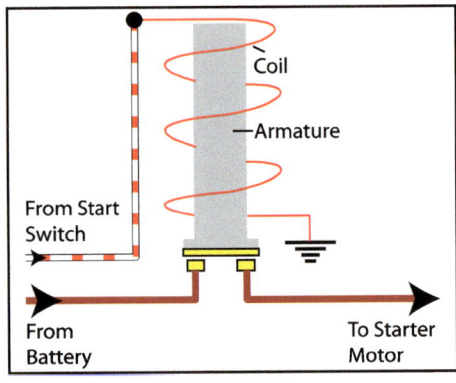

Figure 10.8. The schematic for the stand-alone solenoid.

Figure 10.9. This starter solenoid is shown separated from the starter motor of which it is a part.

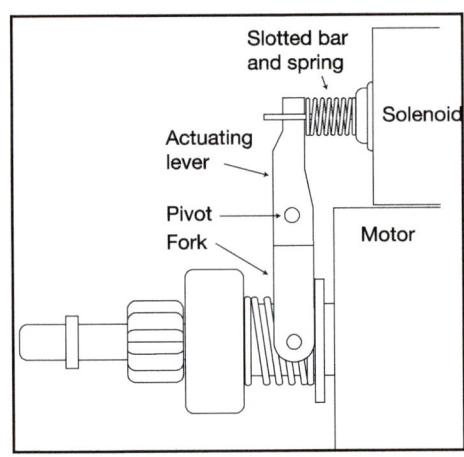

Figure 10.10. The slotted bar of the solenoid moves to the right when energized. It interlocks with a pivoted lever that forces the drive dog forward, pre-engaging it with the flywheel ring gear before full power is applied to the starter motor.

Figure 10.6. A rear view of the second generation solenoid. The top stud is connected to the battery and carries spade terminals that allow battery power to be distributed to the rest of the vehicle's electrical system. The bottom stud goes to the starter motor input cable and the small stud on the left connects to the ignition switch starter feed.

Figure 10.7. The early starter solenoid.

Solenoid 1968-1980

The solenoid in later cars, Figure 10.9, is more aptly named, being a true actuating device a well as a switch.

The slotted bar and spring, arrowed in Fig 10.9 and labelled in Figure 10.10, interlocks with a pivoting lever in the starter motor. On the other end of the lever is a fork, not unlike a small version of that on the car's clutch actuating lever. When the solenoid is actuated, the bar, which is attached to the armature, moves inward into the body and as it does so it pulls the lever back, causing the fork on the other end of the pivot to move forward, pushing the pinion gear into the flywheel ring gear.

The spring and slot on the bar form what is known as a lost motion device, allowing the bar to immediately act on the pre-engagement mechanism when energized, but to have to move some distance before it causes disengagement. The purpose is to make sure that the electrical contacts in the solenoid separate before the pinion disengages from the flywheel gear; avoiding the possibility of the starter motor over revving if it were to operate with no load.

The solenoid illustrated in Figure 10.11 is of the latest type, having four terminals. The power-in, power-out and actuate terminals operate just as they do in the earlier solenoid discussed above. However, late cars, from 1974½ onward (with rubber bumpers) have a solenoid with a terminal marked IGN that goes to the ignition coil. The purpose of is to shunt a resistor out of circuit during starting in order to supply more energy to the coil. This system is fully described in the Ignition section page 95.

Cars from 1967 onward can all use the post 1974 starter motor solenoid assembly. However, if a rubber bumper car is fitted with an older solenoid, it will not have an IGN contact. The technique of using a diode or a relay, described on

STARTING SYSTEM

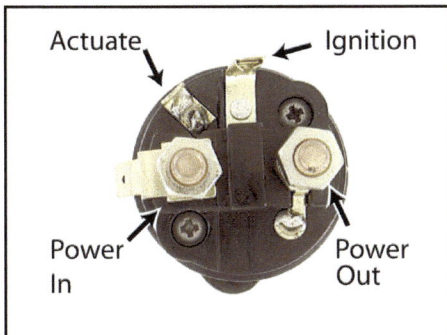

Figure 10.11. The latest solenoid has an ignition terminal that provides full battery voltage to the coil during cranking, bypassing the ignition system's ballast resistor. It is easy to confuse this terminal with the actuate contact that is fed from the starter relay.

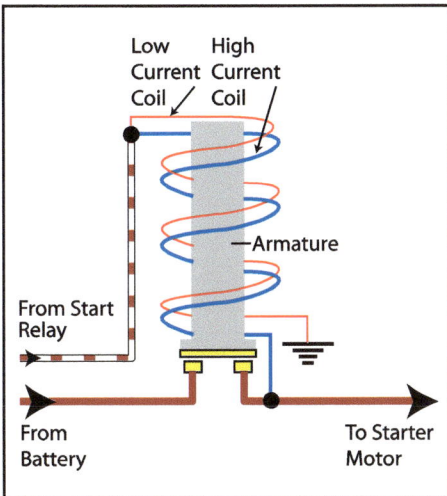

Figure 10.12. The pre-engaged starter motor solenoid has two windings, a low current coil that achieves the pre-engagement of the starter motor gear with the vehicle's flywheel ring gear, and which then switches in the high current coil that drives the starter motor at full power.

through the high current coil also goes through the starter motor, the latter begins to turn, although only slowly since the solenoid coil in series with it reduces the available voltage.

The currents passing through both solenoid coils produce sufficient magnetic force to make the armature move and operate the pre-engaging mechanism of the starter motor, the slowly rotating motor allowing the gears to more easily mesh or pre-engage. Once the armature reaches full travel, the main contacts become joined by the armature contact. Full current then passes to the pre-engaged starter motor and it cranks the engine with full force. Note that the high current coil now has full battery voltage on both sides, effectively shunting it out of circuit and so that it no longer operates. Once the tougher job of pre engaging the pinion gear is done, the solenoid only needs the low current winding to hold it in. Further, since only the low current coil is operating, when the start key is released, the relay only has to break a low current, minimizing arcing and increasing its life considerably.

It is possible to dismantle the later solenoid. It is unusual for either of the coils to become open circuit, and if they do so, the cause is often a connection problem at the terminal. The contacts can erode badly but it is possible to clean them to a degree. Note that the black plastic insulators are very brittle and often crack during disassembly. New insulators and contacts, like those in Figure 10.13, are however available if required.

Solenoid diagnostics

One cause of failure to start the car may be that the solenoid contacts are totally or partially burned out. To check for this, temporarily take the solenoid out of circuit. Brave souls can do this by bridging the large solenoid terminal lugs with a screwdriver. This produces some spectacular sparks, but unless accidental contact is made to earth, is harmless. Otherwise, proceed and test as follows:
1. Remove the earth connection from the battery or isolate the input power by using the battery disconnect switch if fitted.
2. At the solenoid, remove the nut and ring terminal of the cable that is incoming from the battery.
3. Remove the nut from the outgoing terminal of the solenoid and temporarily

Figure 10.13. The pre-engage starter solenoid contacts are replaceable items.

place the ring terminal from the incoming battery cable on the stud.
4. Replace the nut on the outgoing terminal of the solenoid.
5. Make sure the car is in neutral and the handbrake is applied.
6. Momentarily reconnect the earth terminal on the battery. If the starter spins the engine, then the solenoid, now eliminated from the circuit, is the culprit component. An attempt may be made to recondition it, but any improvement is often short lived and not usually considered worthwhile.
7. If the engine still does not turn properly, then suspect the starter motor.
8. Return the solenoid cables in their original positions.

If, during normal attempts to crank the engine the familiar solenoid click is not heard, it may not be getting any energizing current to its magnetizing coil. To check:
1. Remove the push on spade connector with a white/red wire (pre '67 cars) or white/brown wire (post '67 cars) from its terminal on the solenoid.
2. Using any spare piece of wire 18AWG (1mm^2) size or larger, make a connection to the small spade terminal from which the wire was removed, you may re apply the female connector if you wish to hold the temporary wire in

81

MGB ELECTRICAL SYSTEMS – THE ESSENTIAL MANUAL

place. Make sure no spare wire strands are touching anything else.
3. Make sure the car is in neutral and the handbrake is applied.
4. Take the other end of the temporary wire and touch it to a fuse clip or terminal to which a brown wire is connected.
5. If the starter motor operates normally, then the problem is the ignition switch, the white/red wire from the ignition switch or, on 1970 and later cars, the start relay or its circuit.
6. Use a circuit tester to check if power is getting to the small terminal on the solenoid when the key is turned to start.
7. If the circuit tester shows current is getting to the coil then the solenoid may be jammed, or the solenoid coil may be faulty, necessitating replacement of the complete unit.

Should the solenoid appear to be physically jammed, which is more likely on post 1967 cars that have a pre-engaged starter:
1. Check the car is in neutral and the handbrake is applied.
2. Grasp the solenoid.
3. Get an assistant to turn the key to the start position.
4. It should be possible to feel the solenoid trying to move.
5. If the solenoid does not move then the coil of the solenoid may be burned out. Try the test in the section above to check for a faulty solenoid.

STARTER RELAY

The starter relay was fitted from 1970 onward. It is usually located just to the rear of the fuse block, see Figure 10.14. However, late RHD cars with brake servos required that the starter relay be moved in front of the fuse block. Because the wires from the harness emerge from the same point to connect to the identical starter and ignition relays, it is often found that the wires have been swapped from one to the other. The starter relay is normally that

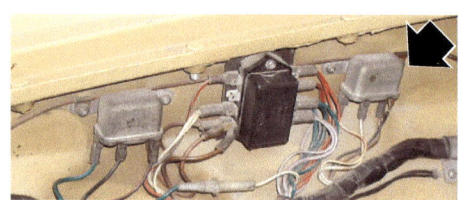

Figure 10.14. The rectangular box style (arrowed) is often mounted upright, with contacts pointing to the back of the car, or the relay may be cylindrical.

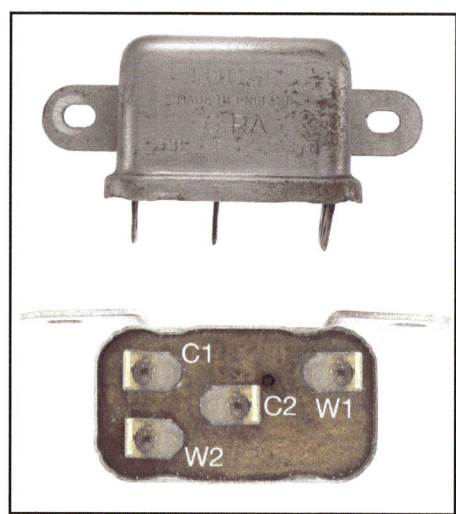

Figure 10.15. Side and base views of the 6RA rectangular box style of starter relay.

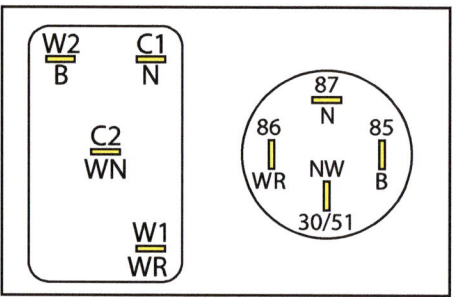

Figure 10.16. Connection for the rectangular and circular base starter relays.

nearest the rear of the car, but it is best identified by the wire colours attached to it. The starter relay's purpose is to switch relatively high current through the solenoid by utilizing only a small current from the ignition switch.

1970-1974½

The original Lucas 6RA relay is contained in a plated steel box like that shown in Figure 10.15. The terminal blades accept standard ¼in (6.35mm) push-on contacts.

Referring to Figure 10.16:
- Terminals W1 and W2 are the coil winding terminations.
- Terminals C1 and C2 are the relay power contacts.

The original connections are shown but the wires to C1 & C2 or those to W1 & W2 may be reversed without affecting normal relay operation.

If the relay coil is good, its resistance, measured from W1 to W2, should be about 40Ω.

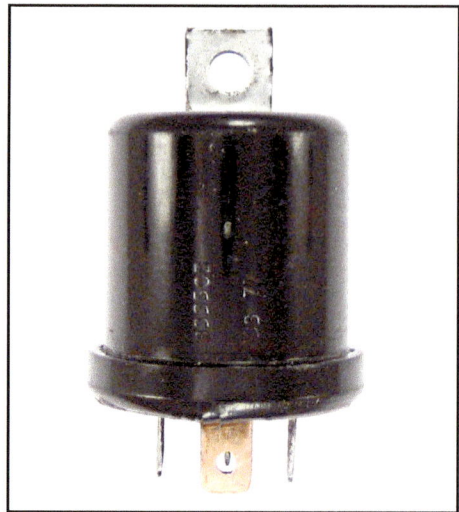

Figure 10.17. Late cars used a cylindrical 26RA relay.

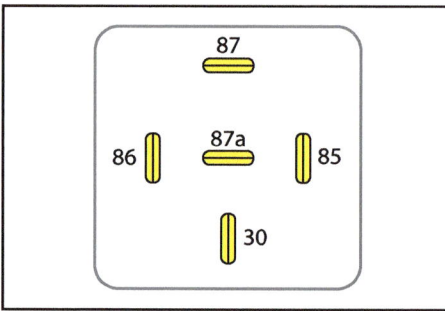

Figure 10.18. A modern and inexpensive ISO, often called 'ice cube', relay can be substituted for either the box or cylindrical original relays. Wiring colours are as per the circular base relay shown in Figure 10.16. Contact 87a may not be present; if it is, leave it unterminated.

1974½-1980 relay

Though its location is the same, the relay found in late cars will be the Lucas 26RA cylindrical format, shown in Figure 10.17.

The terminal marking on this relay is like the ISO type used today and which is described below and in Appendix 1.

Alternative relay

Should the relay fail, and there is no concern about keeping original style components, a regular ISO relay as described more fully in Appendix 1 can be used to replace it for about a tenth of the cost.

One of the mounting holes vacated by the old relay may be used to attach the ISO relay, although this may

82

STARTING SYSTEM

necessitate increasing the size of the hole in the relay bracket. Connections are shown in Figure 10.18. Note the ISO relay used may or may not have a contact 87a. If it is present, leave it unterminated.

Checking the relay
1. Identify the starter relay (see Figure 10.14 and 10.17). The starter relay has black, brown, white/brown and white/red wires connecting to it.
2. Disconnect the white/brown wire from the relay.
3. Using any spare piece of wire, 18AWG (1mm²) size or larger, make a connection to the female spade terminal on the wire just removed. Make sure no errant wire strands are touching anything else.
4. Put the car in neutral with the handbrake applied.
5. Take the other end of the temporary wire and touch it to a fuse clip or terminal to which a brown wire is connected.
6. If the starter motor does not turn then the problem is downstream of the relay and so the starter/solenoid requires checking.
7. If the starter turns, remove the temporary wire and re-apply the red/brown wire to the C2 terminal on the starter relay.
8. Remove the white/red wire from the starter relay.
9. Using any spare piece of wire, 18AWG size (1mm²) or larger, make a connection to the small spade terminal from which the wire was removed, you may re-apply the female connector if you wish to hold the temporary wire in place. Make sure no wire strands are touching anything else.
10. Take the other end of the temporary wire and touch it to a fuse clip or terminal to which a brown wire is connected.
11. If the starter motor does not turn the problem is the relay.
12. If the starter motor does turn, the white/red wire is not being energized by the ignition switch. With the help of Figure 10.3 or 10.4, check the connections of the white/red circuit all the way to the ignition switch.

STARTER MOTOR
The starter motor, while not unlike a dynamo in design, is a 430A intermittent usage machine, as opposed to the dynamo used in early cars which is a 22A constant usage. For this reason it has to be extremely robust, taking as it does, many bursts of very high-energy. For the same reason, it is not an easily serviceable device, even brush changing requiring very high power soldering equipment. For most owners with a failed starter motor, an exchange unit is the best option.

Schematic
The schematic, Figure 10.19, is essentially the same for all starter motors.

Current from the solenoid enters the motor and travels through two pairs of field windings. Current exiting each pair is taken via brushes and the commutator through the armature windings. The current leaves the armature windings through the commutator segments and two more brushes that connect to earth via the motor casing.

This arrangement is called a series-parallel wound motor because a set of two field and one armature windings are connected in series and then connected in parallel with an identical set of field and armature windings. This type of motor has a very high starting torque that reduces as speed increases; characteristics ideal for the purpose of starting an engine.

Early motor
The original motor, Figure 10.20, was installed from 1962-1967 and is of the inertia type. The pinion gear rides on a very coarse thread known as a Bendix or Eclipse drive. The very high torque

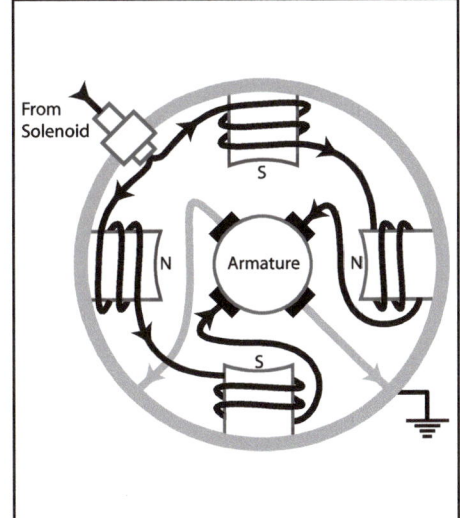

Figure 10.19. The field windings of the starter motor are connected in series with the armature windings.

motor starts extremely rapidly, but because of its inertia, the pinion gear is literally left standing and rides down the Bendix thread toward the motor. At the end of its travel, the pinion gear meshes with the ring gear on the flywheel and turns the engine. Once the engine fires and runs faster than the starter motor, the pinion is thrown back down the thread where it is arrested by the cushion spring.

The resistance of the starter motor is so low that only specialist resistance-measuring equipment is capable of distinguishing winding resistance from a short circuit. Open circuits can be checked, however, and this being a series motor, any opens may be due to brush, armature or field winding problems. Access to the brushes is possible via the ports revealed when the brush cover band is removed. From there any problem can be isolated because the field windings can then be checked separately and the brushes and commutator inspected. The brushes can be changed if a high power soldering iron is available. The commutator is of the cylindrical type and can be serviced similarly to the dynamo (see page 60), which it closely resembles.

Later motor
The motor used in cars after 1967

Figure 10.20. The early starter motor with no integral solenoid.

Figure 10.21. The later pre-engaged starter has a solenoid attached that pre-engages the gear before applying full turning power.

MGB ELECTRICAL SYSTEMS – THE ESSENTIAL MANUAL

(Figure 10.21), is distinguished by having the solenoid activated pre-engagement mechanism.

The two long fixing bolts that go the length of the motor body will be evident on the rear cover, (Figure 10.22), and need to be removed before the brushes can be accessed. The spring steel clip on the shaft has also to be removed. It is very stubborn and brittle and may well break during removal.

Once the cover is removed, Figure 10.23, the commutator and brushes are revealed. From 1975, the motor had a face-type commutator like that shown here, as opposed to the cylindrical type found in all earlier motors and typified by that found in the dynamo, (see page 61).

As was shown in the schematic Figure 10.19, two sets of brushes are in parallel and so two others have to connect to the field windings, as shown in Figure 10.23. It is interesting that Lucas chose to ultrasonically weld the brush wires to the terminal. When replacing brushes terminated this way, the old ones will have to be cut off and a lot of soldering heat used to install the new ones. Care should be taken to ensure there is no danger of a short between the resulting solder mound and the brush cover when it is replaced.

The unusual-shape brushes are shown in Figure 10.24. They can be simply pulled out of their housings. Two brushes go to the field winding as illustrated immediately above, while two go to the input terminal.

The long screws that hold the motor together also retain the front

Figure 10.23. Two brushes have to join to the field winding connection tab.

Figure 10.24. The unusual-shaped brushes in the pre-engaged starter.

housing. When reassembling the three sections, front housing, body sleeve (with field windings) and brush housing, take care to locate the small pin and hole keys sited on the edges of each part and align them. The keys are there to ensure correct orientation of all the sections.

Why starter motors fail

The biggest single cause of failure of starter motors is trying to crank the engine with a low battery.

Starter motors often mysteriously fail after the car has been left unused for several months, usually at the end of winter. Cold, thick oil and dry cylinder walls result in very high energy demands on the starter motor. At the same time, a neglected battery will have self-discharged, or worse, sulphated, and may not have sufficient energy to turn the starter motor. The battery may nevertheless have enough charge to supply plenty of power which, while not enough to crank the engine, will turn into heat in the starter motor and burn out windings should repeated and prolonged attempts be made to crank the car.

Another common cause of failure is worn starter motor brushes. They require changing about every 80,000 miles (130,000km).

UPGRADING FROM AN INERTIA TO A PRE-ENGAGED STARTER

A number of companies offer pre-engaged starter motors, often gear-reduction machines, that can replace Lucas inertia-engaged motors.

It is essential that the battery be disconnected before proceeding. The job is largely a mechanical one, and the original power cable from the start switch or solenoid should fit the new solenoid's power input terminal bolt without problem.

However, the solenoid piggy-backed onto the motor needs power for its actuation too. There are a couple of ways to do this, both illustrated in Figure 10.25. That labelled 'Method 1' is technically preferred because it takes

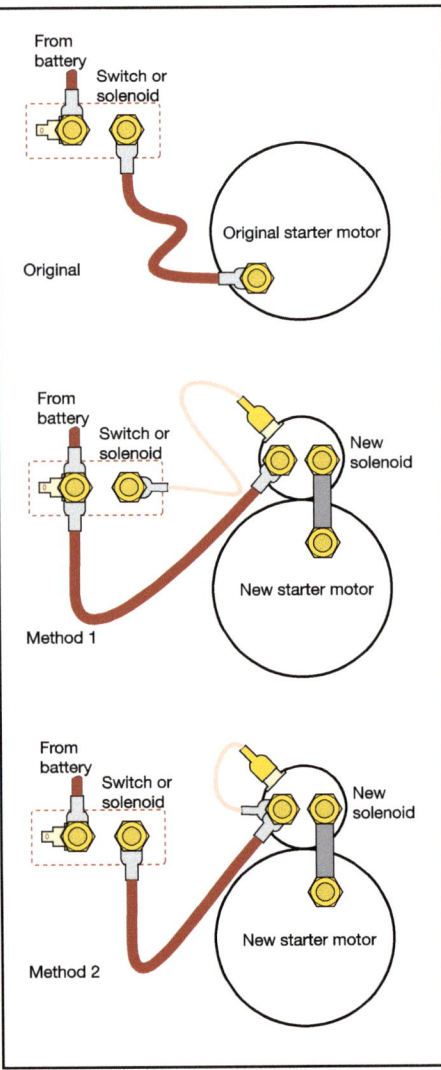

Figure 10.25. Two methods of connecting a pre-engaged starter motor in place of an inertia type.

Figure 10.22. Access to the brushes necessitates removing the long bolts from the holes arrowed in black and the spire clip arrowed in red.

STARTING SYSTEM

the original solenoid or switch out of the main power route and so lowers the resistance path and improves system reliability. 'Method 2' is easier and more discreet and will appeal to those who want to upgrade their classic cars without the changes being too obvious.

For space reasons, the scale and relative positions of the starter motors and switches or solenoids have been changed. In practice, the relative distance between the two components is much greater.

The top illustration shows the original wiring.

In the centre drawing, the pre-engaged starter is installed and the power input cable that was removed from the original motor has been attached to its power input terminal. The starter switch or solenoid has been taken out of the power circuit by moving its output connection to the same post to which the battery input cable is attached. A new link wire shown in pink, which in reality is quite long, has been attached between the output terminal and the small contact on the new starter motor solenoid. When the original switch or solenoid is activated is now only switches a relatively small current to the new solenoid. The main power contacts close and the motor is supplied current directly from the battery.

In the lower drawing, a short link wire, again shown in pink, has been attached between the new solenoid's power input and solenoid actuation terminals. When the original switch or solenoid is activated it supplies both the low current for the new solenoid and, a fraction of a second later, the high current for the new starter.

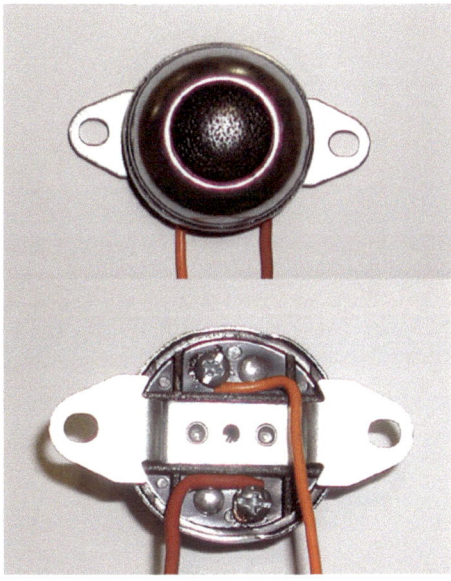

Figure 10.26. Front and rear views of a horn switch that can be used for remotely cranking the engine.

ADDING A REMOTE CRANKING SWITCH

Figure 10.5 shows a solenoid with a button that allows the starter motor to be operated from under the bonnet. With the ignition off, this button will crank the car but will not start it; a useful feature when checking dwell angle, doing a compression test or carrying out fault diagnostics.

For those cars with no such solenoid, a simple momentary switch – one that only operates while being manually depressed – can be fitted so that it provides the same utility.

The switch shown in Figure 10.26 is an inexpensive horn switch and is one of many types of momentary

Figure 10.27. A typical non-permanent remote cranking switch.

switches suitable for use as a starter switch. Do make sure that any switch used for this purpose is a momentary type. Any switch that can accidentally be flipped on and left on is both dangerous and damaging to the starter and ring gear.

Situating the switch depends on the style actually purchased but it is advised that, for ease of wiring, it be close to the starter relay or solenoid, and in a location that will not result in it being pressed unintentionally.

Wiring is simple. One wire from the switch goes to the white/red wire on the solenoid or relay and the other to a brown wire found on the same device.

Alternatively, a non-permanent switch, like that in Figure 10.27, may be bought that uses alligator clips to connect to the car's wiring system. In order to crank the car using this switch, connect one clip to the terminal that carries a white/red wire at the starter solenoid of pre 1969 cars or the relay of all later cars. The other clip should be attached over the clip of the fuse which has a brown wire going to it.

MGB ELECTRICAL SYSTEMS – THE ESSENTIAL MANUAL

STARTER CIRCUIT FAULT-FINDING

Symptom	Possible causes	Action
Starter will not turn. No sound is heard.	Totally exhausted battery.	Charge or replace battery.
	Faulty ignition switch.	Try cranking the car without using the ignition switch. To do this, use a jumper wire between the white/red wire at the starter solenoid of pre 1970 cars, or the relay of all later cars, and the fuse clip that has a brown wire going to it.
	Relay coil is bad.	See page 82.
	Totally open battery connections or battery earth connection	See if other high power functions, like the headlamps work. If not, clean and tighten the battery connections and that of the earthing cable where it joins the car body.
Starter will not turn. A clicking sound is heard.	Solenoid coil is bad.	See page 79.
	Relay contacts are bad.	See page 82.
Starter will not turn. A clonking sound is heard.	Low battery.	Charge battery,
	Poor battery connections.	Immediately after attempting to crank the car, check to see if the battery terminals are warm. If so, remove them, clean them and the battery posts and reconnect them tightly. See page 49. Also check that the earth connection to the car frame is tight and clean.
	Solenoid contacts are bad.	See page 79.
	Starter failure.	Check and change brushes if necessary. See page 84. Replace the starter if non serviceable.
	Starter pinion is jammed in ring gear.	Place the car in fourth gear and rock it back and forward to free the pinion.
Starter runs continuously.	Solenoid or relay stuck closed.	Disconnect battery. Replace solenoid or relay.
	Brake system blocking diode failed.	If releasing the handbrake stops the motor, see page 131.

Table 10.1. Starter system fault-finding chart.

Chapter 11
Ignition system

CONVENTIONAL IGNITION

High voltage is necessary to produce a spark with sufficient magnitude to jump the plug gaps and ignite the fuel mixture. With only two electrical power sources in the vehicle, the battery and the generator, which are linked together and can be considered low voltage systems, the high voltage has somehow to be derived from them.

Recapping on the discussion in Motors and Generators (page 57), Michael Faraday found that when a magnet and wire are moved relative to one another, such that the magnetic field crosses the wire, electricity is generated. Making many wires for the magnetic field to pass through, by winding it in a coil, and increasing the rate at which the field cuts the wire, Faraday found, increases the voltage generated. These two principles — having a magnetic field cut lots of wires, and doing so very quickly — are the means by which the high ignition voltage is generated.

Three steps are taken to achieve the high voltage pulse required.
1. A coil of a few turns of thick wire, which can pass a high current from the battery, is wound around a magnetic material core, thus forming an electromagnet capable of producing a strong magnetic field. This coil is referred to as the 'primary winding'.
2. A second coil is wound, using many turns of fine wire wound around the same core. This coil is referred to as the 'secondary winding'.
3. The power to the primary winding is cut, and the magnetic field collapses very quickly. The large number of turns on the secondary winding, and the high rate at which the collapsing magnetic field cuts it, causes a very high voltage to be 'induced' in it.

The rate at which the magnetic field collapses around both windings also results in a high voltage being induced in the primary winding, but not as high as that in the secondary. In fact, the voltages induced in each winding are directly related to the relative number of turns of wire in each coil. A typical coil might have 70 times as many turns on the secondary winding as on the primary, and this will result in 70 times as many volts being induced in it as in the primary winding. If the sparkplug requires the voltage to rise to 20,000V to jump the gap then, with a 'turns ratio' of 70:1 the primary winding will produce 20,000V ÷ 70, or approximately 300V.

The device carrying the primary and secondary windings, which, in a vehicle, is misnamed a coil, is in fact a transformer, not unlike the device that plugs in the wall as a battery eliminator to many household and office products. If an ignition system relied on transformer action alone, and not the quickly collapsing magnetic field, the coil would only produce about 12V × 70 = 840V; not enough to jump the sparkplug gap.

Note that the magneto, used in non-battery machines, such as lawn mowers and string-trimmers, does have a true coil. Rapidly spinning the poles of a magnet past its many turns produces the high voltage required for ignition. The principle is the same therefore; a magnetic field rapidly crossing many wires produces high voltage pulses.

The circuit in Figure 11.1 shows a typical ignition system similar to that found in MGB/Cs.
L1 = Primary winding of the coil
L2 = Secondary winding of the coil
The solid lines between the coils represent the magnetic core.
CB = Contact-breaker (sometimes called points)
C = Capacitor (sometimes called a condenser)
D = Distributor

The dashed line indicates that the contact-breaker is mechanically linked to the 4-lobe cam in the distributor.

When the ignition switch is closed, a voltage is applied to the top of the coil primary winding L1. As the 4-lobe cam

MGB ELECTRICAL SYSTEMS – THE ESSENTIAL MANUAL

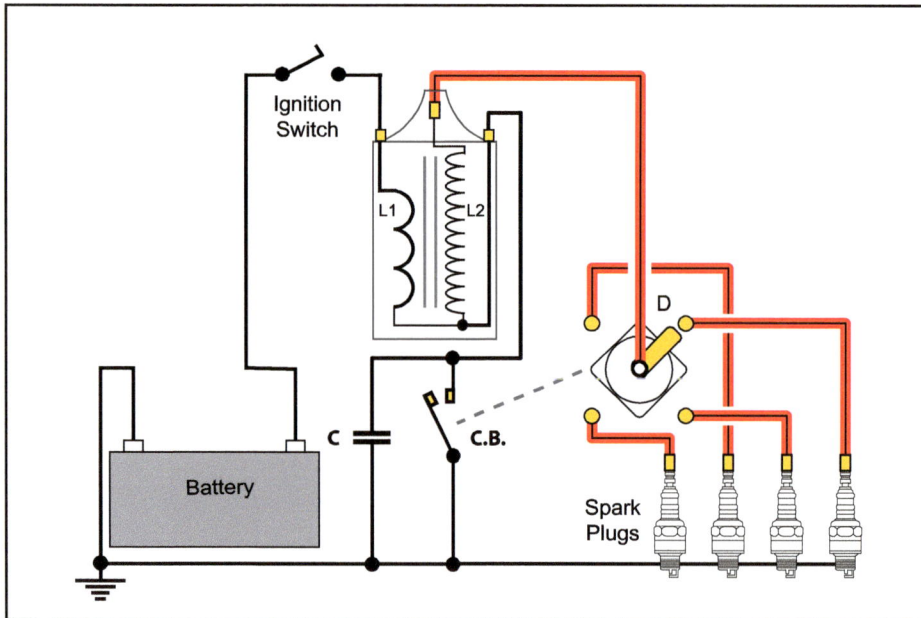

Figure 11.1. The basic ignition schematic for a four cylinder engine.

in the distributor turns, it opens and closes the contact-breaker. When they close, a current can flow through the coil to earth.

A coil can be considered the electrical equivalent of mass, having as it does a property called inductance that is rather like inertia. Remembering our physics, one of Newton's laws was that every force has an equal and opposite reaction. The inductance of a coil also produces an opposite reaction in the coil, generating a current that tries to oppose that coming in. This electrical inertia results in the coil current building up very slowly, just as you have to build up momentum to get the mass of a heavy object like a car moving. This relatively slow build-up of current results in a slow rise in magnetic field strength and in turn, a relatively low voltage is induced in both coils.

Continuing the analogy of a car that exhibits inertia to get it moving, we all know that it stores all that energy once it is rolling. We can stop it relatively benignly by applying the brakes and slowly converting the energy to heat, or, we could run it into a wall and release the energy suddenly and spectacularly. Similarly, in the ignition system, when the distributor rotates further, the contact-breaker opens and the current generating the magnetic field is cut, causing the field to collapse and to release all its stored energy very rapidly. A high voltage is thus induced in the secondary winding (and a somewhat lower one in the primary winding which, remember, has many times fewer turns of wire). This high voltage tries to go wherever it can, taking the course of least resistance, which is from the top of L2 to the distributor rotor arm, across the small gap to whichever plug lead the arm is closest to it, to the plug and across the plug gap.

In physics, you cannot get something for nothing; therefore the energy that comes out of the secondary winding can be no greater than that went into the primary winding. In fact it is somewhat less because of inefficiencies in the transformation from one side of the coil to the other. So, whereas the power from the secondary winding is derived from a very high voltage and a very low current (remember volts × amps gives watts), at the primary winding, there is 70 times less voltage present but at least 70 times as much current available. The not insignificant primary voltage of some 300V and the available current can pull an arc across the contact-breaker like a very tiny lightning strike. An arc occurs when a gas, like air, conducts through a process called ionization, and is familiar to us in photographic flashguns, fluorescent lights and neon signs. We want the arc to occur as sparks at the plugs, but an arc at the contact-breaker points has several deleterious effects:
1. The current continues to flow in the arc, so that the rapid magnetic field collapse is slowed down, reducing the output voltage.
2. The system energy gets dissipated at the contact-breaker, rather than at the plugs.
3. The heat in the arc burns and erodes the contact-breaker.

These problems are largely resolved by use of a capacitor (also known as a condenser) across the contact-breaker points. A capacitor is rather like an electrical spring. If we put springs on the bumper of the car before we ran it into the wall, they would absorb some of the force of the impact. Similarly, the capacitor absorbs some of the energy at the contact-breaker, but its value is very critical. If it is too small, the arc will not be quenched. If too big, it will take a long time filling up and slow the all-important collapse of the magnetic field. A very common problem with ignition systems is that a large capacitor, used to absorb, or more properly suppress, ignition noise on the car's radio, is inadvertently put on the contact-breaker side of the coil, reducing the high-tension voltage substantially.

Although the Figure 11.1 shows the high-tension wires as thick lines, as stated earlier, the current is very low, the wires' thickness mostly being made up of insulation. In fact, the core of the high voltage wires is often made from a resistive material like carbon and may have a resistance in the order of 50,000Ω; the purpose is to prevent the ignition from radiating high frequency signals that interfere with radios and TVs. We talked of the coils as having characteristics not unlike those of a mass. We also compared the capacitor to a spring. Just like a car with a given mass, suspended with springs, it will bounce and oscillate. Adding shock absorbers, which provide resistance to movement, will damp out the oscillations. That is exactly what the resistance in the plug lead does; it damps the system and stops it from oscillating and emitting radio waves. Instead of resistance leads, an alternative is to use standard metal cored wires but have the resistance added at the sparkplug connector cap on to the end of the lead or even in the plugs themselves.

ELECTRONIC IGNITION
Contact-breakers are at best a fairly mediocre means of switching coil current. They erode and pile due to

IGNITION SYSTEM

arcing, bounce, oxidize, are almost impossible to adjust accurately or with any repeatability and the cam follower on which they run wears down. No wonder all new cars, without exception, have abandoned the mechanical contact-breaker switch in favour of a breaker-less, electronic and no-touch sensor driving a semiconductor; robust versions of which were only available toward the end of the MGB's production life.

Not only does an electronic system eliminate wear and thus the need for adjustment and eventual replacement, but the current flow to the coil is also cut off much more sharply. The voltage produced by the coil is proportional to the rate of change of its magnetic flux when the current is cut. By cutting the current more rapidly than the combination of a contact-breaker and its required capacitor, electronic ignition can result in higher ignition voltage; and perhaps make that important difference when conditions are at their worst.

Variable reluctance pick-ups

Variable reluctance pick-ups are coils that exhibit different electrical characteristics when a rotating metal component, having a lower magnetic resistance (or more properly reluctance) than air, is in close proximity. This is the same principle that allows a guitar pick-up to detect a closely situated vibrating metal string, even though the string itself is not magnetized.

The Lucas OPUS (Oscillating Pick-Up System) was a complex version of the variable reluctance pick-up and was fitted to MGBs headed for certain territories from 1975 to 1979. An electrical signal of 470kHz was generated to supply a winding situated in the distributor that linked the signal to a second closely located winding. The signal received from the second winding told the electronics to provide the ignition coil with current. A rotating ferrite rod, placed where a cam lobe would normally reside, would then come around and direct the magnetic field produced by the oscillator to a third winding rather than the second. The signal from the third winding told the electronics to break the coil current, and thus produce the spark. The use of the past tense is very appropriate when discussing OPUS; it was so unreliable few are still in use.

Constant energy ignition

The later Lucas CEI (Constant Energy Ignition) system had a simpler magnetic pick-up and was more reliable. As is discussed in the section concerning dwell angle, page 102, the faster the engine rotates, the less time the coil has to charge, even though the actual dwell angle remains constant. Less time to charge the ignition coil means less energy is stored that can be later discharged as a spark. CEI systems are normally used with low resistance, low inductance coils that can be rapidly stored with energy until they reach a maximum saturation point. Since the maximum level of stored energy can be reached, even at high engine speeds it is deemed 'constant'.

Magnetic pick-up coils

Magnetic pick-up coils were used on some early electronic distributors. Here a 4-pole rotating magnet replaces the cam and, as its magnetic field crosses coils fixed to a plate, it causes an electrical impulse, which is used to trigger the switching transistors.

Hall effect sensors

Hall effect sensors (after the discoverer of the phenomenon, Dr. E. H. Hall), as used in the PerTronix Ignitor and Luminition Magnetron systems, incorporate a rotating multi-pole magnet assembly (Figure 11.2) like the magnetic pick-up system but instead of coils the system utilizes a special crystal – the Hall effect sensor – to provide a precise and readily usable signal.

The small signal current is amplified by transistors to provide a sufficiently large current to operate the coil. Modern electronics have allowed the devices to be miniaturized to a point where the whole unit now fits within the standard size distributor, in contrast to the early Lucas breakerless systems.

From the point of view of engine timing, a Hall effect ignition system is potentially less accurate than an optical system. There are a number of reasons for this:
1. The difficulty in setting the magnets at exactly 90° (for a 4-cylinder engine) from one another.
2. The difficulty of ensuring that the magnets are of exactly equal strength.
3. The effect of temperature on the sensitivity of the Hall effect pick-up sensor.

Optical ignition switching

Optical systems, as made by Luminition and MSD (Autotronic Controls Corp.) and others, use a rotating shutter (sometimes called a chopper) to alternately allow a photocell receiver to be impinged upon by infrared light from a light emitting diode (LED) sender, or to be in shadow.

The shutter may be a bladed type like that in Figure 11.3, or a slotted disc like that in Figure 11.4.

The amplifier needed to increase the current from the photocell cannot generally be contained within the distributor, and room has to be found, therefore, for an external module. This can affect price. However, the optical system has the advantage of inherently greater timing accuracy than other systems, including that of the Hall effect type. This is because once a very accurate tool is made to

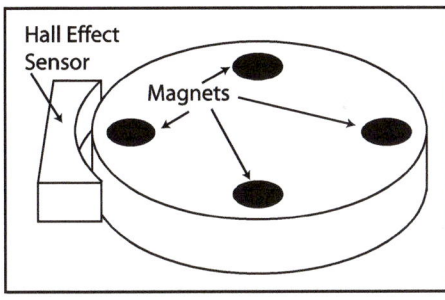

Figure 11.2. In a Hall effect ignition system, the sensor is triggered by magnets embedded in a disc, which is installed over the original contact-breaker cam. The sensor causes a semiconductor to alternately open and close the current path to the coil.

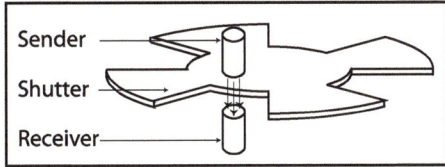

Figure 11.3. In an optical system the trigger signal comes from a photo-transistor that receives light from a light emitting diode. The rotating shutter blade alternately obscures and reveals the light to the transistor.

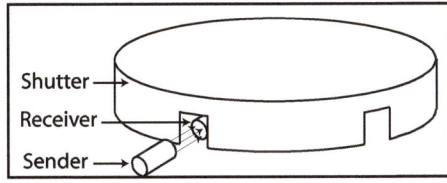

Figure 11.4. An alternative form of optical shutter formed by notches or slots in a rotating disc.

MGB ELECTRICAL SYSTEMS – THE ESSENTIAL MANUAL

stamp or mould the chopper (or shutter) blade, so that it has accurate and equal apertures and angles, there are few other variables that can affect the system's ability to fire the engine at the same time for each cylinder and from one engine revolution to the next.

Capacitive discharge ignition
Capacitor discharge ignition (CDI) systems address the problem of only having a fixed voltage (that supplied by the battery/generator/alternator system) available. Increasing the voltage is one method of increasing the energy of the spark. In a CDI system, an electronic boost circuit, not unlike that used in a photographic flashgun, is used to produce a voltage supply in the hundreds of volts. Again, as in a flashgun, the high voltage charges a capacitor, an electrical spring or energy reservoir, and a special semiconductor called a silicon controlled rectifier (or SCR) is then used to suddenly release the energy stored in the capacitor – this time, however, not through a flash tube but via a specially designed ignition coil.

CDI systems produce a very high energy, short duration spark. This makes them suitable for vehicles with very tightly controlled combustion systems such as may be found in a fuel injected racing engine. With more traditional carburation, longer duration sparks are generally preferred because they give more opportunity for the variable mix of fuel vapour to be in the right place and consistency for ignition.

Electronic ignition sparkplug gap
Most electronic ignition manufacturer's instructions advise that to take best advantage of the system the sparkplug gap should be increased, usually to about 0.040in (1mm). A wider gap means that the voltage has to rise to a higher level in order to fire, which aids starting. A conventional ignition system cannot reliably produce a spark that can jump a wide gap under all conditions, whereas an electronic system can.

There is also some small advantage to a wide gap in that it provides a greater chance of combustible fuel being in the spark path at idling speeds when fuel turbulence is poor, and at cruising speeds when the fuel mixture is weakened for economy reasons. Consideration has to be given to whether or not the plug is suited to wide gapping. See 'Sparkplugs' page 109.

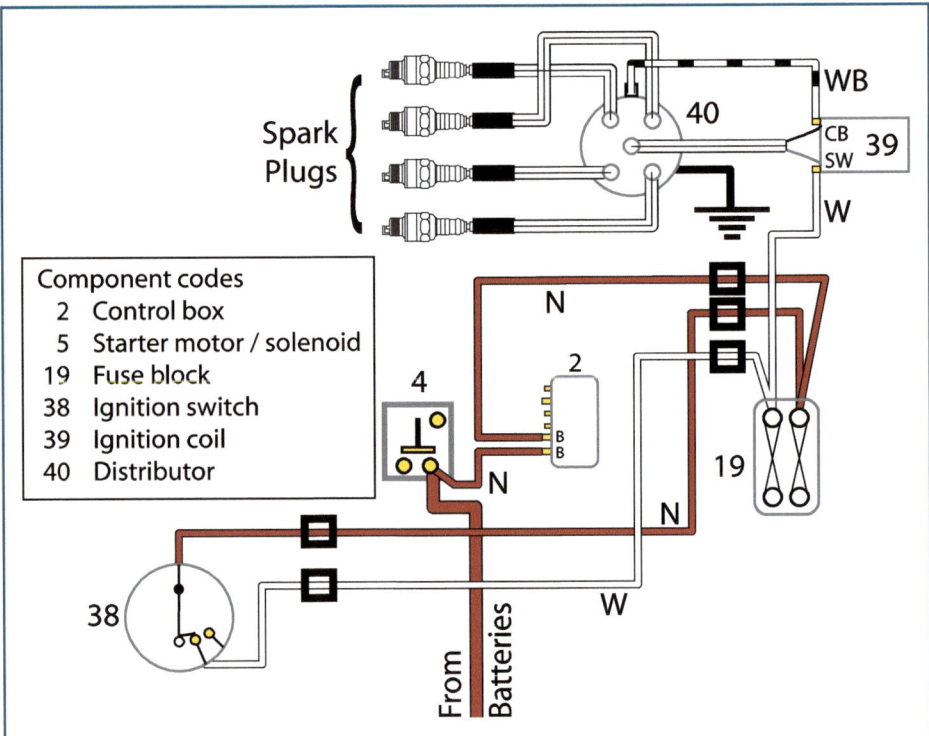

Figure 11.5. The 1962-1964 ignition system was a carry-over from the MGA.

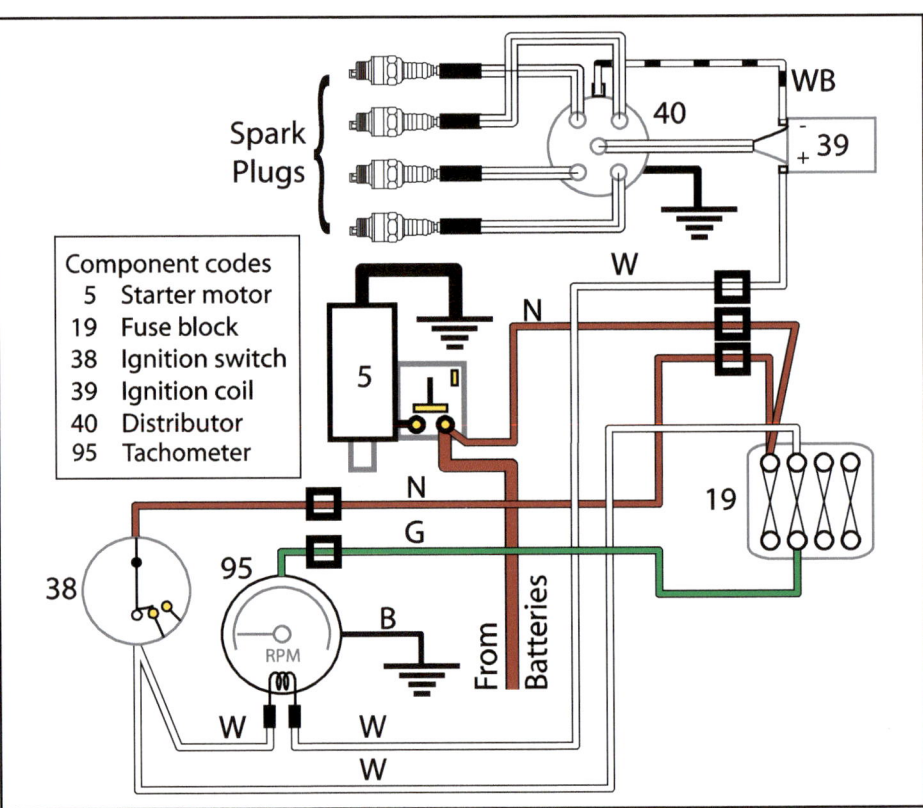

Figure 11.6. In 1964 the first electronic tachometer was introduced. Soon after the car switched to negative earth, requiring a change to the ignition coil.

IGNITION SYSTEM

Further benefit may be gained from the use of an electronic ignition system by changing the coil and adding a ballast resistor; see page 96.

IGNITION CIRCUIT 1962-1964
Circuit description

The very earliest form of the MGB ignition system is distinguished from later vehicles in that, as originally supplied, it is only driven from a positive earth power system and the mechanical tachometer requires no input from the ignition to drive it.

Referring to Figure 11.5, current flows from the batteries on a large cross section area cable to the starter solenoid (4), which is used as a securing point. There it connects to a thinner brown (N) wire that goes to the fuse block (19).

At the fuse block, another brown wire takes current to the ignition switch (38). When the ignition switch is on, current can flow from the ignition switch on a white (W) wire and back to the fuse block. The white wire goes to the SW side of the coil (39) primary winding.

The CB side of the coil is connected via a white/black (WB) wire to the distributor (40), which makes a connection to the contact-breaker.

The high voltage connection from the coil goes to the centre of the distributor cap where the rotor arm 'distributes' the spark to each of the 4 wires going to the sparkplugs.

IGNITION CIRCUIT 1964-1974½
Circuit description

In 1964 the first electronic tachometer was introduced on the MGB. This first version senses the pulses as the ignition coil draws current from the ignition switch. Soon afterward, the system polarity was changed from positive to negative earth, requiring an internal change to the tachometer (see page 152). The illustration shows the fuse block having 4 fuses. Prior to that time, only 2 fuses used, so that part of the circuit was as shown in Figure 11.5.

Referring to Figure 11.6, current flows from the batteries on a large cross section area cable to the starter motor/solenoid (5), which is used as a securing point. There it connects to a thinner brown (N) wire that goes to the fuse block (19).

At the fuse block, another brown wire takes current to the ignition switch (38). When the ignition switch is on, current can flow from it on a white (W) wire and back to the fuse block. There a fuse connects to a green wire that provides power to the tachometer (95).

The ignition switch also provides power to the ignition coil via a white wire that connects through a tachometer sensing coil that may be internal or external to the instrument, depending on model. The white wire from the tachometer goes to the '+' side of the coil (39) primary winding.

The '–' side of the coil is connected via a white/black (WB) wire to the distributor (40), which makes a connection to the contact-breaker.

The high voltage connection from the coil goes to the centre of the distributor cap where the rotor arm "distributes" the spark to each of 4 wires going to the sparkplugs.

IGNITION CIRCUIT 1974½-1977
Circuit description

In mid 1974 the current sensing tachometer was replaced by a superior design that senses voltage pulses from the contact-breaker. At approximately the same time, the coil was changed to one requiring a ballast resistor.

Referring to Figure 11.7, current flows from the batteries or battery on a large cross section area cable to the starter motor/solenoid (5), which is used

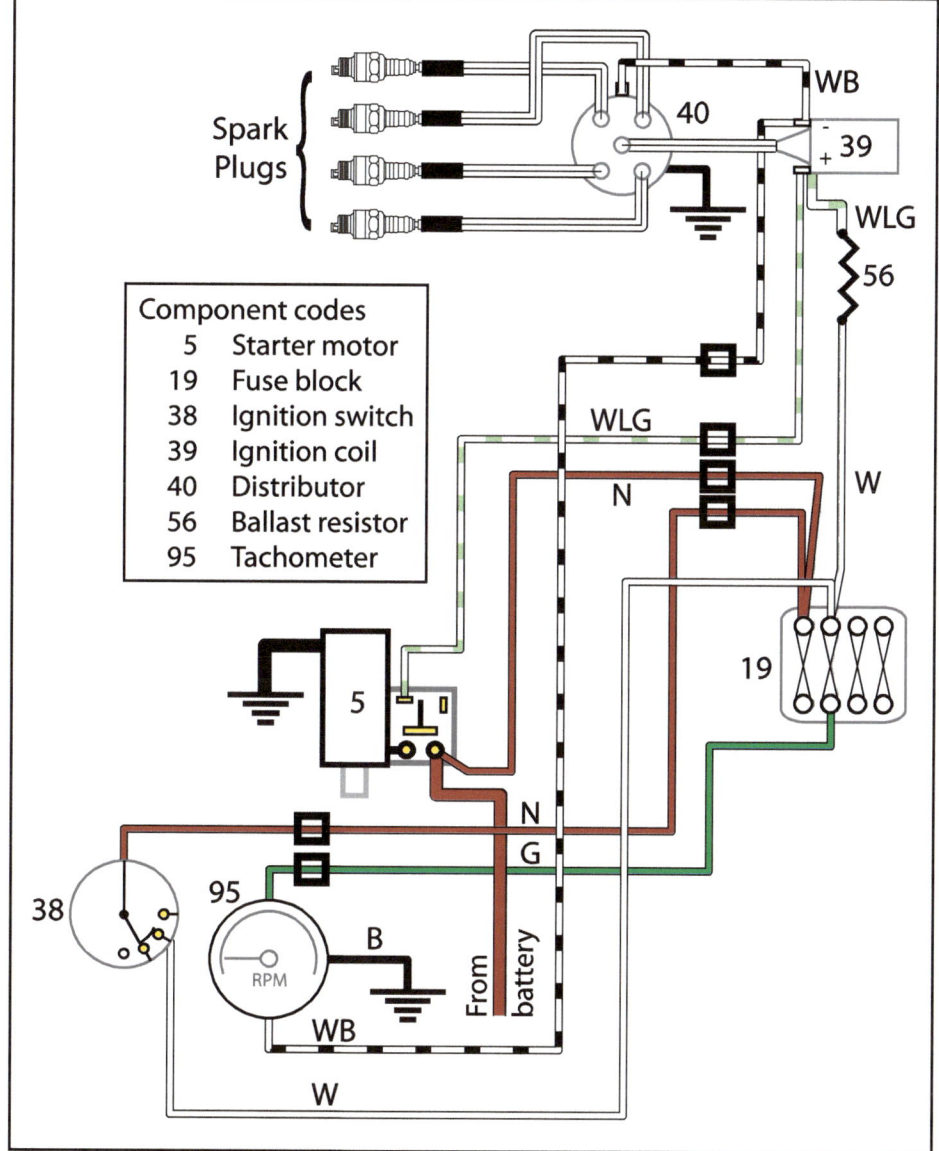

Component codes
- 5 Starter motor
- 19 Fuse block
- 38 Ignition switch
- 39 Ignition coil
- 40 Distributor
- 56 Ballast resistor
- 95 Tachometer

Figure 11.7. Rubber bumper cars introduced in 1974 gained a ballasted ignition coil and a voltge sensing tachomter

MGB ELECTRICAL SYSTEMS – THE ESSENTIAL MANUAL

as a securing point. There it connects to a thinner brown (N) wire that goes to the fuse block (19).

At the fuse block another brown wire takes current to the ignition switch (38). When the ignition switch is on, current can flow from it on a white (W) wire and back to the fuse block. There a fuse connects to a green wire that provides power to the tachometer (95).

A white spurs off from the fuse block to supply current to the coil (39) '+' terminal via a ballast resistor (56) and white/light-green (WLG) wire. However, during cranking, the coil is supplied full voltage via a white/light-green wire from the starter/solenoid (5), effectively jumping the ballast resistor out of circuit. The ballast resistor may be either a length of resistance wire or a discreet electrically resistive component.

The '–' side of the coil is connected via a white/black (WB) wire to the distributor (40), which makes a connection to the contact-breaker.

The high voltage connection from the coil goes to the centre of the distributor cap where the rotor arm 'distributes' the spark to each of 4 wires going to the sparkplugs.

IGNITION CIRCUIT 1977-1980 (EXCLUDING NORTH AMERICA)
Circuit description

In order to keep the MGB competitive, improvements were made to the car, some of which included the addition of more ignition dependent electrical loads, most notably the electric cooling fan. The point had been reached when the ignition switch could no longer carry all the current directly, and so an ignition relay was incorporated in the circuit.

Referring to Figure 11.8, current flows from the battery on a large cross section area cable to the starter motor/solenoid (5), which is used as a securing point. There it connects to a thinner brown (N) wire that goes to the fuse block (19). At the fuse block another brown wire takes current to the ignition switch (38). When the ignition switch is on, current can flow from it to the W1 coil connection on the ignition relay (42). The relay becomes energized and the resulting electromagnetic force pulls the contacts connected to C1 and C2 together allowing current to flow from the always live brown circuit to a white/brown wire (WN) that goes back to the fuse block. There a fuse connects to a green wire that provides power to the tachometer (95).

A white/brown wire spurs off from the fuse block to supply current to the coil (39) '+' terminal via a ballast resistor (56) and white/light-green (WLG) wire. However, during cranking, the coil is supplied full voltage via a white/light-green wire from the starter/solenoid (5), effectively jumping the ballast resistor out of circuit. The ballast resistor may be a length of resistance wire or a discreet component.

The '–' side of the coil is connected via a white/black (WB) wire to the distributor (40), which makes a connection to the contact-breaker.

The high voltage connection from the coil goes to the centre of the distributor cap where the rotor arm "distributes" the spark to each of 4 wires going to the sparkplugs.

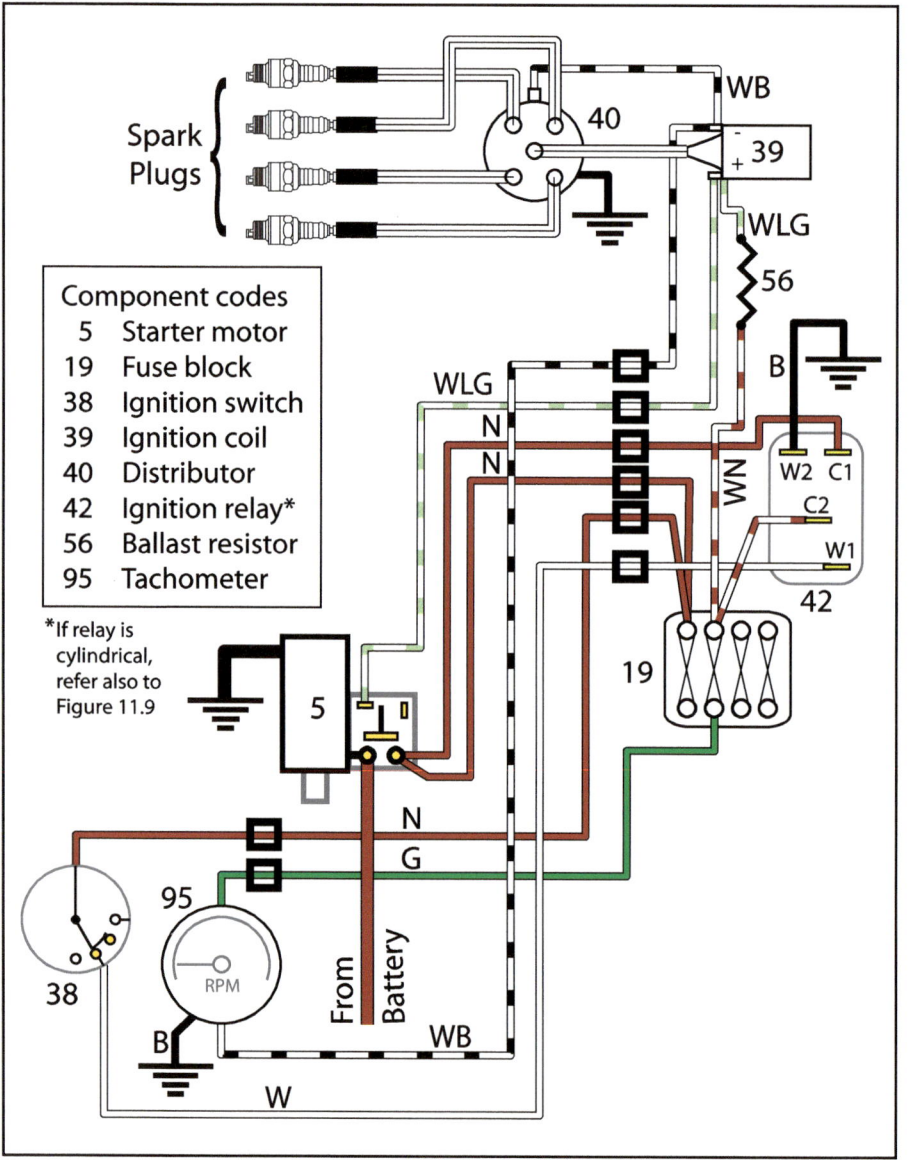

Figure 11.8. By 1978, the increasing number of electrical loads in the vehicle necessitated a relay to switch ignition loads.

IGNITION CIRCUIT 1977-1980 (NORTH AMERICA)
Circuit description

This period was one of steep increases in fuel cost and the introduction of unleaded fuel. Regulatory standards were tougher too and MGBs meeting the California, and later US federal

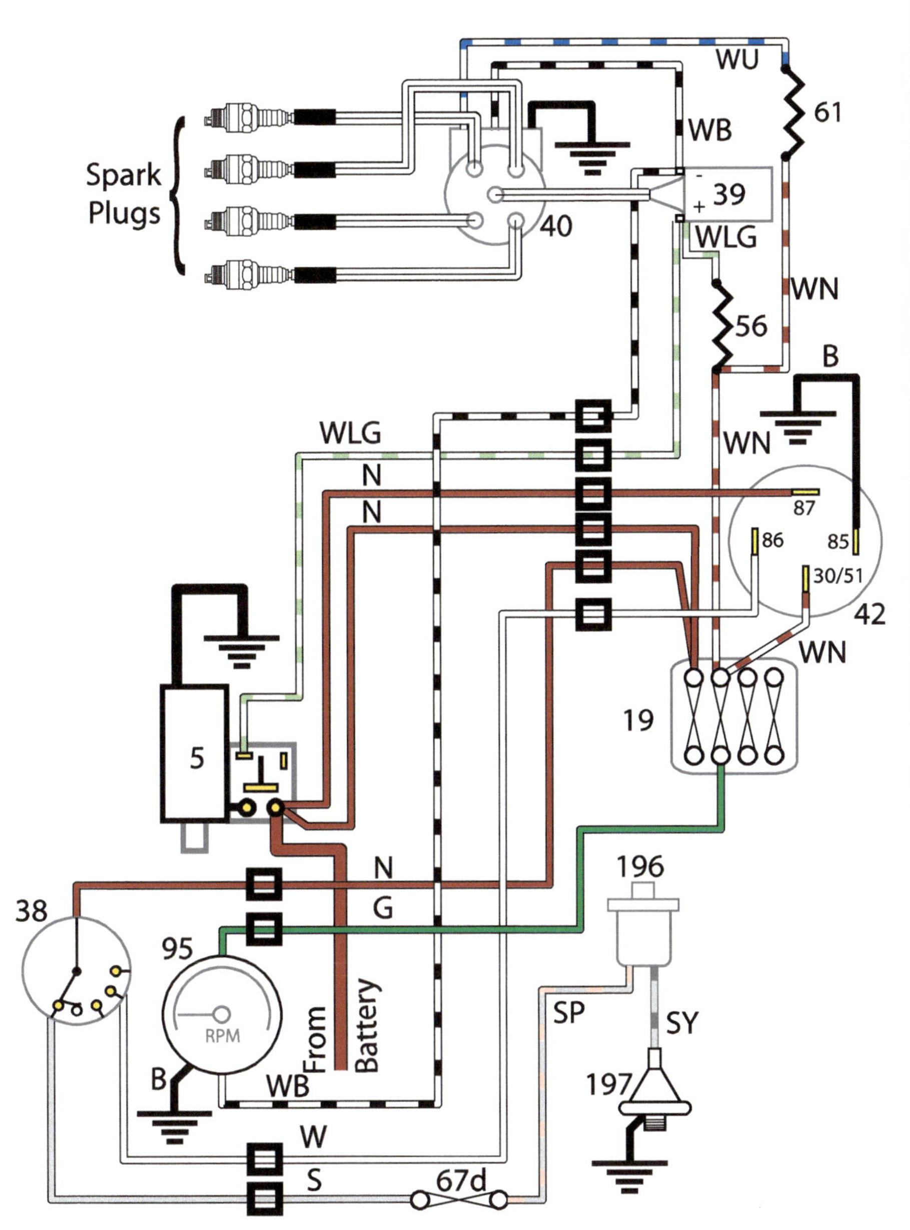

IGNITION SYSTEM

standards were supplied, commencing in 1975, with an electronic ignitions system housed within the distributor.

Referring to Figure 11.9. The original Lucas OPUS (oscillating pick-up system) also known as the electronic ignition distributor (EID) system had a current amplifier incorporated into the distributor but required an external power feed resistor (61) to supply the power output transistor. The product proved troublesome and was replaced by the constant dwell angle design that provided constant energy ignition and so became know as the CEI system.

The Lucas CEI distributor was only installed as original equipment in 1980 but many cars originally supplied with the OPUS distributor were retrofitted with the CEI type. The CEI is distinguished by having an external amplifier box.

Other than for the electronic distributor, the circuit description and operation is identical to that for non-North American vehicles.

Running-on became a problem with unleaded fuel and so in mid-1977 a running-on valve was fitted that ports air to the inlet manifold and float chambers on switch-off. This system is described more fully on page 109.

IGNITION COMPONENTS

Ignition relay

The ignition relay was fitted to MGBs from about mid-1974 onward. Its purpose is to relieve the ignition switch of the burden of carrying the total current of all the components that require to be switched on and off with the ignition. The decision to add the relay coincided with introduction of the electric radiator cooling fan that is a particularly high current device.

The fact that the wiring for current flowing to accessories does not have to route from the fuse block into the

Component codes

Code	Component	Code	Component
5	Starter motor	56	Ballast resistor
19	Fuse block	61	Ignition resistor
38	Ignition switch	67d	Line fuse
39	Ignition coil	95	Tachometer
40	Distributor	196	Running-on valve
42	Ignition relay	197	Oil pressure switch

Figure 11.9. Although not introduced at exactly the same time, this circuit includes electronic ignition and an anti ron-on valve. Both were needed to better handle the newly introduced U.S. unleaded fuel and new emissions requirements.

Figure 11.10. The usual ignition relay location is arrowed but may be differently positioned on some cars. Check the wire colours to positively identify which relay is which.

MGB ELECTRICAL SYSTEMS – THE ESSENTIAL MANUAL

cabin and back again reduces wire length, and the numbers of connectors in a circuit. The result is that not only is the life of the ignition switch extended, but also that voltage drop is reduced and accessories can operate more efficiently.

Figure 11.10 shows the location of the ignition relay. The MGB-GT V8 was fitted with an ignition relay from its introduction in 1973 and the photograph shows that installation. In MGBs, the 6RA rectangular box style, often mounted sideways on, was used up until 1976, after which all cars were fitted with the cylindrical design, which Lucas called the 26RA, shown in Figure 10.17. The ignition relay is identical to the starter relay, pictures of which can be seen on pages 82. That can cause confusion on late RHD cars where the brake-servo location required that the starter relay be moved to a point adjacent to, but still to the rear of, the ignition relay. In this case, check the colours of the wires against the identical circular relays as they may well have been swapped over.

The connections to both rectangular and circular relays are shown in Figure 11.11.

Alternative relay

An alternative ISO relay, also called the Lucas 28RA, like that described on page 82 for the starter relay, can also be used for the ignition relay, the wiring colours to contact numbers being identical to that for the circular relay shown in Figure 11.11. However, be more circumspect in replacing the ignition relay with a modern one, or even a new original style product, as without the addition of a diode, running-on problems can occur.

Running-on, the phenomenon where the engine continues to turn after the ignition is switched off, can happen when using a new relay because the amount of energy required to keep it closed is much less compared to that of the Lucas relays originally used by MG. After ignition switch-off, the engine normally continues to turn for a few revolutions and so the alternator continues to generate current. A sneak current (see Chapter 5) can find its way through the charge warning lamp back to the ignition circuit and is sufficient to keep the relay closed, so keeping the engine running. The same phenomenon can occur even with the standard relay if a more powerful alternator is installed.

Figure 11.12A shows how it is possible for current to flow from the alternator, through the charge warning lamp and to earth through the energizing contact of the relay.

If the starter relay is original then that may be used as the ignition relay, and the modern ISO relay can be substituted for the starter relay.

Another solution, illustrated in Figure 11.12B, is to fit a diode in the brown/yellow circuit to block current flowing from the alternator to the ignition relay yet allow current to flow from the ignition switch to the alternator and light the warning lamp when the battery voltage is greater than that being generated. The diode is best situated in the more benign environment close to the warning lamp rather than under the bonnet. An inexpensive 1N4002 or 1N4003 diode will work well. It should be insulated and supported with heat shrink tubing or tape. For more information regarding diodes, see Appendix 2 and page 132.

IGNITION COIL

The principle of operation of the coil is described at the beginning of this chapter.

Why ignition coils fail

Heat and vibration are enemies of a coil. Fortunately, MG minimized both by mounting the coil on the frame rather than the engine block as is common on Triumph cars of the same era.

Under normal engine operation the coil is conducting primary current via the contact-breaker for about 67% of the time. However, if the ignition switch is left on while the car is not running, current can flow for 100% of the time increasing the power dissipated in the coil by 50% compared with that when the engine is running. When an engine is switched off, it tends to settle with the pistons about halfway up the cylinder bores because as it finally stops turning, any compression in a cylinder tends to push the compressing piston back down. That happens to be a point in the cycle when the contact-breaker is closed and conducting

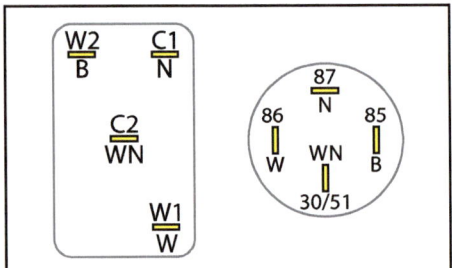

Figure 11.11. Contact and wire colour identification for both rectangular and circular ignition relays.

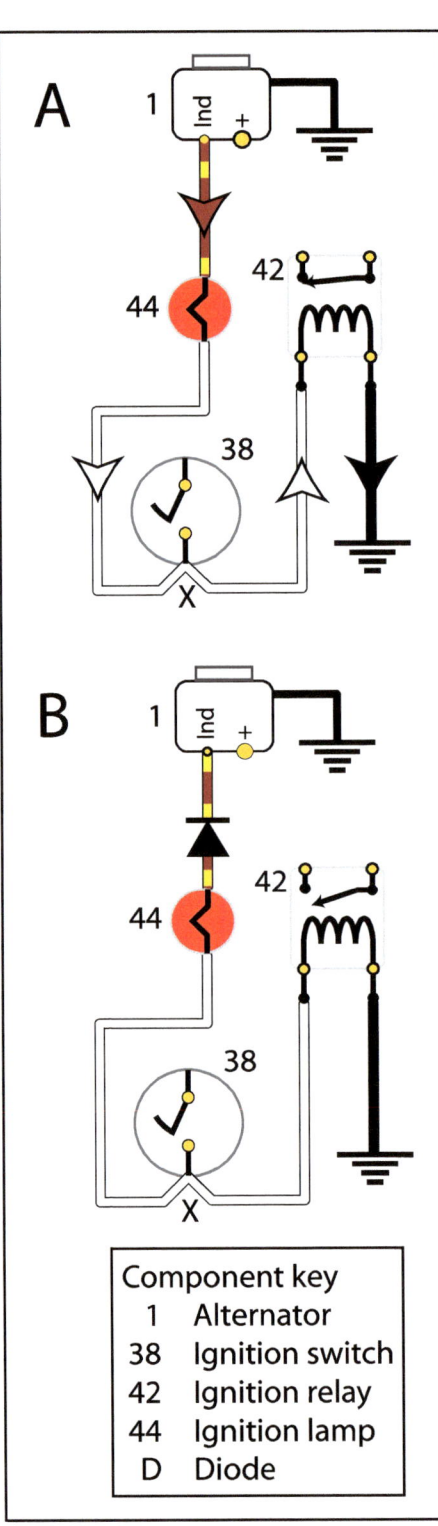

Component key
1 Alternator
38 Ignition switch
42 Ignition relay
44 Ignition lamp
D Diode

Figure 11.12. Relay sneak currents.

IGNITION SYSTEM

current, so if the ignition is on, and the engine is not turning, the probability is that the coil will get hot. This is bad practice; the coil may not fail the first time but will certainly be degraded and could fail later. Moreover, the contact-breaker also becomes hot and the battery can run down to a point where the car may not start.

A coil that fails open-circuit because of overheating will often temporarily repair itself when it cools down and the broken wires retouch as the assembly contracts. Suspect the coil whenever a car exhibits missing or total engine failure when hot, but starts or works normally again when allowed to cool down.

Tracking – a phenomenon where a spark occurs across an insulator forming an initial carbon track or fissure in the insulator for subsequent sparks to more easily jump across – can occur in coils, most often from the coil tower to one of the low-tension terminals.

Figure 11.13 shows how such a spark can travel down the track formed on the tower of the coil and then jump across to a terminal. This nearly new coil failed while in an MGB but the problem was hard to see in daylight and the earth field effect caused the spark to occur on the terminal closest to the panel metal so it was hidden from view.

This particular failure was thought to have occurred because of a loose plug lead. The spark, unable to get to the plug had to find somewhere to go and so took the next easiest route. Moisture on the coil can cause the same effect. If spotted early, the track can often be scratched out with a knife but repeated arcing deepens the track to a point where it is permanent and the coil must be replaced. Not all tracking is on the surface; imperfections in the plastic moulding can cause internal failure of an insulator. Minimize the chance of such failures by keeping plug leads secure, not pulling plug leads off to check for a bad cylinder and by keeping the coil dry.

The coil in Figure 11.13 failed in the field but could not be encouraged to do so for the camera until the rubber boot, Figure 11.14, that would normally support, insulate and seal the high voltage wire to coil tower junction, was removed. The boot is effective in discouraging tracking so make sure one is fitted where applicable and that it is in good condition and properly installed.

Coils fitted up until 1967 have screw-in high-voltage cable attachments and will benefit from dielectric grease being inserted into the cavity before the cable is screwed in, as shown in Figure 11.15. Some will emerge from the gap between the cable and screw as it is fastened, indicating that the gap is properly filled. Wipe off any surplus so that it does not attract dirt.

Most coils are oil filled as part of the internal electrical insulation system. As the MGC and many MGB coil installations have the coil tower pointing down, oil leakage can sometimes occur with the end result of coil failure. Such leakage is usually obvious when the coil is inspected because of the visible oil around the top seal.

BALLAST RESISTOR AND LOW RESISTANCE COIL

An ignition coil with fewer turns exhibits both lower resistance (R) and lower inductance (L). Inductance, remember, is an electrical quality not unlike inertia in a mechanical system. The time (t) the coil takes to charge with magnetic flux is proportional to: $L \div R$. If, as in a typical low resistance coil, the number of turns were halved both L and R would be approximately halved too and there would be no benefit to such a coil; both the numerator and denominator of the equation having halved, the time (t) would remain the same. However, if we then add some resistance, in the form of an external ballast resistor, to double the resistance (R) to its original value, the time (t) will be halved. At high engine speeds, when the coil has little time to charge, such an arrangement can result in a more reliable ignition.

Why not just make the coil using a higher resistance wire rather than use an external ballast resistor? That could be done but the amount of heat generated in the coil would be difficult to dissipate and it could be short lived. There is another benefit too. Having an external ballast resistor gives the option of using it when wanted but of selectively taking it out of circuit during starting. The low inductance, low resistance coil described above is very much like the type of coil used on 6V ignition systems. When cranking the engine, the system voltage can be as low as 9V and applying that directly to what effectively is a 6V coil drives up the energy level stored in it and aids starting. The coil and contact-breaker do of course overheat under such over-rated voltage and current conditions, but since the extra stress is applied only for short periods during cranking, no permanent damage occurs.

Figure 11.14. The rubber boot around the tower of the coil and outlets from the distributor helps prevent the onset of arc tracking.

Figure 11.13. Although this photograph was taken in the workshop, this coil originally failed in an MGB, immobilizing it.

Figure 11.15. Ignition coils and distributors with screw-in high-voltage cables will benefit from dielectric grease injected where indicated by the arrow.

MGB ELECTRICAL SYSTEMS – THE ESSENTIAL MANUAL

	Standard coil		Performance coil	
	No ballast	Ballasted	No ballast	Ballasted
Turns ratio	60 to 70 :1	80 to 90:1	>90:1	>90:1
Primary resistance	>3Ω	1.3 to 2Ω	2 to 3Ω	0.5 to 1.2Ω
Inductance	>14mH	>8mH	10 to 13mH	5 to 7mH

Table 11.1. Many exaggerated claims are made concerning coil performance. This table gives some guidance regarding what really constitutes a performance coil as compared to a standard one. The sign > means greater than.

Ballast resistors are installed in late MGBs in the form of a long resistance wire, but note that this brittle wire may well have been replaced by a discreet component. They can be seen as component 56 in schematic Figures 11.7, 11.8 and 11.9. Note how the starter motor has a special contact that supplies full system voltage to the coil during cranking, effectively jumping the ballast resistor out of circuit.

Coil selection

Do you need a special coil? Perhaps, but you might find that the one you have in your MG, or that one you can pick up at a breaker's yard is almost, if not as good, as a shiny new one that claims to be the Holy Grail of coils.

For the MGC and early MGBs, a low resistance coil with a ballast resistor as was fitted to later MGBs, may well be worthwhile. Besides offering easier starting, a ballasted coil has a lower electrical inductance that allows the coil to build more energy in the short time available, a feature most beneficial at high rpm. It also discharges more quickly, producing a higher voltage. If the coil has a low inductance the current can build quickly; that's important because the energy stored is proportional to the square of the current (double the current and the energy goes up 4 times). As a trade-off, the energy stored is proportional to the inductance, so halve the inductance and the energy stored is also halved. This explains why some high current, low inductance coils are no better than some high inductance low current coils.

High performance coils are constantly being brought to the market or being superseded by newer types and what is available varies by territory, so no brand or model recommendations will be given here. However, some guidance to reading coil specifications will help selection.

1. Stay with the standard cylindrical style coil.
2. Do not take any notice of the hyped voltage specifications.
3. Choose the finish, paint colour or chrome, to suit your own taste and pocket. It makes no difference to the performance.
4. Use the Table 11.1 as a guide to specifications.

Adding a ballast resistor

In order to use a ballast resistor on an MGB/C, which was not originally fitted with one, requires that a connection be made to the starter-motor to jump the ballast resistor out of circuit during cranking and so apply the full system voltage to the coil. Changing the starter motor for a later type is not usually practical and it isn't possible to simply join a wire from the starter relay or solenoid to the coil. That would certainly provide the requisite full voltage to it, but it would also mean that, with ignition on, current from the coil would flow back down the wire and keep the solenoid, and hence the starter motor, energised. A method of isolating the reverse current from the coil is needed, and either a diode or an additional relay will achieve that objective.

Figure 11.16. Ballast resistors come in many shapes. They become quite hot in use and so are often encased in ceramic. They should be firmly fixed to the flattest metal surface that is convenient in order to most efficiently dissipate heat.

Ballast resistor

Don't be too concerned if the ballast resistor you buy doesn't look very much like that shown in Figure 11.16, which was bought from an auto spares department; various styles are available and all will work well. If you can, check the resistance, it should be between 1.2 and 2Ω.

Diode ballast isolation

Although reference was made above to using a diode to stop current feeding back from the coil to the starter solenoid, sufficiently high current diodes, although common in industry, are not readily available to the consumer. Lower current diodes can, however, be wired in parallel to achieve the requisite 12A rating, more information about which can be found in Appendix 2.

For positive earth vehicles refer to the original circuit Figure 11.5 and to Figure 11.17A.

The white wire from the fuse block to the coil (39) SW terminal has been cut at a convenient point and the ballast resistor (56) has been wired in between the cut ends.

A new wire has been connected from the contact on the starter solenoid that carries the white/red wire. The new wire has a diode inserted in the line with the anode toward the SW contact of the coil to which it is connected.

When the starter solenoid is energized, current can flow from it to the coil via the diode, supplying full system voltage to the coil's SW terminal. However, when the white wire on the fuse block is energized, current going to the coil has to flow through the ballast resistor, which drops the voltage down to the normal running voltage of the coil. Current cannot flow back through the diode to the starter solenoid because the diode is connected in such a direction as to prevent it.

For negative earth vehicles refer to the original schematics in Figures 11.6, 11.7, 11.8 or 11.9 and to Figure 11.17B. The circuit installation and operation is identical to that described above for the positive earth system except that the diode are connected with its cathode toward the coil where it connects to the '+' terminal and ballast resistor.

Relay ballast isolation

For more information concerning relays, please see Appendix 1.

For positive earth vehicles refer to the original schematic Figure 11.5 and to Figure 11.17C.

IGNITION SYSTEM

DISTRIBUTOR

The distributor is the jack of all trades of the ignition system. At one and the same time it is mechanically rotates a cam that operates an electrical switch (the contact-breaker) that feeds a low-tension circuit to the coil. The coil transforms the voltage to high-tension, which is fed back to the distributor's mechanical rotor arm from where it is distributed to each sparkplug. While doing all this, the cam can move relative to its driving shaft by centrifugal force and the plate that retains the contact-breaker can be moved by vacuum – or more accurately differential pressure – both mechanisms advancing and retarding the timing of the opening and closing of the contact-breaker according to engine conditions.

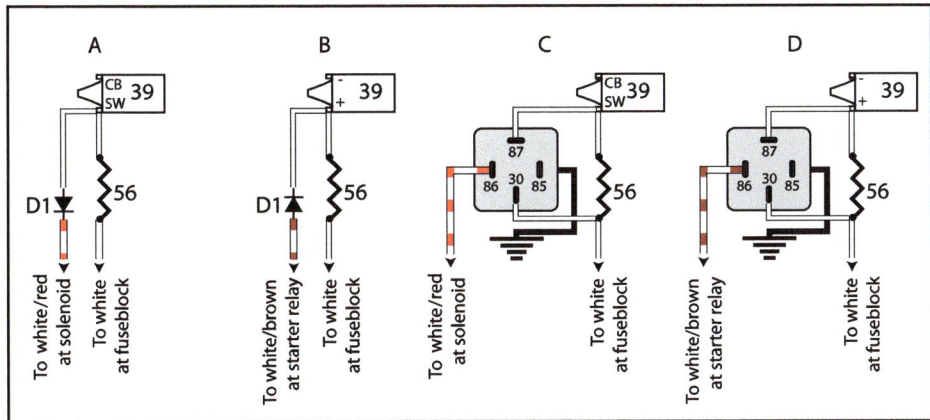

Figure 11.17. Fitting a ballast resistor to a car without a special contact on the starter solenoid requires using diodes or a relay.
Circuits A and B use a diode for positive and negative earth connections respectively.
Circuits C and D use a relay for positive and negative earth connections respectively.

Description

Figure 11.18 shows an internal view of the Lucas 25D4 distributor that was fitted to MGAs and MGBs until 1974 and which is typical of many of its era.

The distributor illustrated is actually a 25D4 meant for the 4-cylinder MGB and therefore has a 4-lobe cam. The MGC distributor was a 25D6, the only significant difference for these 6-cylinder cars being the number of lobes on the cam, as per Figure 11.19, which also shows an 8-lobed cam for reference. After 1974, MGBs were fitted with the 45D distributor, described below. MGB-GT V8 cars used the Lucas 35D8 distributor, which is very different from the 25D and 45D designs, and is described later in this chapter.

The description of conventional ignition in page 87 describes how the contact-breaker switches current to the coil to charge it with energy and then opens to discharge it as a spark at a plug. Referring to Figure 11.17, the connection from the coil is made via the power input connector, through a short wire to the contact spring and so to the moving contact via a rivet that passes through the cam follower. The contact spring tends to push the moving contact toward the centre of the distributor and thus also toward

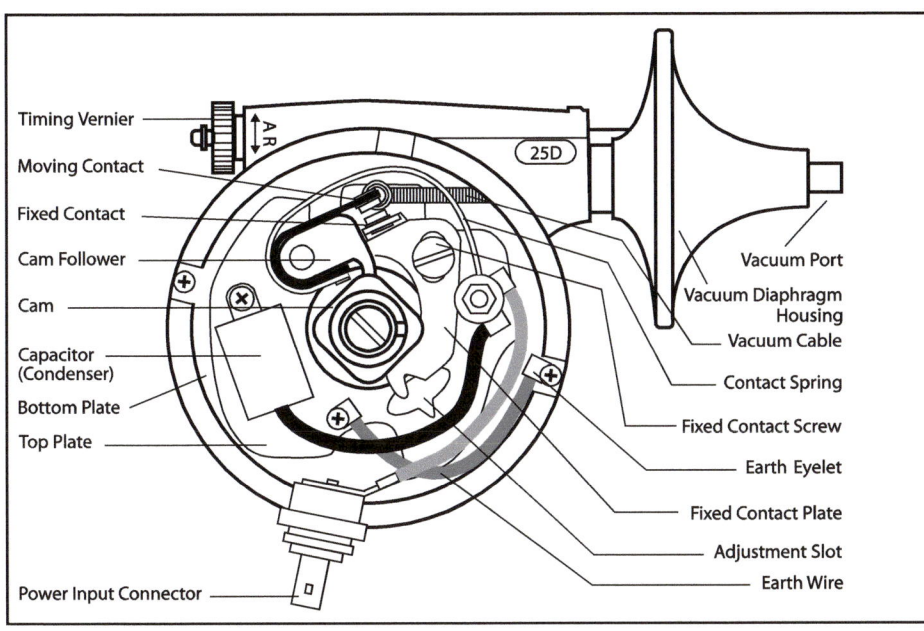

Figure 11.18. The Lucas 25D4 distributor with the cap removed.

The white wire from the fuse block to the coil (39) SW terminal was cut at a convenient point and the ballast resistor (56) has been wired in between the cut ends. A relay has also been installed with its power contacts, terminals 30 and 87 wired across the ballast resistor.

A new wire has been connected from the terminal on the starter relay that carries the white/brown wire. The new wire is connected to the relay coil terminal 86. Relay terminal 85 has been connected to earth.

When the starter relay is energized, current can flow from it to the new relay coil and from there to earth, thus energizing it, closing its power contacts and joining its terminals 30 and 87, thus allowing full system voltage from the fuse block to be applied to the coil's '+' terminal. However, since there is no direct connection on the new relay from terminal 30 to 86, there is no danger of power from the fuse block inadvertently energizing the starter relay.

For negative earth vehicles refer to the original schematics in Figures 11.6, 11.7, 11.8 or 11.9 and to Figure 11.17D. The circuit installation and operation is identical to that described above for the positive earth system except that the ballast resistor and new relay are connected to coil's '+' terminal.

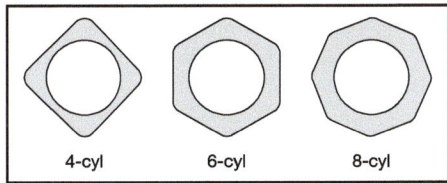

Figure 11.19. Comparitive cam profiles for different cylinder counts.

97

MGB ELECTRICAL SYSTEMS – THE ESSENTIAL MANUAL

the fixed contact, which is electrically connected to earth via the top plate and an earthing wire that is secured to the distributor body at an eyelet. The cam drive is geared so that it rotates at half engine speed. As it does so, it alternately forces the cam follower to rise and fall and the moving contact to open and close the connection to the fixed contact.

Rotor arm
A notch in the top section of the cam serves as a key into which to lock the rotor arm, Figure 11.20. As each of the 4 lobes of the cam causes the contacts to open and a spark to be produced, the rotor arm points towards a different contact in the distributor cap, each of which is attached via the ignition cables to the sparkplugs. Note that the rotor arm does not touch the high-tension contacts in the cap; it passes so close, however, that the spark can jump the gap. Note that the rotor arms for 6 and 4-cylinder cars will fit in either car's 25D distributor, but they are different and only the correct arm should be used.

Because the distributor cam rotates at half engine speed, it provides a spark to each plug only every other engine revolution, as per the principle of the 4-cycle (or stroke) engine.

Capacitor
The capacitor, once known as a condenser, is a compromise device. It effectively sustains current conduction for a short period after the points open and thus lessens arcing and erosion. If its capacitance is too small it will be less effective and the points will have a very short life; if too large, the rate of change of collapse of the coil's magnetic field is too slow, and the high voltage output is reduced. Electronic ignitions do not require a capacitor; they can switch without arcing and have a sufficient, but small, amount of inherent capacitance to allow the ignition system to ring (oscillate) more rapidly. The result is a higher voltage output than can be produced by a system with a capacitor. The capacitor value is usually 0.2 micro-Farads (µF).

Capacitors are often suspected when ignitions go wrong, but rarely are they the cause. Early capacitors used a paper insulation (more correctly called a dielectric) that could not always withstand the severe conditions of use. That poor reliability has been a stigma for the component ever since, even though since the 1960s, advances in polymer chemistry have resulted in extremely reliable dielectric materials that shrug off heat, vibration and humidity. Problems with capacitors are now almost wholly restricted to the connecting wire that can short or open due to being, or having been, trapped between the distributor body and cap. Poor connection of the wire to the contact-breaker points may also be a source of problems.

Distributor variants
The 25D distributor was produced over a long period and some small detail modifications were made that will make some versions look a little different from that shown in Figure 11.18, particularly in respect to the vacuum diaphragm.

The 45D distributor, Figure 11.22 differs a little from the 25D.

The major differences are:
- The distributor cap has top outlets, rather than the side outlet common on the 25D (see Figures 11.40 and 11.41).
- The vacuum advance operator is a rod that fits under a pin on the top plate, rather than a cable that fits over a pin.

Figure 11.20. The rotor arm from a 25D4 distributor. Contact is made with the centre of the arm by a spring-loaded brush in the distributor cap.

Figure 11.21. A typical capacitor, also often called a condensor..

Figure 11.22. There are detail differences between the 45D distributor shown here and the 25D shown in Fig 11.18, but the principal of operation is identical.

Figure 11.23. The Lucas Opus electronic distributor is based on the conventional 45D platform.

IGNITION SYSTEM

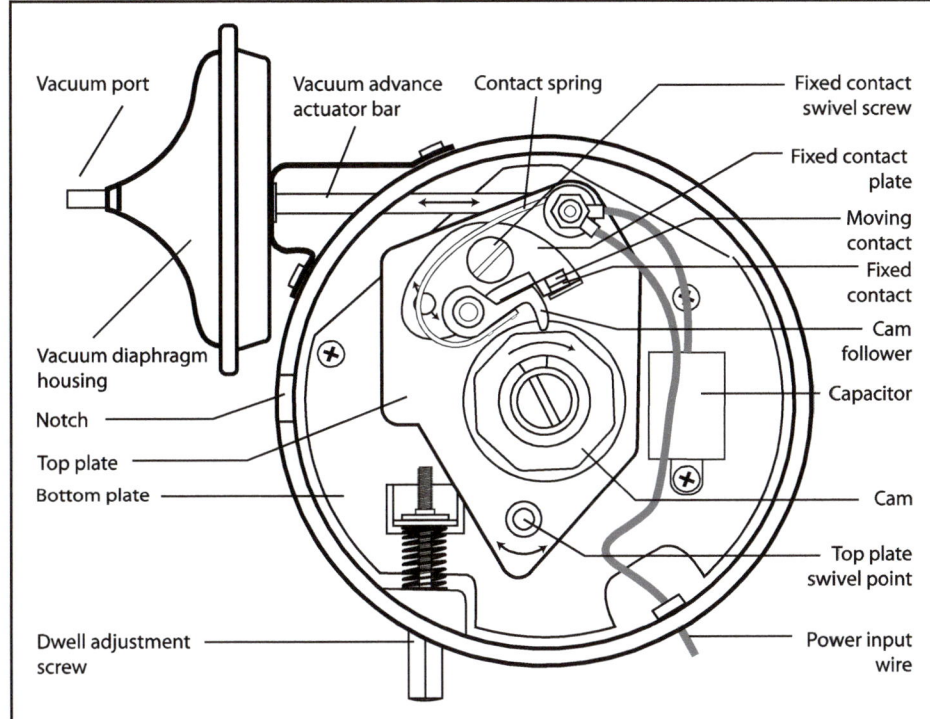

Figure 11.24. The Lucas 35D8 distributor with the cap removed.

- The power input is via a cable rather than a connector.
- There is no timing vernier.

The Lucas OPUS and CEI distributors, fitted to California cars from 1975 and all US cars from 1977, are based on the 45D and look similar. The OPUS has an amplifier box attached as shown in Figure 11.23. See also pages 89 and Figure 11.9.

The Lucas 35D8 distributor, used in the MGB-GT V8 and illustrated in Figure 11.24, is quite different from the 25D and 45D, having adopted some features from the Delco-Remy distributor that was originally used on the car's Buick designed engine. Most notable is the dwell angle adjustment screw, which is external to the body. As will be discussed later in this chapter, contact breaker points gap, dwell angle and engine timing are intrinsically linked, making dwell angle an important parameter to keep constant. To adjust the dwell angle of the 25D and 45D distributors, it is necessary to remove the cap, adjust the points gap, then replace the cap, start the engine and check the dwell. If it's wrong, the process had to be repeated. With the 35D8, the dwell angle can be adjusted without stopping the engine and dismantling the distributor. Even if a dwell meter isn't available, the adjusting screw allows much more precise and repeatable adjustment of the contact-breaker points gap. Turning the screw moves a bar that slides under the bottom plate, emerging under the fixed contact-breaker plate and attaching to it. As the bar moves, it causes the fixed contact-breaker plate to rotate about a swivel screw, moving its contact closer or further from the moving contact.

The vacuum advance system is also different from that in the 25D and 45D. Rather than the vacuum advance mechanism rotating the moving plate around the centre of the distributor, it swivels about a point on the opposite side.

Lastly, unlike the other distributors discussed here, the 35D8 rotates clockwise when viewed from the top.

DISTRIBUTOR ADVANCE MECHANISMS

As is the case with almost all conventional ignition systems, there are two advance mechanisms in the Lucas distributors used in MGBs and MGCs.

Centrifugal advance

The centrifugal advance mechanism causes the spark to occur earlier in the cycle as engine speed increases. Once the sparkplug ignites the fuel mixture, the vapour expands and builds up pressure in the cylinder. The rate of expansion does not vary very much with engine speed, while of course, the speed of the piston does.

Ideally, to achieve maximum engine torque, pressure in the cylinder should peak at about 10° after the piston has reached top-dead-centre (ATDC). In order to ensure that this happens, the fuel mixture must be ignited some time before top dead centre (BTDC) is reached. As the piston speed increases, so ignition must occur earlier and earlier to ensure that maximum pressure is reached in time. The centrifugal advance achieves this.

During starting, the concern is not with achieving maximum torque but of getting the engine to run and sustain itself. Very early cars, with no centrifugal system, would have a driver operated lever that could adjust the ignition timing. The lever was placed in a position providing little or no ignition advance to start the car but once the engine was running, the lever could be moved to advance the ignition much further. The Lucas distributors used in MGBs and Cs provide the same function automatically and then further provide progressive ignition advance up to a certain maximum.

Figure 11.25 shows the 25D4 distributor with the upper components removed. The mechanism can be seen more clearly in Figure 11.26 The cam (C) rotates on an upper spindle together with the plate and stop bar (SB), to which it is attached. Two weights (W) are attached to it and pivot at points (P). Two springs (S), which are fixed at one end to the lower rotating plate (LP), tend to pull the stop bar clockwise, which in turn pulls the weights against cam blocks (CB) and hold them inward.

The lower diagram of Figure 11.26 shows the change in condition when the distributor rapidly rotates, and this being a 25D, the direction of rotation is anti-clockwise. This throws the weights outward so that their rearward faces roll back against the cam blocks at the points marked X. In rolling back, the weights pull the stop plate, and the cam with it, further anti-clockwise up to a certain maximum when the stop bar contacts one of the spring posts.

The result is that the cam lobes contact the cam follower earlier than they otherwise would, thus advancing the ignition timing. Note how the red dashed line shows how much the cam lobe has moved relative to its rest position shown by the blue dashed line.

Figure 11.25. The 25D distributor with the top plate removed. Note the two weight restraining springs are different from one another.

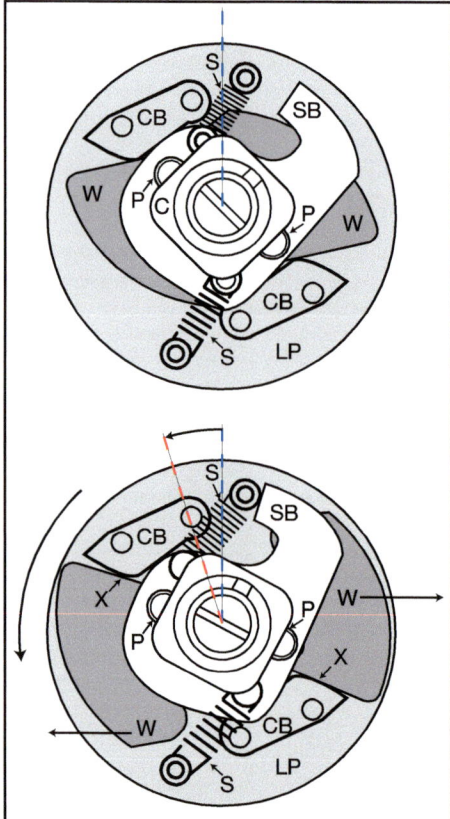

Figure 11.26. Centrifugal advance mechanism for the 25D distributor.

Figure 11.27. The 45D distributor with the top plate removed. Note that in this case, the two weight restraining springs are not noticeably different from one another.

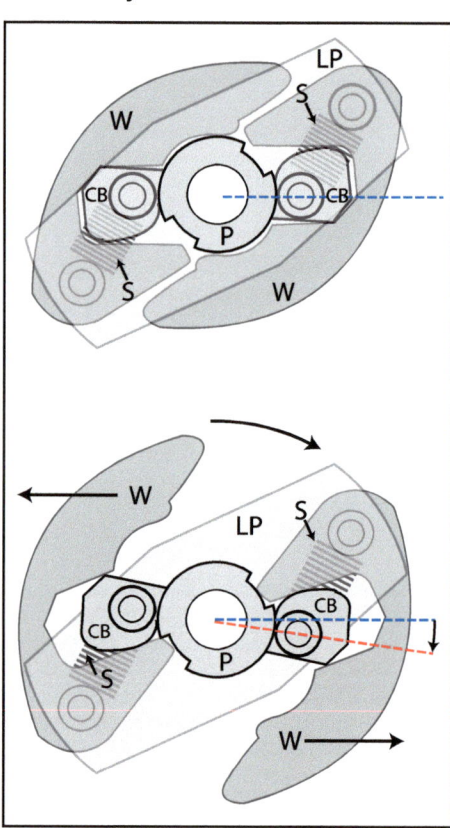

Figure 11.28. Centrifugal advance mechanism for the 45D distributor illustrated from underneath. That for the 35D is similar, but the mirror image.

There are two restraining mechanisms that prevent the weights flying out too soon and too far. Firstly the weights move together against the tension of two different springs shown in Figure 11.25. Spring A is very light and holds the weights inward while the engine is stationary but is not strong enough to restrain them past idling speed. Spring B is much stronger but has elongated hooks that result in the spring initially sitting loosely on its retaining posts. The weights initially move only against the force of spring A. The result is that when the car is cranking, the ignition advance is only that set when the engine was static. However, as soon as idling speed is reached, some initial centrifugal advance is provided as spring A elongates. Past that point, however, the slack in spring B's hooks is taken up and as it comes under tension, higher speeds are required to throw the weights further outward.

As noted above, the stop bar (S) limits the maximum centrifugal advance. It is mechanically locked to the cam and moves anti-clockwise as more centrifugal advance is applied. It eventually contacts the nearest spring retaining post and prevents further advance. The stop bar in the example illustrated in Figure 11.25 is marked 10°, (equating to 20° of crankshaft advance because it rotates twice as fast) which indicates that it limits the centrifugal advance by that much. Different distributors will have different stop bar lengths that are marked accordingly.

The 45D and 35D distributors have a somewhat different mechanism using claw shaped weights that operate on cam blocks that cannot be seen in Figure 11.27 because they are below the weights and much closer to the centre than is the case with the 25D. Also, unlike the 25D, these weights pivot on the lower rotating plate (LP). Because the advance mechanism operates below the weights, Figure 11.28 shows an underside view (with some parts omitted for clarity).

Referring to both Figures 11.27 and 11.28, again the springs (S) tend to hold the weights inward as they pull them against the cam blocks, which are part of the assembly that retains the cam (C), the stop bar (SB) and a plastic collar (C).

The lower diagram of Figure 11.28 shows the change in condition when the distributor rapidly rotates, and this being a 45D, like the 25D, the direction of rotation is anti-clockwise. However, because the view is of the underside, the direction of rotation appears as being clockwise. The rapid rotation throws the weights outward so that their claws roll around the cam blocks (CB). In doing so, the weights rotate the cam blocks, collar, stop plate and cam (all of which are attached) relative to the rotating lower plate. Thus the stop plate, and the cam with it, rotate further anti-clockwise (but clockwise in Figure 11.28, due to the underside view) up to

IGNITION SYSTEM

a certain maximum when the stop bar contacts one of the spring posts.

The result is that the cam lobes contact the cam follower earlier than they otherwise would, thus advancing the ignition timing. Note how the red dashed line shows how much the cam lobe has moved relative to its rest position shown by the blue dashed line.

Within all distributor families, Lucas produced many different advance characteristics, some of which are illustrated in Figure 11.50. These variations were largely achieved by changing the characteristics of the weight restraining springs. Note that the two springs in Figure 11.25 are quite different from one another, both in strength and attachment method whereas those in Figure 11.27, are almost identical. The centrifugal advance characteristics of these two distributors would therefore be very different.

The 35D8 distributor has claw style centrifugal advance weights rather like those in the 45D. Refer therefore to the illustrations for the 45D, always remembering that, because the 35D8 rotates clockwise, the actual mechanism appears to be the mirror image of those shown.

Vacuum advance

Largely for economy reason, most cars are designed so that at cruising speeds, the mixture is quite lean: that is, it has a higher air to fuel ratio. Lean mixtures burn slower than rich ones and so some additional ignition advance is needed to ensure that maximum cylinder pressure is achieved at the optimum time in the combustion cycle.

The MGB and C have a vacuum port on the carburettor (or on the rear carburettor if there are two and on the left one of the MGB-GT V8) just behind the throttle butterfly.

Figure 11.29A. At idle speeds, with the throttle almost completely closed, the vacuum port, being on the air-cleaner side of the butterfly, is not exposed to the high vacuum that results from the engine trying to inhale against the closed butterfly disc.

Figure 11.29A. At part throttle the vacuum port becomes exposed to both the inlet manifold depression and to venturi effect as air flows over its orifice. The port is thus exposed to vacuum, which it transmits via a tube to the distributor spring loaded vacuum diaphragm contained in the vacuum housing of the distributor (Figure 11.18).

The top and bottom plates shown in Figure 11.18 are attached at the centre in such a way that the top plate can swivel relative to the bottom one. When the vacuum diaphragm moves, it pulls the vacuum cable (or rod in the case of a 45D distributor), which rotates the top plate clockwise, moving the cam follower, fixed contact and moving contact with it. In so doing, the cam follower contacts the anti-clockwise

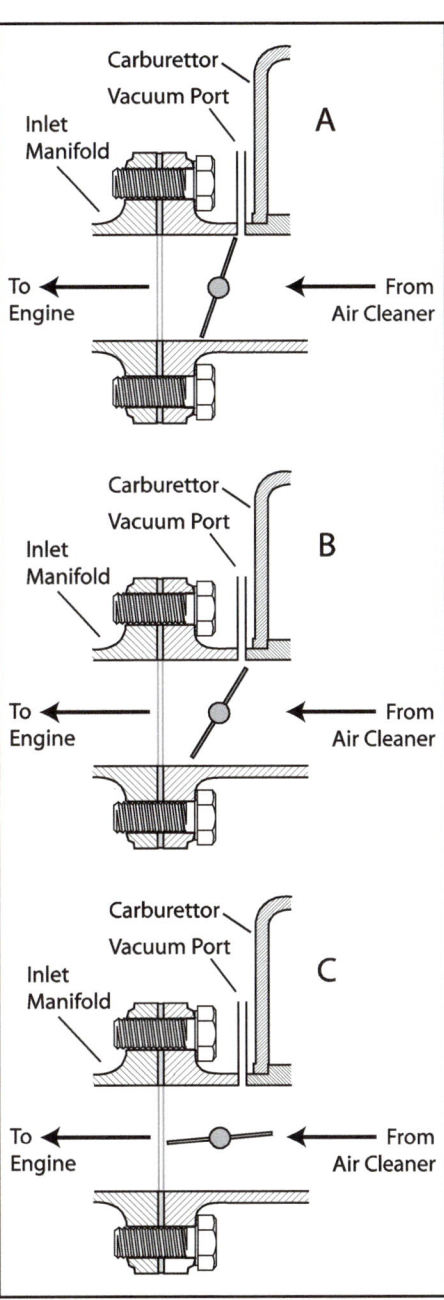

Figure 11.29. The amount of vacuum ignition advance is a function of the position of the carburettor butterfly valve.

rotating cam earlier than it would otherwise, and the ignition timing is thus advanced. Vacuum advance is not limited by the centrifugal advance stop bar but by a stop inside the diaphragm housing that restricts it to a maximum of about 10° at the crankshaft.

Figure 11.29A. At full throttle, the vacuum port is fully exposed but the wide open area causes overall vacuum to be low.

It is easy to test the vacuum advance. Anybody with reasonably healthy lungs can pull the vacuum tube from the port on the carburettor and, with the distributor cap removed, be able to observe the top plate swivel as they suck on the tube.

If the suction required is high or the plate does not move, it may be seized against the bottom plate and need removing and lubricating. Also check that the cable or rod from the vacuum diaphragm is properly attached to the top plate.

Should sucking on the tube be easy and there is an evident leak, the tube may be cracked or badly connected. A broken vacuum diaphragm will also leak.

Many cars have had carburettor transplants and/or removal of emissions equipment. Not all carburettors that may have been fitted will have vacuum ports and removal of emissions equipment may expose other ports to which it is tempting to attach the distributor vacuum tube. Unless the port is correctly located behind the carburettor butterfly, vacuum will not be applied to the distributor under the correct engine conditions.

Electrical vacuum advance (TCSA)

From 1977, with soaring fuel cost and more stringent emissions regulations in the USA, a better way was needed to achieve the benefits of being able to burn leaner fuel at cruising speeds than was possible with carburettor butterfly valve control.

MG responded by applying vacuum advance to the MGB whenever the car was in 4th gear, a system they referred to as 'transmission control spark advance'. IIn 1977 cars fitted with the system, a micro-switch is bolted to the transmission that can detect if the car is either in 2nd or 4th gear by operating when the gear stick is in the rearward position. The overdrive gear switch, which detects if the car is in 3rd

101

MGB ELECTRICAL SYSTEMS – THE ESSENTIAL MANUAL

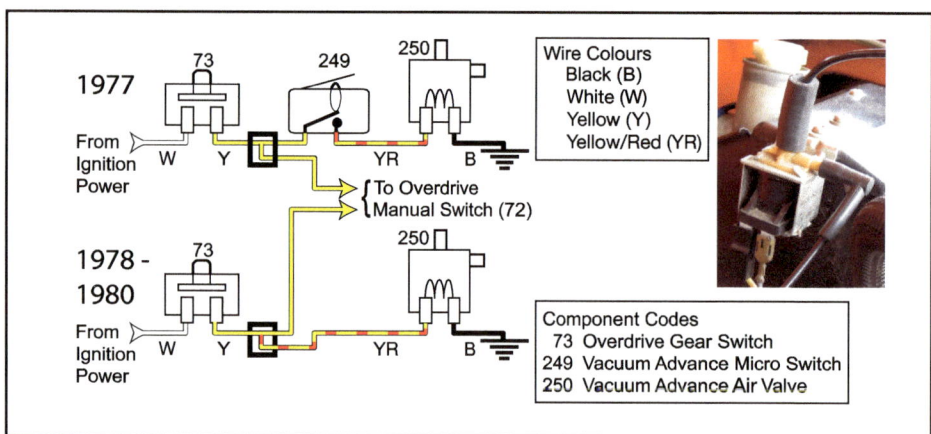

Figure 11.30. The 1977 and 1978+ transmission control spark advance circuits. An actual air valve is shown on the right. See also Figure 13.5.

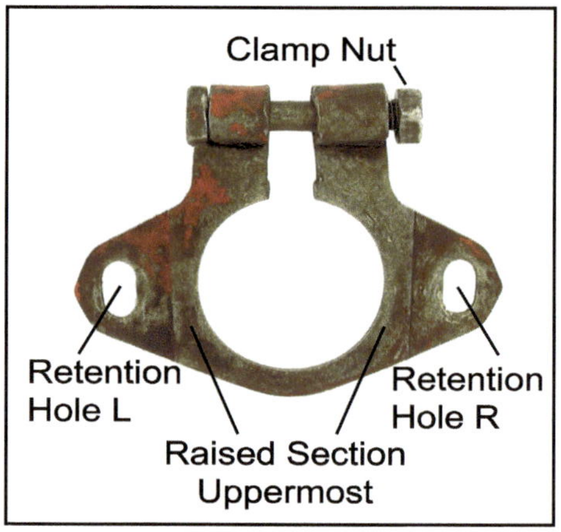

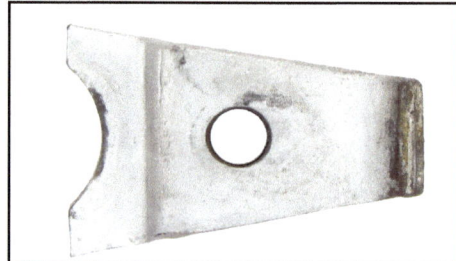

Figure 11.32. The 25D and 45D distributor clamp.

or 4th gear, was also fitted to all cars. With the two switches in series, when power is applied, current can only flow when the car is in 4th gear and both are closed. That current is then directed to an air valve that links a vacuum feed from the manifold to the vacuum diaphragm of the distributor. In cars from 1978 on, a modified gear selector that only operates the overdrive switch in 4th gear was installed, and the micro-switch was removed.

The circuits for these systems is shown in Figure 11.30.

Distributor drive orientation

If the 25D or 45D distributor has been disassembled, it is necessary to ensure that the drive dog is in the correct position relative to the rotor arm.

When assembling the distributor, in order to keep the centrifugal advance weights together, hold it with the top downward. To get the orientation correct, place the rotor arm on the camshaft with its drive key properly located. As the camshaft, weight and rotor are assembled to the drive shaft and body, ensure that the rotor arm blade is uppermost and that the offset drive dog is to the left; see Figure 11.31.

Distributor clamp

The apparently simple clamp that holds the distributor, Figure 11.32, can cause some problems because it is shown incorrectly placed in some workshop drawings.

It is important that the slightly raised centre section is outward, away from the engine block. This ensures that the retention bolts can secure the clamp tightly against the block, that the clamp can compress around the centre

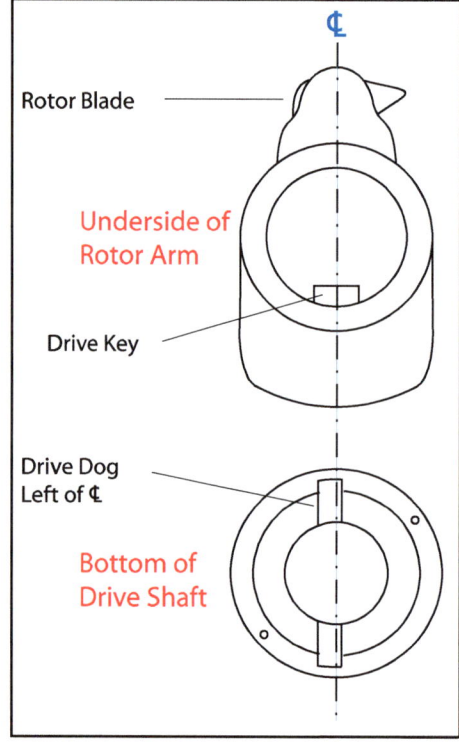

Figure 11.31. It is important that the drive dog at the base of the distributor is correctly aligned with the rotor arm.

of the step on the distributor to which it clamps, and that the clamp nut is in the most accessible position.

When releasing the distributor, not only does the clamp nut need to be slackened but at least one of the bolts in the clamp retention holes has to be loosened in order that the clamp can open. All require a 7/16in A/F wrench. The smaller diameter of the 45D distributor makes access to the clamp retention bolts much easier than is the case with the 25D. It is therefore not necessary to slacken the clamp and the distributor may be removed for service and replaced without affecting its orientation and thus the ignition timing.

There are no real issues with the single bolt fixing, two pronged distributor clamp on the MGB-GT V8 (Figure 11.33). Its design doesn't allow removal of the distributor without losing ignition timing, so try and put an alignment mark on it and the part of the block adjacent to it.

Figure 11.33. The MGB-GT V8 distributor clamp.

Dwell angle and contact-breaker gap

Most people know that if the car has a mechanical contact-breaker then the points gap has to be set. The gap itself is not the important thing; it is the dwell angle that is effectively being adjusted.

The dwell angle is the angle of rotation of the distributor cam during which the contact-breaker contacts, usually referred to as points, 'dwell' together. For a 4-cylinder engine, each cam lobe opens and closes the points for a total angle of 90° of rotation per cylinder, for 6-cylinders the total angle is 60° and for 8-cylinders it's 30°.

IGNITION SYSTEM

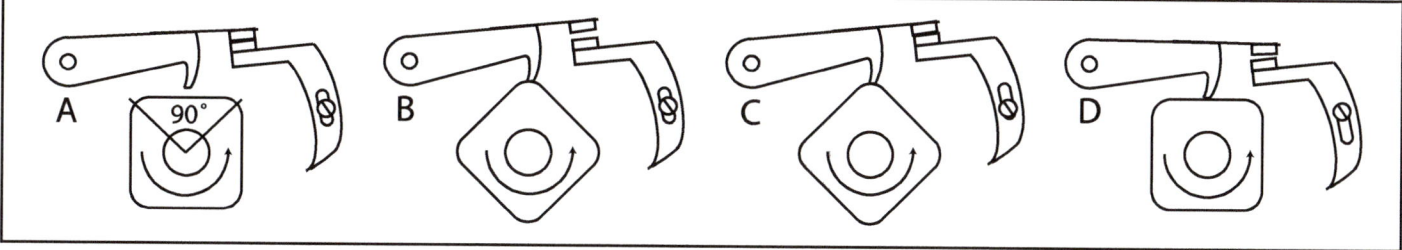

Figure 11.34. While the contact-breaker fixed contact can be adjusted to change the measured gap, this is only a means to an end, the real objective being to set the dwell angle. Changing the gap also has the secondary, but critical, effect of changing the ignition timing.

Manufacturers generally specified that the points should dwell together for about ⅔ of the total rotation. BMC/BL came close to the ⅔ rule, but in order to standardize maintenance procedures across vehicle models, settled on the nearest value that would result from using a 0.15in (0.38mm) feeler gauge, the outcome being the dwell angle values listed in Table 11.2.

Using a 4-cylinder example for simplicity, Figure 11.34 shows how changing the contact-breaker gap, changes the dwell angle.

Figure 11.34A. The fixed contact has been set at about halfway along the adjustment slot. With the cam at a low position relative to the cam follower, the points are closed.

Figure 11.34B. The fixed contact adjustment has not been changed but the cam has rotated so that the cam follower causes the points to open. With the fixed contact adjusted in this way, the points are dwelling together for some portion of the 90° angle and being opened for the remaining portion.

Figure 11.34C. The fixed contact is at the upper extreme adjustment position, so that the contact-breaker gap is zero, and even with the cam follower at the highest point on the cam lobe, the points will not open and so dwell together for the full 90°.

Figure 11.34D. The fixed contact has been moved to the other extreme of its adjustment and the contact-breaker cannot close, even when the cam follower is at its lowest position. When the cam rotates to move the cam follower to its highest position the points gap will be very wide. Because the points never actually dwell together the dwell angle is 0°.

During the dwell period, the coil builds up magnetic energy which it then dissipates during the open period. The actual dwell angle really only matters at high engine speeds when, should the dwell be too short, there may be insufficient time available for energy to be stored in the coil and so produce a strong spark to reliably fire the engine. If the dwell is too long, there may be insufficient time at high engine speeds to dissipate all the stored energy. A very long dwell may also mean that the contact-breaker points gap is so small as to never separate enough to quench arcing between them.

Table 11.2 shows the dwell time for each car and distributor family. The time 'ms' means milliseconds or thousandths of a second. The standard, non ballasted, Lucas ignition coil can charge to ⅔ of its maximum capacity in about 4.5ms. The table would give the impression that it falls short at high engine speeds but the coil is capable of producing about 33 times as much energy as is generally considered necessary to fire a sparkplug, so that even though it may not fully charge it nevertheless can charge sufficiently, even at the highest engine speeds for the V8 engine.

Figure 11.34 showed how adjusting the contact-breaker gap also adjusts the dwell angle. The actual dwell angle value isn't very important, what is crucial is that it is kept constant, because a change in the dwell angle will

	Actual times for specified dwell angle							
	MGB 25D4 60° dwell		MGB 45D4 51° dwell		MGC 25D6 35° dwell		MGB-GT V8 35D8 27° dwell	
Engine (rpm)	Dwell (ms)	Open (ms)	Dwell (ms)	Open (ms)	Dwell (ms)	Open (ms)	Dwell (ms)	Open (ms)
1000	20	10	17	8.5	12	5.8	9	4.5
3000	6.7	3.3	5.7	5.7	3.9	1.9	3	1.5
5000	4	2	3.4	1.7	2.3	1.2	1.8	0.9

Table 11.2. A fixed dwell angle doesn't mean that the time the points dwell or open is fixed too. They are also a function of engine speed. (ms = thousandths of seconds).

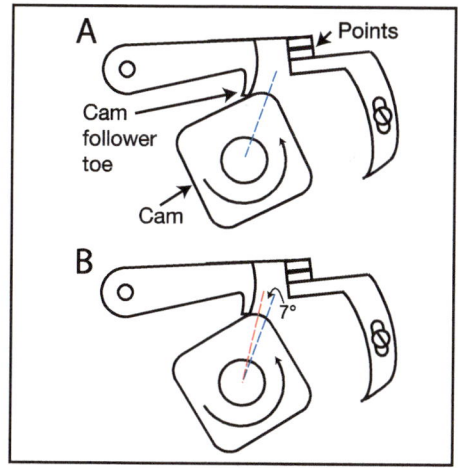

Figure 11.35. Contact-breaker gap and dwell angle affect ignition timing.

result in a change in the ignition timing. Fig 11.35A shows a 4-lobe cam at the point where it is just about to open the contact-breaker points, which would cause the coil to fire a sparkplug. The blue dashed line shows the angle of the cam lobe at this position.

In Figure 11.35B, the toe of the cam follower has been shortened, as it might be after some considerable wear. The blue dashed line again shows the

103

angle that the cam lobe was at in the upper diagram without the cam follower wear. However, with cam-follower wear, the cam no longer opens the contact-breaker points until it reaches the red dashed line, representing, in this hypothetical example an ignition retardation of some 7°, an amount that would significantly affect engine performance.

Setting the dwell angle

Setting the contact-breaker gap is a crude method of setting the dwell angle, but is perfectly adequate. Do not try to set the gap if the surfaces of the contacts do not appear to be smooth. New contact sets are inexpensive and easy to change.

Figure 11.36 shows a representation of how arcing between the contacts causes the phenomena of pitting on the lower contact and piling on the upper one. When the contacts separate a small spark or arc occurs between them. This is caused by electrons boiling from the surface of the more negative contact and being attracted to the more positive one. The electrons hit atoms of air molecules and knock other electrons from them which, in turn, rush towards the more positive contact and in doing so hit more atoms. The deprived atoms, having lost a negative electron, are unbalanced and have a more positive charge; they are now called ions. The process is called ionization and the energy released by the impacts results in heat and light being produced, which we see as a small spark. The relatively heavy, positively charged ions are attracted to the more negative electrode, to which they rush and collide. The collision causes metal vapour to be dispersed from the bombarded contact. The vapour flies off and deposits itself on the nearest object — the other contact — that thousandths of a second beforehand, separated from its mate. Arcing can only be sustained while the contacts are still very close together so very little metal exchange occurs at each contact separation. However, at an engine speed of 3000rpm, the contacts separate about 1 million times every 3 hours, so over time the small effects of pitting and piling become significant. (Note that the polarity of the contacts during arc discharge is not the same as the vehicle battery polarity.)

Trying to measure the contact-breaker gap for a pair of contacts like that shown in Figure 11.36 is, of course futile, hence the need to replace them. Replacement is much easier today than was the case in the original car, since any contact-breaker set purchased new will be a pre-assembled, one-piece design on which the contact spring is secured to a plastic post. If by chance an older design is found with a metal post, refer to Figure 11.37 for guidance concerning the order of assembly. Adjusting the contacts is relatively easy.
• For 4 and 6-cylinder engines.
1.   Refer to Figure 11.18. Remove the distributor cap and
 turn the engine until the cam follower is at the peak of any lobe. (Getting the cam to this position can be tricky.) The engine can be turned more easily if the sparkplugs are removed, which is a good safety measure in any event. The engine can be most easily turned by placing the car in 4th gear and nudging it either forward or backward as required. The engine can also be turned while in neutral using a 1⁵⁄₁₆in A/F wrench on the crankshaft pulley

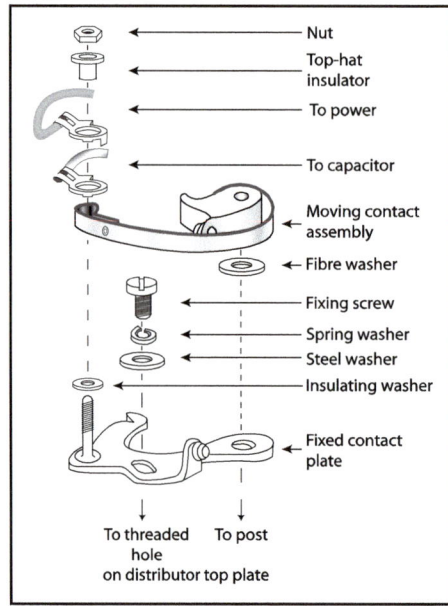

Figure 11.37. The original contact-breaker's assembly order.

nut. Alternatively, some people prefer to remove the distributor from the car altogether and make the adjustment in the comfort and visibility available in a workshop. This can be done without changing the ignition timing adjustment so long as the distributor clamp is removed along with the distributor as discussed in page 102.
2.   Slacken the fixed contact screw so that the fixed contact plate can be moved with just a little resistance.
3.   Place a large bladed screwdriver in the adjustment slot. It will be seen that by twisting the screwdriver blade the contact gap can be opened and closed.
4.   Use a 0.15in (0.38mm) feeler gauge together with the screwdriver to find a point where the feeler gauge just moves with some resistance in the gap.
5.   Carefully withdraw the feeler gauge and screwdriver and re-tighten the fixed contact screw.

It can be very frustrating when the action of tightening the screw moves the contacts just a little. Don't be too concerned; the gap and the dwell angle that it adjusts are not very important in themselves. What is important is that changing the contact-breaker gap also changes the ignition timing, and an adjustment to that may well be necessary after any adjustment to the contact-breaker points.
• For 8-cylinder engines.
1.   Refer to Figure 11.24. Remove the distributor cap and turn the engine until the cam follower is at the peak of any lobe. The engine can be turned more easily if the sparkplugs are removed, which is a good safety measure in any event. As with the other engines, it can be most easily turned by placing the car in 4th gear and nudging it either forward or backward as required. The engine may also be turned by placing are bar between the raised lugs on the crankshaft pulley (labelled L in Figure 11.48). Making adjustments to the contact-breaker gap is so easy with the 35D8 distributor that, unlike the case with the smaller engines, it is not generally worthwhile removing the distributor from the engine and losing the ignition timing as a result.
2.   Use a 0.15in (0.38mm) feeler gauge, together with turning the dwell adjustment screw, to find a point where the feeler gauge just moves with some resistance in the gap. Turning the screw clockwise increases the gap, and vice versa

As previously stated, contact-breaker gap affects dwell angle, which

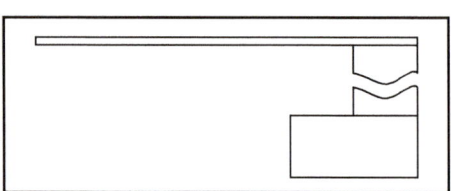

Figure 11.36. In normal operation, one breaker contact tends to pit while the other piles, making adjustment with a feeler gauge very difficult.

IGNITION SYSTEM

in turn affects ignition timing. Also, the points erode and the cam follower wears. With these things in mind, the popularity of electronic breakerless and hence zero maintenance ignition systems is understandable.

The best way to check and adjust dwell directly is with an instrument, not surprisingly called a dwell meter. However, again, the gap and the dwell value are not in themselves that important. That they are kept the constant, or if not, that the ignition timing is adjusted afterward, is essential.

Dwell meters vary somewhat in their connections. Most have only two wires. If the car has a negative earth system, then the red wire goes to the "–" terminal of the coil and the black wire to body metal. For positive earth cars, black goes to the CB terminal on the coil and red to body metal. Some meters have 3 wires because they need a source of power. In that case connect the red wire to a 12V point, by a brown wire on the fuse block is fine, and black to the chassis for negative earth cars and vice versa for positive earth. The third wire, usually green, goes to the CB or "–" terminal on the coil.

Run the car and measure the dwell angle. If the meter indicates it needs adjusting, then for V8 engines simply turn the adjustment screw (Figure 11.24) clockwise to reduce and anti-clockwise to increase the dwell angle. For all other cars, it is possible to check dwell with the engine cranking. Removing the sparkplugs makes this easier because the engine cranks faster and the battery is under less strain. Unless you have a solenoid like that in Figure 10.5 or a remote switch like one of those in page 85, then you'll need an assistant to turn the key. Connect and watch the dwell meter while adjusting the contact-breaker points as described above. Making the contact-breaker points gap smaller, increases the dwell angle and widening the gap decreases the dwell.

The Lucas electronic distributors do not have a contact-breaker and should need no maintenance. The electronic amplifiers are epoxy potted and are not serviceable. If it is desired to check the gap between the rotor and pick-up sensor, make sure the ignition is off, otherwise a metal feeler gauge will trigger the ignition. Remove the rotor and flash shield. Use a feeler gauge to check that the gap is as per the Lucas recommendation of between 0.010in and 0.017in (0.25mm and 0.43mm). If not, slacken the pick-up retention screws to make the appropriate adjustment.

Drive gear position

The distributor drive gear is driven at half engine speed from the camshaft via a helical gear. Should the gear be inserted in the wrong position, the distributor orientation in the engine may be such that the ignition cannot be correctly timed; the vacuum advance housing fouling one or other engine components.

In order to check that the orientation is correct, or to change it should some addition to the engine make re-orienting the distributor advantageous, the engine must first be set at top dead centre for cylinder #1's compression stroke (TDC). Refer to Figures 11.45 to 11.48 to find TDC but remember that the crankshaft's TDC mark may indicate that #1 cylinder is at the top of its exhaust stroke. If possible, set the engine to TDC for #1 cylinder before removing the distributor. To do so, set the timing mark on the crankshaft to TDC and then remove the distributor cap to see if the rotor arm is pointing to the ignition wire that goes to cylinder #1. If it doesn't, rotate the crankshaft by a full turn. If the engine rotation must be disturbed after removing the distributor, there are basically two ways to tell which of of two possible cylinders is at TDC. One method is to remove the valve cover and see which of the cylinders has both valve rockers still free and able to move a little. That is the cylinder with both valves closed and under compression. Alternatively, with plug #1 removed, place a thumb over the plug hole as the engine is rotated clockwise (looking from the front). If the pressure blows air past the thumb, #1 cylinder is coming toward TDC. If there is no pressure, then it is on its exhaust stroke and that valve is open; the crankshaft must be rotated 360°.

The distributor and its clamp, Figures 11.32 and 11.33, must be removed by removing the retaining bolt(s).

Under the clamp on 4-cylinder engines will be found a plate, Figure 11.38, which has a tube projecting from it. The tube goes into the distributor drive shaft hole and prevents the gear and its attached drive dog from riding upward. With the distributor clamp removed, the plate assembly

Figure 11.38. Below the distributor clamp is a plate and tube that retain the drive gear shaft.

Figure 11.39. The distributor drive gear can be lifted and re-aligned using a bolt as a tool.

can be seen to be retained by a single countersunk screw. Remove the screw and withdraw the plate. On 6-cylinder engine, removal of the distributor clamp reveals an extension tube, retained by two more bolts. Remove this part too.

The drive dog can be rotated to the correct position by lifting it, turning the unmeshed gear and replacing it in a new mesh position. A tool is required to reach the deeply set gear and that for the 4-cylinder cars is simply a 5/16in UNF × 3in or longer bolt which screws into a hole in the centre of the gear. Only a couple of hand tight turns are required and so a 5/16in UNC or an M8 × 1.25 × 75mm or longer will work fine too. For the MGC, a 7/16in bolt is ideal, but again, equivalent UNC or metric sizes will suffice.

Figure 11.39 shows the bolt inserted into the drive and with drive dog in the correct position for a 4-cylinder car, that is with the larger of the two segments upward and the slot at about the 2:40 position on the clock. If it is not correct, check again that piston #1 is at TDC and then lift the gear to unmesh it by turning the temporary bolt clockwise and lifting slightly at the same time. Note that because of the helical gear, the drive will have to be positioned at about one hour of the clock forward from the final position, so if it re-enters at 3:45 it will fall back to 2:40 on the clock as the gear meshes.

Note that the distributor drive position is 180° different on the MGC, the larger segment being set away from the engine block. When reinstalling the distributor on either the MGB or C engines, as distributor is inserted into the engine, turn the rotor arm shaft until the drive dog is felt to locate in its mate.

There are two important difference on the V8 engine that make the distributor orientation process very different. First, the distributor is driven from a helical gear already attached to it. Secondly, the drive dog is symmetrical and drives the oil pump. To install the distributor:
1. Set the crankshaft to the 6° BTDC mark (see Figure 11.48).
2. Take the distributor, with the cap removed and the rotor arm pointing toward the notch in the body shown in Figure 11.24.
3. Point the notch and rotor arm toward the left side of the car and observe the position of the distributor's drive dog at this point. The distributor will enter the timing cover in this position so the oil pump's drive slot must be turned with a long screwdriver to be about 30° further clockwise than the dog on the end of the distributor shaft. This is because the distributor shaft will turn clockwise by this amount as the helical gears mesh.
4. Satisfy yourself that the distributor

Figure 11.41. Connections for a 4-cylinder top entry distributor cap.

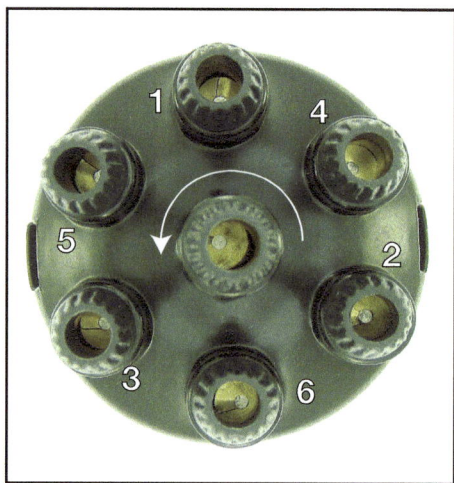

Figure 11.42. Connections for an MGC 25D6 distributor cap.

has seated properly. If it has not, then the oil pump drive dog has probably not engaged in the oil pump. This is best remedied by rotating the crankshaft until the distributor drops fully down.

Firing order

The cylinders are numbered as per Figure 11.44. The firing orders are:
4-cyl   1 – 3 – 4 – 2.
6-cyl   1 – 5 – 3 – 6 – 2 – 4.
8-cyl   1 – 8 – 4 – 3 – 6 – 5 – 7 – 2.

The 4 and 6 cylinder car distributors rotor rotates anti-clockwise and that for the 8-cylinder engines rotates clockwise. Note how the number orders in Figures 11.40 through 11.43 reflect the firing order for the each type.

IGNITION TIMING

When MGBs and Cs came off the production line decades ago they were clones of one another and the ignition timing was set to a value determined to be optimum by the manufacturer for the average conditions of use. Today, both the cars and the fuel they burn have changed. Each car has experienced different amounts and patterns of wear, some have been rebored and/or had the cylinder head skimmed. Moreover, the high-octane lead laden fuels are no longer available. It may also be the case that the average conditions for which the ignition timing was determined do not pertain to a particular car's environment; for example, it may primarily be used at high altitude or perhaps in very hot conditions. For these reasons, it is suggested that the textbook timing should be regarded only as a starting point and you should afterward determine the optimum setting for your vehicle, its environment and the available premium fuel.

Before attempting to time the

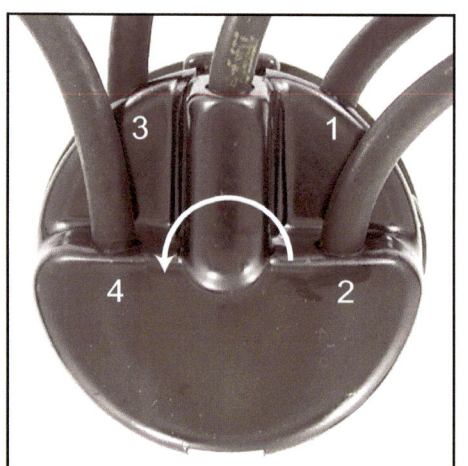

Figure 11.40. Connections for a 4-cylinder side entry distributor cap.

Figure 11.43. Connections for an MGB-GT V8 35D8 distributor cap.

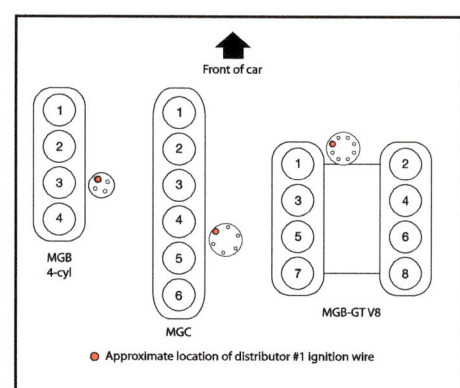

Figure 11.44. Cylinder numbering.

IGNITION SYSTEM

ignition, make sure that the advance mechanisms in the distributor are working as described on page 99 or by using a timing light (see page 108).

Approximate timing

If just getting an engine going is required, all that is often needed is approximate timing. There are four general requirements.
1. If the 25D or 45D distributors have been disassembled, then the drive dog and rotor arm key-way must be correctly aligned relative to one another. See Figure 11.31
2. If the engine has been dismantled then the distributor drive gear should have been correctly oriented. See page 105.
3. The wires exiting the distributor cap must go to the correct sparkplugs. See Figures 11.40 through 11.43
4. The distributor should be positioned as shown by the red dot in Figure 11.44.

Static timing

Most 4-cylinder MGBs will run well, without risk of damaging knock or pinking (pinging), if statically time to 10° BTDC. For the MGC and MGB-GT V8, a good static timing point is 8° BTDC.

Using the Figures 11.45 to 11.48, locate the timing marks on the front cover and crankshaft pulley, and highlight them using bright paint. It will be required that the engine be precisely turned; see the methods suggested in setting the points gap on page 104.
1. Connect a circuit tester (see page 11) between earth and the white/black wire either at the coil or at the distributor, whichever is easiest.
2. For safety reasons and to relieve engine compression, remove the sparkplugs, which makes turning the engine much easier.
3. Remove the distributor cap.
4. Using the chosen method, turn the engine clockwise (looking from the front) until the timing marks align for the required degrees of static timing.
5. Switch the ignition on. Try to minimise the time you keep the ignition powered because the coil and contact-breaker can overheat. The circuit tester light should not be illuminated. If it is, move the engine back (anti-clockwise) until it extinguishes.
6. Whenever, in this process, it is necessary to turn the engine backward, use finger pressure to push the rotor arm of the distributor clockwise (anti-clockwise for the V8). This simulates it being dragged or trailing as it is rotated by the engine.
7. Nudge the car forward until either the circuit tester lights or the required timing mark and pointer align. Some estimation will be required where there is no exact timing mark for the required number of degrees of ignition advance.
8. In the event that you go past the mark, back up some so that when you come forward again, any backlash in the system is taken up.
9. If the light illuminates before the mark corresponds to the selected number of degrees of advance, then the engine is too advanced and requires retarding.
10. If the light has not illuminated by the time the mark has reached the correct point, then the engine is retarded and requires advancing.
11. Change the ignition timing by slackening the distributor clamp and, with the timing groove on the crankshaft pulley in-line with the chosen mark, rotate the distributor clockwise to advance the timing or anti-clockwise to retard it (vice versa for the V8). At the same time, put gentle clockwise (anti-clockwise for the V8) pressure on the rotor arm (to take up slack) and watch the timing light. When the light status changes stop turning the distributor and re-tighten its clamp.

In the case of the 25D distributor, small changes in timing can be made by rotating the vernier anti-clockwise to advance and clockwise to retard the engine. It takes about 18 clicks of the vernier to adjust the timing just 1°. Counting clicks is tedious; instead you can mark the vernier wheel with typist's correction ink or paint and work in full turns. There are 35 clicks per turn, which equates to 2°. With about 6.75 turns available the vernier can adjust the timing a little under ± 6.5° from its centre point. Whereas the distributor is turned clockwise to advance ignition timing, rotating the vernier in that

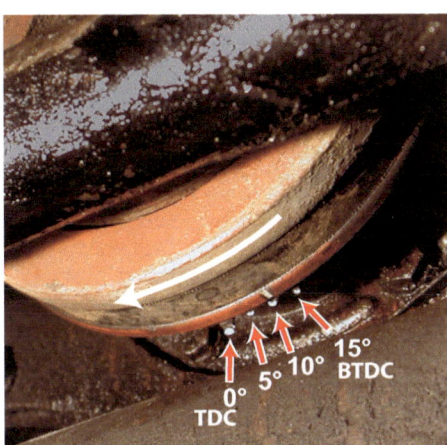

Figure 11.45. Timing marks for chrome bumper 4-cylinder MGBs are inconveniently situated under the car.

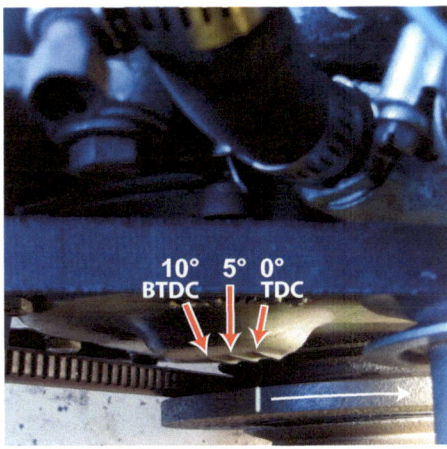

Figure 11.47. The MGC timing marks are located on the upper right side of the front cover.

Figure 11.46. Rubber bumper MGBs have timing marks that can be easily viewed from the top.

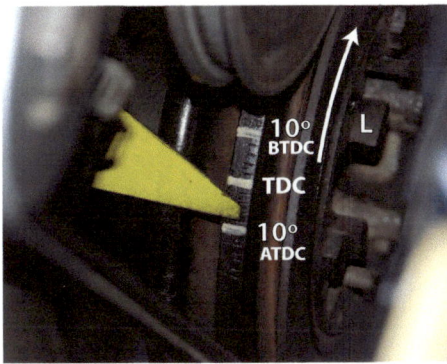

Figure 11.48. MGB-GT V8s timing marks are on the top left of the pulley, but here the pointer is static and the scale rotates.

direction retards the timing. This can be confusing but the distributor body, close to the vernier wheel, carries helpful arrows with the markings A & R for advance and retard.

Dynamic timing

It can be argued that static timing is unrealistic since the ignition isn't actually working unless the engine is turning. Dynamic timing, on the other hand, looks at the ignition operation of the working engine and can be used to verify the proper operation of the centrifugal and vacuum advance systems.

This method of ignition timing requires the use of a timing light. Figure 11.49 illustrates one type that is somewhat more sophisticated than most. Timing lights are usually pistol shaped and have a clamp with a sliding opening, shown at the bottom-left of the illustration, which is usually put around #1 cylinder sparkplug wire. The timing light illustrated has a lot of extra features, the most useful of which are a measure of rpm and a set-back control that allows the actual degrees of advance before top dead centre (°BTDC) to be read directly from the dial.

A timing light is not unlike a camera flashgun that is triggered by the electrical pulse going to a sparkplug. By shining it on a mark on the rotating crankshaft pulley, it is possible to make it appear stationary, the light only illuminating it every time the sparkplug fires on the particular cylinder to which the timing light clamp is attached.

Besides the clamp shown in Figure 11.49, which is slipped over #1 plug lead, most timing lights will require a power supply and so have red and black coloured alligator connectors that have to be attached to a vehicle power source and earth according to the battery polarity of the car under test. The fuse block is a convenient point for the power cable, see page 42, while any bare metal component to which the other clip can attach will suffice as an earth connection.

Dynamic timing requires that the engine be running, so please review the safety rules discussed in chapter 1. Be careful using a timing light, particularly on those cars where the marks are underneath, because it is very easy to let the cables dangle too close to the alternator, fan and its belt.

Once the car is started the timing light will flash synchronously with the firing of the #1 sparkplug. The light is then shone on the timing marks illustrated in Figures 11.45 to 11.48. So long as the ambient lighting is not too bright, the mark on the pulley should appear stationary.

If the centrifugal advance is working correctly, as the engine speed is increased the mark on the pulley will appear to slide anti-clockwise as the spark advances and the light flashes a little earlier. Removing and attaching the vacuum advance hose with the engine revving should cause the mark to move noticeably, thus verifying that this system is working too. Should the pulley mark not appear stationary and instead jitter, wear in the distributor is usually the cause. Distributors are expensive so if you decide that the problem is so bad that a transplant is necessary, check first that the key that locks the inexpensive rotor arm, Figures 11.20 and 11.31, to the distributor shaft is in good condition.

Figure 11.50 is a graph showing the published advance characteristics for a number of Lucas distributor part numbers. Note that these are centrifugal advance values only and the static timing must be added to arrive at the total advance with the vacuum hose removed. The number can be found stamped on the side of the distributor. Although the amount of advance MG selected over the years changed frequently and seems fairly arbitrary, it is an useful exercise to use a timing light to compare a distributor's advance characteristic with its original specification.

To do so, remove the vacuum hose from the distributor and either adjust the idle screw (only one need be adjusted on ganged dual carburettor cars) or have an assistant operate the accelerator pedal to raise the engine speed to 1000, 2000, 3000 and if you can stand the noise 4000rpm. At the same time, note where the pulley mark is against the scale on the engine block.

It's very likely that a distributor that is well used will have weak centrifugal advance springs (Figure 11.25) and the resulting advance will be much greater than indicated in the graph. New springs are, unfortunately, hard to obtain.

If you decide to adjust the timing at one point, then the following BTDC values are suggested with vacuum advance disconnected:

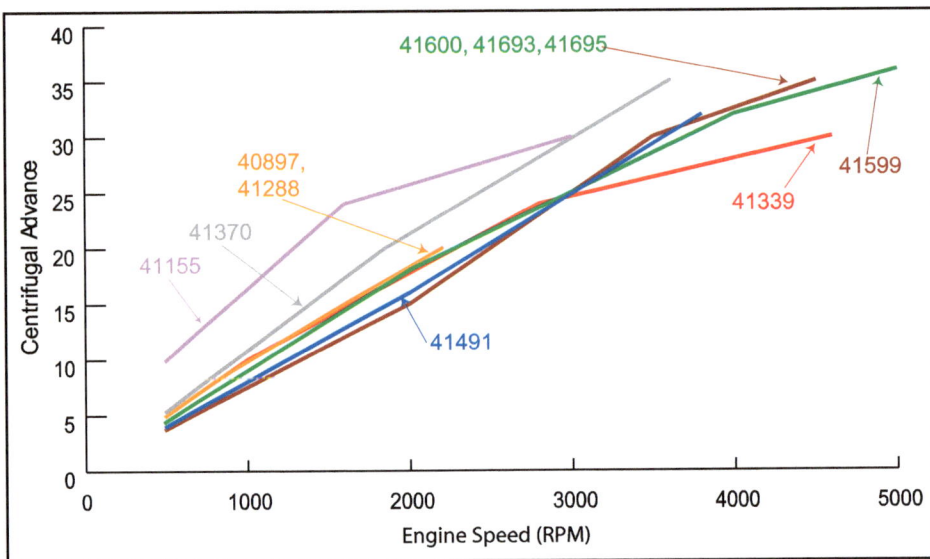

Figure 11.50. A graphical representation of Lucas distributor centrifugal advance characteristics for a series of part numbers.

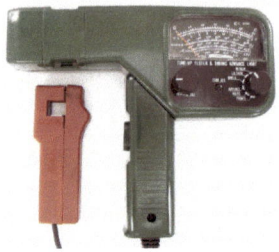

Figure 11.49. A timing light and pick-up clamp. This model has extra features including a meter that can measure engine speed, contact-breaker resistance, dwell angle, degrees of advance and voltage.

IGNITION SYSTEM

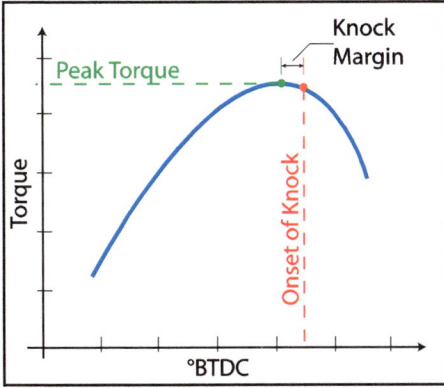

Figure 11.51. As the ignition is advanced so the available engine torque increases. However, at the onset of knock, torque decreases sharply.

- 4-cyl cars   30° @ 4000 rpm
- 6-cyl cars   20° @ 1000 rpm
- 8-cyl cars   28° @ 2000 rpm

Optimizing the timing

Different fuel types and mixtures have a different burning rates and so require a different ignition setting to ensure maximum combustion pressure is reached at about 10° after TDC. There is no point in trying to find the optimum timing for the car unless the carburettors have been properly tuned beforehand and the same octane rating fuel is always used. Note that MG recommend 98 octane for high compression engines and 93 octane for the low compression engines both measured by the RON system. This equates to 93 and 88 octane respectively when measured by the North American (RON + MON)/2 method.

Figure 11.51 shows how engine torque varies as the ignition timing changes in degrees before top dead centre (°BTDC). Note that as the ignition timing is advanced, the engine torque increases until a point is reached when the spark occurs too early and the onset of 'knock' is heard. Knock and pinking or pinging are technically different phenomena but for most purposes they can be considered the same thing. Once knock occurs, torque – and brake-horsepower with it – reduce substantially and piston damage may occur. The so-called knock margin is very small on high compression engines and so the peak torque point can usually be established by finding the timing setting that produces knock and then retarding the ignition timing just enough to eliminate it.

To find the optimum timing for a particular car, with a tank full of premium fuel, drive the car uphill and try to accelerate without changing down a gear. Do you hear pinking (pinging) (a tinkling or rattling sound) that disappears when you decelerate or shift down?

- If so, try retarding the engine until the noise no longer occurs. If it is evident that retarding the engine is futile, the pinging persisting but the engine losing power, then you need to use an octane booster, your local premium fuel not having sufficient anti-knock qualities. Remember that pinging is extremely harmful and every effort should be taken to avoid it.
- If there is no pinging, gradually advance the ignition timing until it can just be perceived, then back it off until the effect disappears.

This method of timing, although not textbook, results in the best timing for your car and with your fuel, without damaging knock or ping.

ANTI RUN-ON VALVE

Figure 11.52. When energised, the anti-run-on valve joins a pipe from the inlet manifold to another that goes to the carburettor float chamber.

Figure 11.53. An oil pressure switch is situated in series with the anti-run-on valve.

Late model MGBs, particularly those destined for North America, were loaded with anti emissions equipment and required to operate on low octane unleaded fuel. Run-on, sometimes called dieseling, the phenomenon by which the engine continues to run after ignition switch off, became a normal part of the car's operation but was nevertheless a nuisance. To eliminate it, an anti run-on valve was fitted.

The circuit diagram in Figure 11.9 shows the valve (196) and its associated components: an oil pressure switch (197), an in-line fuse (67d) and a modified ignition switch (38). In operation, upon switch off, the ignition switch supplies power, via the in-line fuse, to the anti run-on valve, Figure 11.52, and to earth via the oil pressure switch, Figure 11.53, which, with oil pressure present, is closed. The anti run-on valve is thus energized and opens. In doing so it joins a vacuum pipe from the manifold via the absorption canister to the float chamber of the single carburettor. With the throttle butterfly valve closed, the depression in the float chamber is very much higher than that trying to draw fuel into the carburettor. The engine becomes starved of fuel and so stops. Once the engine stops turning, oil pressure drops and the oil pressure switch opens, breaking the circuit energizing the anti run-on valve. Without the oil pressure switch, the anti run-on valve would continue operating with the ignition off, resulting in a constant current drain that would run the battery down.

SPARKPLUGS

Sparkplugs have to work in one of the most severe environments imaginable. In a four stroke cycle the pressure and temperature may vary between 13psi at 150°F (0.9 bar at 65°C) at the bottom of the induction stroke to 660psi at 5400°F (45 bar at 3000°C) at the peak of the power stroke, and all this is repeated in a high vibration, corrosive environment 25 times every second at 3000rpm.

While the sparkplug manufacturer takes care of the complex chemistry and manufacturing of the insulator and electrodes, the user has a choice in terms of heat range, electrode type and gapping.

Heat range

The temperature at which a sparkplug runs is a function of several factors including:

MGB ELECTRICAL SYSTEMS – THE ESSENTIAL MANUAL

- Thread length. Don't use either longer or shorter than that of the standard ¾in (19mm) specified for the 4-cylinder MGB and the MGC or ½in (13mm) for the MGB-GT V8.
- Thread diameter. That for the MGB/C sparkplugs is 14mm, with hex across flats ¹³⁄₁₆in (21mm).
- Electrode projection
- Electrode material
- Insulator length. This is the primary method of changing the thermal characteristics of the plug.

Referring to Figure 11.54, the cold plug on the left has an insulator that has a short distance, or heat path (L1), from its tip to the point where it contacts the metal body. In contrast, that on the right, a hot type plug, has a relatively long heat path (L2) from tip to body. Most sparkplug manufacturers use a number code to indicate heat range. While all use increasing numbers to represent higher heat ranges, they do not use the same scale. For example, the heat range recommendation for an MGB/C sparkplug from AC Delco is 2, NGK and Autolite are 6, Bosch is 7, Champion is 9 and Denso is 20. Changes to the engine such as super-charging or higher compression will increase combustion chamber temperature and may require a cooler running – lower heat range – plug. Similarly, leaner fuel mixtures will require cooler plugs and richer mixtures a higher heat range.

Certain running conditions, such as the length of the average journey, average sustained speed, altitude of operation, available fuel, ambient temperature, amount of engine wear, air/fuel mixture, or compression ratio may make a change to the recommended plug temperature appropriate. Check your plugs by removing them and inspecting each insulator around the centre electrode; they should appear light brown. Before changing plug type, ensure that the fuel mixture is properly set. As a stopgap measure, a higher temperature plug can ameliorate some of the ignition problems arising from an oil-burning engine.

Too low a plug temperature can result in a plug fouling, evident when sticky black material is deposited on the internal insulator rather than being burned off.

Too high a plug temperature, indicated by light grey or white deposits on the internal insulator, results in pre-ignition and sparkplug insulator failure, with potentially dangerous consequences to the engine should the ceramic material fall into the cylinder bore.

- A 'hot' high power engine requires a 'cold' plug.
- A low power engine requires a hot plug.

So important can plug temperature be that some vehicles have different plug types in different cylinders.

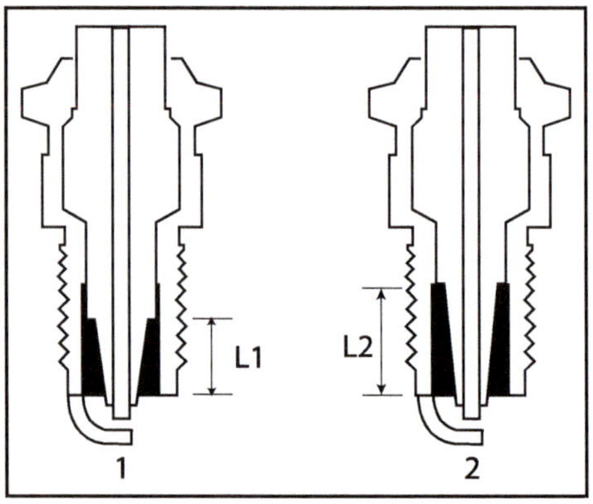

Standard plugs

The sparkplug in your lawn mower probably looks much like that on the left in Figure 11.55. The electrode projects only about ¹⁄₁₆in (1.5mm) into the combustion chamber. The plug is often used in small engines where the plug is centrally mounted over the piston and so cannot project too far for fear of a piston collision.

Figure 11.54. The major contributing factor to how a sparkplug removes heat from its tip is the distance between the tip and where the insulator contacts the metal body.

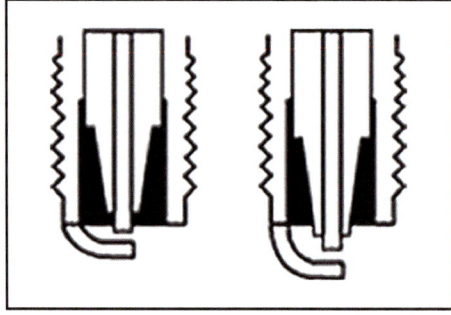

Figure 11.55. The low projection plug on the left is often used in low performance engines such as garden equipment. The projected nose plug on the right is the type used in MGB and C engines. It projects into the cylinder so that it can better ignite the fuel/air mixture.

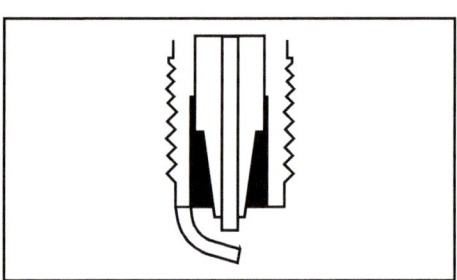

Figure 11.56. Some sparkplug designs are hard to wide-gap, the earth electrode becoming non-parallel. The spark will occur at the closest point, which may not be that which is most conducive to the best chance of fuel ignition. Electrode erosion will occur much faster at the smallest gap point.

Projected nose plugs

MGBs and Cs use a projected nose plug, like that on the right in Figure 11.55. It is sometimes called a Y type because of its identifying letter in the Champion sparkplug part numbering system. This projects about ⅛in (3mm) into the combustion chamber. The tip is thus closer to the centre of the fuel/air mixture, aiding the speed of combustion and making the engine more tolerant to mixture variation. It is also more easily cooled by the incoming fuel.

Plug gap

The standard gap for plugs used in MGB/Cs is 0.025in (0.6mm).

Electronic ignition permits the gap to be increased to between 0.030in (0.75mm) and 0.040in (1mm). Unfortunately, most plugs do not 'over-gap' well, the earth terminal becoming non-parallel, as shown in Figure 11.56. Only a single point is correctly gapped, resulting in premature erosion there. Don't over gap plugs by more than 5 thou (mils) (0.12mm). There are special plugs that are designed to be gapped wider than standard, see Table 11.3.

Given a certain amount of energy, an ignition system can produce a high voltage spark for a certain amount of time or a lower voltage one for a longer period. There are trade-offs and benefits to both high voltage and long spark duration. If you have higher than standard energy available, see coil selection page 96, then by all means widen the plug gap if you can do so at the same time as maintaining reasonable plug electrode geometry. It should be remembered that if the gap is widened, then the electrical

IGNITION SYSTEM

stress on all the high-tension side of the ignition system is increased and any deficiencies will quickly exhibit themselves. It is particularly important to keep the MGB/C plug leads away from pipes and cables because the increased voltage could punch through aged and heat hardened cable insulation.

Widening the plug gap can often smooth an uneven idle. However, since the coil has to produce a higher voltage to jump a wider gap, and voltage declines with engine speed, the penalty can be misfiring at high engine revolutions. Electronic ignition allows over-gapping without penalizing high-speed performance.

Recommended plugs

Table 11.3 lists some common sparkplugs that may be used in MGBs and MGCs. Many other part numbers are also suitable, most having additional features. These may include an internal radio suppression resistor, long life electrode metals or multiple electrodes.

SPARK POLARITY

Although, as far as the low-tension (12V) system is concerned, the vehicle polarity is usually negative earth, the coil is connected so that the earth is positive relative to its high voltage output. This is important because electrons, which are negative, leave hot surfaces, like the plug's centre electrode, more readily because they are already 'boiling' close to the surface.

IGNITION WIRES

High-voltage wire deterioration is a frequent cause of problems with the ignition system. The inner cores are often made from a carbon-plastic construction to increase resistance and so reduce radio frequency interference (RFI). Operation in the high under-bonnet temperature and vibration can eventually cause cracks to occur in the conductor that propagate because of flexing and because of erosion from the sparks that jump across them. The outer insulation can also become worn from rubbing against other objects or brittle with age, making it less effective at doing its job of containing the high voltage inside the wire and keeping moisture out. To avoid these problems it is worthwhile changing the ignition wires every 5 to 10 years irrespective of the amount of usage the car has undergone. The method of terminating ignition wires is dependant on the component to which they attach. The early distributor cap shown in Figure 11.42, and ignition coils with similar screw-in connections are intended for use with a stranded wire that is stripped, passed through the screw-in ferrule and the strands spread across the face of a copper washer, as illustrated in Figure 11.57.

The terminating method for the side entry cap shown in Figure 10.31 is illustrated in Figure 11.58. The wires are cut to length with the ends as square as possible. They inserted into the blind holes on the outside of the cap and pushed in all the way until they butt the end of the cavity. A special piercing screw, provided with the cap, is then screwed into each of the holes (arrowed) so that it makes an electrical connection to the wire core and mechanically restrains it.

Both this type of cap and the screw-in connection type will benefit from some dielectric grease being applied so that it fills the gap between the ignition wire and the cap or screw-in ferrule. The grease has better insulating properties than humid air and will block any actual water entry.

Sparkplug cap connections for the stranded wires used with the screw-in distributors and coils were usually made by literally screwing the cap onto the wire, the cap containing something not unlike a woodscrew to do the job. This type of plug cap does not work well with solid metal or carbon cored wires.

Both the previously described methods of terminating ignition wires has been superseded by the use of a copper plug-in connector that can be straight or right-angled and that pushes into the cavities of the coil and distributor or over the top of the sparkplug. Figure 11.59 shows how the core is folded back over the (red) wire and crimped (blue wire). Note that the red wire has a carbon core and the blue one a solid metal core. Before crimping, the wire is turned so that the folded core is to the closed face of the crimp.

When buying new wires it is easy to be seduced by exaggerated claims of high performance due to the use of space-age polymers and alloys as well as special construction methods such as high tensile strength cores spirally wound with special metallic conductors to deliver full power to the plugs with low RFI. While there is some merit in some of these claims, the differences that will be noticed in the performance of a vehicle, are negligible.

Most of the special wires are delivered in a kit and the user has to cut them to length, terminate them and stretch rubber boots over the ends. Without special tools and skills, this is no easy task; without them it is recommended that only pre-made sets of wires be used. If you can also get the following features in order of priority, and you have the budget, then by all means do so:
1. Silicone rubber insulation for superior high temperature and fluid resistance performance.
2. 8mm rather than 7mm diameter wire for higher voltage capability. Don't use a wire any wider than 8mm,

MGB and MGC Sparkplugs	
Brand	Part #
AC Delco	42XLS
Autolite	AP63
Bosch	W7DC
Champion	N9YC
Denso	W20EP-U
Motorcraft	AGS22C
NGK	BP6ES
MGB-GT V8 Sparkplugs	
Brand	Part #
AC Delco	R43FS
Autolite	275
Bosch	W6BC
Champion	L92YC
Denso	W16FP-U
NGK	BP5HS

Table 11.3. Recommended sparkplugs.

Figure 11.57. Terminating a screw-in distributor or coil connector.

MGB ELECTRICAL SYSTEMS – THE ESSENTIAL MANUAL

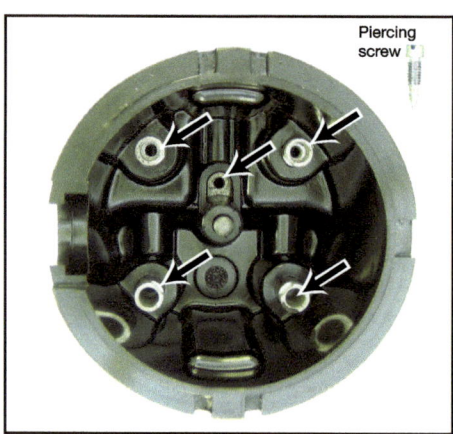

Figure 11.58. A side-entry distributor cap terminated with a special piercing screw.

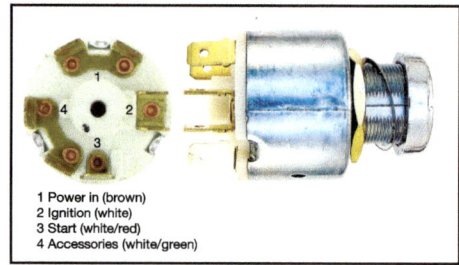

Figure 11.60. Dash mounted ignition switch.

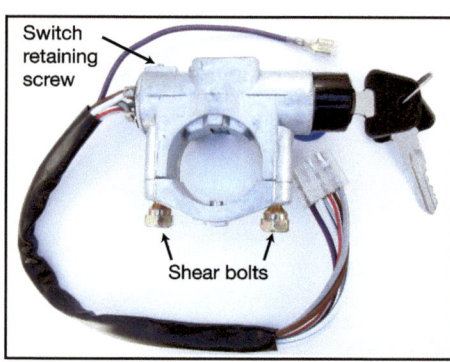

Figure 11.61. Steering lock with integral ignition switch.

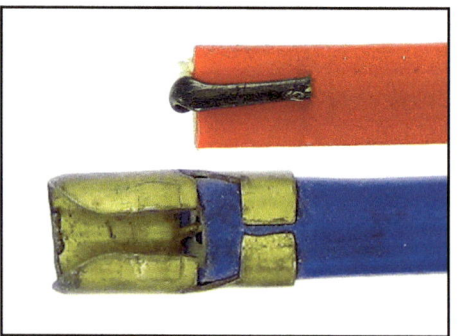

Figure 11.59. Ignition wire connection.

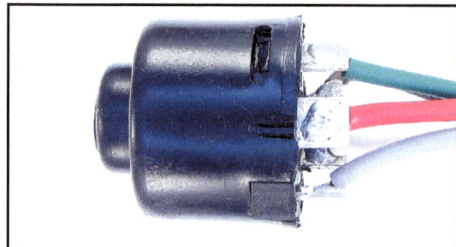

Figure 11.62. The electrical switch that installs in the steering lock.

unless you are sure it will fit into the top of the coil and distributor cap.
3. Spirally wound conductor of any alloy to provide a more robust core and better RFI suppression.
4. Kevlar or fibreglass core over which the conductor is wound providing very high tensile strength.

IGNITION SWITCH
There were many different ignition switches used on MGB and MGCs. They differed mechanically because of their location in the cockpit and electrically because they performed different functions over the years of manufacture and for the territories to which the cars were shipped.

Dash mounted switches
From 1962 to 1967, the ignition switch was mounted on the dash. The earliest versions had only 3 positions: off, ignition and start. However, some of the last of those fitted had an accessory position between off and ignition so that the heater fan, wipers and a radio, if installed, could be operated without the ignition system being powered.

The lock mechanism can usually be removed from the switch body by depressing a sprung peg, which is accessed via a hole in the side of the switch, while at the same time gently pulling the lock barrel out with the key.

Column mounted ignition switch
The column mounted ignition switch was introduced on the MGC in 1967 and MGB in 1968. Originally, there was no steering locking mechanism and the ignition switch was essentially the same as that in Figure 11.60.

After 1970, the steering lock, Figure 11.61 was introduced. Again, there were many different types, mostly varying in the number of electrical functions performed and/or the electrical connectors used for joining to the vehicle harnesses. All had accessory, ignition and start positions but some North American cars had a running-on preventer in the 'off' position (see page 109) and most had some key-in detector that sounded a buzzer or worked with the sequential seat belt system (see page 183).

Sadly many steering locks have been drilled and ground off, (the security fixing bolt heads having been sheered off during installation) because it wasn't realized that the electrical part of the switch (Figure 11.62) can be withdrawn simply by removing its retaining screw.

IGNITION SYSTEM

IGNITION SYSTEM FAULT-FINDING

Some ignition faults are very difficult to differentiate from those associated with fuel mixture and starvation. If the ignition system is suspect, first check for a spark as described on page 23 and ensure that the timing is at least approximately correct, as discussed on page 106.

Symptom	Possible causes	Action
No spark. Also consult section below. Many 'no spark' faults have the same root causes as 'misfiring or uneven running'.	No power to coil.	Check for power at coil + or SW terminal. Check power feed wire/ballast resistor.
	Contact-breaker not working.	Check that power cycles on and off at coil '–' or SW terminal as the engine is cranked.
	Coil failure.	Change coil.
	Rotor arm key sheared.	Replace rotor arm.
Misfiring or uneven running.	Fouled or inoperative plug or plugs.	Inspect or change sparkplugs.
	Tracking in distributor cap or rotor arm.	Inspect cap and rotor arm for moisture, tracking marks or cracking. Substitute if suspect.
	Insulation of wires in distributor worn and touching metal casing.	Check wires from capacitor and power input (see Figure 11.18).
	Firing order incorrect.	See page 106.
	Timing incorrect.	See page 106.
	Rotor arm key worn.	Change rotor arm.
	Spark tracking from ignition wires or coil tower.	Crank or run engine in dark when sparks can often be seen. Listen for ticking noise made as sparks are produced. Inspect wires and coil for cracks and tracking traces and change if suspected.
	Capacitor failure or radio suppression capacitor incorrectly fitted.	See page 88.
	Distributor drive gear worn.	Change distributor.
	Faulty electronic tachometer.	Try running car with tachometer out of circuit. Repair or change if necessary.
Running-on.	Low octane fuel.	Use premium fuel or add an octane booster.
	Running-on valve circuit (where fitted) inoperative.	See page 109.
	Plug temperature type too low.	See page 110.
	Ignition timing retarded.	See page 106.
	Engine requires decarbonizing	Remove the cylinder head and clean the combustion chambers.
	Ignition relay or alternator changed from standard.	Use a standard relay or install a blocking diode as per page 94.

MGB ELECTRICAL SYSTEMS – THE ESSENTIAL MANUAL

Symptom	Possible causes	Action
Engine stops when hot.	Coil or fuel pump failure.	Change coil or service fuel pump. See page 169.
Misfiring at high engine speed.	Dwell angle too low.	See page 102.
	Spark gap too wide.	See page 110.
	Rotor arm blade eroded.	Change rotor arm.
Points erode quickly.	Bad capacitor.	Change capacitor.
	Low resistance coil used without a ballast resistor.	Install ballast resistor or use a higher resistance coil. See page 96.
Poor fuel economy at cruising speeds.	Vacuum advance inoperative.	See page 101.
Low engine power.	Timing retarded.	See page 106.
	Centrifugal advance inoperative.	See page 99.
Engine fires only when starter is running.	Ballast resistor or ballast wire failure.	Replace with new resistor. See page 96.
Pinking (pinging).	Low octane fuel.	Use premium fuel or add an octane booster.
	Ignition timing too advanced.	Reset ignition timing. See page 106.
	Centrifugal advance springs weak or broken.	Replace springs.
Uneven idle.	Plug gaps too small.	Increase gaps. Verify engine does not then misfire at high engine speed.

Table 11.4. Ignition system fault-finding chart.

Chapter 12
Lighting

FILAMENT LAMPS

Automotive lamps are simply very thin tungsten wires, called filaments, enclosed in a glass envelope containing a gas. When current is forced through them by the pressure of the applied voltage, they heat up to white-hot temperatures. At these temperatures, even tungsten would burn quite quickly if oxygen were present, so an early development in lamps was to put the filament in a partial vacuum, enclosed by a glass bulb. Unfortunately, just as water boils at a lower temperature in the low pressure at high altitudes, in a near vacuum a tungsten filament will vaporize at the comparatively low temperature of about 3600°F (2000°C). A quickly vaporizing filament deposits its condensate on the glass bulb, blackening it quickly as the filament rapidly depletes toward failure.

The first attempts to increase the pressure by adding an inert gas, such as nitrogen or argon, failed because the gas moved over the filament by means of convection, cooling it very efficiently. However, the American Irving Langmuir (1892-1957) discovered that if the filament is tightly coiled, gas doesn't pass between the coils and cool it, so the filament can reach temperatures in the order of 4500°F (2500°C). Some of the filament still boils off, but most of it collides with gas molecules before it hits the glass, reducing blackening.

The benefits of the inert gas soon diminishes if attempts are made to run the filament even hotter, as will happen if bulbs are subjected to higher than design voltage. Conversely, lamps will last much longer than normal if operated at lower than design voltage. For this reason, daytime running lights, safety headlamps that switch on with the ignition, have a voltage reducing circuit in series with them to increase lamp life. Full voltage is still used for operation at night.

If the inert gas is replaced with one which is highly reactive, such as one of the halogens, iodine being most frequently used, the filament vapour reacts with the gas before it gets to the bulb glass, some of it re-depositing itself back on the filament. This results in a bulb capable of being run hotter, and so brighter and whiter, without shortening its life. The regeneration of the filament only happens when the bulbs are running at very high temperatures, so to keep the temperature high, the glass envelope is usually smaller than on standard bulbs. Indeed, the quartz glass becomes so hot that the oils from any finger marks can burn into the surface and cause obscuration.

Filament lamps are also referred to as tungsten or incandescent lamps.

Figure 12.1. The dash bulb on the right still works, but evaporation of the filament has gradually reduced its brightness.

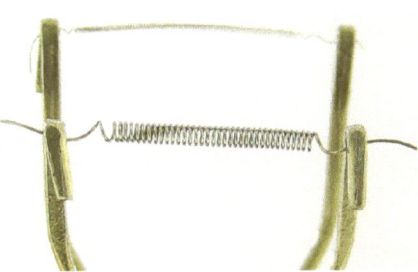

Figure 12.2. Coiling the lamp filament reduces the cooling effect of gas convection.

115

Voltage effect on brightness

Voltage changes have a very marked effect on the brightness of filament lamps.

Figure 12.3 graphs the relative brightness of a lamp with changes in voltage. In this graph the brightness factor is normalised to 1 at 13.5V, the design voltage for an automotive light bulb and the approximate voltage in a running vehicle. For those interested in calculating the changes for themselves, the graph follows the formula:

Brightness factor = $(V/13.5)^4$

Some testing was performed on a left hand drive MGB, which has rather longer wire runs than on the right hand drive version, to find the voltage drop and calculated relative brightness factors for some lighting functions. In each case the measurement was made at the left hand lamp, and in the case of the turn signal the rear of the two. The results are tabulated in Table 12.1. The voltage drops were shown to be shared among all the wires, switches and connectors in the wiring circuit with no particular item contributing much more significantly than any other. It is quite alarming that both the turn signal and brake (stop) lamps work at less than half the lamps' design brightness.

In each of the sections concerning headlamps, brake and turn signals, some suggestions are made for improving the lamp brightness.

Brightness perception

The term 'brightness' as used here refers to the measured light output that would be recorded by a light meter calibrated in candela or candlepower. This roughly equates to perceived brightness, but viewing conditions, the fact that the eye is such a complex organ and that human perception is so varied and variable, mean that some care should be taken in interpreting the term.

When viewing turn signals and brake lamps the eye looks at the light source, whereas headlamps are used to reflect light from the road and objects ahead. If one were to shine a headlamp on a totally matt black non-reflective surface, then no matter how bright the headlamp is, no light would be reflected back and so increasing the lamp brightness would be totally ineffectual.

The eye receives light by two devices: rods that do not distinguish colour and have their peak sensitivity in the green region, and cones that can distinguish colour, operate at normal and high light levels and have their peak sensitivity in the yellow region. They thus differ from one another in absolute and relative spectral sensitivity with light wavelength. Using these along with the iris and a process called dark adaption in the brain, the eye can see an enormous range of illumination levels. After ten minutes in darkness, the eye becomes 10,000 times more sensitive, and a million times after 30 or 40 minutes. This is why it is so important to have good signal lights, bright sunlight making it very difficult for the eye to see a brake or turn lamp illuminate.

Although Figure 12.3 and Table 12.1 only reference brightness, lowering the voltage to a bulb also increases the wavelength of the light output toward the red band of 647 to 723 nano metres (nm). At this frequency, the eye is only about 1/10 as sensitive as it is to the green-yellow band at about 600nm. Even behind red or amber lamp lenses, these differences are somewhat apparent. Redder light may, however, be preferable for dash illumination; the retina's cones are sensitive to red and have a short recovery time after exposure to light. The eye's rods are not sensitive to red, and thus maintain their dark adaption for seeing ahead. It is for this reason that weapons control rooms in ships are illuminated with red light.

Voltage effect on lamp life

There is some benefit to be gained by running filament lamps at less than their design voltage because the operational life increases enormously. On the other hand, running a lamp at voltages greater than that for which it was designed will have the opposite effect, shortening its life dramatically. In fact, the life of a bulb changes by the 12th power of the voltage change: a whopping variation. Figure 12.4 graphs the relative life of a filament lamp with changes in voltage. As was done with the brightness graph, life factor is normalised to 1 at 13.5V. For the mathematicians, the graph follows the formula:

Life factor = $(V/13.5)^{-12}$

Page 123 describes how to fit daytime running lamps (DRLs) to an MGB/C. Because most drivers use their vehicles more often in daytime, using DRLs at full lamp brightness would increase the frequency of headlamp failure, so it is usual, and sometimes mandated by statute, to run them at lower than standard vehicle voltage. Canadian law, for example, requires

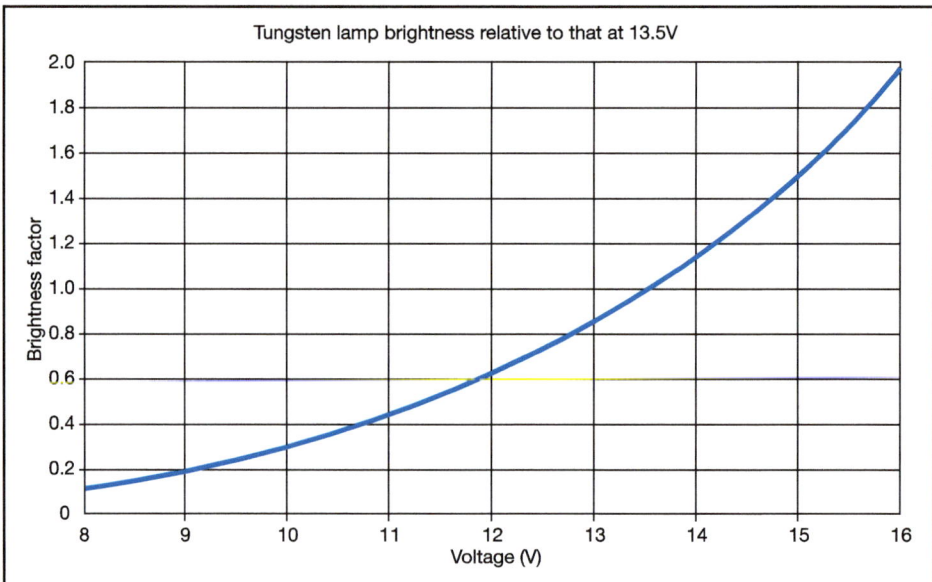

Figure 12.3. A graphical depiction of the relative brightness of an automotive filament lamp compared to that at 13.5V.

Function	V drop	Bf
Headlamp	1.53	62%
Turn Signals	2.22	49%
Brake	2.31	47%

Table 12.1. The measured voltage drop and calculated relative brightness factors (Bf) of some MGB lamps.

LIGHTING

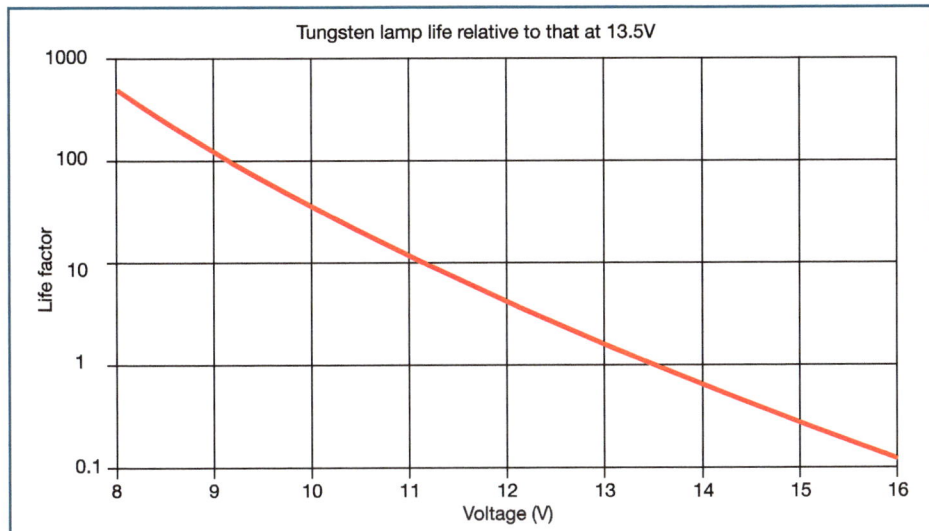

Figure 12.4. A graphical depiction of the relative life of an automotive filament lamp compared to that at 13.5V.

Figure 12.6. This LED replacement for a standard automotive lamp was found to produce adequate light directly in front of it, though the light output fell off significantly when viewed even slightly from the side.

Figure 12.7. To better emulate the wide light emittance angle from an incandescent lamp, this LED assembly emits from the periphery as well as the front.

that DRLs be operated at a maximum of 92% of vehicle system voltage, resulting in a brightness reduction to 72% but a lamp life increase to 271% of design life.

LIGHT EMITTING DIODES

At the time of writing, light emitting diode (LED) technology is progressing rapidly. LEDs are a form of diode and, as such, drop a given amount of voltage when passing current. Some form of series voltage dropping device must be used in order to ensure that an LED is not operated at a higher current than it should be. The voltage a given LED drops will be defined in its specification and labelled V_F for forward voltage. A red LED typically has a V_F of 2.5V while that for a green, blue or white device may be around 3.6V. Should you want to experiment with LEDs it is essential you find out the value of V_F for the device you are using. The voltage is most easily dropped with a resistor. If,

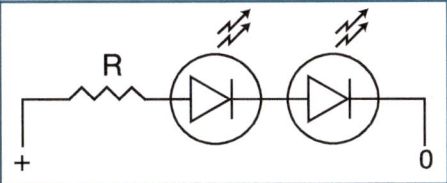

Figure 12.5. LEDs need a series voltage dropping device to limit the current that passes through them. This is usually a resistor but may also include additional LED(s) as shown, or a more complex constant current electronic circuit.

referring to Figure 12.5, we had two red LEDs each with an V_F of 2.5V, each had a maximum forward current (I_{Fmax}) of 0.025A (25mA) and we are to supply it with 14V maximum, the value of the resistor R can be easily calculated. With a supply voltage of 14V and the LEDs dropping 2.5V each, the resistor must drop the remaining 9V. If we wish to limit the LED current to 0.025A then the resistor value is:

$R = V \div I = 9 \div 0.025 = 360\Omega$

Running the LED at a higher current will increase its brightness but limit its life. When operated at the recommended I_F an LED should last indefinitely.

As a precaution, also calculate the power the resistor will dissipate. The power will be the voltage across it multiplied by the current flowing through it, in this case:

$9 \times 0.025 = 0.225W$

Resistors typically come in wattage ratings of 0.25W, 0.5W, 1W, 3W and greater, so in this case a 0.25W would be adequate.

The author's tests on LED lamps have shown those available offer no major benefit over incandescent lamps, but that situation may change as the technology improves. At present, LED lamp assemblies with adequate brightness, like that shown in Figure 12.6, have such a narrow emittance angle that their performance is not acceptable when viewed off axis. Where there is space, the use of multiple LEDs placed at different angles can help. The stop/tail lamp from

Classic and Vintage Bulbs of South Australia, Figure 12.7, is about as good as a standard 5W/21W stop tail lamp when viewed at any angle, and has very good contrast in brightness between running as a tail lamp and when the current is boosted to operate it in stop mode. Although this bulb assembly uses 13 LEDs, it consumes less than 25% of the current of a standard bulb. That can be an issue when substituting an LED turn signal lamp for a standard bulb. Many turn signal modules require a certain amount of current draw to operate, and that used by LED lamps is insufficient. An electronic flasher module can resolve this problem (see page 128), or a dummy load can be incorporated in the LED turn signal lamp.

Attempts to replace the inadequate instrument bulbs with LEDs have been wholly unsuccessful. Improving both brightness and the need to replace these hard to access bulbs would be very beneficial. Unfortunately, all MGB/C instrument lamps rely on a wide angle of emittance so that the light can bounce around the white inner walls of the gauge and produce an even glow across the dial face. The brightest LEDs

MGB ELECTRICAL SYSTEMS – THE ESSENTIAL MANUAL

that are small enough to pass through the hole in the back of the instruments and that have a diffused lens to improve emittance angle have proven to be insufficiently bright and too blue in colour to read the instruments well. Halogen instrument bulbs are still a better alternative.

LIGHTING CIRCUITS

There are many lighting variations that may be observed from model year to model year and from territory to territory. The number of permutations is too large to allow every circuit combination to be illustrated here. Between the two diagrams provided, it should be possible to understand all possible circuit combinations that might be found. The MGC wiring is as per 'early car' diagrams. The MGB-GT V8 is as per the 'late car' diagrams

Early car lighting circuit

Current flows from the batteries (3) via the anchor points of the starter solenoid (4) and control box (2) to the fuse block (19). From there a brown wire (N) goes to the lighting switch (6), which has three positions:
1. Off.
2. Park. Current goes to a red (R) wire that routes it to the parking lamps (11, 12, 16 & 17), number plate lamps (15) and side marker lamps (170, 171, 172, 173) where fitted. A red wire also feeds current to a dimming device called a rheostat or to a switch (see Figure 12.9 and 12.12) that in turns supplies panel lamps via red/white wires (RW).
3. Headlamps. Current goes to the same destinations as in park but also is directed on a blue (U) wire to the headlamps full (high) / dip (low) beam switch (7), located on the floor. Depending on the position of the dip switch current may also flow to the headlamps' (8 & 9) dip beam filaments on blue/red (UR) wires or the full beam filaments and indicator lamp (10) on blue/white (UW) wires.

In some vehicles the front park lamps may be a separate bulb fitted into the side of the headlamp reflector, may be a double filament lamp as per (11) or separate bulb from the turn signal as in (12).

Late car lighting circuit

Current flows from the battery (3) via the anchor point of the starter solenoid to the fuse block (19). From there a brown (N) wire goes to the lighting switch (6), which has three positions:
1. Off.
2. Park. Current goes to a red/green

Component Codes					
2	Dynamo control box	10	Full beam lamp	17	LH stop/tail
3	Battery	11	RH front park lamp	19	Fuse block
4	Starter solenoid	12	LH front park lamp	170	RH front side marker
6	Lighting switch	13	Panel lamp rheostat or switch	171	LH front side marker
7	Dip switch	14	Panel lamps	172	RH rear side marker
8	RH headlamp	15	Number plate lamps	173	LH rear side marker
9	LH headlamp	16	RH stop/tail		

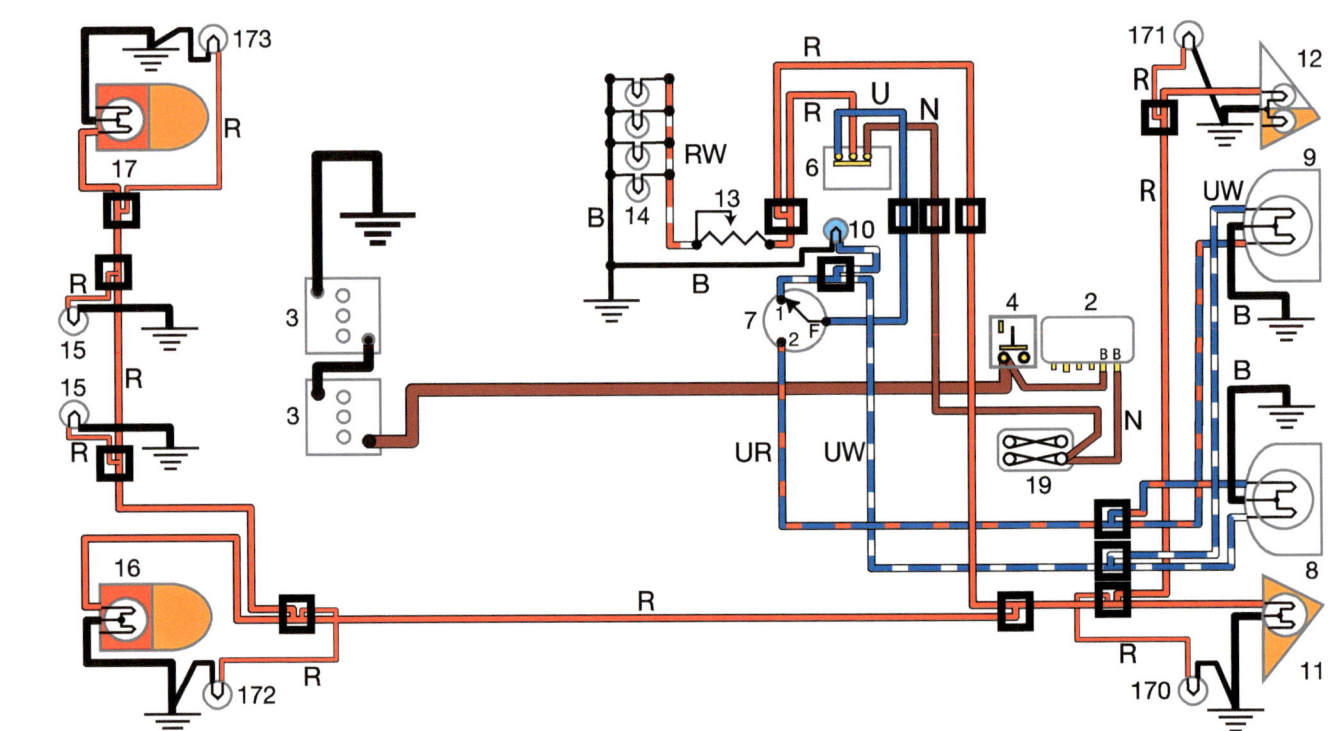

Figure 12.8. A lighting circuit for an early car.

LIGHTING

(RG) wire that routes it to the top two fuses of fuse block (19), which have a link bar between them. However, some cars with only two fuses in the fuse block utilise instead two in-line fuses located below the fuse block. Current from the two fuses routes separately to the left hand (11 & 16) and right hand (12 & 17) parking lamps and left and right number plate lamps (15). A red/green wire also feeds current to a switch or to a dimming device called a rheostat (see Figure 12.8 and 12.12) that in turns supplies the panel lamps via red/white (RW) wires.

Unlike the early car, the rear stop/tail lamps are located in the upper section of the rear lamp assembly.
3. Headlamps. Current goes to the same destinations as in park but also is directed on a blue wire to the headlamps full (high) / dip (low) beam switch, located in the steering column mounted multi-function switch (26). Depending on the position of the dip switch, current may also flow to the headlamps' (8 & 9) dip beam filaments on blue/red (UR) wires or the full beam filaments and indicator lamp (10) on blue/white wires (UW).

The multi function switch assembly, which also includes the horn and turn signal functions, has an extra contact that allows current from the purple fused wire that is routed from the fuse block to be momentarily switched to the blue/white wire, providing a full beam headlamp flash facility irrespective of the state of the lighting or ignition switches.
In some vehicles the front park lamps may be a double filament lamp as per (11) or separate bulb from the turn signal as in (12).

LIGHTING SWITCHES
There were a large variety of lighting switches used in the MGB over its lifetime and in different territories. The connections should be recognizable by reference to one of the diagrams in Figure 12.10.

Unfortunately, the terminal numbers are sometimes impossible to read, some switches have very different contact numbers and some aftermarket switches do not follow any convention.

Should Figure 12.10 not reference a particular switch, as long as the wires are not allowed to touch chassis metal, no harm can be done by trying different permutations of connecting the three wires to different switch terminals and

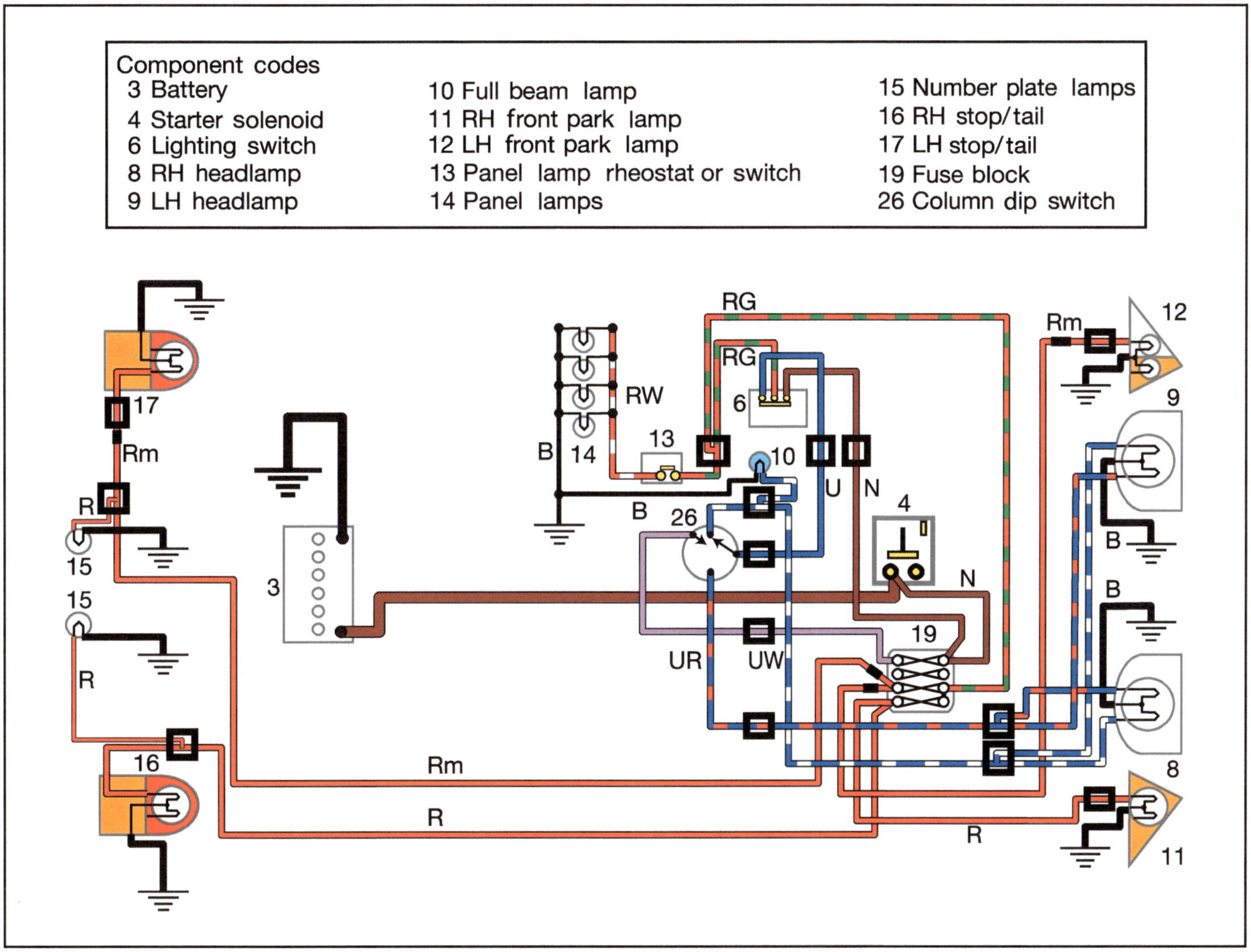

Component codes
3 Battery
4 Starter solenoid
6 Lighting switch
8 RH headlamp
9 LH headlamp
10 Full beam lamp
11 RH front park lamp
12 LH front park lamp
13 Panel lamp rheostat or switch
14 Panel lamps
15 Number plate lamps
16 RH stop/tail
17 LH stop/tail
19 Fuse block
26 Column dip switch

Figure 12.9. A lighting circuit for a late car.

MGB ELECTRICAL SYSTEMS – THE ESSENTIAL MANUAL

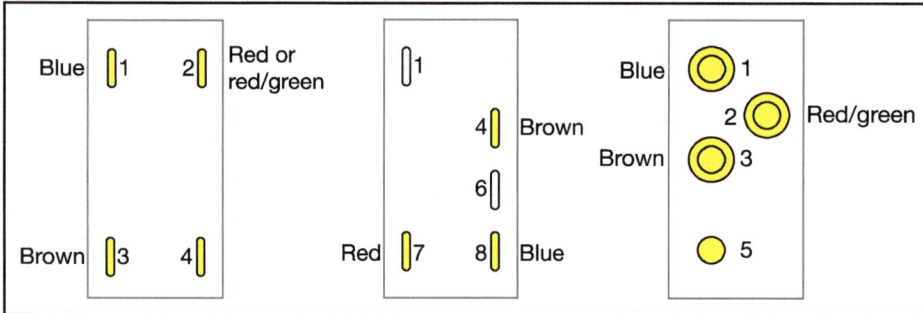

Figure 12.10. Lighting switch connections.

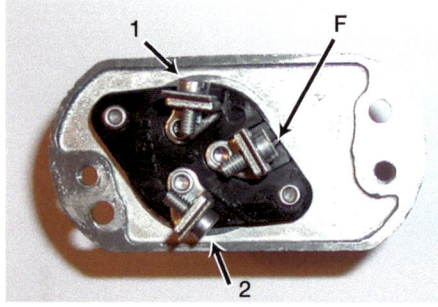

Figure 12.11. A floor mounted dip beam switch.

Figure 12.12. Panel lamp rheostats.

testing the switch to see if it works in the sequence of off, park only and park + headlamps. The process is made easier by the fact that the red (or red/green) and brown wires can be swapped without affecting switch functionality.

First connect the blue wire to one of the switch terminals and then connect the other two wires to the remaining terminals. If the switch does not function correctly, then move the blue wire to a different terminal and try again. If the switch has only three terminals then the correct connection can be found in a maximum of three tries. More switch terminals make the process a little more tedious. Having a multimeter with a continuity tester helps tremendously.

Dip switch
A floor mounted dip or beam switch was fitted until 1967. It has three terminals as shown in Figure 12.11.

It is most important to identify the common terminal F, which is connected to the blue wire. The other two wires, the blue/white and blue/red, go to terminals 1 and 2 in no particular order.

After 1967, the dip switch was moved from the floor to be part of the multi function switch on the steering column that also operates the turn signals, horn and headlamp flash functions. That switch has wire terminations and reference should be made to Figure 12.9 in order to identify those associated with the dip switch function.

Parking lamps
The need for parking lamps varies, not only from country to country but also from city to city and even, as in some parts of the UK, to whether or not the street is part of a bus route. For that reason the style of the front parking lamp is different in North America, where parking lamps are not generally required. In early cars at least, a single lamp unit with a double filament bulb was used behind an amber lens. The lamp assembly then functioned as a running lamp and turn signal. In other territories the lamp assembly was divided into two, the outer and larger segment being covered in a white lens for parking and the other segment being under an amber lens and working as a turn signal. The same lamp unit was later supplied to North America but with amber lenses on both segments.

Instrument lamps
MGCs and many MGBs were fitted with a dimming device for the instrument lamps, which is rather a cruel joke as even at full brightness the lamps are woefully inadequate. This control is called a rheostat and it will also switch the panel lamps completely off at one extreme of its travel, allowing the driver to save battery power when parked. Some MGBs simply have a slide switch for this purpose.

Figure 12.12 shows two styles of rheostat. Both have two pairs of terminals. So long as only red or red/green wires connect on one pair and red/white wires connect to the other, the device will be correctly wired.

It is not always immediately obvious how to remove the control knob from the rheostat. Like those for the heater control, a thin rod – the short end of a small Allen key is ideal – should be pushed through the small hole in the side to depress the spring loaded pin on the shaft as, at the same time, the knob is gently pulled off.

Side marker lamps
Side marker lamps were fitted to many North American 4-cylinder MGBs but serve very little useful purpose and waste battery power if lamps are required to be used when parked at night. Many owners have regarded them as ugly appendages and have removed them when having any work done to the wings (fenders). Amber lenses are available for them and it is a very simple matter to swap the side marker wires from the bullet connectors linking them to the parking lamps and to join them to the turn signals instead. Alternatively, the marker lamps can be linked to the headlamps so that they do not operate with the parking lamps.

HALOGEN BULBS
Using halogen bulbs offers an easy way to improve the brightness of MGB/C lamps. Halogen bulbs have 20% to 50% greater luminous intensity than conventional tungsten of the same wattage. They are also available in higher wattages, offering the possibility of even brighter operation. However, some caution is needed when using higher wattage bulbs because:
1. Higher wattage means more heat. Too high a wattage can result in scorched lamp lenses and melting

LIGHTING

Figure 12.13. Halogen bulbs have a smaller glass envelope than standard filament bulbs.

of the diffuser lenses used in the instruments of late model cars.

2. Higher wattage also means higher current that will increase heating at any points of resistance in the supply circuit. This is particularly evident where passing the higher current through an old lighting switch can quickly bring it to its demise. In order to get full benefit from halogen headlamps and to avoid damage to the lighting switch, it is recommended that relays be fitted to more directly supply the current and to require the switch to provide the very small relay coil current, possibly increasing its life (see page 122).

Halogen bulbs have a smaller glass envelope (Figure 12.13) than standard filament lamps, which results in the surface temperature being much higher; around 570°F (300°C). The heat is essential to the chemistry of the bulb but it does mean that any fingermarks on the glass surface will turn white and prevent some light emission. The bulbs are usually supplied with an expanded polystyrene (Styrofoam™) sleeve over the glass that protects it during transit and provides a method of safe handling. Should the glass be accidentally touched, clean it thoroughly with methylated spirit (denatured alcohol).

The recommended maximum bulb wattages are as follows:
- Turn　　　　　　　　35W
- Stop/tail　　　　　　35W/5W
- Instruments pre '74　5W
- Instruments post '74　3W

Fitting halogen headlamps

If your car already has sealed beam headlamps, converting to halogen is an easy and inexpensive way to improve the quality and safety of driving at night. Even if you have an older vehicle with ordinary dual filament bulbs, rather than a sealed reflector unit, a halogen unit may well very easily fit. The type with a spring clip retaining the bulb has an identical connector to that on the halogen units and should just plug straight in. If you have a bayonet retention system for the bulb, that is, the type you have to push in, then turn, the conversion is a little trickier, requiring a new connector.

Halogen headlamp units can be obtained at most automotive outlets worldwide under type # H6024 and/or 2D1.

The chrome plated headlamp rim must first be removed. It is retained by two tabs at the top placed at about the 11 and 1 o'clock positions and it snaps over matching clips at the bottom. Prising them off is not easy on

Figure 12.14. The headlamp fixing and adjustment screws.

Figure 12.15. The headlamp unit removed.

the MGB/C because the body styling does not allow easy access to the lowest part of the rim. A proper pry tool with a cranked shaft works much better than a flat screwdriver. Pry as far down the lamp rim as possible and use something behind the tool to work as a pad to protect the paintwork.

The headlamp unit is retained by three screws identified by the red arrows in Figure 12.14. The black arrows indicate the headlamp adjustment screws. The screws are in exactly the same locations for both left and right lamps.

Once removed, the sealed beam unit connector will be revealed as in Figure 12.15. It is a simple matter to remove the connector and plug it into the halogen unit.

Should there be no connector, as may be the case if a pre focused bulb is found, then a connector may be purchased and spliced in or individual standard, but hard to find, 5/16in (8mm) female blade connectors can be used. Figure 12.16 shows how the wires are connected.

Beam alignment

1. Measure and note the distance from the ground to the centre of each headlamp.
2. Locate the car on level ground, facing a vertical wall and as far from it as is practical.
3. With the headlamps on high (full) beam, measure the distance from the ground to the centres of the beams of light thrown on the wall; they should fall at the same height as the headlamp centres.
4. If the beam for a lamp falls too low, turn the slotted head screw located at the top of the lamp unit clockwise; if too high, turn anti (counter) clockwise.

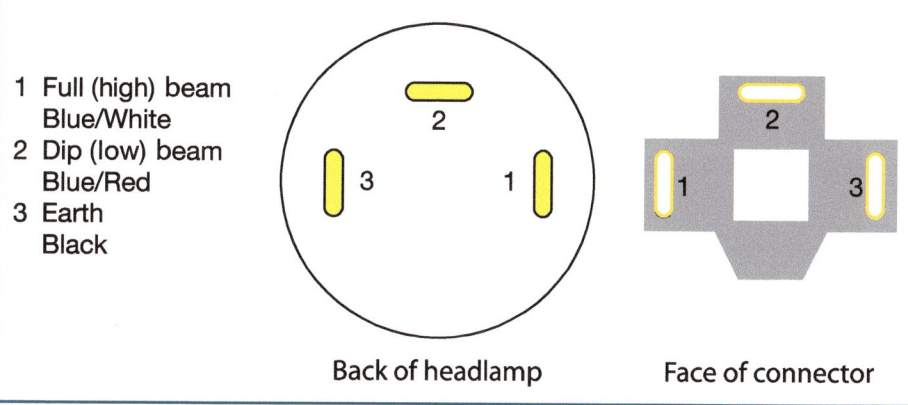

Figure 12.16. Headlamp connections.

1 Full (high) beam Blue/White
2 Dip (low) beam Blue/Red
3 Earth Black

MGB ELECTRICAL SYSTEMS – THE ESSENTIAL MANUAL

5. Checking the horizontal alignment is more of judgement than measurement: the beams should point straight ahead. If in doubt, make the lamps tend toward the kerb side rather than toward oncoming traffic.

6. Screw the slot headed screw on the left side of each lamp clockwise to move the beam to the right and anti clockwise to move it left.

7. Refit the outer rim, making sure any weld seam is at the bottom and so out of sight. Rims simply snap on, but make sure they are firmly located by hitting around the periphery of each with the heel of the hand.

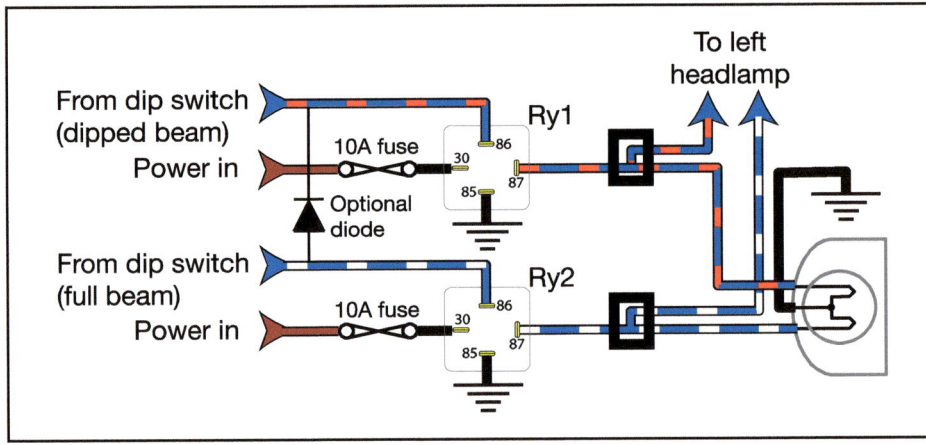

Figure 12.17. Headlamp relay circuit. An optional diode may be used as described on page 123.

HEADLAMP RELAYS

The current consumed by headlamps makes them one of the highest consumption loads in the car, and vulnerable to high voltage drop that can cause very significant reduction in brightness. To minimize voltage loss, almost every modern car uses relays to switch the headlamps and avoid the need to route their full current through the lighting switches.

MGB/Cs can benefit from adding headlamp relays, too. Not only will the lamps be significantly brighter, but the lighting switch life will be greatly extended. This modification is especially recommended when halogen headlamps are fitted as, not only will it derive maximum benefit from their use, but since most manufacturers supply them at 60/55W power rating, as against the original lamp rating of 50/40W, the current drawn from the two headlamps rises by 20% and heating in the switches by 44%. On the MGB tested, lamp brightness loss due to voltage drop decreased from 38% to 9% by simply adding relays. By using both relays and halogen headlamps, brightness more than doubled compared to the conventional system.

Installing headlamp relays

Figure 12.17 illustrates the headlamp circuit with the relays installed. Refer to Appendix 1 for more information concerning relay selection and how to terminate them. The modifications to the standard circuit are:

1. A new power feed must be provided for the power-in line to both relays. This is best taken from where brown wires are connected to the starter solenoid because it both provides a very good low loss supply and has minimal effect on any other

Figure 12.18. Headlamp relays (and one used for another purpose) installed by the fuse block.

system. It is recommended that the power feeds be individually fused at 10 amps as the power line will be live at all times. More information on auxiliary fuses can be found in Chapter 7. Use 14AWG (2.5mm^2) wire or larger.

2. Both the blue/red dip beam and blue/white full beam wires must be cut at a convenient position where it is intended to install relays Ry1 and Ry2. Figure 12.18 shows an installation made by Bob Muenchausen of Boise, Idaho. The relays, only two of which are for the headlamps, have been positioned close to the bonnet stay fixing and above the wiring harness from which the blue/white and blue/red wires have been teased. In order to be able to pull through sufficient length of wire that can be cut, terminated and connected to the relays, it may be more convenient to install them closer to the front of the vehicle where a taped harness can be more easily unwrapped and more free length of wire is available.

In operation, the dip switch, which is supplied from the lighting switch, provides power to the relay coils via terminal 86, the earth return being terminal 85. Once energized, the relays switch power to either the full or dip beam headlamp filaments by taking power in to terminal 30 and switching it to terminal 87. Again, these two connections can be reversed if convenient.

DAYTIME RUNNING LAMPS

Motorcyclists, recognising the small visual target their vehicles present, have long understood the value of operating headlights in daylight. Although somewhat bigger, MGB/Cs and other small sports cars also have a relatively small frontal area and in addition are lower to the ground than the average vehicle. Daytime running lights or DRLs may well make these cars more visible and hence increase safety.

The evidence that the increase in conspicuousness that DRLs offer is a safety benefit, greater than that which is provided by anti-lock brakes for example, is compelling. Some countries have had laws requiring the use of headlights in daylight for some time, and to this end, vehicles supplied there have been equipped with headlamps that switch on automatically during daylight. Finland, Sweden, Norway, Iceland and Denmark have such laws. Poland and Hungary require DRLs outside of cities. Canada, taking a slightly different legal tack, required all vehicles manufactured after December 1, 1989 to be equipped with DRLs. DRLs, although not mandated by law in the USA, are nevertheless fitted by some manufacturers, notably GM and VW.

Here are some, very much

LIGHTING

summarised, examples of the recorded reduction in multi-vehicle crashes when DRLs were used:
1. Finland. 21% on rural roads in winter
2. Sweden. 11%
3. Norway. 14%
4. Denmark. 7% overall but a 37% reduction in left turn collisions with oncoming vehicles.
5. USA. 18% on a small fleet study.
6. Canada. 11% (excludes rear-end collisions).
7. Avis car rental. DRL equipped cars involved in accidents required 45% less cost of repair over those that did not have DRLs.

It should also be said that there is a vehement and vocal anti-DRL lobby. The concern seems to hinge on freedom of choice issues and the fact that DRLs are often criticized for causing driver distraction as a result of dazzle, especially when the system is connected to the full (high) beams.

Headlamp life is obviously reduced when they are used for both day and night driving. However, as discussed on page 117, if the circuit includes some mechanism for reducing voltage then the lamp life reduction will be minimised.

DRLs consume about 5A and may not be a good choice for car with a dynamo, rather than an alternator, which has marginal capability to recharge the battery.

As far as fuel consumption and power are concerned, the power used to run DRLs is not free but even at about 40% alternator efficiency, DRLs will use just 0.25 horsepower, which equates to 0.26% of the total engine brake horsepower.

Installing DRLs

There are a number of different ways to reduce the voltage to the lamps.
1. Silicon diodes (see Appendix 2) drop about 0.6V when conducting, a value that is almost independent of the current flowing through them. Two or three diodes in series would be suitable for DRL voltage dropping. Even if one headlamp fails, the other will continue to receive almost the same voltage. Unfortunately, diodes that can pass about 5A are not easy to find in the consumer market and the power that each dissipates (3W at 5A) requires that they be fitted to a heat sink of some sort and at the same time electrically insulated from one another.
2. Pulse width modulation (PWM) is a

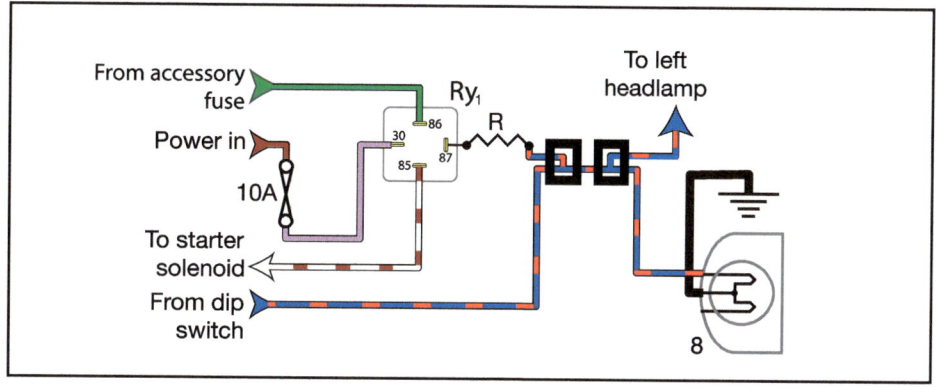

Figure 12.19. Daytime running lamp circuit.

system that switches the lights on and off hundreds of times per second and so can keep the lamps' off to on ratio (duty cycle) at a predetermined level. If the lamps are off for 10% of the time and on for 90% of the time the effect will be the same as reducing the voltage by 10%. PWMs are very efficient and little energy is lost as heat. The circuitry is sophisticated and is best bought as a module from a manufacturer such as Hamsar of Burlington, Ontario.
3. Resistors are simple, relatively inexpensive and, if bought in the correct format, easy to heat sink. The voltage they drop is proportional to the current flowing through them so that if one bulb fails the voltage to the remaining bulb will increase as that dropped across the resistor decreases. Despite this disadvantage, resistor voltage dropping is the easiest do-it-yourself method of installing DRLs and will be used here.

Suggested circuits for adding DRLs are shown in Figures 12.19 and 12.21.

It may appear that, in order to run DRLs, it would be possible to simply connect the resistor from the dip lamp filament to a white or green wire that is only energized when the ignition switch is on. That would work but it would add a heavy loading to the ignition and accessory circuits, detrimentally affecting, and probably overloading, the systems attached to them. It would also mean that the DRLs would be on when the engine cranks, depriving the starter motor of energy at a critical time and that the lighting circuit could sneak current back to the ignition system, causing strange effects. Both circuits shown use a relay to switch a preferred source of lamp power using a small current taken from elsewhere. Refer to Appendix 1 for information regarding the selection and termination of relays.

A power feed must be provided for the power-in wire to the relay (Ry_1) terminal 30 (sometimes marked 30/51). This is best taken from the brown wire that connects to the starter relay or solenoid because in these circuits, the starter and DRLs never work at the same time. If headlamp relays have already been installed then this power input can use the same fuse and wire that is used to supply Ry_1 in Figure 12.17. Whether shared or dedicated to the DRL circuit alone, the wire should be fused to 10 amps. More information on auxiliary fusing can be found in Chapter 7.

The power output from relay Ry_1 terminal 87 passes through the resistor (R), which slightly dims the dipped headlamp beam and extends the life of the lamps. The value of the resistor should be between 0.3Ω and 0.5Ω and it should have a power capability of 5W or greater (a calculation would indicate 8W as the minimum rating, but a 5W resistor, of the type recommended here, may be re-rated to 8W at the temperatures found under-bonnet in MGB/Cs). While suitable resistors are made in a wide number of values, distributors and stockists that sell in small quantities only keep a limited range and in fractional resistance values, 0.5Ω is that most often available. The recommended style should be like that in Figure 12.20. This has a finned aluminium housing that can be screwed down to flat vehicle sheet metal in order to remove the heat generated. Consult the Internet to find suppliers in your region. Some suitable manufacturers and 5W, 0.5Ω resistor part numbers are:

* Vishay Dale   RH005R5000FE02
* Clarostat   778-CMC5.5
* Huntingdon   TMC-5-05
* Ohmite   805J0R5

MGB-ELECTRICAL SYSTEMS – THE ESSENTIAL MANUAL

Figure 12.20. The recommended style of DRL resistor has its own heat sink housing.

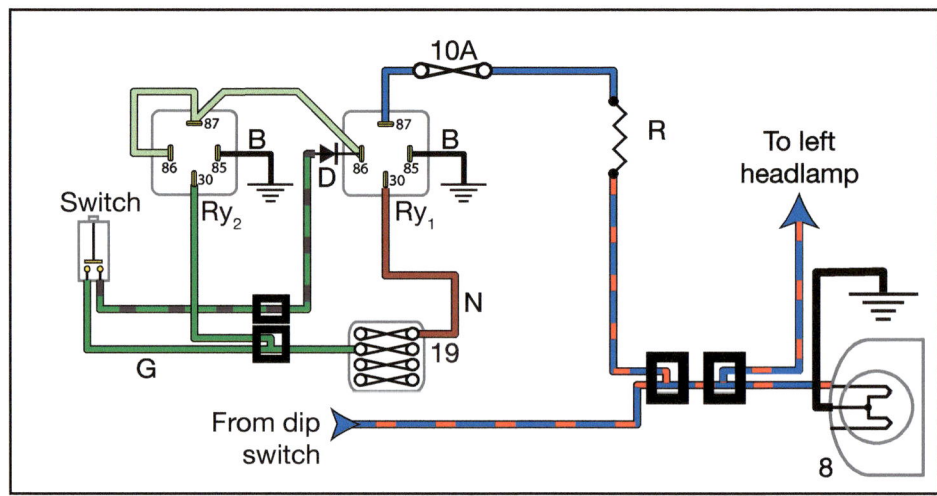

Figure 12.21. A DRL circuit that is initiated by a switch.

If a suitable resistor cannot be found then about 25ft of 22AWG (8m of 0.35mm²) wire can be substituted and distributed discreetly around the under-bonnet area of the car so that the heat it produces is not concentrated at any single point.

The relay has to be energized in order to close the contact and connect the lamps to the resistor fed power. This is where the circuits differ from one another. In Figure 12.19, in order to do this whenever the car is running, a wire is taken back to the green or white ignition power wire at the fuse block. Refer to the circuit diagrams in Chapter 11 to locate the correct point on your car. The system would work if terminal 85 were simply earthed and that is an option that can be considered. However, the starter motor needs all the energy it can get when cranking and some method of turning off the DRLs during starting is advantageous. The starter solenoid is of such low resistance that the 0.2A or so of relay coil current is hardly affected by it and that amount of current doesn't affect the solenoid either. In Figure 12.19 the relay has been earthed by taking it back through the starter solenoid. The connection there is made with the white/brown (brown/white in late cars) wire at the starter motor relay or, if the car has no starter relay, with the red/white wire at the starter motor solenoid. Refer to the relevant circuit for your car in Chapter 10 in order to identify the correct connection point.

When, still referring to Figure 12.19, the ignition is switched on, the relay terminal 86 is supplied battery power via its connection to a white or green vehicle wire. The relay coil becomes energized as its terminal 85 is earthed through the very low resistance of the starter solenoid. However, when cranking the car, the starter solenoid terminal that connects to the DRL relay (Ry$_1$) is taken to battery voltage too. With battery voltage on both sides of the relay coil, there's little or no voltage difference across it, so no current flows, the relay is de energized and the DRLs switch off during engine cranking.

There are some disadvantages to the DRL circuit in Figure 12.19. Because the DRLs are on at any time the ignition switch is closed, they will be draining the battery if it is necessary to power the ignition to work on the car. At night, the fact that the headlamps are on when the engine has started, can make the driver think he has already switched the main lighting on, and it is all too easy to drive off with no lights showing to the rear of the car. The driver, being used to the dim dash lighting, is not alerted by any clues from that source.

A method of switching the DRLs at some other time may be advantageous. Figure 12.21 adds a second relay (Ry$_2$) that accepts a trigger pulse from a chosen source to its coil at terminal 86. When the relay power contacts close, its terminal 87 closes and then both feeds power back to its own coil, latching the contacts closed, and energizes the coil of Ry$_1$. Ry$_2$ remains closed, keeping the DRLs powered until the ignition is switched off. The diode D is required so that Ry$_2$ cannot feed power back and affect any other function of the initiating switch.

Some sources for the trigger signal might be:
• The green/purple stop lamp wire. Using this, the DRLs would turn on at first use of the brakes. Of course, if you are in the habit of starting the car with your foot on the brake pedal, this trigger source is not for you.
• The green/red or green/white turn signal wires. The DRLs would illuminate when the chosen direction signal is first used. To work with either signal, two separate diodes would be required on terminal 86 of Ry1, one connected to the green/red circuit and the other to the green/white.
• Cars with transmissions made between 1971 and 1976 have an inhibitor switch (see page 142) that is closed and supplies power when any gear is engaged.
• The overdrive switch that may be fitted to your car even if you have no overdrive, see Chapter 13, can provide a trigger source from its yellow wire. Depending on the overdrive wiring in your car, use of the overdrive, or selecting 3rd or 4th gear, will trigger the DRLs to illuminate.

Relay terminal 87 takes the power from the relay to the dipped beam lamps. If the relay you use has a centre contact 87a, then it may be ignored for the purposes of this circuit.

LINKING LIGHTING RELAYS

Diodes (see Appendix 2) are devices that pass current in one direction only. This feature allows diodes to link electrical circuits so that when circuit A is switched on, circuit B will also operate, however, because current cannot flow in the opposite direction, when circuit B is on, circuit A will not operate.

In principle, any two circuits could be linked in this way but the current that most vehicle functions consume and that would have to pass through the diode would make it large, costly

LIGHTING

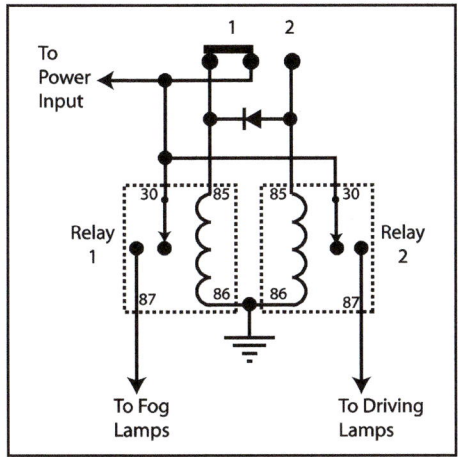

Figure 12.22. Fog and driving lamp relays linked by a diode.

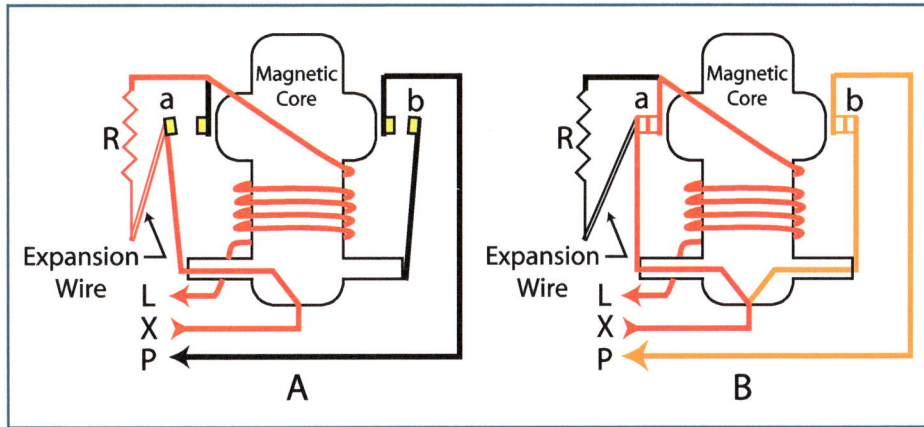

Figure 12.23. A 3-terminal thermal flasher that uses an expansion, or 'hot wire' actuator.

and necessitate that it be fitted to a heat sink. Putting the diode in a relay coil circuit, on the other hand, permits the use of very small and inexpensive diodes. If in figure 12.17 for example, the optional 1 Amp diode, which may be a 1N4001, 1N4002 or 1N4003, were used between terminals 86 of relays Ry1 and Ry2, with the anode toward that of Ry2, when full beam is used and Ry2 is energized, current could flow through the diode to also energize Ry1 and the dipped lights would operate at the same time. The reverse, however, is not true. When dipped beam is selected, current cannot flow backward in the diode and cause the full beam to operate.

The circuit in Figure 12.22 was devised for an MGB user who wanted his fog lights to operate every time the driving lights were on, but when he moved the switch to position 1, he wanted only the fog lamps to operate. The existing switch was not capable of performing the function but since the relays were already in place, the diode was an effective solution.

TURN SIGNALS AND HAZARD FLASHERS

The turn signal module is the heart of the turn or flasher circuit.

Flasher module

The original MGB/C modules were of the thermal type. This technology has some inherent benefits yet can cause some problems:

- The flash rate is dependant on the current drawn so that it will increase and indicate a turn signal bulb failure.
- It is voltage sensitive so may slow down to a very long flash rate or not flash at all at traffic lights with the engine at idle and with loads such as brake lamps and headlamps also operating.
- When first switched on, the turn signals will be off and will take a half cycle, up to 0.5 seconds to come on. At 50mph (80kph) that equates to a distance travelled of over 73ft (22m).
- Many are very quiet in operation providing no audible warning to the driver should a turn signal be left on.

Figure 12.23 shows the principle of operation of the thermal flasher module. In circuit A, current flows in at terminal X, sometimes marked B, where it joins to a metal component called the magnetic core. Current can flow to the lever arm of contact 'a' which is attached to the core, through an expansion wire, a resistor 'R', a coil around the magnetic core and out to the turn signal lamps via terminal L. The resistance of the expansion wire and the resistor R reduces the current so much that, although current flows to the turn signal lamps, they are not perceptibly illuminated. That current is, however, sufficient to heat the expansion wire so that it does indeed expand until, under the spring force of the lever to which contact 'a' is attached, the contact closes and the current is shunted around the expansion wire and R, so that the circuit looks like that in B.

Without the expansion wire and R in circuit, the current increases dramatically so that the turn signal lamps illuminate, and the current in the magnetic core provides strong magnetic attraction to the levers of contacts 'a' and 'b' holding them in.

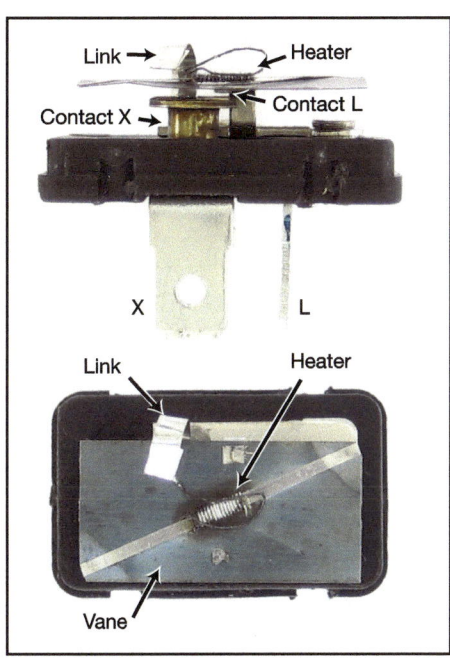

Figure 12.24. Side and top views of a 2-terminal vane type flasher unit.

Because contact 'b' is closed, current can now also flow via the metal core through 'b' to the flasher indicator (or pilot) lamps via terminal P.

With no current in the expansion wire it contracts, pulling hard on contact 'a' until the force is sufficiently strong for it to overcome the magnetic force holding it closed. As it does so, the circuit reverts to that in A and the cycle restarts.

When one of the two turn signal lamps on each side fails, the current in 'a' is reduced by about half, as is the magnetising force that is holding it closed. The expansion wire will thus be able to overcome that force much sooner in its cooling cycle and so the flasher rate increases, indicating the lamp failure to the driver.

The 3-terminal flasher with a pilot or P terminal was normally only used in circuits that had a single turn signal indicator lamp, the P terminal being energized irrespective of the left or right position of the turn signal direction switch. As shown in Figure 12.25, MG nevertheless chose to use it on the early MGB, possibly as a carry-over from the MGA, even though there were both right and left turn signal indicator lamps on the dash. As a result, the turn signal direction switch required extra contacts to earth one or other of the indicator lamps and switch it in circuit. As can be seen in Figure 12.26, that was later rectified when a 2-terminal flasher unit was used and each dash indicator lamp was connected directly to the main turn signal lamp on its respective side.

The dash lamp power is so low relative to the main lamps that the additional load they put on the flasher module is negligible.

Another type of flasher module, used for 2-terminal systems, is the vane type illustrated in Figure 12.24. It incorporates a spring steel vane or diaphragm that is formed in such a way that it snaps up and down as it is heated. On its underside is a contact.

Current from the input terminal X is passed via a flexible link to a resistance heater mounted on the vane and from there via a connecting bar to the lamp terminal L. The current is insufficient to light the turn signal lamps but it can heat the vane sufficiently to make it snap downward, usually with an audible click. The contact of its underside makes a direct connection to terminal X effectively joining it to terminal L and so illuminating the turn lamps. The heater becomes bypassed and so cools, as does the vane which snaps back, again with an audible click. The cycle then restarts.

Electronic flasher modules

Not many modules that describe themselves as electronic truly meet that description if 'electronic' is taken to imply that transistors are used. Most use a relay that cycles as the result of the charging and discharging rate of a large value capacitor, some 1500μF, through a relay coil. This makes it voltage sensitive but impervious to load changes, and so it is incapable of detecting lamp outage. This can have advantages if a trailer lamp loading is added for example, if other types of lamps are used such as halogen or LED, or if turn signal relays are fitted. See also page 128.

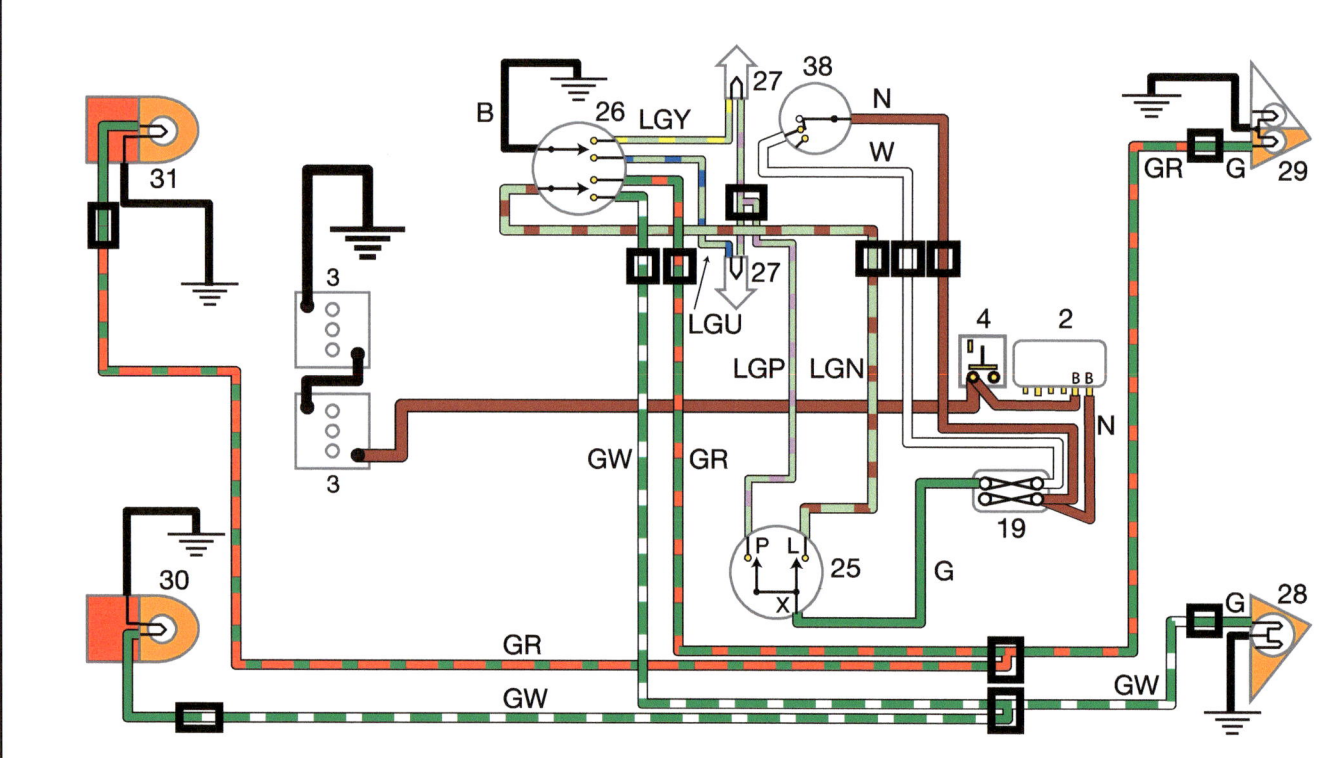

Figure 12.25. The turn signal circuit for an early MGB.

LIGHTING

EARLY CAR TURN SIGNAL CIRCUIT

There are many iterations of the turn signal circuit. Those illustrated in Figures 12.25 and 2.26 between them show most of the changes. The early circuit shown in Figure 12.25 is distinguished by having 2 fuses, a 3-terminal flasher module and no hazard flashers.

Power from the batteries (3) is routed by a large cable to the starter motor solenoid (4) that acts an anchor and termination point. It then goes on brown (N) wires via the dynamo control box (2), which is also used as a wire anchoring point. The current is taken to the fuse block, (19) yet another anchor point, and to the ignition switch (38). When closed, the ignition switch directs the current via a white (W) wire, to the fuse block and through a fuse where it exits on a green (G) wire that goes to the 3-terminal flasher module (25).

When a current passes through the flasher module it cycles it on and off. That current can flow when the turn signal direction switch (26) is operated in either direction to direct the current to the turn signal lamps via green/red (GR) wires for a left turn or green/white (GW) wires for a right turn.

In the early car the turn signal bulb was situated in the upper half of the rear lamp units. Differences may also be found in the front lamp units, European vehicles having separate bulbs under amber and white lenses for the turn and park lamps as per component 29 while most North American cars had a single amber lens over a dual filament bulb that served for both turn and park as per component 28.

When the turn signal switch is operated another set of contacts earths light green/yellow (LGY) or light green/blue wires (LGU) from the dash mounted turn flasher indicator lamps (27). This allows them to pass current that is supplied via a light green/purple LGP) wire from the P terminal of the flasher module and so they flash in time with the main flasher lamps. Should there be a turn signal bulb failure, the signals will operate at a higher rate but the indicator lamps may not work at all.

LATE CAR TURN SIGNAL CIRCUIT

The late turn signal and hazard circuit shown in Figure 11.26 is distinguished by having four fuses, a 2-terminal turn flasher module and hazard (4-way) flashers.

Power from the battery (3) is routed by a large cable to the starter motor solenoid (4) that acts an anchor and termination point. The current is taken to the fuse block, (19) used as another

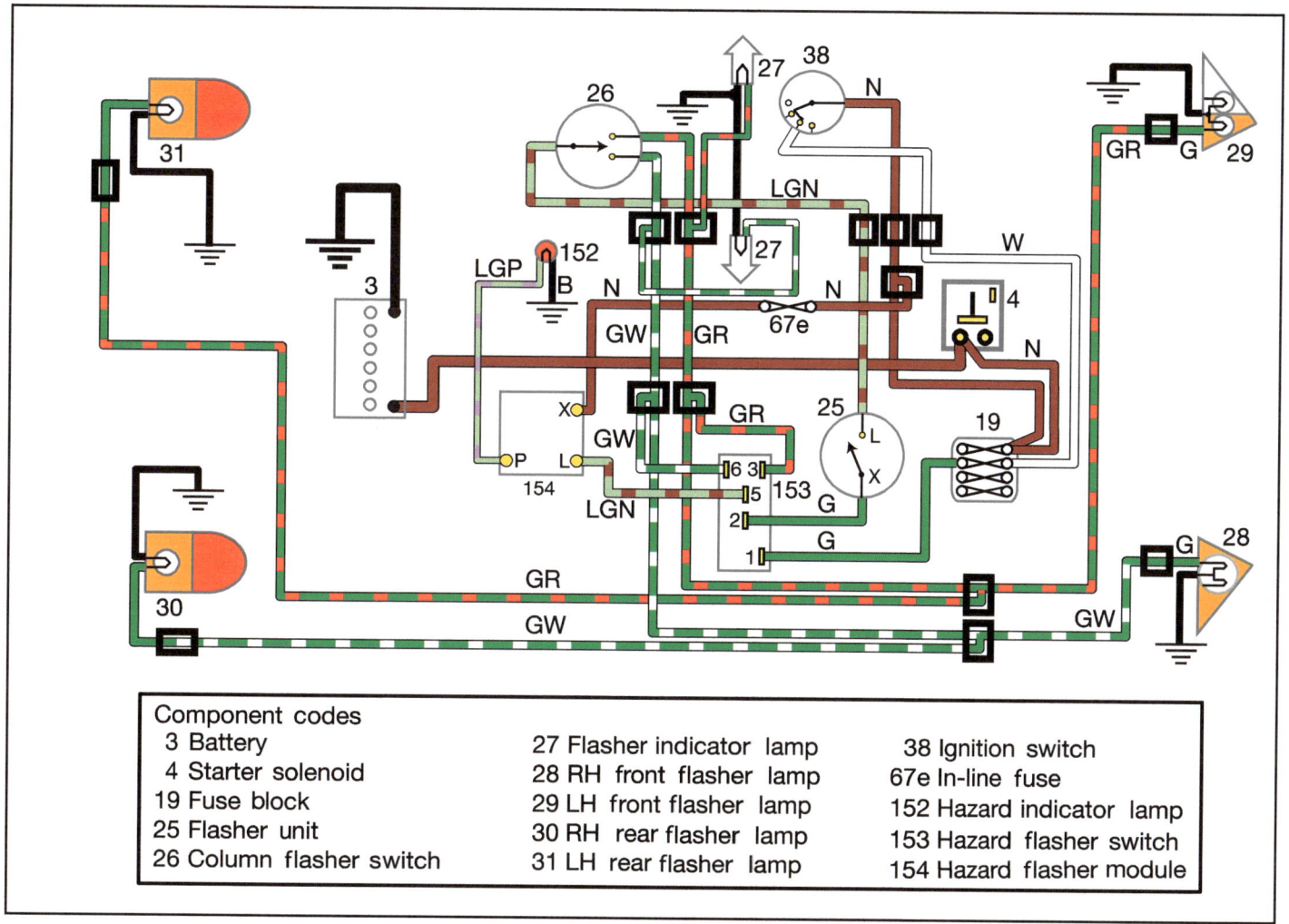

Component codes
- 3 Battery
- 4 Starter solenoid
- 19 Fuse block
- 25 Flasher unit
- 26 Column flasher switch
- 27 Flasher indicator lamp
- 28 RH front flasher lamp
- 29 LH front flasher lamp
- 30 RH rear flasher lamp
- 31 LH rear flasher lamp
- 38 Ignition switch
- 67e In-line fuse
- 152 Hazard indicator lamp
- 153 Hazard flasher switch
- 154 Hazard flasher module

Figure 12.26. The turn signal circuit for a late MGB.

anchor point, and to the ignition switch (38). When closed, the ignition switch directs the current via a white (W) wire, to the fuse block and through a fuse where it exits on a green (G) wire that goes to the hazard flasher switch (153). The purpose of bringing this power feed to the hazard flasher switch is to disable the turn signals when the hazard flasher is operated. If the hazard flashers are off, the two green wires going to the switch are joined and power from the fuse block is routed to the 2-terminal flasher module (25).

When a current passes through the flasher module it cycles it on and off. That current can flow when the turn signal direction switch (26) is operated in either direction to direct the current to the turn signal lamps and indicator lamps via green/red (GR) wires to for a left turn or green/white (GW) wires for a right turn.

The hazard flashers must operate even when the ignition switch is off and as stated before, in order to take control of all four turn signal lamps and both turn indicator lamps, the hazard switch must disable the turn signals.

On switching the hazard lamp switch on, the green wires on its terminals 1 and 2 disconnect from one another. At the same time, switch terminals 3, 5 and 6 join. This allows a brown (N) – always live wire – supplied with power via a fuse (67e), to pass current through the 3-terminal hazard flasher lamp module (154), to the hazard flasher switch on a green/brown (GN) wire to all the turn signal lamps via the green/red and green/white wires.

The hazard flasher module is especially designed to be able to supply four lamps rather than only two at one time, as is the case with the turn signal flasher module. The 3-terminal type powers the hazard flasher indicator lamp from its P terminal via a light green/purple (LGP) wire. A 2-terminal module may also be found, in which case the hazard flasher module terminal L supplies the indicator lamp as well as the switch.

A different style of hazard switch may be found on some cars. The connections for the alternative switch are shown in Figure 12.27.

There have been problems obtaining replacement hazard switches in some countries and so commonly available alternatives have to be used. A double pole (a device having two mechanically linked but electrically separated switches in one), double throw (each being capable of switching to one circuit or another) switch is required. The shorthand used in specifications for all such switches is DPDT.

Figure 12.28 shows a DPDT switch being used in this way. Although this circuit requires no diodes, it is quite difficult to wire because the red/green and red/white turn signal lamp wires have to be separated from the turn signal direction switch at a point distant from the normal hazard switch position. Figure 12.29 uses two diodes of at least 3A rating (see Appendix 2) but uses the wire connections that were used on the original switch.

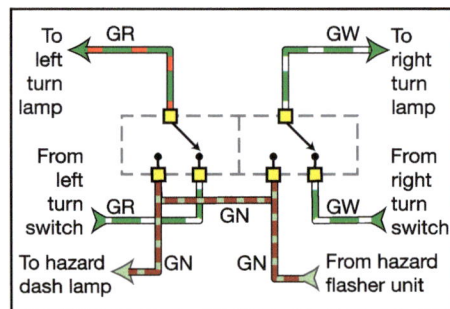

Figure 12.28. A hazard switch using a standard DPDT switch and no diodes.

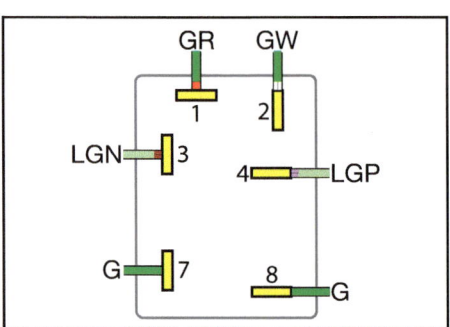

Figure 12.27. A variant of hazard flasher switch shown in Figure 12.26.

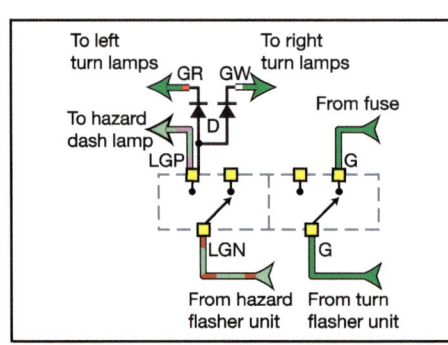

Figure 12.29. A hazard switch using a standard DPDT switch and diodes.

Using an electronic flasher module

Electronic turn signals can solve many of the problems that were associated with the thermal devices, namely:
1. They illuminate immediately the direction indicator switch is operated, giving other drivers a significant ½ second earlier warning of the intention to turn.
2. A true electronic module can work at voltages down to 8V and not change its flash rate. Unfortunately, many so-called electronic modules are equally susceptible to voltage changes that can reduce the flash rate considerably under adverse conditions.
3. They are available in versions that change the flash rate in the event of lamp outage and versions that do not. There are benefits to both systems depending on the circumstances. If a module is of the type that does indicate a bulb failure it should be stated on its casing, or at least marked on the packaging.

Those that don't change their flash rate with loading are useful for non-standard loads such as relay switched signals, described later in this chapter, halogen bulbs, LEDs and trailer-tow lamps. Such a module is shown in Figure 12.30. It has three terminals and can be directly substituted for 2 or 3-terminal thermal flasher modules. That illustrated is a true electronic module and its clever circuitry requires no earth connection. It is almost impervious to voltage variations and will keep the turn signals flashing at a constant rate, shrugging off the effects of an idling engine and heavy demands on the electrical system.

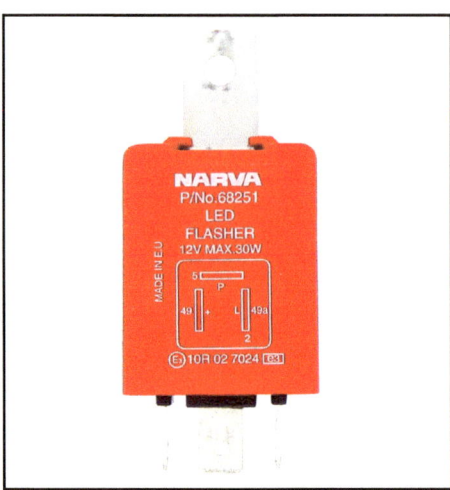

Figure 12.30. This 3-terminal electronic flasher does not require an earth

LIGHTING

MAKING TURN SIGNALS MORE AUDIBLE

The early 3-terminal flasher module is very quiet in operation, and engine noise and hearing impairment can make an improved audible warning desirable. Fortunately, it is very easy to fit a buzzer to this kind of module. Your car may already have a redundant buzzer somewhere, perhaps behind the dash or centre console. MG installed them for key-in, door ajar and seat belt undone warnings and most no longer work or were disconnected because of the nuisance they invoke. Alternatively, magnetic and piezoelectric buzzers, like that illustrated in Figure 12.31, are very inexpensive and readily available. Most are specified to work between 3V and 18V and so work well at automotive voltages. Although small, the sound output level of 70dBA or more should be heard over normal interior MGB/C noise or a loud radio. The piezoelectric type is high pitched and, while described by its manufacturers as a buzzer, the noise is more of a beep, if not a screech. The biggest limitation is the strength of the connecting wire, which is usually of very small gauge and not really rugged enough for use in cars, so care must be taken to place any such buzzer where they will not be snagged. One way to do this is to mount the components on some kind of circuit board, in the manner the circuit in Figure 12.34 has been constructed in Figure 2.28, page 17.

The circuit for installing a buzzer in cars with a 3-terminal flasher module is shown in Figure 12.32. The red wire of the buzzer simply connects to the P terminal of the module and the black wire is earthed. However, a different route to earth, for the buzzer – through the brake (stop) lamp switch – is also shown in the diagram. This alternative circuit was devised by Rich Wagner of Walled Lake, Michigan, who installed a buzzer in his Triumph TR-3A. While he found it useful, it also proved very annoying if he had to wait at a light for a prolonged time when making a turn. By connecting the earth side of the buzzer to the brake lamp switch, he created a sneak path (see Chapter 5) for the current to flow to earth. However, if, at a traffic light, the brake pedal is depressed, the brake lamp voltage, as well as that at the black wire of the buzzer, become the same as that on the red wire of the buzzer. becomes the same as that on the red wire of the buzzer. With equal voltage on both its terminals, no current flows in the buzzer and it mutes. Once the traffic light goes green the brake pedal is released and the buzzer pulses again and reminds the driver that the turn signal is operating.

Most buzzers are polarity sensitive, so on positive earth cars, reverse the buzzer connections so that red goes to earth.

If the flasher module is of the 2-terminal type, without a P contact, then the circuit in Figure 12.33 should be used. Making this circuit mute when the brake is pressed is a little more complicated. One alternative is to fit a

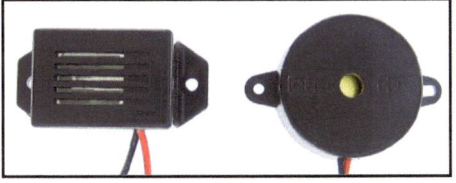

Figure 12.31. Typical buzzers. Magnetic (left) and piezoelectric.

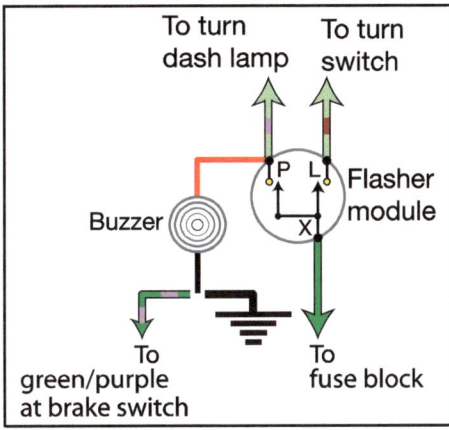

Figure 12.32. Connections for a turn signal warning buzzer for cars with a 3-terminal flasher module.

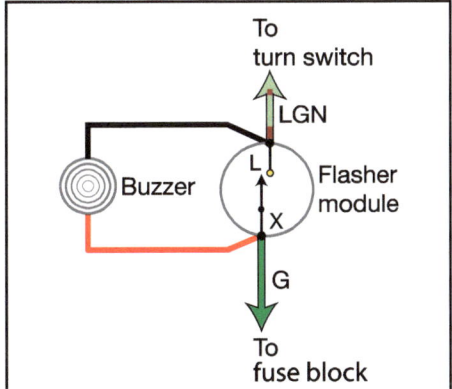

Figure 12.33. Connections for a turn signal warning buzzer for cars with a 2-terminal flasher module.

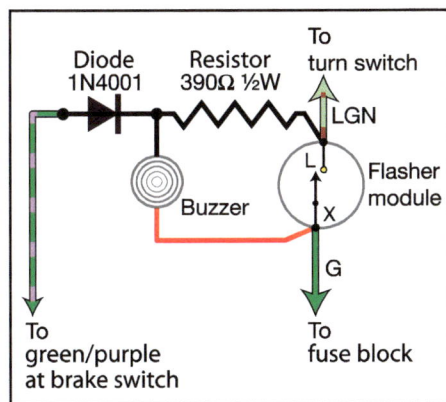

Figure 12.34. The circuit of Figure 12.33, modified to provide brake muting.

modern 3-terminal flasher module like that in Figure 12.30 and use the circuit in Figure 12.32. If that isn't an option, then Figure 12.34 shows one way to achieve muting.

Here the buzzer operates just as is does in Figure 12.33, but its current also passes through a 390Ω resistor. So long as the buzzer is one of the types shown in Figure 12.31, or similar, it draws so little current that its loudness is hardly affected by the resistor. The diode 1N4001, (see Appendix 2) is wired in such a direction that it does not allow current to pass to the brake switch. When the brake is pressed, the diode, being a one way device, does allow current to potentially pass to the buzzer's black wire from the brake circuit. However, this voltage is approximately the same as that at the buzzer's red wire, which is fed from the same green wire circuit that powers the brake lamps. With near zero voltage difference across the buzzer, it mutes. Without the resistor in circuit, the brake circuit would sneak current to the turn signal circuit, but in this case, the 390Ω resistor is very significant, only allowing about 2% of the normal lamp current to flow by that route, and so the resistor effectively isolates the brake and turn signal circuits

In the unlikely event that a 2-terminal flasher module is fitted to a negative earth car, the diode and the buzzer connections will require reversal.

BRAKE LAMPS

The brake (stop) lamp circuit is basically simple but became complicated by regulations, mostly in the USA, that required that the brakes had dual independent hydraulic circuits and that a warning system, with facility to verify the lamp integrity, be installed.

MGB ELECTRICAL SYSTEMS – THE ESSENTIAL MANUAL

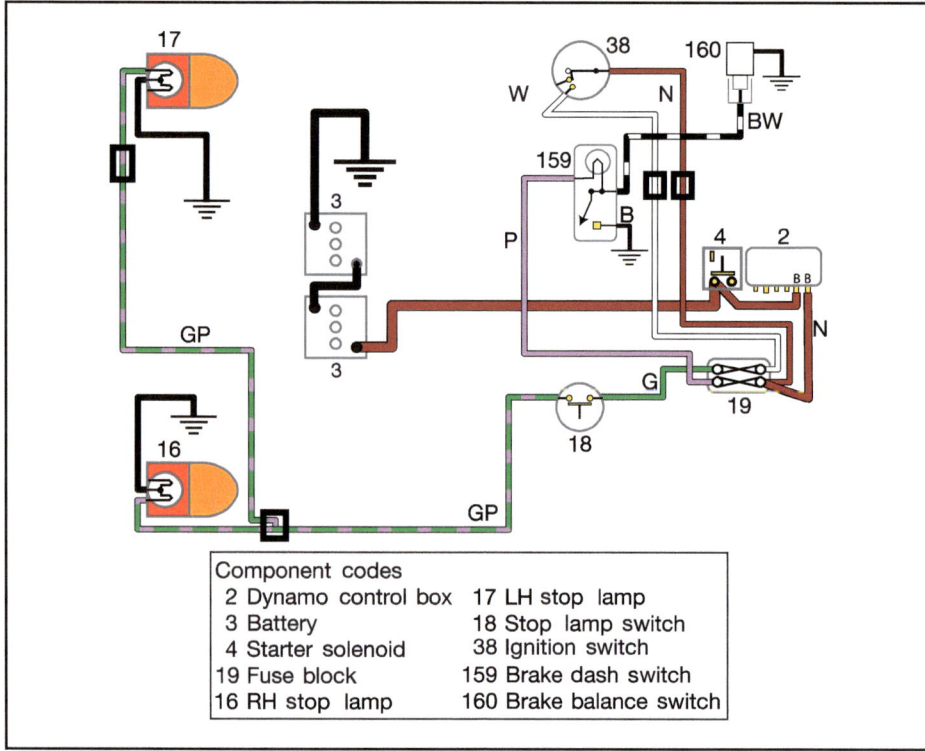

Figure 12.35. Early brake circuit, including brake pressure balance check system where fitted.

that goes to the brake lamp switch (18). Early cars had a carry over system from the MGA, which uses a hydraulic switch (Figure 12.36), located at the union where the brake pipes meet. The switch closes under brake fluid pressure, routing current on green/purple (GP) wires to the brake lamps (16 & 17).

On some vehicles, a dash mounted lamp, incorporated in a switch (159) is connected to a fused, but always powered, purple (P) wire. The other side of the bulb is joined, via a black/white (BW) wire, to a pressure differential switch that detects when a shuttle valve moves off centre as a result of unequal pressure in the independent brake lines. If this happens, the switch is actuated and it earths one side of the lamp in the switch, illuminating it and alerting the driver. As a check that the bulb is not blown, the driver can press the switch to illuminate it. Note that this check on the integrity of the brake pressure balance circuit requires driver action and would not detect if the black/white wire became disconnected.

The use of silicone brake fluid is a common cause of hydraulic brake switch failure. Silicone oil is very invasive, and can find its way into the

Figure 12.36. An hydraulic brake switch.

Early brake circuit

Figure 12.35 shows an early brake circuit. Not all components were fitted to all vehicles.

Power from the battery (3) is routed by a large cable to the starter motor solenoid (4) that acts an anchor and termination point. The current is taken to the fuse block, (19) used as another anchor point, and to the ignition switch (38). When closed, the ignition switch directs the current via a white (W) wire, to the fuse block (19) and through a fuse where it exits on a green (G) wire

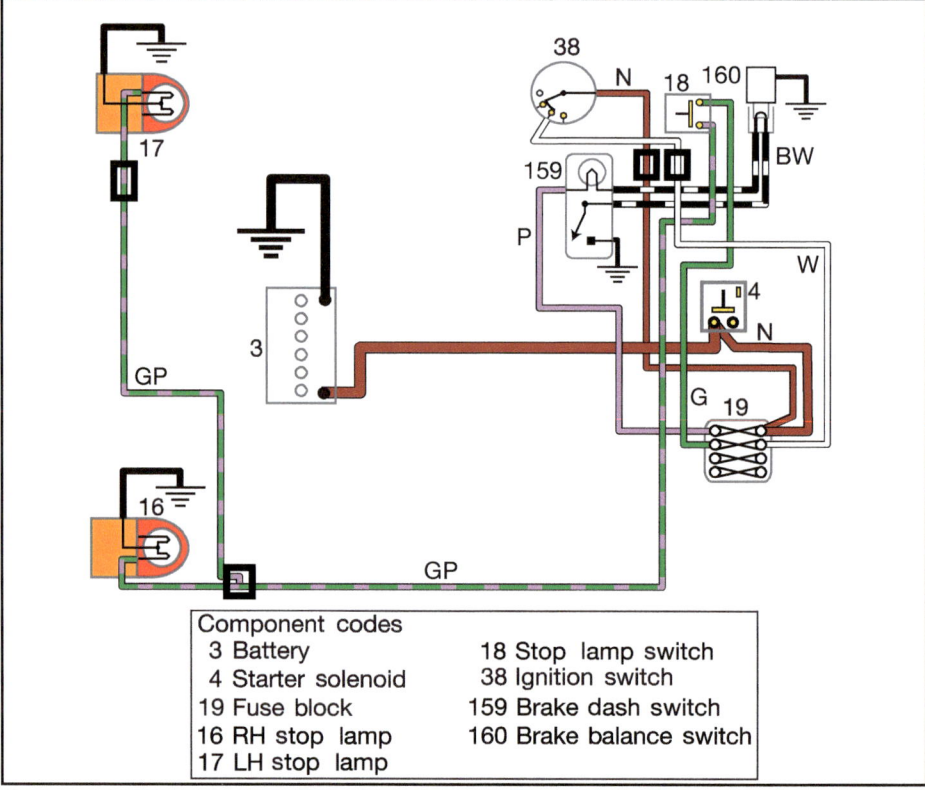

Figure 12.37. Later brake circuit, including brake pressure balance check system where fitted.

130

LIGHTING

electrical part of the switch mechanism. Either the fluid itself or its vapour can get onto the switch contacts. The superheating effect of the small spark that occurs between the contacts as they open turns the silicone into silica, a form of glass – a very good insulator. The switch is thus rendered inoperative.

Later brake circuit

The basic brake circuit, illustrated in Figure 12.37, has changed only in detail. The hydraulic brake switch has been replaced by one installed on the pedal box (Figure 12.38). It is normally depressed and open. The action of lifting the brake pedal lets the switch button release and closes the switch. It can be adjusted by screwing it in or out of the pedal box, a lock-nut being used to fix the final position. Disconnect the bullet connectors supplying the switch before adjusting it, otherwise the wires will become twisted and over stress the connections to the switch, which may later fail.

The later circuit shows that the position of the brake lamps was moved to the lower section of the rear lamp assembly.

Changes were also made to the brake balance detection circuit so that a limitation of the former test switch circuit would be overcome. Driver intervention is still needed but failure of the connecting wires would be detected.

An extra contact was added to both the dash test switch Figure 12.39 and the balance switch Figure 12.40, those on the latter switch having a jumper link between them.

When the test switch (159) is pressed, in order for the lamp to become earthed and illuminate, current must be able flow on the black/white

Figure 12.38. The mechanically operated brake switch (black arrow) and pressure balance switch (red arrow).

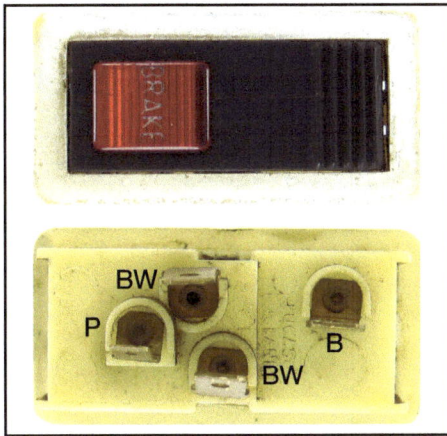

Figure 12.39. Front and back views of the brake balance test switch. The letters indicate wire colours. Early switches have only three terminals.

Figure 12.40. An example of a brake balance detection switch.

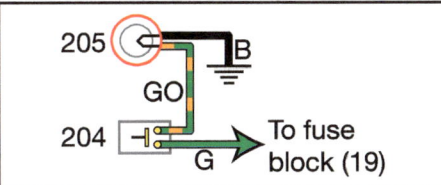

Figure 12.41. The handbrake warning lamp circuit location.

wires to the balance switch (160), through the link and back to the dash switch. In the event that the wires from the dash switch to the balance switch become disconnected, the lamp will not light.

Brake lamp circuit with handbrake warning lamp

A very simple circuit, illustrated in Figure 12.41, was used in some late cars to illuminate a lamp and warn the driver should the handbrake (parking brake) be left on. A green (G) wire from the fuse block, which is fused and only powered when the ignition is on, feeds power to the handbrake switch (204) shown in Figure 12.42. When the

Figure 12.42. The handbrake switch location.

handbrake is on, the switch is closed allowing it to pass current on a green/orange (GO) wire to a dash-mounted warning lamp (205).

North American models had a far more complex circuit, as illustrated in Figure 12.43.

The objective was to check for failure of the brake pressure warning lamp without the driver having to remember to push a switch. The warning lamp was given double duty as a handbrake warning lamp also.

When the starter motor relay (174) is activated by the white/red (WR) wire, current can also flow through the diode (203) and on green/orange (GO) wires to the warning lamp (205), illuminating it. Thus, every time the car is cranked, if the bulb is good, it will indicate the fact to the driver. Two other components are also connected on green/orange wires to the brake warning lamp: the handbrake switch (204) and the brake balance switch (160). Should either of these switch power to the warning lamp it will light. It is imperative, however, that current from these sources does not find its way back to the starter relay. If it did, the car would crank every time the handbrake was applied, or there was a pressure imbalance between the two brake circuits. The diode blocks the back flow of current, so that, while the ignition switch start contact can supply current to the brake warning lamp, the lamp cannot supply current back to the starter relay.

Failure of the diode is sometimes the cause of a mysterious and very damaging fault. When diodes fail they tend to short circuit in both directions so that the starter may, for no obvious reason, run continuously and burn itself out. It is not an intuitive reaction to release the handbrake when this happens, but it would indeed prevent the starter from running.

Figure 12.44 shows the location of the diode. It can be hard to find,

MGB ELECTRICAL SYSTEMS – THE ESSENTIAL MANUAL

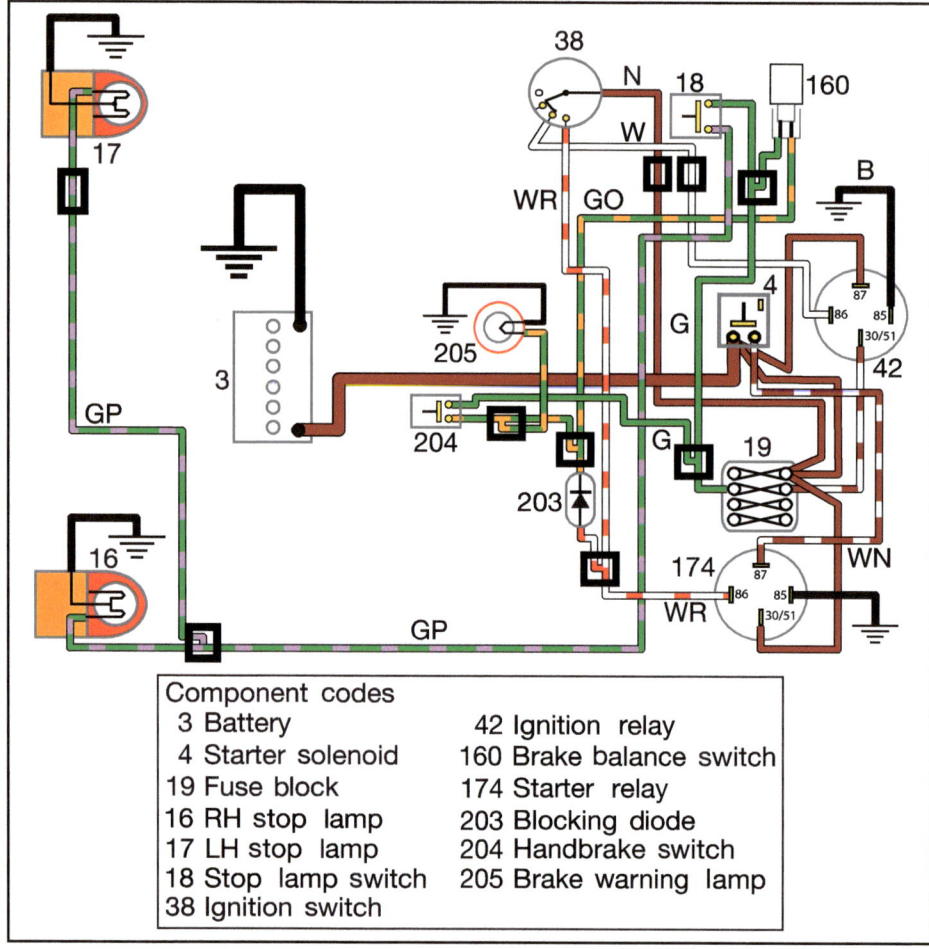

Component codes
- 3 Battery
- 4 Starter solenoid
- 19 Fuse block
- 16 RH stop lamp
- 17 LH stop lamp
- 18 Stop lamp switch
- 38 Ignition switch
- 42 Ignition relay
- 160 Brake balance switch
- 174 Starter relay
- 203 Blocking diode
- 204 Handbrake switch
- 205 Brake warning lamp

Figure 12.43. The handbrake warning circuit with pressure balance detection.

Figure 12.45. The brake diode.

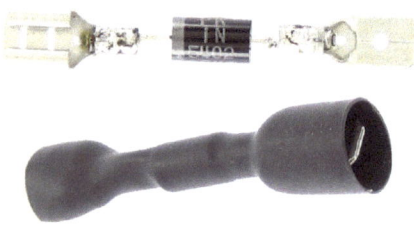

Figure 12.46. A suggested construction for a replacement brake diode.

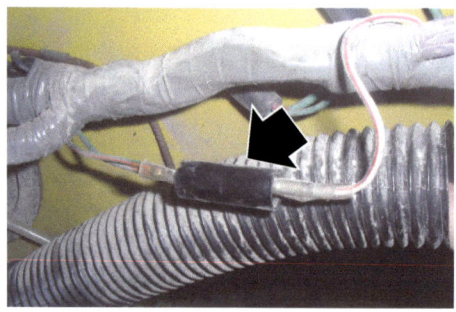

Figure 12.44. The location of the brake diode.

under the dash on the right side of the car, and having an appearance, Figure 12.45, not unlike that of a bullet connector.

Replacement diodes are hard to find and expensive. A diode assembly, that can be made extremely cheaply, will work just as well, and will probably be more robust than the original. A suggested construction is shown in Figure 12.46. Low cost, uninsulated crimp terminals were selected. However, the solid wire of a diode does not crimp well, so the sleeving over the crimp barrels was easily pulled off and the diode soldered to them. The short leads on the diode mean that it will get hot during soldering. Modern diodes are robust and should not be harmed, but it is worth taking some care not to heat them more than is necessary.

The diode is a 3A type 1N5402. A 1A diode would suffice but it was considered prudent to use a physically stronger device. It is very important that the female contact goes to the cathode, the end with a band on it, and the male to the anode. The assembly should be insulated. Do not use tape, it will not last. A piece of small bore hose can be glued or caulked to retain it over the diode so that it looks somewhat like the original. A heat shrink sleeve was used on that in Figure 12.46, some metal tube temporarily used at each end to prevent the sleeve shrinking where access to the terminals is required.

IMPROVING LAMP EARTHING

As discussed in Chapter 5, sneak currents around poor earths in lamp circuits can cause some peculiar effects. The earths are inherently bad on both front and rear side/turn/brake lamp assemblies and improvement can prevent or solve problems and provide more reliable and brighter lamps.

The lamp units have no earth wire and rely on the fixing screws to do the job of joining the lamp unit to chassis earth. The lamps cannot be tightened very much because of the foam seating gaskets. Moreover, the fixing screws themselves are often of a stamped, rather than machined, construction that can accept only limited tightening torque.

Bringing a wire back to a known good earth point is not difficult and is worthwhile. For the rear lamps, the fixing point for the boot lid or rear door latch striker is a good place to choose as an earth. Unlike the boot, at the front of the car there are plenty of good internal panels that can be drilled and fitted with self-tapping screws. See page 15 for a discussion on suitable ring terminals and serrated washers.

Figure 12.47 shows a rear lamp unit. Note there are only two wires going to the stop/tail to supply those two functions and there is no earth

LIGHTING

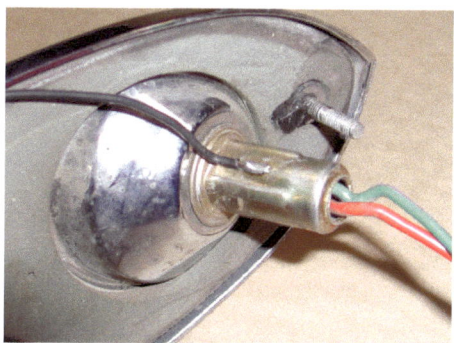

Figure 12.47. In order to improve lamp earthing, a wire can be soldered to a bulb holder.

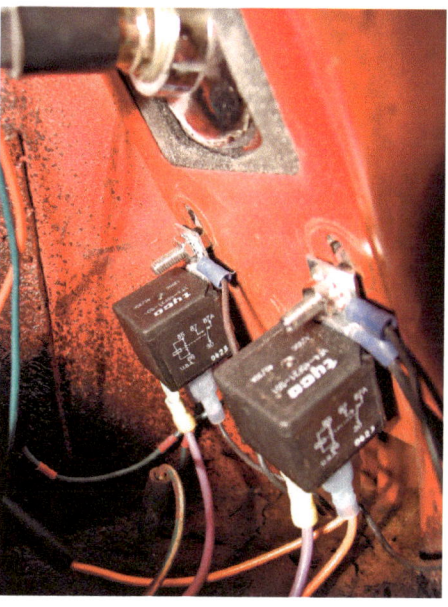

Figure 12.48. Stop and turn relays fitted to a right rear lamp unit.

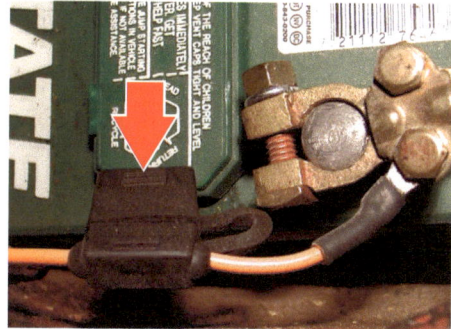

Figure 12.49. Power for the lamps is supplied directly from a fuse fitted close to the battery.

wire. There is also only a single wire to the turn signal bulb holder (not shown). The bulb holder itself does lend itself to soldering and so a wire has been added that be taken back to a secure electrical earth point. It takes quite a lot of heat to solder a plated steel component like the bulb holder and not everyone has the necessary high power soldering iron. An alternative is to use a ring terminal and a serrated washer under one of the lamp housing fixing screws and tighten that up as much as possible.

IMPROVING STOP AND TURN SIGNALS

As was discussed on page 116, the wire lengths, particularly on LHD cars, and the number of switches and connectors in circuit, can cause both the stop and turn lamps to receive too little voltage and to operate at less than 50% of the bulb design brightness. Adding higher powered lamps such as some of the high wattage halogen types becomes counter productive when the additional current only results in more voltage drop. Using relays to switch current directly to the brake and rear turn signals, and using the wires that normally supply the lamps to energize the relays with less than 0.2A, makes a tremendous difference. In addition, the reduced load on the overall turn signal circuit increases the brightness of the front turn lamps too.

Applying relays to the turn signal circuit does require an electronic flasher module that does not operate faster when a lamp is out. The relays take so little current that a thermal flasher interprets the reduction as lamp failure.

The voltage drop problem is much less severe with the tail lamps that have shorter wire runs, less connectors, fewer switches and draw less current. Hence there is less benefit gained from using relays in this application.

There is no point in adding relays if the rear lamp units are not well earthed as described in the preceding section.

Figure 12.48 shows stop and turn relays supported by the fixing screws for the right hand rear lamp assembly. Which relay is used for which of the two functions is not important. The brake relay is used for both right and left hand lamps, so only a single relay, for the left turn signal, is needed on the left of the car. Indeed, if there were room, all three relays could be fitted on the right side.

The lamp power is supplied from the battery, which being at the back of the car, permits the use of a very short wire run to the relays. A pre wired proprietary automotive fuse of 20A rating has been used in the example shown in Figure 12.49. One end of the fuse wire has been crimped to a ring terminal and fitted to the hot side of the battery. The other end of the fuse wire has been spliced to a 12AWG (4mm²) wire and taken into the boot area through a hole into which a protective grommet is fitted. During wiring, the fuse should be removed.

Figure 12.50 shows the circuit. For each function, the bullet connector joining the lamp to the harness has been disconnected, the male bullets removed and a spade terminal substituted.

Power from the fuse has been brought to each relay by daisy-chaining (Figure 2.13) 14AWG (2.5mm²) wire between terminals 30 of each one. An alternative method would have been to butt-splice (Figure 2.17) the wire from the fuse to individual wires to each relay.

The relays have been earthed at terminal 86. As can be seen in Figure 12.48, the earth connection is achieved via a ring terminal fixed to the same screw as the relay support. A serrated washer is used under the fixing to provide both good electrical connection and inhibit rotation. It is essential that this connection be firmly tightened. Some thread lock used sparingly on the thread and around the nut would offer additional security to the connection.

Each harness wire is brought to terminal 85 of a relay.

Wires from the four lamps are brought to terminal 87 of the respective relay, the two brake lamp wires sharing a contact or being spliced together elsewhere.

Operation is simple. When a stop or turn signal is operated, power, constant or pulsed, is applied to terminal 85 of the respective relay coil, energizing it and closing the contact between terminal 30 and 87. Current from the battery can travel the short distance through the fuse to the splice, through the relay and from there to the lamp.

COURTESY LAMPS

Most of the electrical circuits in an MGB/C are high side switched; that is to say, power input from the battery, be it direct, via the ignition switch or a fuse, is passed through a switch that either allows the current to travel to a load, or interrupts it. The load is earthed so that current flowing in it can return, via the vehicle frame, to the low side of the battery.

For some loads, it is much more

MGB ELECTRICAL SYSTEMS – THE ESSENTIAL MANUAL

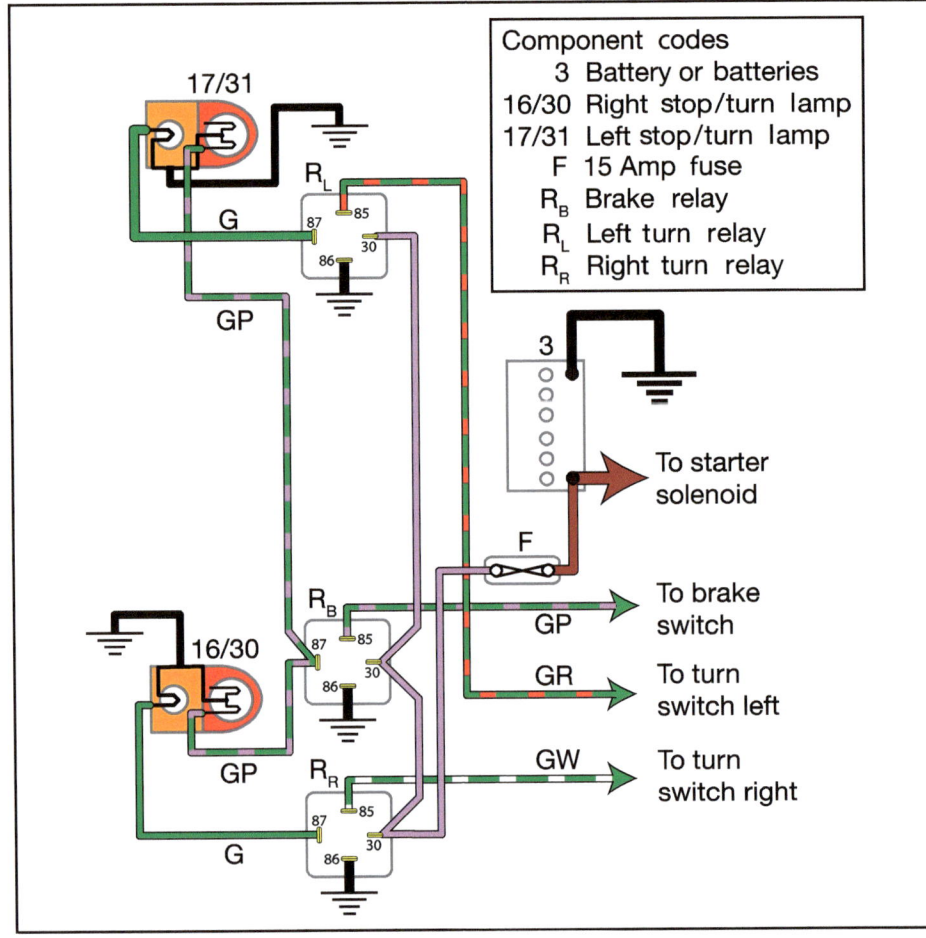

Figure 12.50. Relays added to the stop and rear turn signals to improve lamp brightness.

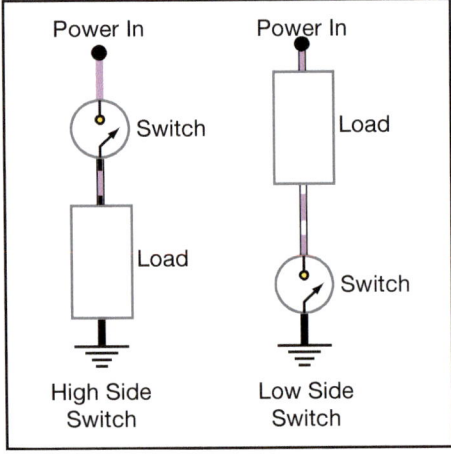

Figure 12.51. High and low side switching circuits.

harmless event for an interior lamp.

In the MGB/C virtually all the courtesy switches are supplied by the fused, always hot, purple line. All the wires from the lamps to the switches are purple/white. If the courtesy lamps fail, check the operation of the horn and the clock, if there is one. These are on the same fuse and their coincidental failure would make that suspect.

With the possible exception of light bulb failure, the predominant problem with courtesy lamps is door switch failure caused by corrosion. A typical door switch is shown in Figure 12.52. This example is retained with two screws into the A pillar. To remove it just undo the screws and withdraw it just enough to reveal the bullet connector pushed onto the back. It is worthwhile tying a piece of string at least 18in (45cm) long to the wire before removing the connector, because the wire has a habit of springing back into the pillar and becoming lost inside. Corrosion may make removal of the contact quite difficult, and cause some to doubt that the connector really does pull off the back off the switch.

Any plastic switches in the door pillar are not intended for operating courtesy lamps. These are fitted for functions that require a switch that is insulated from the body metal. Once such example is connected with the system that warns of a key left in the ignition and on cars with the sequential seat belt system (see page 183), the switch status being one of the many data inputs.

Some cars have a switch fixed by a threaded barrel, as in Figure 12.53. The operation of the switch is identical to that with screw holes but more care must be taken in removing it. Use an open-ended spanner on the nut while at the same time gripping the plunger with pliers to stop it rotating. Failure to do so will result in the wire twisting and possibly breaking as the switch is unscrewed.

Figure 12.53 shows a switch in the closed and open positions. Pressing the plunger pushes it, and the wire attachment, backward against the force of a spring. Some fine oil may be needed in order to get the button and its spring moving freely. Contact is made at the points arrowed and corrosion on these surfaces will prevent the switch from working. As the plating will have already gone from a corroded switch, any repair is usually temporary but can be fairly long lasting, so is worth a try.

convenient to use low side switching. As shown in Figure 12.51, in low side switching, the positions of the load and the switch are reversed, the switch allowing, or not, the current to pass to earth. Low side switching is particularly useful where a single load may be connected to several switches, as is the case with courtesy lamps. A single lamp load may be operated by one of a number of switches in the low side of the circuit, such as those on the two passenger doors, the hatch of an MGB/C-GT and possibly a switch on the dash or in the roof of the GT. Wire length is saved because each switch needs only a single feed from the load.

Low side switching is used on modern cars because functions are often switched electronically using a field effect transistor (FET). It happens that N-channel FETs, the type used for low side switching in negative earth cars, are cheaper than the P-channel FETs required for high side switching.

Although several wires may run from a load to low side switches located in difficult to access parts of the car, increasing the probability of a short circuit, any that occur simply switch the load on. That's a comparatively

LIGHTING

Figure 12.52. A courtesy door switch with screw fixing.

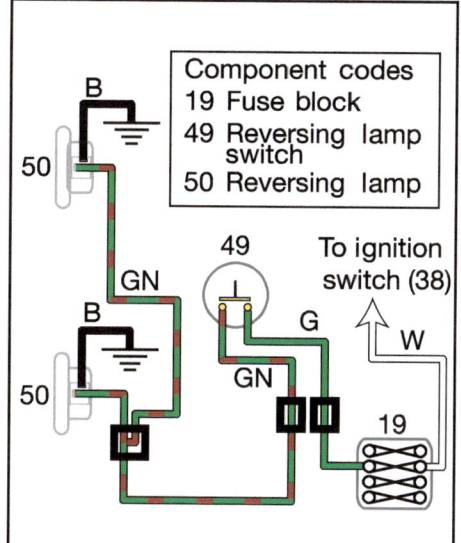

Figure 12.54. The reversing lamp circuit.

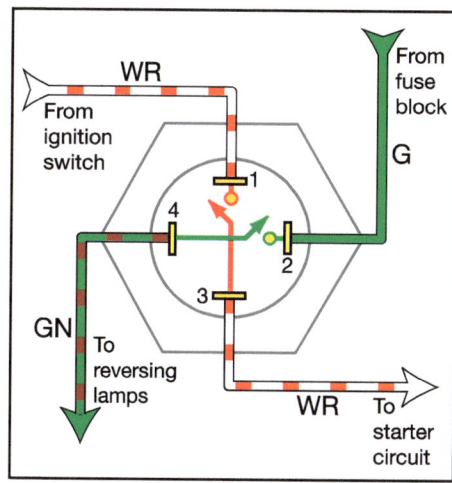

Figure 12.55. The combined automatic-transmission reversing lamp and starter inhibitor switch.

Figure 12.56. A view of the inverted reversing lamp housing showing the wire terminations.

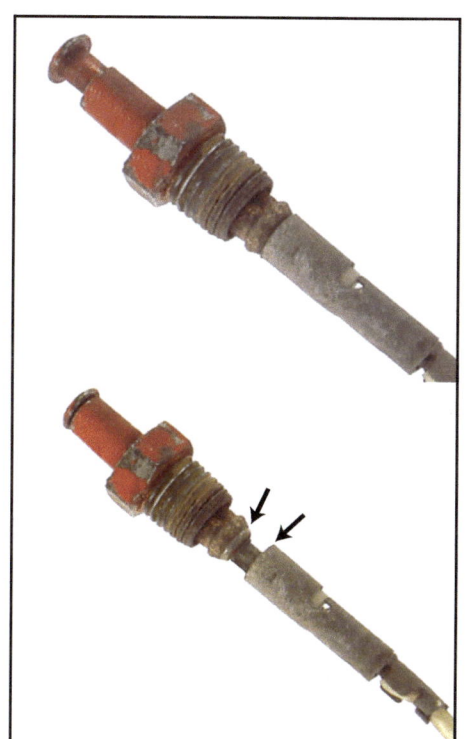

Figure 12.53. A courtesy door switch with threaded fixing.

Clean the surfaces by making one contact face abrade against the other so as to bed them together and achieve more points of contact. One way to do this is to clamp and rotate the plunger in a slow speed chuck, like that of a power screwdriver, while the switch body is held stationary.

Battery run-down will occur if a courtesy lamp switch does not properly open. This is an unusual fault that may not be noticed in the case of the boot-mounted lamp. Removing a reversing lamp provides an easy method to look inside the boot to check that the lamp extinguishes.

REVERSING LAMPS

Reversing (back-up) lamps were fitted from 1967 on. The circuit, Figure 12.54, is extremely simple. Current from the ignition switch is carried to the fuse block (19) and from there on a green (G) wire to the switch (49), which is mounted on the gearbox. When reverse gear is selected, the switch closes and current can flow to the reversing lamps (50) on green/brown (GN) wires.

The major problems with this circuit come from switch failure. The switch is mounted in a very inhospitable area under the car. Early switches were not splash-proof and water can enter, causing the springs to corrode and the contacts to oxidize. Switch replacement and refurbishment is discussed in Chapter 13.

Automatic-transmission vehicles have a combined reversing lamp and starter inhibitor switch shown in Figure 12.55 and also discussed in Chapter 13.

All reversing lamp connectors are vulnerable to disconnection or even damage from moving objects in the boot. The connector can be replaced with individual 3/16 inch (4.75mm) insulated female blade connectors. The original two way connector ensures that the earth and power wires are correctly inserted. If they are not, a short circuit will occur. Should individual connectors be used, it is very important that the earth and power wires are connected to the lamp as per Figure 12.56.

MGB ELECTRICAL SYSTEMS – THE ESSENTIAL MANUAL

LIGHT BULB CHART

Application	Fitting	Power	UK #	Euro #	US #
Back-up/reverse	Festoon SV8.5	18W or 21W	270, 273	C21W	6411
Courtesy	Festoon SV8.5	5W or 6W	239, 254 or 258	C5W	6418
Turn signal	SBC bayonet Ba15s	21W	382	P21W	1073 or 1156
License plate '70 US split bumper	Capless	5W		W5W	194
Number plate '62 -'74.5	MCC bayonet Ba9s	6W	207	T4W	53 or 1895
Number plate '74.5-'80	Festoon	18W or 21W	273	C21W	6411
Map '62-'70	Edison screw E10	2.2W	987	E10	52
Map '71-'80	Festoon SU8	5W or 6W	239, 254 or 258		6418
Panel illumination	Edison screw E10	2.2W	987	E10	52
Parking – front '62-'69	MCC bayonet Ba9s	6W	989	T4W	1895
Side marker '70-'80	MCC bayonet Ba9s	6W	989	T4W	1895
Side/indicator – front '70-'80	SCC bay15dt	5W/21W	380	P21W	1157
Stop/tail – rear	SCC bay15dt	5W/21W	380	P21W	1157
Boot/trunk (roadster) / tailgate (GT)	Festoon SV8.5	5W or 6W	239, 254 or 258	C5W	6418
Headlight	Sealed beam	50W/40W		H4	H6024
Headlight	BPF cap retained	45/40	410	-	
Headlight	UEC 3 blade contacts	45/40	411	P45t-41	R2

Table 12.2. Replacement bulb chart.

LIGHTING FAULT-FINDING

Symptom	Possible causes	Action
Any lamp failure.	Light bulb failure.	Replace the bulb.
	Switch failure.	Jumper across the relevant switch. If the lamps then work then change the switch.
Turn, brake or reverse lamp failure.	Fuse failure.	Whichever function has failed, check first if the other two functions work. If not, change the fuse or clean fuse block contacts. See page 43.
Peculiar lamp operation. Switching one lamp on causes another to fail.	Sneak currents around poor earth connections.	Check and remake the earth connections to affected lamps.
Turn signals do not work.	Turn signal module failed.	Replace the module.
	Hazard switch bad.	Remove the green wires from the hazard switch and join them together. If turn the signals work, replace hazard switch.
Courtesy lamps failure.	Switch failure.	See page 133.
	Fuse blown.	Check if the horn, and clock if fitted, work, If not change fuse or clean fuse block contacts. See page 43.

Table 12.3. Lighting fault-finding chart.

Chapter 13
Overdrive & gearbox

OVERDRIVE

The overdrive is controlled by a solenoid that, when powered, closes a dump valve, thus causing hydraulic pressure to rise and engage the system. Because hydraulic pressure is needed to run the overdrive, operation from the starting gears, 1st and 2nd, is inhibited using a switch that closes when the car is in 3rd or 4th gear (4th gear only in V8s and after '77). The same switch also prevents damage that could occur should overdrive operate in reverse gear.

Changes to the overdrive and some regulatory requirements, unrelated to the overdrive itself, resulted in changes to its electrical circuit.

The original 'D' type overdrive has a control circuit that includes a vacuum switch and latching relay. The purpose of these components is to prevent the overdrive disengaging when the vehicle is in overrun and using engine braking. If the vacuum switch detects a high manifold depression as a result of the carburettor butterfly valves being closed while the engine is turning at a reasonable speed, it energizes the self-latching relay that holds the overdrive in engagement, irrespective of commands to release it from the driver's switch, but not incidentally, the gearbox switch. When the overdrive was changed to the 'LH' type in 1968, the vacuum switch and its relay were not considered necessary and they were removed.

PRE-1968 OVERDRIVE CIRCUIT

Figure 13.1 shows the circuit for cars made through 1967 using the 'D' type overdrive unit.

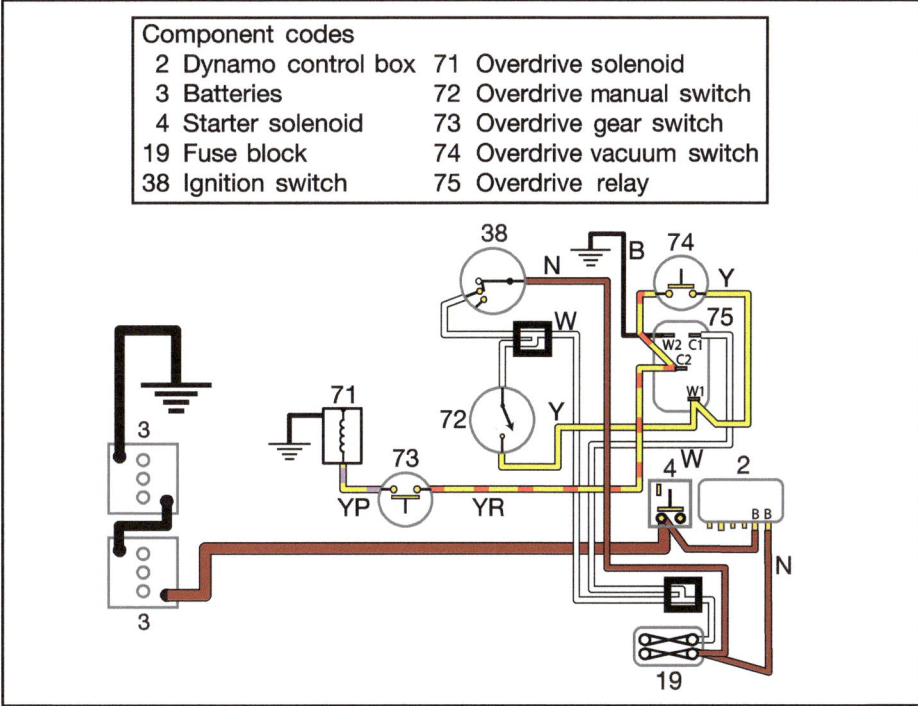

Figure 13.1. The pre-1968 overdrive circuit.

MGB ELECTRICAL SYSTEMS – THE ESSENTIAL MANUAL

Power from the batteries (3) is routed by a large cable to the starter motor solenoid (4) that acts as an anchor and termination point. It then goes on brown (N) wires via the dynamo control box (2), which is also used as a wire anchoring point. The current is taken to the fuse block, (19) yet another anchor point, and to the ignition switch (38). When closed, the ignition switch directs the current via a white (W) wire, to the fuse block (19).

A tap from the same white wire directs current to the overdrive manual switch (72), which at this time, was usually dash mounted. When the driver engages overdrive, the switch is closed and current flows on a yellow (Y) wire to the coil of the overdrive relay (75), shown in Figure 13.2, energizing it and closing its contacts. This action allows current taken from another tap on the white wire to flow from relay contacts C1 to C2 and then on a yellow/red (YR) wire to the overdrive gear switch (73). If the car is in either 3rd or 4th gear, this switch is closed and current is directed on a yellow/purple (YP) wire to the overdrive solenoid (71) that operates and engages the system.

Similarly, if the driver chooses to disengage the overdrive by opening the manual switch, the circuit is broken and the overdrive solenoid is de-energized. If, however, prior to the driver opening the manual switch, the car is in overrun, using engine breaking with the throttle closed, there will be a high depression in the inlet manifold and vacuum switch (74), shown in Figure 13.3, will be closed. It will then take current from the powered C2 terminal of the relay and feed it back to the coil, latching the relay on and overriding the driver's switch until the throttle is opened and the manifold pressure rises.

POST 1968 OVERDRIVE CIRCUIT

With the changed to the 'LH' overdrive the circuit that inhibits overdrive disengagement during overrun was deemed unnecessary and so the vacuum switch and relay were removed from the circuit as shown in Figure 13.4.

Power from the battery (3) is routed by a large cable to the starter motor solenoid (4) that acts as an anchor and termination point. The current is taken to the fuse block, (19) used as another anchor point, and to the ignition switch (38). When closed, the ignition switch directs the current via a white (W) wire, to the ignition relay (42) or, in cars without an ignition relay, directly to the overdrive manual switch (72). The ignition relay, where fitted is energized at any time the ignition switch is closed and it passes current from the fuse block to the manual switch on a white/brown (WN) wire.

Figure 13.2. The overdrive relay.

Figure 13.3. The overdrive vacuum switch.

Figure 13.5. The LH overdrive solenoid.

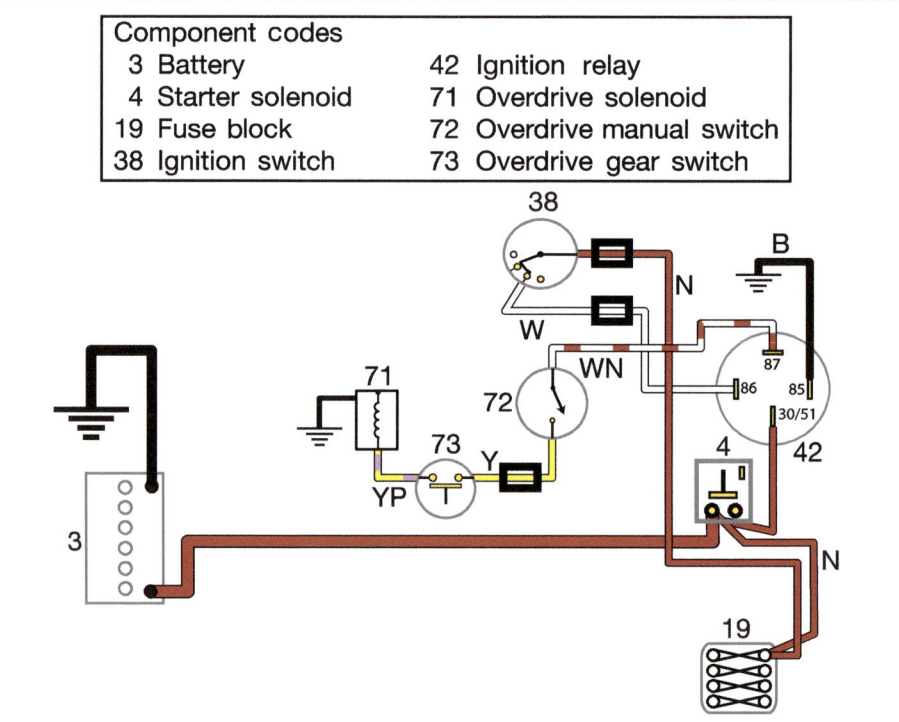

Figure 13.4. The 1968 overdrive circuit.

Component codes
- 3 Battery
- 4 Starter solenoid
- 19 Fuse block
- 38 Ignition switch
- 42 Ignition relay
- 71 Overdrive solenoid
- 72 Overdrive manual switch
- 73 Overdrive gear switch

OVERDRIVE & GEARBOX

When the driver wishes to engage the overdrive, the manual switch, now usually part of the column mounted wiper switch, is closed and current flows on a yellow wire to the overdrive gear switch (73). If the car is in either 3rd or 4th gear, this switch is closed and current is directed on a yellow/purple (YP) wire to the overdrive solenoid (71) that operates and engages the system.

The LH solenoid is mounted on the bottom of the overdrive, Figure 13.5. The earlier D solenoid is cylindrical and mounted on the right hand side.

POST 1977 NORTH AMERICAN OVERDRIVE CIRCUIT

The introduction of TCSA (see page 101) required a method of detecting when the car is in 4th gear. The overdrive gear switch, which was by this time fitted to all cars with the electrical advance system irrespective of whether or not an overdrive was installed, was used for this purpose (together with a micro-switch in 1977 cars). The modification necessitated a rearrangement of the overdrive switches, essentially reordering them so that the gear switch was placed upstream of the manual switch.

Power from the battery (3) is routed by a large cable to the starter motor solenoid (4) that acts an anchor and termination point. The current is taken to the fuse block (19), used as another anchor point, and to the ignition switch (38). When closed, the ignition switch directs the current via a white (W) wire,

Figure 13.7. The gear stick-mounted overdrive switch.

to the ignition relay (42). A tap on the same white wire takes power to the fuel cut-off inertia switch (70) (see page 167) and on to the fuel pump (41). Because this wire runs to the back of the car it is convenient to tap off it so as to provide power to the overdrive gear switch (73). If the car is in either 3rd or 4th gear, this switch is closed and current is directed on a yellow (Y) wire to the overdrive manual switch and the vacuum advance micro-switch that is part of the electrical vacuum advance mechanism.

When the driver closes the overdrive manual switch, which is a slide switch mounted on the gear lever (Figure 13.7), current is directed on a yellow/purple wire to overdrive solenoid (71) that operates and engages the system.

OVERDRIVE PROBLEMS

Failure of the overdrive may well be caused by a mechanical problem that will require fairly major work, including removing the engine and transmission before the overdrive can even be properly accessed. It is prudent, therefore, to first check that the electrical system is working properly.

There are a number of electrical switches in series that provide power to the solenoid and failure in any one switch, its connectors or wiring, will prevent the overdrive solenoid from being energized. Referencing the relevant circuit diagram, it is worth probing each connecting point with a circuit tester in order to establish where any break might be. It will be necessary to have the ignition on, the driver's overdrive switch closed and the car in 3rd or 4th gear while doing this. As both a safety precaution, and to prevent the ignition coil from overheating during prolonged fault diagnosis, the low-tension wire or wires from one side of the coil should be removed.

Although not perhaps the easiest part of the car at which to start, the probability is that the fault lies under the car so it is actually worthwhile working backward from the solenoid. It may be possible to hear the operation of the 'D' overdrive solenoid when an assistant operates the driver's switch. Unfortunately, the 'LH' solenoid operates inside the overdrive, is immersed in oil and is almost silent.

The 'D' overdrive actuating rod can be observed in operation by removing a cover plate on the right hand side. There is also an adjustment method to the mechanical actuation that is outside the purview of this book.

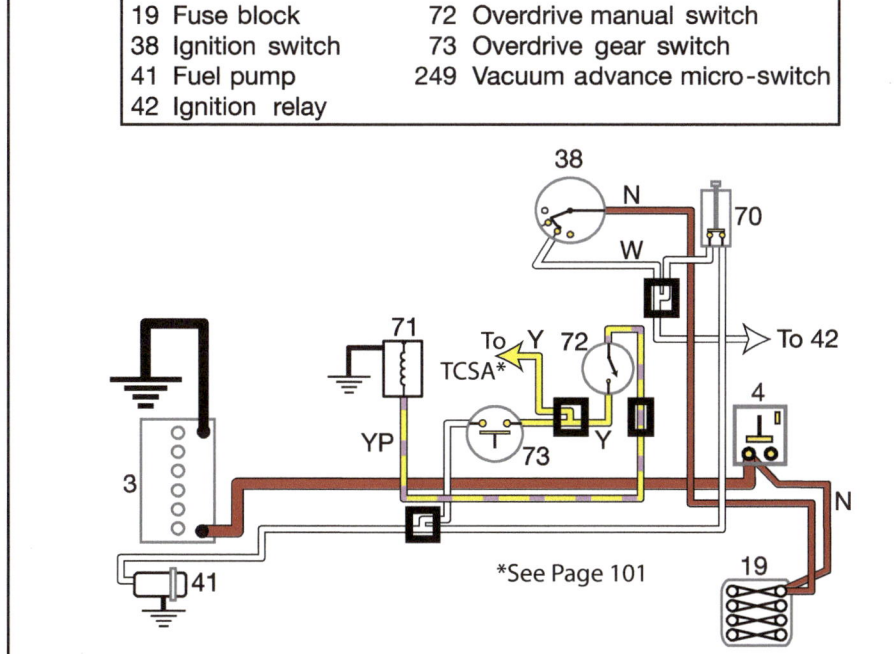

Component codes	
3 Battery	70 Fuel cut-off switch
4 Starter solenoid	71 Overdrive solenoid
19 Fuse block	72 Overdrive manual switch
38 Ignition switch	73 Overdrive gear switch
41 Fuel pump	249 Vacuum advance micro-switch
42 Ignition relay	

Figure 13.6. The North American overdrive circuit from 1977.

MGB ELECTRICAL SYSTEMS – THE ESSENTIAL MANUAL

Figure 13.8. The location of the gearbox switches.

Figure 13.11. Caulk can be used to seal the switch. That used here is of a type which cures clear so that the final switch will not look so messy.

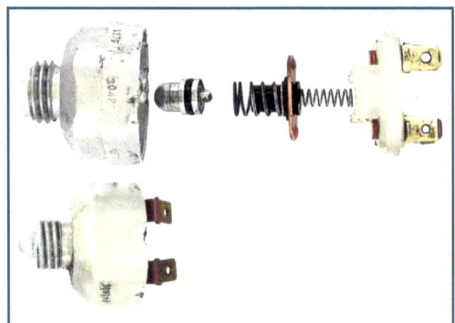

Figure 13.9. The reversing/overdrive switch.

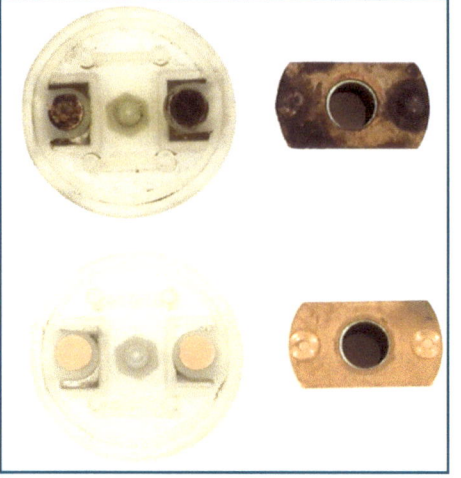

Figure 13.10. A switch as first disassembled (top) and the same switch cleaned.

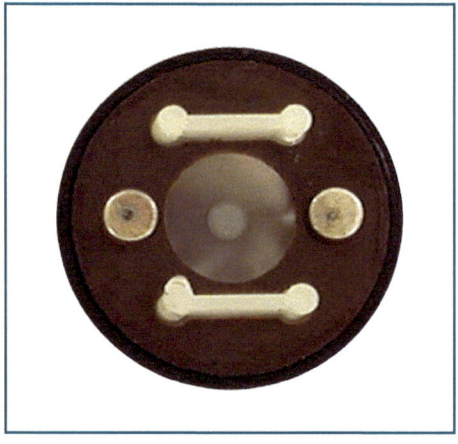

Figure 13.12. The later reverse and overdrive switch had a sealing washer fitted. This example shows the effects of some contact arcing but no corrosion damage.

Only remove the solenoid from the 'LH' overdrive if power is shown to be getting to its connecting wire and that it is obviously not damaged along its length. The overdrive runs in the same oil as the gearbox and dirt can cause solenoid operating problems. Be prepared to lose some oil, and for the coil bobbin and a small ball bearing to fall out. Note that it is all too easy to lose the ball bearing and to break the wire connection to the coil.

By far the biggest cause of failure in the overdrive circuit is failure of the gear switch. Those made before about 1974 were not well sealed and the switch is in a splash zone. Any water in a switch will result in reduced pressure on the contacts due to spring corrosion, as well as oxidization and erosion of the contacts, all of which increase contact resistance, often to the point where the switch is effectively open circuit.

Gear and reversing switches

The switch used for reversing (backup) lamps and that used to activate the overdrive are identical. The reversing lamp switch can be removed with the transmission in situ but the overdrive switch is extremely difficult to access. Figure 13.8 shows the positions of all the switches that may be found on an MGB/C. Not all switches will be installed on all cars.

The switches, once removed, can be disassembled. The aluminium body around the hexagonal section is peened over the plastic insulator, and can be pulled back with pliers until the insulator is freed. Be careful that no springs fly out as the switch is opened. Figure 13.9 shows the order of the internal components.

If there was any need to open the switch then in all probability the contacts will look like that at the top of Figure 13.10. General cleaning of all parts is advantageous but the electrical contact areas need most attention. The fixed contact surfaces will no doubt be pitted, and some gentle work with a fine flat rat's tail file or an emery board will be required to get them smooth and square. The moving contact is too thin to file and so needs attacking with a wire brush and fine sandpaper.

OVERDRIVE & GEARBOX

Once all switch parts are clean, put a little grease on the plunger O-ring to keep it moving and to repel water.

Reassemble the switch and peen the edges of the aluminium housing over the plastic insulator. To prevent future failure some caulk can be applied around the interface between the housing and the insulator as shown in Figure 13.11.

Figure 13.12 is provided for reference, the expectation being that this type of switch will not require opening. It has a rubber diaphragm over the insulator that seals against a ledge on the interior of the housing, keeping moisture out.

INHIBITOR SWITCH

The inhibitor switch is installed on cars with the sequential seatbelt system. That system was troublesome, but whether or not it still works, the switch can be useful for other applications.

The switch, which closes its contacts whenever the car is in gear, was installed from 1971 to 1974 and is located on the gearbox selector housing (Figure 13.8) in the same position that previous cars had a detent ball and spring under a brass cap nut. Unfortunately, the switch cannot be retrofitted to older gearboxes because the thread size of the switch is much smaller than that of the nut.

Figure 13.13 shows a replacement switch, which unlike the original has a degree of sealing. In the event that this switch is hard to find, it is also listed as the reversing lamp switch for MG Midget, A-H Sprite and Triumph Spitfire.

The inhibitor switch is accessible from under the car and like the other gearbox switches, it can be opened by prising back the metal that is peened over the insulator. The failed switch shown in Figure 13.14 had severe pitting on the surface of the copper annular moving contact. It and the fixed contact were cleaned, the switch reassembled and sealed with caulk before being reinstalled in the car where it has since proven reliable.

To check the operation of the switch before use in the following projects or for any other reason, look for a pair of wires, one green the other yellow/orange, bundled with at least a green/purple from the reversing lamp, coming from under the car and terminating in the junction area below the fuse block. The green wire should be plugged into a bullet connector,

Figure 13.13. This replacement inhibitor switch has sealant around the wires and interfaces.

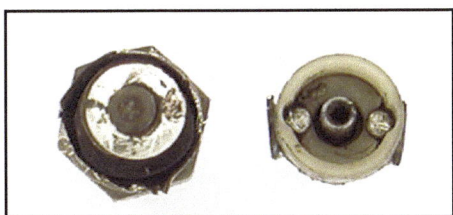

Figure 13.14. Inside an inhibitor switch that failed.

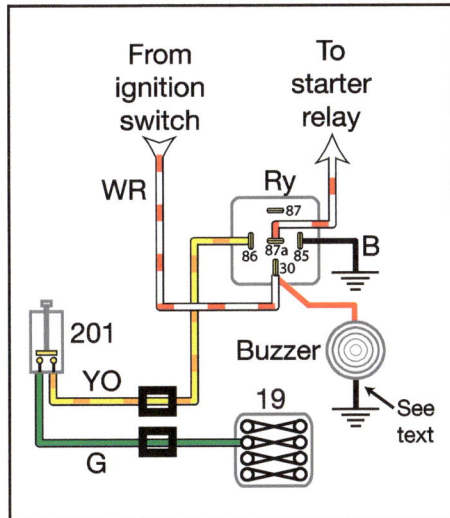

Figure 13.15. Using the inhibitor switch: this blocks any attempt to start the car while in gear.

joining it to other green wires. With the ignition switch on and the car in gear, probe with a circuit tester to verify that there is power at the yellow/orange wire. Check in every gear and make sure that any power found is not present when the gearbox is shifted into neutral.

Automatic transmission inhibitor and reverse switch

Automatic transmission cars have a combined reversing lamp and inhibitor switch, the latter only allowing current to flow to the starter relay when the car is in Park or Neutral (see Figure 12.55). The switch is located on the left side of the transmission. Other than the fact that it has 4 terminals, it is not unlike the standard reversing lamp switch in Figure 13.9.

Adjusting the switch requires moving the transmission out of Park, so make sure the handbrake is applied. Terminals 1 & 3 are for the starter inhibitor and 2 & 4 are for the reversing lamp. Some kind of continuity tester is required to indicator when a connection is made by the internal contacts between terminals 1 & 3 or 2 & 4. This may be a lamp and battery or a multimeter with a buzzer. Remove the connectors from the switch and loosen the lock nut holding it in place. First check the switch operation by removing it from the transmission and in turn, connecting the continuity tester across opposite contacts while operating the plunger.

With the plunger fully out, there should be continuity between terminals 2 & 4 and none between 1 & 3. When the plunger is pressed, the path between 2 & 4 should be broken and that between 1 & 3 made.

With the selector in the D, L2 or L1 position and the continuity tester across terminals 2 & 4, screw the switch into the transmission until the contacts open. Use a marker pen to indicate the position of the switch at this point. Now move the continuity tester to contacts 1 & 3. Continue to screw the switch into the transmission until this switch closes. Mark this point. Now slacken the switch to a position half way between the marks. Tighten the lock nut and reconnect the wires as per Figure 12.55.

Check that the starter only operates when the selector is in the P or N positions and that the reversing lamps only illuminate when the selector is in the R position.

Making a start-while-in-gear prevention circuit

Most MGB/C drivers have, at one time or another, decided to supplement the handbrake by putting the car in gear. Others may engage a gear in order to avoid using the handbrake when the car is to be parked for a long period, the premise being that the pressure of the

MGB ELECTRICAL SYSTEMS – THE ESSENTIAL MANUAL

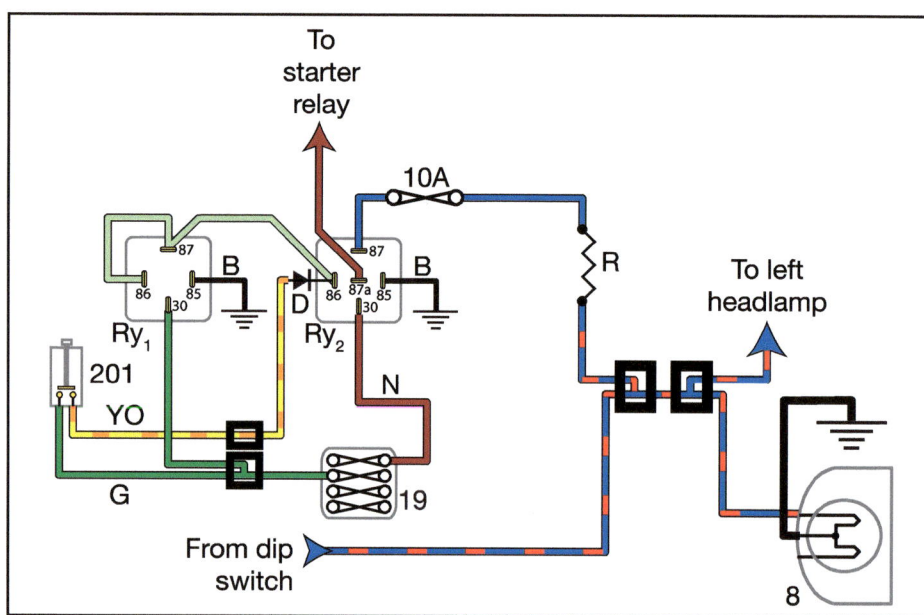

Figure 13.16. This circuit combines features of those in 12.22 and 13.14 so that the inhibitor switch (201) facilitates both DRL switch-on when the car is put into gear but prevents the car starting in gear.

brake shoes will oval the brake drums. When using the gearbox as a parking brake we swear we will remember to put the car in neutral before starting, but it is all to easy to forget and for the car to buck forward, alarmingly and sometimes dangerously, as we crank the engine.

The circuit in 13.15 uses a 5-terminal relay and makes use of the NC contact (87a), which is the one that is closed even when the relay coil is not energized. The white/red (WR) wire that energizes the starter relay is simply taken through this closed pair of contacts on its way to the relay. In practice, this means locating the new relay Ry close to the starter relay and moving the white/red wire from its original position on that relay to terminal 30 of Ry. A new link wire is then made from terminal 87a of Ry to the terminal on the starter relay vacated by the white/red wire. In this way, any reliability problems with the inhibitor switch do not affect the all-important operation of starting of the car.

When the car is in gear, the inhibitor switch closes and powers the coil of relay Ry. In doing so it opens the white/red circuit to the starter relay, preventing the starter motor from cranking.

An optional buzzer warns the driver something is wrong. As drawn, the buzzer will operate every time an attempt is made to crank the car, whether or not the car is in gear. If the car is in neutral, the noise of the car cranking will probably drown out the buzzer and should not be noticed. If it is preferred that the buzzer only operate when the car is in gear and there is a failed attempt at cranking, then instead of earthing the black wire of the buzzer, join it to the brown/white (NW) wire of the starter relay (white/brown (WN) on earlier cars). A piezoelectric buzzer placed under the bonnet and conveniently close to the starter relay is loud enough to be heard in the cockpit of the car.

Using the inhibitor switch to initiate DRLs

The circuit in Figure 12.21 can be used with the inhibitor switch to trigger the operation of DRLs as soon as the car is put into a gear and thereafter latch them on until the ignition is turned off. That circuit can be combined with that in Figure 13.15. If relay Ry_1 is substituted for a 5-terminal type and the brown power feed to contact 30 is that which would normally go to the starter motor relay, then a new power wire can be installed from the vacated terminal on the starter relay to the 87a terminal of Ry_1.

The full circuit is shown in Figure 13.16. A buzzer can be placed between the white/red and brown/white (white/brown on some cars).

Flip-on, flip-off, overdrive circuit

The overdrive makes MGB/C driving much more enjoyable. However, it can be annoying when, after having changed down through the gears, the car then suffers a sudden drop in acceleration when shifting back up again. This occurs because the system drops out as it should in the non-overdrive gears, but the driver often forgets to switch the system off. The transmission then makes a big ratio change from 2nd to overdrive-3rd gear or, in V8s and 1977+ cars, from 3rd to overdrive-4th gear.

The circuit in Figure 13.17 eliminates this problem by requiring that, after having moved out of an overdrive gear, the driver must flip the overdrive operating switch off and on again to get the system to re-engage.

Closing the driver's switch connects it to a 250µF capacitor (C,) which as it charges draws a short pulse of current through the relay coil, and to briefly close its contacts. However, if the car is in an overdrive gear, they do not reopen because it latches 'on', when current from the solenoid flows back to terminal 85 via the diode (D).

When the driver's switch is opened, power to the relay and solenoid are removed, disengaging the overdrive and unlatching the circuit.

When a non-overdrive gear is selected, power to the relay via the diode is removed, so again it unlatches. Moving back to an overdrive gear does not re-engage the overdrive until the driver's switch is flipped open and closed again, allowing the capacitor to discharge via the resistor (R) and on re-closure of the switch, recharging the

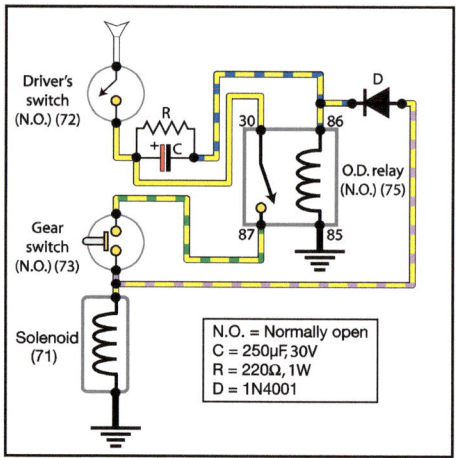

Figure 13.17. Flip-on, flip-off overdrive circuit.

OVERDRIVE & GEARBOX

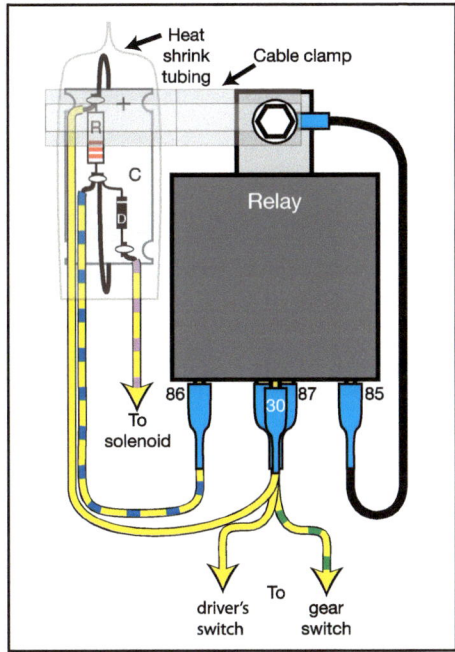

Figure 13.18. A suggested component layout for Figure 13.10.

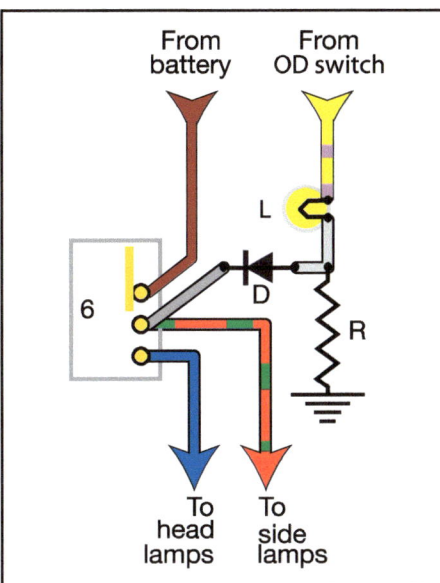

Figure 13.19. Overdrive warning lamp dimming circuit.

capacitor and so again energizing and latching the relay,

The capacitor is chosen to be of a value that can close the relay, which in this case is an ISO type (see page 185) with a 80Ω coil and a 7 thousandths of a second closing time. A lower resistance and/or slower relay will require a larger value capacitor that draws a higher current for a longer period. The resistor value of 220Ω is such that it will discharge the capacitor very quickly during the brief time that the driver's switch is moved from 'on' to 'off' and to 'on' again to re-engage the system. Too low a value resistor could bleed sufficient current to energize the relay and would result in it dissipating more power, requiring a larger, higher wattage device. The diode 'D' prevents the capacitor from charging up through the solenoid rather than the relay.

Figure 13.18 shows a suggested component layout. The capacitor, resistor, diode and their associated wires have been soldered together and enclosed under a piece of heat shrink tube pinched off at the top like that in Figure 2.25, the assembly being retained and supported by a large cable clamp like those in Figure 2.26, which is retained by the same screw that holds the relay.

Night dimming a overdrive warning lamp

Fitting a warning lamp that informs the driver that the car is in overdrive is a useful adjunct. To provide this function, a suitable dash lamp simply has to be installed with one wire going to earth and the other to either end of the yellow/purple (YP) wire shown in Figures 13.1, 13.2 or 13.6. However, selecting a lamp that is powerful enough to be seen in sunlight can mean that it is annoyingly bright at night. The circuit, shown in Figure 13.19, automatically dims the dash lamp when the main vehicle lighting is operating.

The circuit requires a diode (a 1N4002 will work well, see page 188 Appendix 2) and a resistor. The value of resistor depends on the wattage of the warning lamp and how bright you would like it to be at night. A value of about the same resistance as the lamp when running at full voltage seems to work well, and is a least a good starting point. To find this value, divide the lamp wattage into 180, so for a 2W bulb the value would be 180 ÷ 2 = 90Ω. This value need not be exact, just use the nearest value available. Resistors also have a wattage rating and, in this case, it should be at least half that of the bulb, so in this example, a 1W resistor or greater would be chosen.

When the vehicle lamps are off, the warning lamp (L), fed with current from the overdrive circuit, illuminates at nearly full brightness as the current finds an easy earth return through the diode (D) (shown here connected in the correct direction for a negative earth car) and via the lighting switch (6) to the low resistance of the cold sidelamps. If preferred, the diode can be connected to the headlamp connection instead.

When the lamps are on, the voltage at the switch terminal to which the diode is connected, rises to the system voltage of about 12V. The warning lamp current is now denied any route to earth via the lighting switch and so is forced to take the higher resistance path via the resistor (R). Because the entire lamp current now has to pass through a resistor, it is much less bright.

Chapter 14
Instrumentation

INSTRUMENTATION

The electrical instruments consist of senders, sometimes known as transducers, that measure fuel level, water temperature and engine speed or oil pressure, and change them to an electrical value that can be read by a gauge.

The only true electrical gauging system in the earliest MGBs is that for fuel level measurement. Later, water temperature and oil pressure measurement was also an electrical system, although the oil pressure gauge reverted to a direct hydraulic type after about 1972.

GAUGES

Access to the inner workings of the gauges is by removal of the nuts under the electrical terminals, and rotation of the front bezel until the tabs on its rim line up with the slots in the gauge body.

Moving iron gauge

The moving iron gauge, fitted until about 1967 can be recognized by the fact that it will return to zero very soon after the ignition is switched off. It has the major benefit that it is almost wholly immune to voltage variations. Its main disadvantage, however, is that it is not well damped; that is to say that it responds very quickly. It was used in MGBs for fuel gauging, so a tendency to respond to fuel moving in the tank was somewhat of a nuisance. Its scale is also not very linear, so that a half full reading appears at about the ⅝ point on the scale.

Figure 14.1 shows a schematic of a moving iron instrument. Current from the battery flows into coil W1 and resistor R. The current in W1 magnetises a fixed iron core C1, which tends to attract a moving iron armature M that is joined to the gauge needle. The same current flows into an identical coil W2 and into a variable value resistor that forms the sender. Should

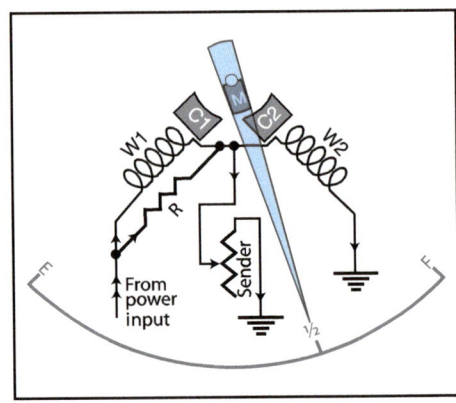

Figure 14.1. A schematic of a moving iron instrument.

resistance of the sender happen to be the same as that of R, the same amount of current will flow in W1 as flows in W2, making the magnetic attraction towards core W1 and W2 identical, and so M will be equally attracted to each, causing the needle to read half scale.

The sender is of a very low resistance when fuel level is low (the opposite is the case with later fuel senders), so most of the current leaving W1 will take the path of least resistance and go through the sender rather than through W2. The magnetic force in C2 will be very low and the moving iron M will be pulled toward C1, making the needle read low.

On the other hand, should the sender resistance be high (if, for example, the fuel level is high), then rather than go through the high resistance sender, W2 will receive almost all the current flowing in both W1 and in resistor R. C2 will attract M more strongly than C1, making the gauge read high.

The moving iron instrument reading depends on the proportions of the sender currents that flow in coils W1 and W2. Those proportions depend on the relative values of R and the sender resistance and are therefore independent of the system voltage.

An actual instrument can be seen

INSTRUMENTATION

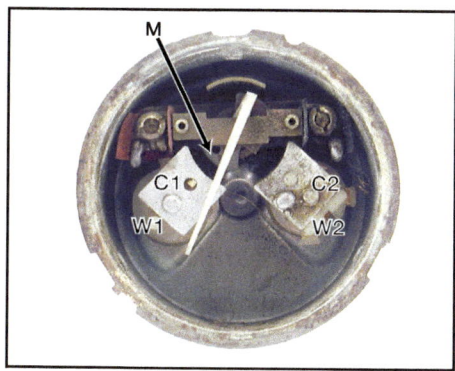

Figure 14.2. An actual moving iron instrument.

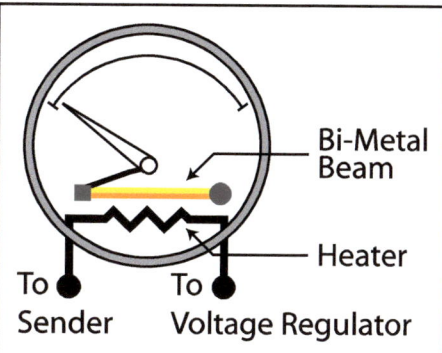

Figure 14.3. A schematic of a thermal instrument.

in Figure 14.2. You will see rust in this example, which is a problem with this type of instrument, using, as it does, soft iron magnetic parts.

To check the gauge, switch the ignition on and remove the green/black wire from the fuel sender behind the rear right wheel. The gauge should read high. Now connect the green/black wire to earth, the gauge should read low.

If you have reason to suspect the gauge, then first check that it is earthed. One method of doing this in a non-invasive way is to verify that the gauge illuminates at night when the lights are on; failure to do so could well be caused by a bad earth. If the gauge has been removed then note that, looking from the back, the right hand terminal, which is often a double connector, should carry a green wire and the left a green/black wire.

The fixing points for coils W1 and W2 are in slotted holes, so that they can be moved closer or further from the moving iron M and adjust the gauge.

Thermal gauges

Thermal gauges are very slow to respond and so are said to be highly damped. This is useful for ironing out the movement of fuel in the tank but is not so effective when required to respond to a sudden loss of oil pressure.

The schematic diagram in Figure 14.3 shows the principle of operation for a thermal gauge, also referred to as a bi-metal gauge because that is its fundamental component. A bi-metal beam is a strip made from two metals with dissimilar expansion characteristics. One is laid on top of the other and the metal that has the greater expansion when heated tends to force the beam to bend. If the higher expansion metal is the lower of the two,

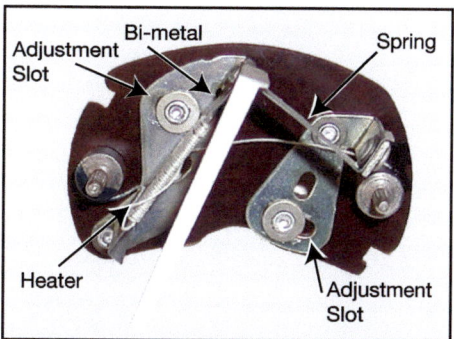

Figure 14.4. An actual thermal instrument.

then the bending motion in response to heating is upward. In figure 14.3, current from the sender is passed through a heater in very close proximity to the bi-metal beam. When the sender resistance is low, the current can flow through it more easily and so more also flows in the gauge heater, which is in series with the sender, causing the beam to bend more. When the sender resistance is high, however, the current is reduced, the heating is less and the beam bends less, and so the gauge reads low.

With this type of gauge, if the battery voltage is high, more current will flow in the system and the gauge will read higher. Conversely, low battery voltage will cause it to read low. For this reason, thermal gauges require a voltage regulator, also called a stabilizer, to keep the voltage reasonably constant. The regulated voltage in MGB/Cs and its contemporaries is 10V.

The actual gauge in Figure 14.4 has the heater wound around the bi-metal beam. The beam moves the indicator needle against the force of a spring, which can be adjusted from the rear by moving its securing point in a slot. Another adjustment slot moves the needle and bi-metal mechanism.

Gauge operation can be checked in the same way as the moving iron type, but note the opposite results. First remove the wire from the sender and check that the gauge does not read. The same wire should then be joined to a good earth point, but this time, do not make this connection for more than a minute because the gauge will be over driven and could overheat. It should read at full-scale.

Unlike the moving iron gauge, no earth connection is required for the thermal gauge and the two wires that terminate to it can be swapped from terminal to terminal without affecting its operation.

Unless there is a severe inaccuracy, it is not recommended that any attempt be made to adjust the gauge, because the two adjustment slots do not work independently of one another. Adjustment of the slot nearest the low end of the gauge tends to adjust the full-scale reading, while that nearest the high end changes the minimum reading. It will be found, however, that getting the gauge to read correctly at one end also has an effect on the other. Adjusting the other end then causes the original adjustment to change. Gauges may be checked and adjusted by applying current from a 10 volt dc source through 2W resistors or a variable resistor of value shown in Table 14.1. The same mechanism is used whether or not it is measuring fuel level, water temperature or oil pressure. If a gauge should fail, therefore, another type may be cannibalized for an internal mechanism.

VOLTAGE REGULATOR

The thermal gauges need a constant voltage in order to read consistently. At the time this type of gauge was introduced on the MGB/C, semiconductors were expensive so

Gauge reading	Resistance ($\Omega \pm 20\%$)
Min	222
¼	105
½	65
¾	35
Full	20

Table 14.1. Required sender or test resistance to produce a particular reading on a thermal gauge.

MGB ELECTRICAL SYSTEMS – THE ESSENTIAL MANUAL

a rather cruder method of voltage regulation was in use.

In many ways the voltage regulator is like the thermal instrument it controls. The regulator is located on the bulkhead behind the instruments. Figure 14.5 shows a LHD installation. Top and side views of the regulator are shown in Figure 14.6. Current from the battery enters on a green wire at the male connector and passes to the lower contact, which is fixed but adjustable in height by means of a screw beneath it.

Current can flow to the moving contact and to the output via the bi-metal beam, the female connectors and light-green/green wires.

Some of the current that passes through the contacts also goes through a heater wire wrapped around the bi-metal beam and to earth. The heater connection to earth is attached to the metal can, which is removed in the illustration. However, note that a good connection to earth is essential in order for the regulator to work, so the screw securing it must be tight and clean. The heater causes the bi-metal beam to bend upward and in so doing break the connection to both the output and to the heater itself. The beam then cools and the contacts close again.

The higher the voltage the quicker the beam heats, and so the 'on time', that is the time power is delivered to the output, is relatively short. At a lower voltage, the heater takes longer to bend upward so the 'on time' is longer. In this way, the average voltage to the instruments is controlled. Ideally, if the input were 14V, the regulator, in order to deliver an average of 10V, should be on for $^{10}/_{14}$ or 71% of the time. At 11V the figure is 91% of the time, and, of course, at 10V the regulator should never open and thus supply power for 100% of the time. For supply voltages below 10V, the regulator again should stay closed for 100% of the time supplying all the voltage available, even though it is less than required to drive the instruments accurately.

Obviously, such a regulator can only be used with a highly damped instrument like the thermal type, otherwise the indicator needle would move constantly and unacceptably as the regulator pulsed on and off. Some movement can, in fact, be seen even on a thermal gauge. Note that because the mechanism relies on a thermal effect, it is sensitive to temperature and will cause the gauges to read low in hot weather and high in cold.

The regulator often caries an "Up" orientation marking, stamped on the insulator. There seems little reason for mounting the regulator one way or another other than it will always hang from its fixing bracket when correctly orientated and may have less tendency to unscrew (the earth connection being via the fixing screw, which is an essential electrical connection).

Check the bi-metal regulator only when you know you have a good battery and the voltage is therefore greater than 12V. Place a circuit tester on the light-green/green wire either at the regulator or at one of the instruments to which it supplies power. The circuit tester should flash on and off as the regulator cycles the power. With the engine started and revving, the battery voltage should rise and the 'on time' of the regulator, as observed on the circuit tester, should shorten in response.

Adjustment is possible if an accurate 10V supply is available. Apply the 10V between the input and earth and monitor the output for the presence of power. At 10V the output should not cycle on and off. The adjustment screw can be used to find the precise point at which it doesn't do so. Turning the screw clockwise will lower the tendency to cycle and vice-versa. Don't expect very great accuracy from this type of device, it is the best system that was available at the time. Attempts by the author to test the accuracy of a bi-metal regulator were frustrated by its erratic and inconsistent behaviour.

Making a semiconductor regulator

Any replacement voltage regulator is likely to be like that shown in Figure 14.7, which takes advantage of technology advances and uses electronic components. Replacing the original bi-metal regulator with a semiconductor type can provide some important advantages, notably:

• Little or no sensitivity to ambient temperature changes.
• Constant voltage with no cycling action.
• Far better accuracy.
• Inherent short-circuit protection.
• If home built, it is much less expensive than replacements.

The semiconductor recommended is a low drop out (LDO) voltage regulator: the National Semiconductor LM2940T-10.0. An LDO is a linear voltage regulator that will operate even when the input voltage only just exceeds the desired output voltage. The LM2940T-10.0 has a drop-out voltage of only 0.5V, which means it will regulate at 10V even with an input voltage as low as 10.5V. It will not actually drop-out when the input voltage falls to below 10.5V, but like the bi-metal regulator will continue to supply a voltage close to that of the input voltage. Although it contains scores of transistors, it cost no more than a hamburger. If there is any difficulty obtaining this LDO, the UA7810CKC, which has a slightly higher drop-out voltage, works well too. Both are only suitable for use on negative earth cars.

Figure 14.5. The location of the voltage regulator.

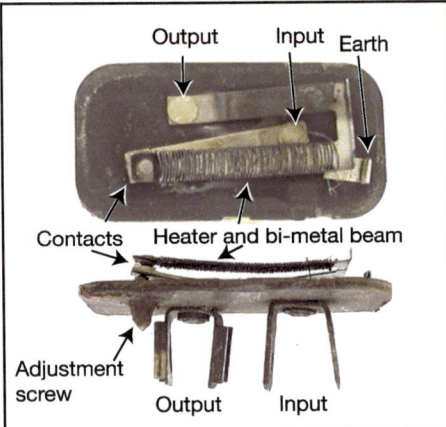

Figure 14.6. The voltage regulator.

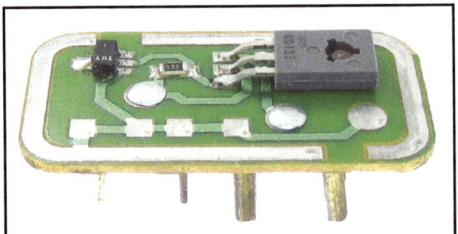

Figure 14.7. A replacement voltage regulator.

INSTRUMENTATION

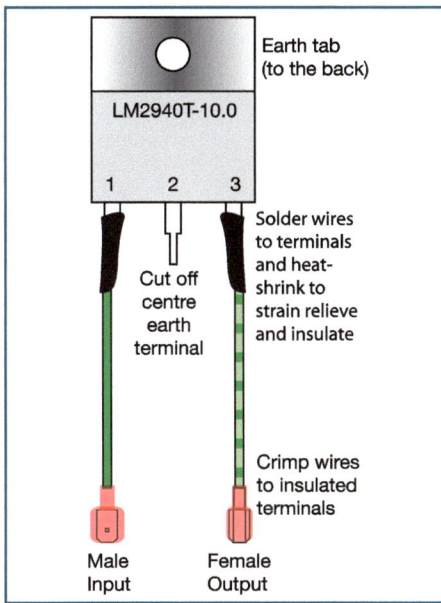

Figure 14.8. An electronic voltage regulator in its simplest form.

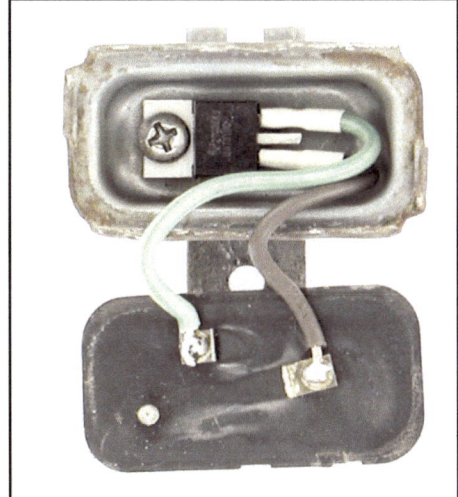

Figure 14.9. The electronic regulator can be installed in the original housing.

The construction shown in Figure 14.8 is simply made by soldering two wires to the outside contacts, adding some heat shrink tubing to insulate and strain relieve them and crimping on male and female spade connectors. It is recommended that the unused centre contact, which in fact is electrically connected to the tab, is cut-off, just to keep it out of the way. The tab, which must be well earthed electrically, is used to heat sink the device, so use a panel screw and serrated washer and screw it down very tightly to the car's panel metal. The two wires simply connect to those from the harness that originally went to the bi-metal regulator.

This construction works well but can be a little fragile due to the weakness of the semiconductor's terminals. If some way is devised to clamp the wires so that snagging them does not cause breakage, then it will work trouble free for the lifetime of the vehicle. Purists will know that it is usually recommended to install a 0.1µF capacitor to the input to stop parasitic oscillation. Bench testing with an oscilloscope and on the road has shown that the nature of the input voltage, the regulator and the load makes this unnecessary in this case.

If the original regulator is still available, it can be cannibalized to provide a housing for the electronic version. The inner workings need to be stripped out, leaving just the internal rivets for the two terminals.

In Figure 14.9 the LDO has been installed in the metal top of the housing by drilling a hole and using a short panel screw, which was then ground off at the back so as to provide a flat external mounting surface (a blind or 'pop' rivet works well here too). Wires have been attached, just as they were in Figure 14.8 but instead of being joined to wire ended connectors, they have been joined to the respective male and female fixed contacts of the original device.

Once reassembled, ensure a good connection to earth by attaching the housing tightly to the vehicle's bulkhead panel, just like the original.

SENDERS
Fuel sender

The fuel sender, shown schematically in Figure 14.10, is very much like a variable resistance used to change the volume of a radio. However, instead of a knob doing the work of sliding a contact across a resistance, a fuel float does it.

The sender includes a wire-wound resistor that is terminated at one end to earth. This termination may be made inside the sender, in which case there is only one external terminal, or outside, requiring two external connections.

The other end of the resistor remains un-terminated. Instead, connection is made by a device known as a wiper that runs along the length of the resistor according to the position of the fuel float, to which it is connected via a pivoted arm. The wiper is connected back to the gauge via the vehicle harness wiring. When the fuel level is high the wiper is very close to the earth connection and the resistance is low. However, when the fuel level falls, the wiper moves toward the far end of the resistor and the resistance between the gauge and earth increases. Note that early cars, with moving iron instruments, had senders that work in the opposite manner, that is a high fuel level results in a high resistance in the sender.

Figures 14.11 and 14.12 show a typical fuel sender. There may be some differences in detail, the most notable being that late versions have a fuel pick-up pipe integrated into the assembly. Note how in Figure 14.12 the pitch and turn length of the resistance wire changes to account for the greater movement of the wiper in the centre of its sweep, the non-linearity of the gauge, and to provide better resolution of fuel level as the tank empties.

Before suspecting problems with the sender, check gauge operation as described on page 145. The sender may be removed from the right side of the car by turning the retaining ring about ⅙ of a turn anticlockwise; the manner in which it retains the sender is not unlike the top of a jam-jar. The tank should be nearly empty before removal is attempted and the car jacked on the right side to force any remaining fuel to the left side. Removal of the right rear wheel facilitates access to the sender. There are one or two wires attached: a green/black wire that goes to the gauge, and in early cars, a black wire that goes to earth.

The resistance values between the terminals should be measurable across the full range of movement of the float,

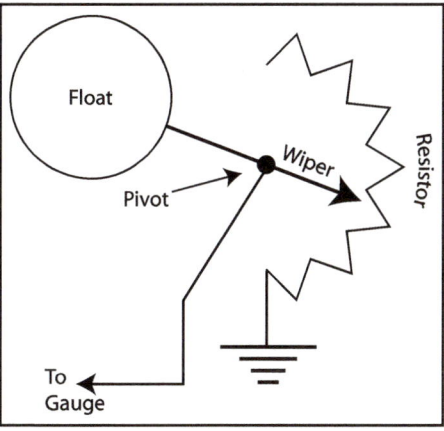

Figure 14.10. Fuel sender schematic.

147

MGB ELECTRICAL SYSTEMS – THE ESSENTIAL MANUAL

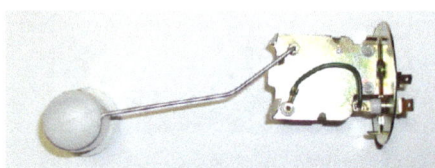

Figure 14.11. A general view of a fuel sender.

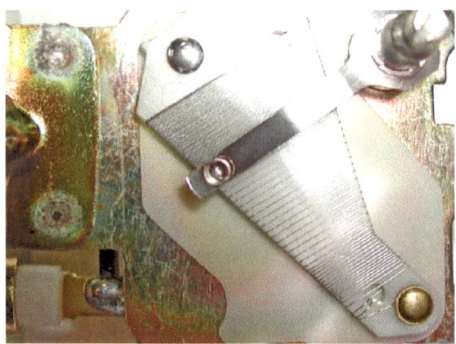

Figure 14.12. A close-up view of the resistor and its wiper, which is attached to the float pivot point.

Float position	Resistance (Ω)	
	Min	Max
High	10	35
Low	210	270

Table 14.2. Minimum and maximum fuel sender resistance that can be expected for high and low fuel sender float positions.

with no breaks or sudden changes. Resistor values measured with the float high and low may be somewhat lower and higher respectively than those required to move the gauge from minimum to maximum, as listed in Table 14.1. That can be the case because the float may not be moved to its full extent of travel when the tank is full or empty.

Expect a lot of variation in resistance from sender to sender. Table 14.2 gives some guidance values based on measurements taken from over a dozen senders.

Temperature sender

The electrical temperature sender was fitted from 1968 on. It varies in appearance slightly depending on model year and whether a non standard replacement has been fitted. Essentially it is a sealed threaded body containing an NTC thermistor. An NTC thermistor (negative temperature coefficient thermal resistor) is a device that changes its resistance downward (in a negative manner) as temperature increases. Being a kind of resistor, the thermistor has two connections. Within the sender, one is earthed to the metal body and the other is joined to a spade terminal on the outside.

In Figure 14.13 the sender on the left has a type of terminal much preferred in comparison with that on the right, which is riveted so that it can swivel for access, but that may come loose and cause a poor or intermittent connection.

NTC thermistors vary in both their resistance at a given temperature and in the rate of change of resistance over a temperature range, known as beta and written as ß. When measured at 68°F (20°C) the resistance of the sender can be expected to be in the range indicated in Table 14.3. Thermistors may be easily measured at room temperature but in this application, the gauge does not start reading until engine coolant temperature is above about 130°F (55°C). If measurements are made at other temperatures, the mathematicians among readers, knowing the resistance at one temperature, can calculate the expected resistance at another using the formula:

Figure 14.13. Two versions of the temperature sender.

Sender for car year	Resistance (Ω@68°F (20°C))	
	Min	Max
1968-1974	800	880
1974-1980	930	1000

Table 14.3. Minimum and maximum temperature sender resistance that can be expected for different vehicle years.

$$R@T_1/R@T_2 = \varepsilon^{\beta(1/T_1 - 1/T_2)}$$

Where:
T_1 is temperature 1 in °K
T_2 is temperature 2 in °K
R is sender resistance in Ω
ε is the exponential constant = 2.718
ß is the thermal coefficient for the NTC and is 5000±250.
°K = °C + 273°C

The wide variation in the resistance and ß of the thermistor, the large differences in the sensitivity of gauges, the poor accuracy of the voltage regulator and the sensitivity of the gauge and regulator to ambient temperature, all combine to make what might be considered the 'normal' gauge reading for one car very different from another. Drivers should therefore make their own assessment of 'normal' running temperature for a particular car so that they may more easily recognize engine overheating.

Oil pressure sender

The electrical oil pressure sender, Figure 14.14, was installed in MGB/Cs from 1967 to 1972. It is not serviceable. In operation it is very much like the voltage regulator, and as such is sensitive to changes in battery voltage. However, because, like the voltage regulator, it pulses power on and off to the gauge, it cannot be used in conjunction with the conventional thermal voltage regulator otherwise it will try to switch power to the gauge at times when the regulator is not supplying it power. If an electronic regulator is used, constant voltage can be supplied to the oil gauge from it, improving its consistency but resulting in a somewhat low pressure reading.

Figure 14.16 shows how current

Figure 14.14. The oil pressure sender.

INSTRUMENTATION

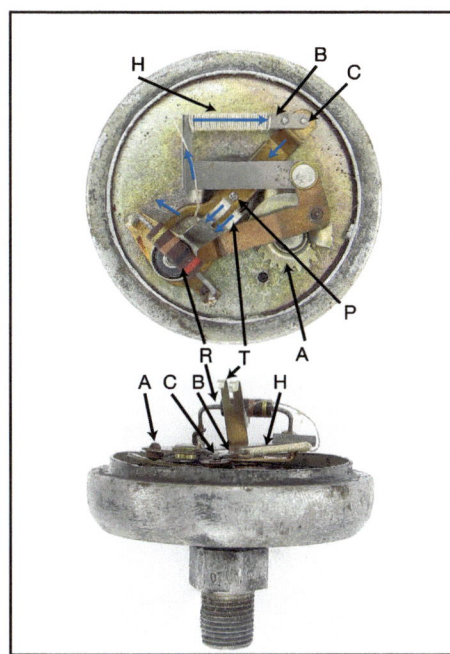

Figure 14.15. The interior of the oil pressure sender.

When the pressure is high, the lower of the two contacts (C) is pushed upward and the bi-metal beam has to heat for longer to bend sufficiently far to open the contacts. As a result, the gauge passes current for longer and reads higher on average. The opposite is the case when the oil pressure is low.

A 200Ω resistor, wired in parallel with the heater, provided the manufacturer with some measure of electrical adjustment to the gauge reading and tended to better iron out the pulsing so that it was less visible to the driver. A mechanical adjustment device (A), not accessible from outside the sealed sender, was used for factory calibration.

Adding an oil pressure warning lamp

An oil pressure light can give the driver immediate warning of oil pressure failure.

Fitting a warning lamp is largely a matter of plumbing and selecting the physical location in the cockpit where any warning lamp might be fitted. The electrical connection is then very simple as shown in Figure 14.16.

The only electrical issue in selection of the switch is that it must be one that closes when the pressure is low. That illustrated in Figure 11.39, for example, is not suitable because it closes when the pressure is high. Connection is simple. The switch is automatically earthed by virtue of its being screwed into a metal fitting. The circuit uses low side switching as per Figure 12.51.

INSTRUMENTATION CIRCUIT

Figure 14.5 shows the instrumentation circuit. Not all cars will have all components installed. Also included is an oil pressure warning system that may be user installed. The vehicle tachometer circuits are not shown here but are included with those for the ignition in Figures 11.6 through 11.9.

Power supplied from the ignition switch via a white (W) wire passes through a fuse located in the fuse block (19) and is carried on a green (G) wire to the voltage regulator. The regulator from the fuse block (19) can flow through the oil pressure gauge (43) and to the oil pressure sender (147). It arrives at the sender via the terminal that can be seen on top of the device in Figure 14.14. Figure 14.15 shows the sender with the top cover cut off. A bifurcated spring pressure contact (T) pushes upward to touch the underside of the terminal and current passes down the contact as indicated by the blue arrows. A link wire from the heater (H) is welded to the contact and so current passes down it, through the heater, the normally closed contact pair (C) and through to a lower spring contact support arm (P), which is attached to a diaphragm (not visible) and which moves upward as oil pressure increases, also moving P relative to the upper of the contact pair C. From there the current can flow to earth via the body of the sender.

Current in the heater causes the bi-metal beam (B) to heat and bend upward. When hot enough, the bending causes the contact pair to separate, with the result that the current flow is interrupted. The unpowered heater cools, the bi-metal beam bends downward and the contacts reconnect, starting the cycle all over.

Internally, the electrical oil pressure gauge is identical to those used for fuel and temperature, and so is of the thermal type and very slow to respond.

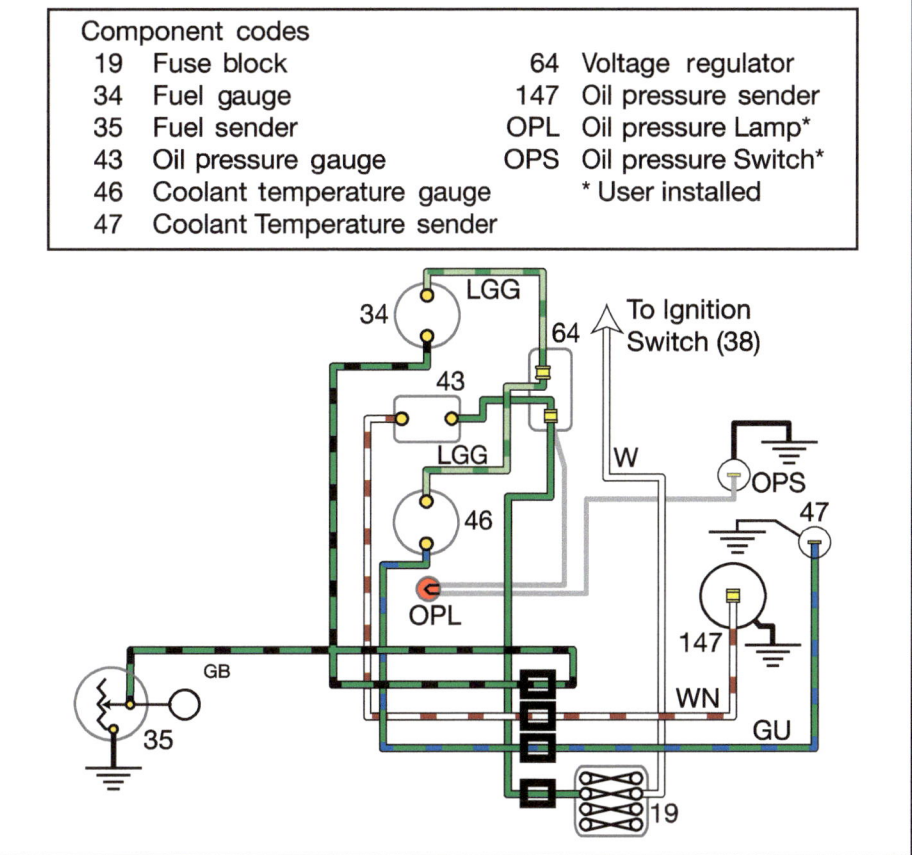

Figure 14.16. The instrumentation circuit.

149

supplies current on a light-green/green (LGG) wire at a voltage of approximately 10V to the fuel (34) and coolant temperature (46) gauges.

Current from the fuel gauge is routed on a green/black (GB) wire to the fuel level sender (35). Depending on whether the fuel level is low or high, the resistance of the fuel level sender will be higher or lower and will allow less or more current to flow in the gauge, making it indicate less or more fuel present.

Current from the coolant temperature gauge is routed on a green/blue (GU) wire to the coolant temperature sender (47). Depending on whether the coolant temperature is low or high, the resistance of the sender will be higher or lower and will allow less or more current to flow in the gauge, making it indicate a lower or higher coolant temperature.

Current from the fuse block is also routed on a green wire to the oil pressure gauge (43) passing through it to exit on a white/brown

INSTRUMENTATION FAULT-FINDING

Symptom	Possible causes	Action
All electrical gauges inoperative.	Fuse failure.	Check if turn signal and brake lamps work. If not, change fuse or clean fuse clips (see page 43).
Fuel gauge (and electrical temperature gauge if fitted) inoperative but turn signals and brake lamps working.	Instrument voltage regulator failure.	Use a circuit tester to check for the presence of power at the green input wire to regulator. If none, check wiring back to fuse. If OK, remove both wires from regulator and plug them together, making sure they cannot touch earth. If gauges work, voltage regulator is faulty. Do not operate gauges for long periods without regulator in circuit.
Temperature and/or fuel gauge read high	Instrument voltage regulator failure.	Check voltage at light green/green wire from the voltage regulator. If it is steady and higher than 10V, replace it or modify it as per page 145.
Single gauge failure.	Gauge or sender failure.	For fuel or temperature gauge problems, check regulator as above. With ignition on, remove the single wire (green/black on fuel senders which may have 2 wires) from sender, gauge should read low. Earth wire removed from sender for no more than 30 seconds. If gauge does read high, then suspect sender, if not suspect gauge or wiring to it. If gauge does read high on last test, suspect sender.
Moving iron fuel gauge only reads maximum.	Gauge is not earthed.	Check if gauge illumination has also failed indicating no earth connection.
Previous tests indicate fuel sender failure.	Bad earth to fuel sender.	Make sure earth connection is good. Verify by using a temporary new wire from sender to a known good earth point.
	Fuel sender wiper making poor connection.	Remove fuel sender, see page 145. Lightly clean the resistor's surface over which wiper travels. Gently bend wiper to increase its pressure on the resistor. Use a resistance meter to verify that gauge sender resistance varies between at least 35Ω and 210Ω. Replace sender if necessary.
Previous tests indicate coolant temperature or oil pressure sender failure.	Unserviceable sender failure.	Replace sender.

Table 14.4. Instrumentation fault-finding.

INSTRUMENTATION

wire (WN) to the oil pressure sender (147). Depending on whether the oil pressure is low or high, the sender will pass current to earth in pulses of less or longer duration causing the slow responding thermal gauge, which responds to the average current, to indicate lower or higher oil pressure. If an electronic regulator is used, the oil pressure gauge power feed can be relocated to the output of the voltage regulator, reducing the system's sensitivity to temperature and voltage changes, albeit with the penalty of a somewhat lower pressure reading.

TACHOMETER

Electronic tachometers were installed in MGBs from 1965 onward. There were four different electrical circuits used as well as some changes in gauge styling.

Due to the technical infancy of transistors and their cost, complex circuits were economically unviable and consequently, the first electronic tachometers were very crude. The result is that the early Smiths tachometers leave a lot to be desired in terms of performance and the problems that drivers often find, with erratic tachometer behaviour, are simply typical of normal operation. Later tachometers used a different measurement means and an integrated circuit (IC). ICs can contain many transistors because each contributes only the cost of a few micro-grams of silicon to the device. Unfortunately, while the instruments containing ICs exhibit a great performance improvement over early models that used discreet transistors, these early integrated circuits were not very robust and are no longer available as replacements.

The tachometer circuits are part of the ignition system, from which they take their engine speed signals. Refer to Figures 11.6 to 11.9

Principle of operation

The tachometer monitors the number of current pulses going to – or voltage pulses at – the ignition coil. It then interprets that as an engine speed. Strangely, although most people refer to engine speed in thousands of revolutions per minute, Smiths gauges are calibrated in hundreds per minute. In a 4 cylinder, 4-stroke engine, the ignition coil has to produce 2 sparks each engine revolution and so supplies that number of impulses to the tachometer. Similarly, 6 cylinder and 8 cylinder 4-stroke engines require

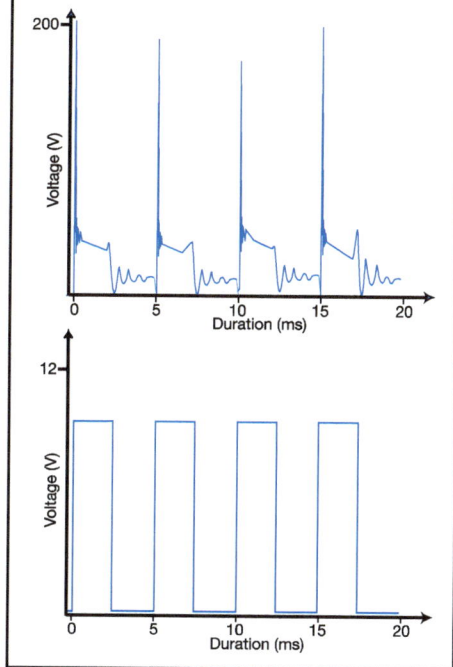

Figure 14.17. Top: a typical spark waveform.
Bottom: the tachometer attempts to turn the upper signal into a cleaner, consistent and more readable form.

the coil to produce 3 or 4 sparks respectively per engine revolution.

The impulses from the coil that are used by the tachometer are very ragged and variable in nature, like that in the upper illustration in Figure 14.17; engine speed, fuel mixture, sparkplug gap and temperature will all change the waveform's shape, amplitude and duration. The tachometer finds this signal hard to interpret in its raw state and attempts to shape it to a consistent and clean format like that shown in the lower illustration of Figure 14.17.

Once the waveform is clean and consistent, the average voltage resulting from the stream of pulses will be proportional to the number of pulses per given time. Figure 14.18 shows how, at low engine speed, the low rate of pulses produces a lower average voltage and the gauge reads low. However, at higher engine speeds the pulse rate increases and current to the gauge is supplied at more frequent intervals and it indicates a higher number of revolutions per minute accordingly. In a tachometer with sophisticated electronics the circuitry will do the work of turning the pulses into a smooth direct current to be read by the meter that forms the gauge. In the MG, the gauge has to do most of that work, relying on the inertia of its indicating needle that cannot move fast enough to respond to each pulse individually. That is most true at high engine speeds, 6000rpm producing 200 pulses per second (4-cyl). At idling speeds of say 750rpm, the number of pulses is only 25 per second and the gauge tachometer needle may often be seen to be responding to this rate and bouncing should there be any missing or other spark irregularity.

When opening a tachometer, turn the front chrome ring until the tabs line up with the slots on the body flange and remove the rim and glass. When removing the casing, it will be seen that some of the screws are recessed and do not secure the case, so do not remove these.

Current driven tachometers

The first electronic tachometers used in MGBs were current driven. The current going to the ignition coil from the ignition switch, is repetitively switched on and off by the contact-breaker forming a stream of pulses. On its way to the ignition coil, the pulsed current

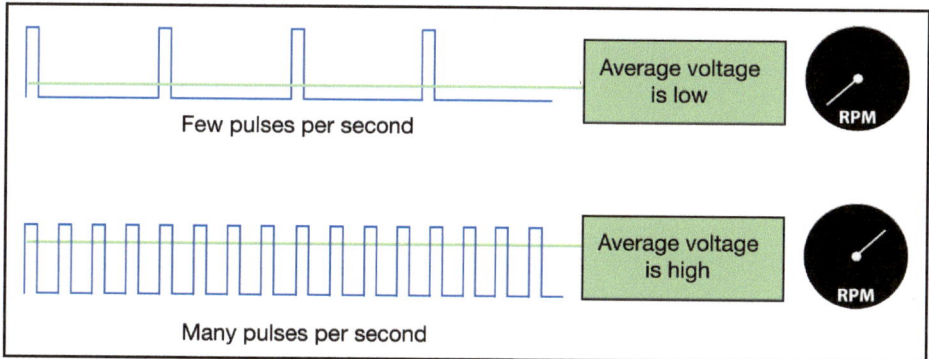

Figure 14.18. Top: a few pulses per second result in a low average voltage.
Bottom: a greater number of pulses results in a higher average voltage.

is passed through the primary winding of a transformer that forms part of the tachometer. While the primary winding may only have one or two turns of wire, the secondary winding has several hundred which transforms the very low voltage, high ignition current signal into a higher voltage, low current signal that can be used by the tachometer electronics.

If a current driven tachometer is removed, the male and female connectors attached to white harness wires that carry the signal current to the tachometer must be joined together if the car is to be used, otherwise no current can get to the ignition coil.

All Smiths tachometers carry a part number at the bottom the dial. Those commencing RV1 are current driven.

RV1 1419/00 tachometer

The RV1 1419/00 tachometer is based on the principle of the monostable multivibrator, which has one stable state and one quasi stable state. The

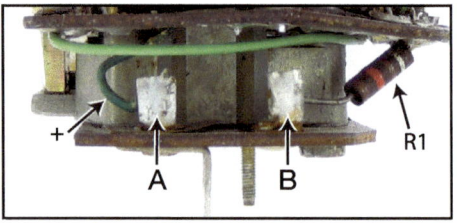

Figure 14.19. Part of the RV1 1419/00 tachometer. This example has already been converted to negative earth.

Figure 14.20. The rear of the RV1 1419/00 tachometer showing the single turn of wire that forms the primary winding of the transformer.

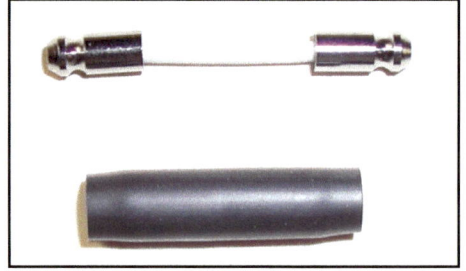

Figure 14.21. A link wire and a female bullet connector can be used to change the polarity of the tachometer input signal.

circuit is normally in the stable state, producing no output. However, when a triggering current pulse from the ignition system is received, the circuit transitions to the quasi stable state for a given time before returning again to the stable state. In this way, each ignition pulse produces a clean pulse of fixed duration that is fed to the gauge mechanism. The more such fixed duration pulses the gauge receives per second, the higher it reads.

The RV1 1419/00 design was used in both positive and negative polarity cars and can be changed in polarity. Figure 14.19 shows a section of the tachometer close to the power input terminal. In the positive earth version the resistor (R1) is connected to terminal A and the small wire (+) to terminal B. In the negative earth conversion shown, the two have been swapped. Making this change provides the correct polarity for powering the instrument's electronics. However, one more step is required; the input signal has to be changed in polarity too.

Figure 14.20 again shows a negative earth tachometer. Note that the wire from the male signal input connector travels anti-clockwise around a plastic former and exits to the female connector. On the positive earth version the direction is the reverse. Swapping from one to another is easier said than done because un-threading the wire is difficult. An alternative, illustrated in Figure 14.21, is to use a link wire with two male bullet connectors attached that can be plugged into the female end of the tachometer wire and a female bullet connector can plug onto the male end, thus reversing the polarity when the gauge is reconnected to the vehicle harness. Note that the bullet connector size may be a little different from those used elsewhere in the harness.

The circuit diagram for the RV1 1419/00 tachometers is illustrated in Figure 14.22.

Current from the ignition switch passes through the single turn current coil of transformer W1 on its way to the ignition coil.

This current is in the form of a

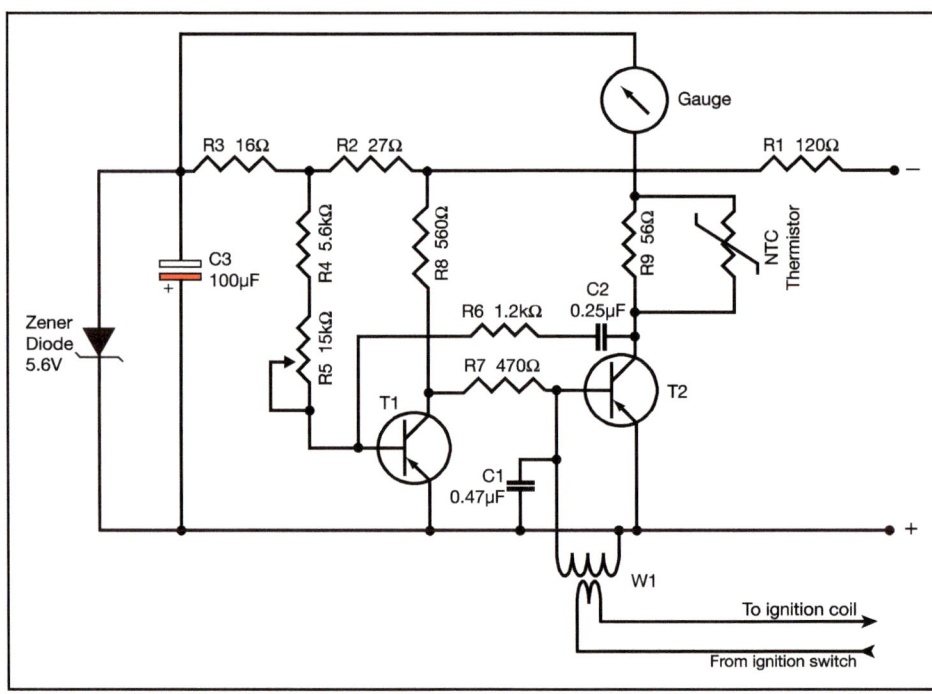

Figure 14.22. Circuit diagram for the RV1 1419/00 tachometer.

INSTRUMENTATION

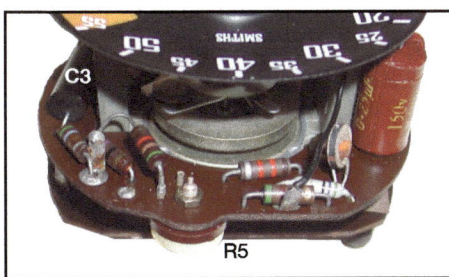

Figure 14.23. The RV1 1419/00 tachometer is adjusted using R5. C3 is the most troublesome component.

pulse, caused when the ignition coil stores its energy. The current pulse is transformed (by transformer action) to a voltage pulse in the voltage coil.

The voltage pulse charges capacitor C1.

As C1 charges it biases the base of transistor T2, switching it on. T2 conducts current from its emitter to its collector, through the parallel combination of the NTC thermistor and resistor R9, to the coil of the gauge and to a stabilized voltage point at the anode of the zener diode.

Also, as it conducts from emitter to collector, T2 takes one end of capacitor C2 close to the potential of the + rail. This tends to bias T1 off because its base is temporarily effectively at + rail potential.

When T1 is off, T2 is held on because base current can flow via R8 and R7. However, C2 soon charges via R4, R5 and R6. It does so at a rate determined by the values of R4, R5, R6 and its own value of C2. It soon reaches a charge level at which the base of T1 can conduct, switching it on. This pulls the base potential of T2 down switching it off. C1 then discharges via R7 and T1 to earth.

Thus one cycle is complete and an ignition pulse of indeterminate characteristics has resulted in a pulse of a known duration and magnitude, passing through the gauge. At each firing of the ignition coil, more pulses of current flow through the gauge. The more pulses pass per given time period, the higher the gauge registers.

Calibration is via R5, which varies the length of the pulse. The higher its resistance the longer the pulse duration and the higher the gauge reads.

The combination of R1, R2, R3, C3 and the zener diode, ensure that the gauge is fed from a fixed 5.6V irrespective of the voltage of the vehicle battery.

Internal to the gauge is a copper wire coil through which the current passes. The resistance of copper increases with temperature. The gauge would thus read lower as ambient temperature increases. However, part of its current passes through an NTC thermistor, a type of resistor that reduces its resistance as temperature increase. The NTC thermistor thus offsets any gauge errors due to coil resistance changes with temperature.

This tachometer is quite reliable. C3 can cause problems; it is a 'wet' electrolytic capacitor that dries out over time. A replacement 100µF capacitor, with a working voltage of 25Vdc or greater, should be easy to find. The capacitor is polarized, that is to say that it must be inserted the correct way round. The replacement capacitor may have the negative side marked with a bar (-), the positive side marked with a plus sign (+) or red colour or both may be marked. The negative end of C3 is shown in Figure 14.23.

RV1 1433/00 tachometer

The RV1 1433/00 tachometer was in no way an improvement on the early type, indeed the change seems to have been made to save money. While the RV1 1419 uses seventeen components, the RV1 1433 tachometer has a far inferior circuit using just seven. This tachometer was never intended for use in positive earth vehicles.

Getting the tachometer to work with so few components meant that it is far less tolerant than any other that was used on MGB/Cs. It may not work well with electronic ignition systems, particularly those, like optical systems, that have a very different dwell angle from that of the original car. Even with

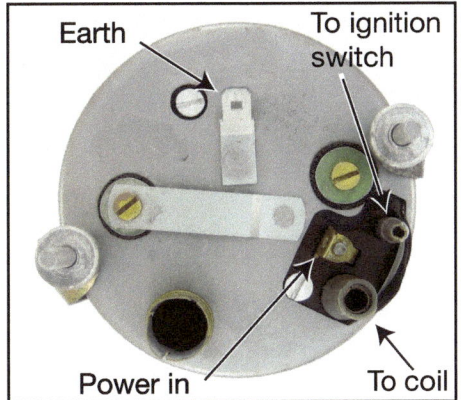

Figure 14.24. The rear of the RV1 1433/00 tachometer.

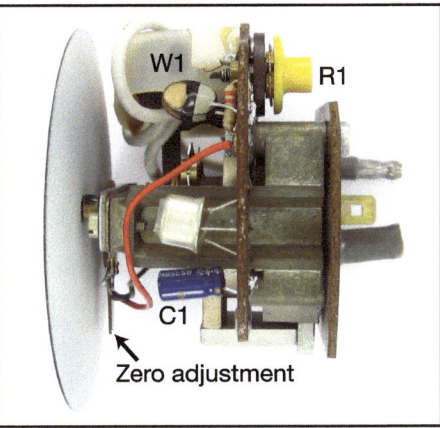

Figure 14.25 The interior of the RV1 1433/00 tachometer.

standard points ignition, it may not work well at idle. It does not work very successfully on 6 or 8 cylinder engines that produce 150% or 200% as many pulses per second as 4 cylinder cars.

Unlike the earlier model, the transformer in the RV1 1419 is wholly located inside the gauge. The signal connections, however, remain as male and female bullet connectors as shown in Figure 14.24

Figure 14.25 shows the interior components. The timing capacitor C1 is a wet electrolytic type and is renowned problem when it dries out. It is also polarised and can sometimes be found to have been inserted the wrong way round during manufacture. It can be replaced with a modern non-polarised type, 50V rated and of value 2.2µF. Adjustment is via R1 and the zero adjustment lever. The lever changes the spring tension that returns the indicator needle back to its rest point. When calibrating the tachometer, use R1 to adjust high readings above 4500rpm. If the calibration at low revolutions, below 1500rpm, is then found to be inaccurate, use the zero adjustment lever to correct it. It will then be necessary to repeat the process using R1 and the lever alternately at high and low rpm until the instrument reads correctly across the full-scale range. On some versions of the tachometer R1 can be accessed by removing a rubber plug from the rear of the instrument. See also calibration page 155.

The circuit diagram is shown in Figure 14.26.

Current from the ignition switch passes through the primary winding P of transformer W1 on its way to the ignition coil. This current is in the form

MGB ELECTRICAL SYSTEMS – THE ESSENTIAL MANUAL

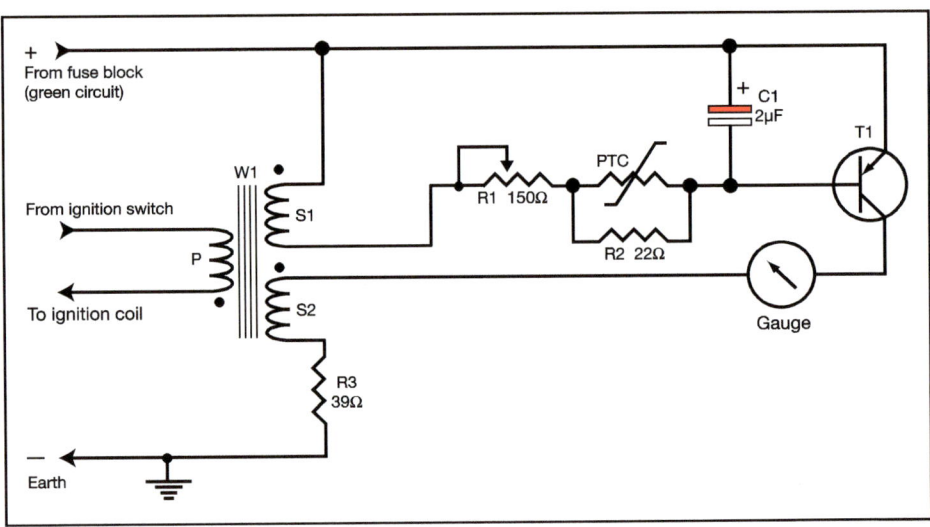

Figure 14.26. Circuit diagram for the RV1 1433/00 tachometer.

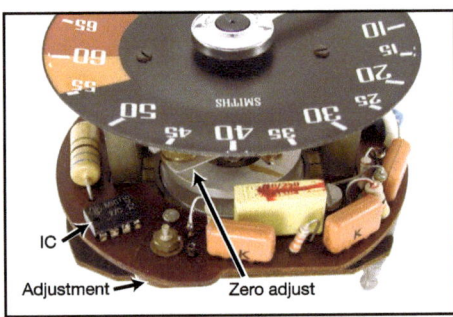

Figure 14.28. Internal view of an RVC 1410/00 tachometer.

Figure 14.29. Internal view of an RVC 1410/00AF and RVC 2432 tachometers.

of a pulse, caused when the ignition coil stores its energy. The current pulse is transformed (by transformer action) to a pulse in secondary winding S1 that charges capacitor C1 via R1 and the parallel combination of R2 and the PTC thermistor.

As C1 charges it reaches a voltage level that allows transistor T1 to conduct base current. T1 switches on and a current flows through the gauge via winding S2 of W1 and R3 to the negative rail. This pulse of current through S2 results in a reinforcing pulse in S1, a process known as positive feedback. This serves to more fully charge C1. Once the pulse decays, C1 starts to discharge to '+' rail potential via R1, R2 and the PTC thermistor. When it is nearly discharged, it switches T1 off and current no longer flows in the gauge.

Calibration is via R1, which varies the length of the pulse. The higher its resistance the longer the pulse duration and the higher the gauge reads. There is no voltage regulation, so the gauge reading will vary with the vehicle battery voltage.

Internal to the gauge is a copper wire coil through which the current passes. The resistance of copper increases with temperature. The gauge would thus read lower as temperature increases. However, part of C1's discharge current passes through a PTC thermistor, a type of resistor that increases its resistance as temperature increase. The PTC thermistor thus causes C1 to discharge more slowly at high temperatures and offsets any gauge errors due to coil resistance changes with temperature.

RVC tachometers

RVC tachometers are very much like those found in modern cars. Rather than sensing the current to the coil, these instruments use a voltage sensing system, getting the signal from a white/black wire on the negative (-) side of the coil (see Figures 11.7 to 11.9). The change was necessitated by the introduction of the ignition relay, which resulted in the ignition switch only carrying the relay coil current and not that to the ignition coil. Routing the high current from the ignition relay under the bonnet, to the tachometer and then back to the coil would have been counter productive.

The RVC tachometers use Texas Instruments integrated circuits (ICs) that are no longer available and for which the manufacturer cannot provide any

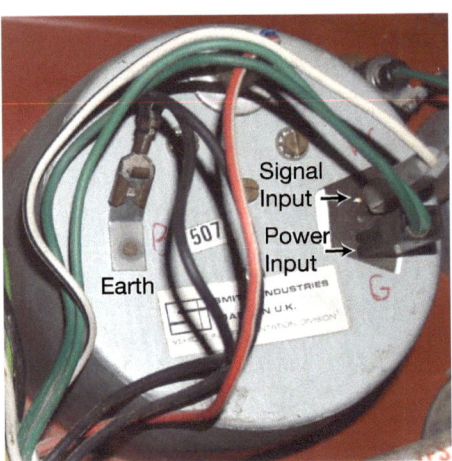

Figure 14.27. Rear view of an RVC 1410/00 tachometer.

data. As a result, no circuit diagram is supplied here (but see http://www.rastley.com/tach-1410.pdf). There is only a signal input, no signal output being required on voltage driven instruments. The connection, however, is still via a bullet style connector as shown in Figure 14.27.

The RVC 1410/00 tachometer has 'through-hole' components placed on a circuit board that wraps around the meter movement. This is a robust design and probably the best of the four different types that were fitted to MGBs. It has an adjustment potentiometer.

The RVC tachometers from 4-cylinder cars are better suited than the RV1 current driven types to modification for use in V6 or V8s. To convert the RVC 1410/00, a 150Ω resistor can be placed in series with one of the wires going to the meter movement. Some calibration will be necessary using the adjustment potentiometer.

The RVC 1410/00AF and RVC 2432 tachometers have similar external connections to the RVC 1410/00 but are quite different from it internally. The components are surface mounted onto

INSTRUMENTATION

Figure 14.30. A potentiometer can be installed in the RVC 1410/00AF and RVC 2432 tachometers in order to make them adjustable for use in V6 or V8 cars.

a rectangular circuit board mounted to one side of the meter movement (Figure 14.29). This model has been shown to be quite unreliable and, with its integrated circuit now unavailable, it is also unserviceable. It has no adjustment potentiometer.

As is the case with the RVC 1410 tachometer, use of the 4-cylinder RVC 1410/00AF and RVC 2432 on V6 or V8 engines requires a resistance in the meter circuit to reduce the output reading; V6 and V8 systems supplying a 150% and 200% greater pulse rate respectively. However, with no adjustment of their own, it is necessary to place a 1kΩ (1000ohm) potentiometer in series with one of the meter wires as has been done to the instrument shown in Figure 14.30. The red wire is easiest to access and there is plenty of space to epoxy adhere a potentiometer onto the white plastic substrate.

Tachometer calibration
The calibration potentiometer can be identified from the respective illustrations of each type of tachometer. The RVC 1410/00AF model was not provided with any means to calibrate it.

Comparison calibration
The preferred adjustment method is to use an external and well calibrated tachometer to compare with that of the car and check at several engine speeds. Remember that external instruments are designed to work on a lot of different cars and may have 4, 6 and 8 cylinder settings. Be sure it is switched to the correct number of cylinders for your car.

Road testing
Whether the tachometer is absolutely accurate is probably not that important, but should you wish to calibrate it, road testing is not recommended for safety

Engine speed rpm	Road speed mph (km/h)			
	1st	2nd	3rd	4th
1000	5 (8)	8 (13)	13 (21)	18 (29)
2000	10 (16)	17 (27)	26 (42)	36 (58)
3000	16 (26)	25 (40)	39 (53)	54 (87)
4000	21 (34)	33 (53)	52 (84)	72 (116)
5000	26 (42)	42 (68)	65 (105)	90 (145)
5500	29 (46)	46 (75)	72 (116)	99 (160)

Table 14.5. Speed in each gear, without overdrive, up to the 5500rpm red-line.

reasons. Moreover, while it is possible, as in Table 14.5, to calculate the road speed in a given gear back to the speed of the engine, the inaccuracy of the speedometer and aspects of the tyres such as size and pressure, make it an unsatisfactory method.

For approximate checking, rather than actual calibration, road testing does have some value. Table 14.5 indicates the road speed for vehicles with standard gearing.

Calibrating with a signal generator
A signal generator is a device that can produce various electrical wave shapes at different amplitudes and frequencies. As such it can somewhat simulate the ignition pulses that normally drive the tachometer.

If you have a computer you can download one of several different free programs that allow you to use it as a signal generator. The one illustrated in Figure 14.31 is the NaTCH Engineering's SigJenny and is available from a number of different sources. Enter SigJenny into any search engine to find it.

When using this program, don't be afraid to play with the settings. Most success has been found using the mark/space setting at 50% but different situations will certainly require adjustment of the output level slider, just to the left of the black square screen.

Note: Although the author has

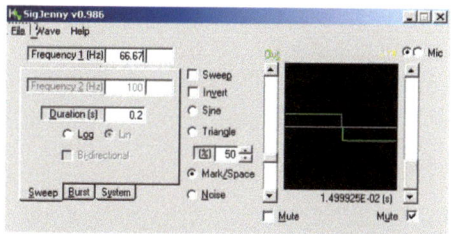

Figure 14.31. The interface of SigJenny, one of a number of signal generator programmes that can be downloaded.

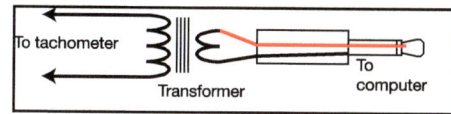

Figure 14.32. The computer output voltage is usually too low to drive the tachometer, so a step-up transformer is required to boost the signal voltage.

used a number of lap and desk top computers with no problems, there are risks associated with driving tachometers using this method of calibration. The sound card in your computer may not be robust enough to drive the tachometer.

A source of 12V power to drive the tachometer electronics will be required. The computer provides the pulse signal, simulating the ignition system. The signal output level from computers is usually of far lower magnitude than produced by the car's ignition system. A small transformer is needed to boost the voltage from the computer to the tachometer. A miniature loudspeaker output transformer can be purchased from electronics suppliers that can boost the output level sufficiently. The plug is a ⅛in (3mm) stereo connector only one channel of which has been connected to the low resistance side of the transformer. The output signal to the tachometer is taken from the high resistance winding, any centre-tap being ignored. Some success has also been achieved using a small mains power transformer. This is a step-down transformer but has to be connected to step-up the voltage in this application, the output being taken from what normally would be the mains voltage input terminals.

Be warned that even after going to all this trouble, variations in tachometers, computers and transformers mean that this method of calibration may not always be successful.

Tach reading rpm	Input frequency		
	4 cyl	6 cyl	8 cyl
500	16.67	25.00	33.33
1000	33.33	50.00	66.67
1500	50.00	75.00	100.00
2000	66.67	100.00	133.33
2500	83.33	125.00	166.67
3000	100.00	150.00	200.00
3500	116.67	175.00	233.33
4000	133.33	200.00	266.67
4500	150.00	225.00	300.00
5000	166.67	250.00	333.33
5500	183.33	275.00	366.67

Table 14.6. The signal generator frequencies, for different numbers of cylinders, necessary to produce a given tachometer reading.

On the RV1 1419, the input signal can be supplied by small alligator jumper leads from the transformer to the output terminals of the tachometer's own transformer. These two terminals carry a red and a black wire. This tachometer may be of either polarity so make sure the power connections made to the input terminal and the tachometer's fixing screws are the correct way round.

Set the output from the signal generator to the correct frequency to produce about 3000rpm reading, see Table 14.6. This rather low calibration point has been chosen because it is a value more likely to be of use than a higher value when changing gears. Adjust the potentiometer to the correct reading on the tachometer scale. Unfortunately, if further testing shows that the readings are not correct right across the scale, there is no method on this tachometer to improve the linearity.

The RV1 1433 is the worst of all the tachometer designs used in MGBs and has proven hard to calibrate. If you want to attempt it then the input signal should go to the output of S1, see Figure 14.27. This tachometer does benefit from having a mechanical zero-adjust lever that allows linearity adjustment. First try adjustment at 5000rpm using Table 14.6 as a guide and the potentiometer for adjustment. Then calibrate at 1000rpm but use the zero adjust lever. Repeat the procedure until no further adjustment is needed.

The RVC 1410/00 tachometers, which have superior circuitry, lend themselves best to calibration. The RV1 1410/00AF and RVC 2432 tachometers can be checked by this means but, unless they are being converted for use in 6 or 8 cylinder vehicles, no calibration, other than mechanical adjustment of the needle movement, is possible. Signal connections are made between the metal frame and the external bullet connector.

Calibration of the RVC1410 series tachometers may be made in the same way as described for the RV1 1433.

Tachometer fault-finding

No fault-finding chart is applicable here. Irregular operation of the tachometer is often the result of misfiring of the engine due to either poor carburettion or ignition problems. Tachometer needle bounce at idling speed is also usually caused by misfiring that can often be rectified by increasing the sparkplug gap.

Electrolytic capacitors failure due to ageing is common. See the relevant RV tachometer section regarding replacement.

The PNP germanium transistors cannot be directly replaced by the now much more common silicon types. Any PNP germanium transistor with a similar physical size to that being replaced and with a maximum collector current (Ic) of 150mA or more should work.

Integrated circuit failure in the RVC tachometers, especially the 1410/00AF and RVC 2432, is common. Replacements are not available. There is a 500µF, 10Vdc electrolytic capacitor between pins 1 and 7 of the IC that can be troublesome, too.

SPEEDOMETER

The MGB/C's speedometer, unlike that in a modern car, is strictly speaking not part of the vehicle electrical system. However, it does work as a result of an electrical mechanism and so deserves consideration here.

Speedometer operation

A rotating cable, driven from the output of the gearbox, enters the back of the speedometer where it connects via a shaft to a magnet that rotates with it. In the discussion concerning generators, page 58, it was shown how a magnetic field that while moving cuts an electrical conductor, will induce a current in it. Moreover, the faster the field cuts the conductor the more current is induced. The magnet in the speedometer is placed very close to an aluminium disc, called a drag cup, which is mounted on a shaft that is coaxial to that of the magnet but not connected to it, see Figure 14.33. The drag cup's shaft also carries the speedometer's indicating needle, which is held toward its zero position by a hairspring that is also connected to the shaft.

The rotating magnet induces a current in the drag cup. The current in the drag cup produces its own magnetic field that is attracted to the rotating magnet and so tries to follow it. However, it is prevented from fully rotating by the hairspring. As the speed of the vehicle increases so does that of the magnet and more current is induced in the drag cup. Thus a stronger magnetic field in the cup is able to better overcome the force of the spring holding it back. As it turns further the needle connected to it also moves and indicates a higher speed reading on the dial face.

Speedometer calibration

If the speedometer and its odometer are grossly inaccurate, it may be that the speedometer assembly or the vehicle's gearbox have been changed and so the gearing in one component is incompatible with the other.

Alternatively, a different differential gear may have been used; that from an MGC for example. Smaller errors may be due to changes to wheel and/or tire size.

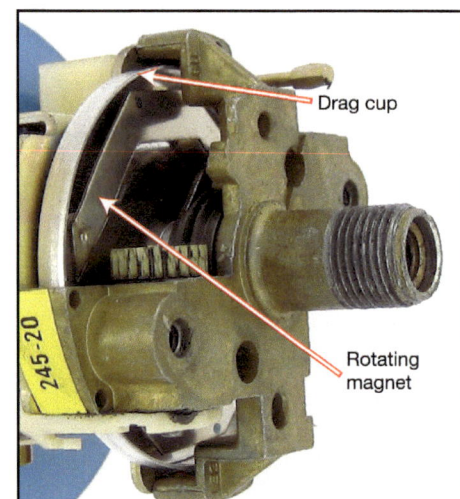

Figure 14.33. Internal view of the speedometer.

INSTRUMENTATION

Figure 14.34. The arrowed number shows the input cable turns per mile or kilometer.

The odometer can be checked against distance markers often found on major roads, or by driving a route previously measured using a computer mapping program or a portable GPS (sat-nav) unit. The speedometer can also be checked by timing between distance markers or by reading directly from a GPS unit.

For the purpose of this exercise it will be assumed that at 50mph (80km/h) the speedometer reads 48mph (77km/h) and similarly, over a 50mi (80km) journey the odometer reads only 48mi (77km).

One way to solve both problems might be to find a used complete speedometer that is more compatible with the car and substitute it. Look at the number at the bottom of the dial, arrowed in Figure 14.34, that indicates the number of cable turns per mile or kilometre, in this case 1000. In our example we would need one that requires less turns per mile (km):

$1000 \times 48/50 = 960$

It may be that there is no Smiths speedometer suitable for an MGB/C with that calibration, but if one can be found with a number closer to 960 than 1000, then the instrument would be more accurate in our example situation.

In the example, the 4% error in reading is relatively small and, if the error in the odometer can be tolerated, that in the speedometer can almost certainly be adjusted out. Larger errors require that the hairspring be changed, which is a job for an instrument maker.

The hard part about calibrating the MGB/C speedometer is often removing it from the car. Once on the bench with the back off, the procedure is quite simple. In the example, the drag cup would be turned so that the speedometer needle indicates 48mph (77km/h). It would then be firmly hand gripped in this position while the needle is moved so that it reads 50mph (80km/h. The needle *should* move

relatively easily on its shaft but there is some risk in doing this as corrosion may have caused it to lock solidly in place.

If you have a variable speed power drill that can rotate *in reverse* at least 1000rpm, a stopwatch and a speedometer cable, then the instrument can be calibrated or checked against the odometer. If the odometer is accurate, set the drill turning at a rate that indicates an easy to calculate speed, such as 60mph (1 mile per min) or 90km/h (1.5km/min). If the odometer completes 10mi or 15km in 10 minutes, then the speedometer is accurate. However, if after the timed period the odometer reads, say, 11mi or 16.5km the speedometer would be reading low. The calculation would be:

At 60mph reading, actual speed = $60 \times 11/10 = 66$mph
or
At 90km/h reading, actual speed = $90 \times 16.5/15 = 99$km/h

The process already described for holding the drag cup at the indicated speed and moving the needle to the actual speed would then be used to make the adjustment.

Should the odometer be known to be reading, for example, 10% too high, it would be necessary to decrease the actual speed calculated above by 10%; conversely, if it were reading 10% too low, then the calculated actual speed would have to be increased by 10%.

CLOCK

A clock was fitted to some MGBs from 1977.

The single biggest problem with the clock comes from the fact that it does not draw sufficient 'wetting' current to overcome any high resistance at the fuse clip. Wetting current is the minimum amount of current required to pass through any oxidization that might occur at a switch or connector contact. Just operating the horn, which shares the same fuse, may burn off any oxides and restart the clock. If the horn does not work either, then the fuse may be blown or there may be a bad case of fuse clip oxidization that requires attention: see page 44.

Unfortunately, clock repair is beyond the scope of most of us and requires the attention of a clock or watch repairer, a rare profession in the era of electronic timepieces.

After-market clocks are available in the approximate style and dial size as MG instruments for replacement or

as an addition, see Figure 1.1. Wiring is simple, the clock needs an earth and a power supply that should come from the purple circuit.

ADDING AN AMMETER

The best advice that can be given to anyone considering installing an ammeter to measure the battery's charge and discharge in amps is "don't."

- Ammeters serve very little purpose.
- Installation is complex.
- The resulting extra length of cable will have a detrimental effect on both the charge and discharge characteristics of the battery.
- The heavy, direct to battery cable behind the dash is a fire hazard.
- The added wiring will decrease reliability.

ADDING A VOLTMETER

For everything said about the ammeter above the opposite is true of a voltmeter.

Installation can be as simple as plugging into a cigar lighter socket like those shown in Figure 14.35. The example on the left is a liquid crystal type and very easy to see in daylight. That on the right has a light emitting diode display and is the easier of the two to read at night. Unless the socket is rewired, they must be removed when the car is parked for a prolonged period because of the consumption from the battery. Rewiring may preclude using the socket for charging the battery (see page 49). If the ignition switch has an auxiliary power position, consider connecting the lighter socket to its white/green wiring.

Traditional style after-market voltmeters – see Figure 1.1 – are inexpensive and simply wire between earth and any ignition-fed power wire, such as a white or green, and alerts the driver if the voltage goes below 11V or above 15V.

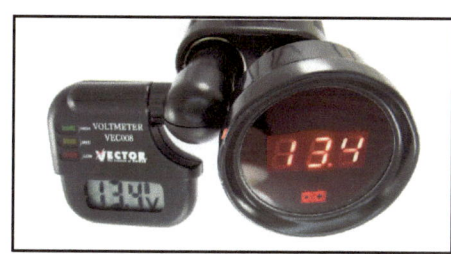

Figure 14.35. Two types of digital voltmeter that plug into a cigar lighter socket.

Chapter 15
Wipers & washers

The first positive ground MGBs, those built from 1962 to 1967, used a wiper motor inherited from the MGA. It was not particularly powerful and MG took the opportunity of changing it when the car went to negative ground and the MGC was introduced in 1967. Early cars had a manual pump action windscreen washer, the move to an electric pump beginning in 1968 for North American vehicles.

For the 1968 model year, that is cars built from October 1967, the new, more powerful motor was introduced that could better propel the three wipers required on roadsters in North America to meet the wiper swept glass area regulations, and the two longer wiper blades for the GT model. This motor took advantage of improvements in magnet technology that allowed the use of permanent magnets, introduced a third brush for two-speed operation, and incorporated regenerative braking to more precisely park the blades, irrespective of friction variations caused by different weather conditions. An electrical washer pump was also introduced at this time.

The wiper switch on early cars was dash-mounted but was later replaced by a column-mounted stalk that was a combined wiper, wash and overdrive switch (where fitted).

1962 to 1967 wiper circuit

Figure 15.1 shows the circuit for cars made through 1967 using the single-speed wiper motor.

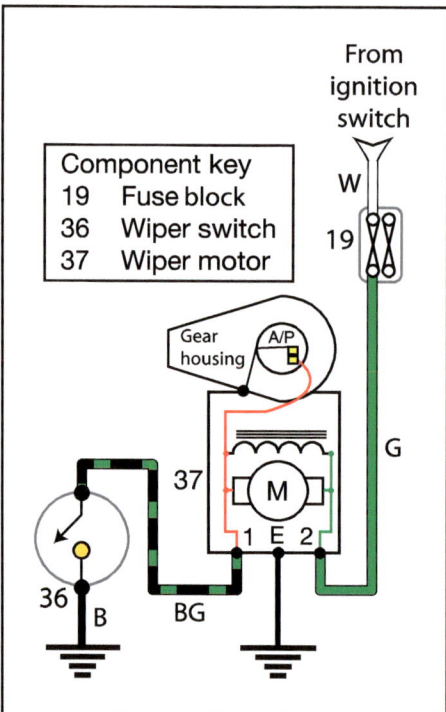

Figure 15.1. Early wiper system circuit diagram.

Power from the batteries is routed by a large cable to the starter motor solenoid (4) that acts as an anchor and termination point. It then goes on brown (N) wires via the dynamo control box (2), which is also used as a wire anchoring point. The current is taken to the fuse block (19), yet another anchor point, and to the ignition switch (38). When closed, the ignition switch directs the current via a white (W) wire to the fuse block.

A fuse supplies current to the windscreen wiper motor (37) via a green wire (G). Closing the windscreen wiper switch (36) allows the current to flow through the motor on a black/green (BG) wire to earth. Opening the switch interrupts the current only if the auto-park switch (A/P) is also open.

Because both the field and armature magnetizing currents would be reversed, no action has to be taken vis-à-vis the wiper motor if the car is converted to negative earth. Although the motor runs a crank, producing a push-pull mechanical output, rotation direction is nevertheless important if the auto-park switch has a trailing switch-blade, as shown in Figure 15.9. It is still very important that the wire connections to terminals 1 and 2 of the wiper motor are correct. Crossing the green and black/green wires will

WIPERS & WASHERS

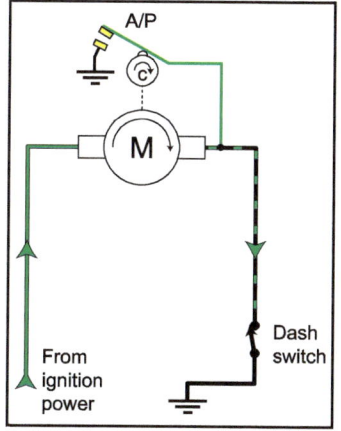

Figure 15.2. The driver closes the dash switch.

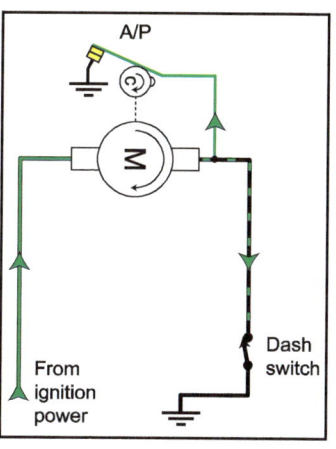

Figure 15.3. The motor begins to turn.

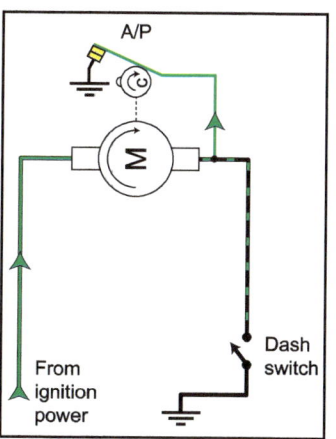

Figure 15.4. The driver opens the dash switch.

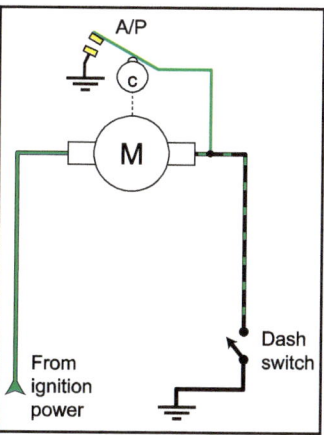

Figure 15.5. The auto-park switch shuts off the motor.

Figure 15.6. Rear view of the early wiper motor.

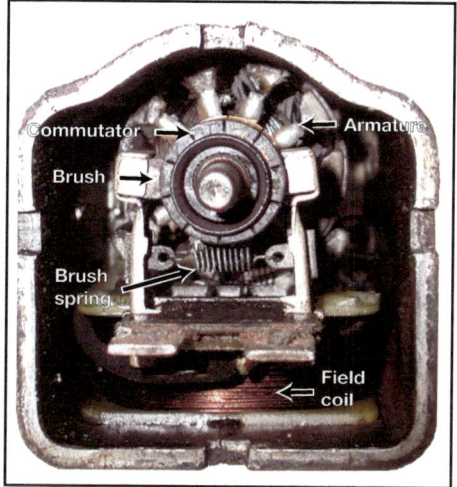

Figure 15.7. Internal view of the early wiper motor.

Figure 15.8. Early motor brush and holder.

result in the A/P switch short circuiting the power to earth. As the motor is mounted in rubber bushes, an earth connection to the E screw is necessary to provide a ground path for the A/P switch.

Auto-park operation

Figures 15.2 through 15.5 show how the early windscreen motor's auto-park system works. For convenience, some licence is taken in these schematic diagrams in the depiction of the auto-park cam and switches. The actual A/P switches used look somewhat different, as illustrated in Figures 15.9 and 15.10.

EARLY WIPER MOTOR

The early motor is a parallel wound, energized field, 5-pole armature brush motor. Whether installed in a left or right hand drive car, the motor is located under the dash at the extreme right.

The most wearable electrical items are the two brushes. Once worn, damage to the commutator ensues and can make the motor unserviceable. Access to the brushes is via removal of the back cover. First remove the two wire fixing screws from terminals 1 and 2 (already removed in Figure 15.6), and then the two screws either side of the terminals. The cover may then be pulled off.

With the rear cover removed access can be obtained to the brushes, commutator and field winding. In the example in Figure 15.7, it is immediately obvious that the right-hand brush is worn down so far that the brush holder is touching the commutator, potentially damaging it.

The brushes may be removed by releasing the spring from its retainers. Note that these small items have a habit of flying off and are easily lost. The now free brush holders can be simply removed from the bottom plate.

If the motor is not running at all, take this opportunity to measure the resistance of the now isolated field winding. It should have a resistance measured between the two terminals of 7Ω to 10Ω.

A sluggish motor may have an open armature winding. Check the resistance between commutator segments that are 180° apart. The resistance should be 1.5Ω to 2Ω.

The brushes simply nest in the brush holders as shown in Figure 15.8. Replacement brushes are costly but almost any motor repair shop can provide inexpensive brushes of almost the same size. Brush material is relatively soft and easy to saw and file to shape. Make the total length no greater than ⅜in (10mm). Use a round file to shape the end that will contact the commutator.

MGB ELECTRICAL SYSTEMS – THE ESSENTIAL MANUAL

If, as in this case, the brushes are so worn that the brush holder has contacted the commutator or it is dirty, use some fine sandpaper to smooth and clean it. You may need to use a sharp blade to remove sanding or other debris from between the segments, as it is essential that they be insulated from one another.

Auto-park mechanism

To access the auto-park mechanism, remove the four screws covering the crank mechanism and fold back the cover to expose the underside, taking care not to strain any wires.

The design of the auto-park switch varies. On that shown in Figure 15.9, a trailing switch contact (A) is joined to the crank wheel, rotating with it and connected to earth through the metal structure.

On the underside of the cover is the static contact (B), which is in the form of a disc with an insulating segment (C) attached to it. A gasket ensures that the disc is not in electrical contact with the crank cover. The disc joins, via an external wire, to terminal 1 of the motor. When the moving contact is touching the disc, the motor will rotate irrespective of the position of the driver switch. However, when it reaches the cut-out section (C), the electrical connection is broken and the motor stops. When the crank cover screws are loose, the cap can be rotated to achieve right or left park positions and to adjust the precise point when the motor stops and the resulting wiper park position. Check that both the moving blade and fixed disc are in good and clean condition. If the motor has been disassembled and rewired incorrectly, it is possible that the motor could rotate in the wrong direction. The gear wheel should rotate clockwise when seen from the tops and hence the moving contact has a trailing action.

Some motors, like that illustrated in Figure 15.10, may be found without a moving blade. Instead the pin (A) that retains the crank arm to the gear wheel contacts a fixed switch (B) in the cap. As it rotates it moves the switch contact and breaks the electrical connection between it and another contact that is joined to the external wire.

Before reassembling the motor, use some lithium grease to lubricate the bearings at each end of the armature shaft and the gearbox.

Regenerative braking

The momentum of the motor, the wiper mechanism and the blades on wet glass tend to keep the system operating for a short time after the electrical power is removed from the motor; the effect being that in some conditions, with wind lift for example, the wiper blades may tend to move past the park position and operate continuously. Regenerative braking can prevent this from happening.

As was described on page 58, a dc brush motor and generator are effectively the same machines and one may be used as the other. Apply electricity to a motor and it produces a mechanical output. Apply mechanical input to a motor and it becomes a generator, producing an electrical output.

In physics, nothing is free. When a generator is loaded such that current can flow in an electrical circuit, it requires extra mechanical input. If the circuit is a short circuit, it will take a large amount of electrical energy from the generator and thus require a very high mechanical energy input.

In the case of the wiper motor, when the motor continues to turn after the circuit is opened, it becomes a potential electrical generator. Apply a short-circuit to it and the required mechanical input is so high that it immediately takes all the remaining kinetic energy away, and effectively acts as a brake.

Later wiper motors with a high-speed switch position are especially vulnerable to running over the park position and so apply the principle of regenerative braking by using a circuit that introduces a short circuit to the motor at the same time the power is removed, causing the wiper blades to stop almost instantly. Regenerative braking was not a feature of the pre-1968 wiper motor, but it may added as described below.

The term 'regenerative braking' is more often heard now in respect to electric and hybrid-electric vehicles. The principle is closely related to that described here but its purpose is very different and the two systems should not be confused. Regenerative braking in vehicles with electric propulsion incorporates electrical generators in the powertrain system that are used to supplement the conventional braking system. Some of the mechanical energy, which would normally be wasted in heat in the brake pads, is converted to electrical energy that recharges the batteries, thus providing greater fuel efficiency.

Adding regenerative braking

If over-run past the park position becomes a nuisance on the early wiper motor, a relay (see Appendix 1), together with some wiring modification can be used to provide regenerative braking.

Figure 15.11 shows the circuit in the rest position. The wiper has stopped after its last use and the relay is unpowered with its power contact terminal 30 connected to the normally closed terminal 87a. Note that under this condition, the two wires from the motor (M) are connected together. Thus, after last use, the motor was shorted out and regenerative braking occurred.

When the dash switch is closed, current can flow from the ignition power input, through the relay coil, thus energizing it. When energized, the connection between power terminals 30 and 87a is broken but terminal

Figure 15.9. One form of auto-park switch.

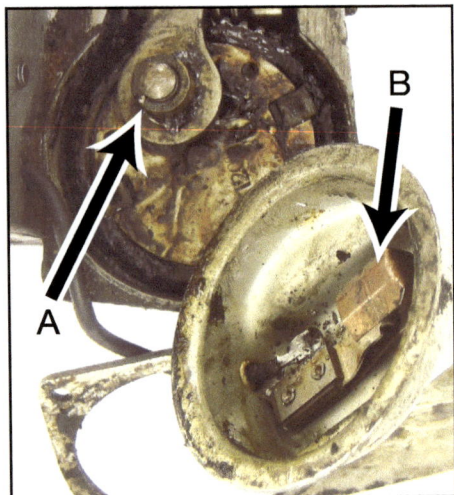

Figure 15.10. A second form of auto-park switch.

WIPERS & WASHERS

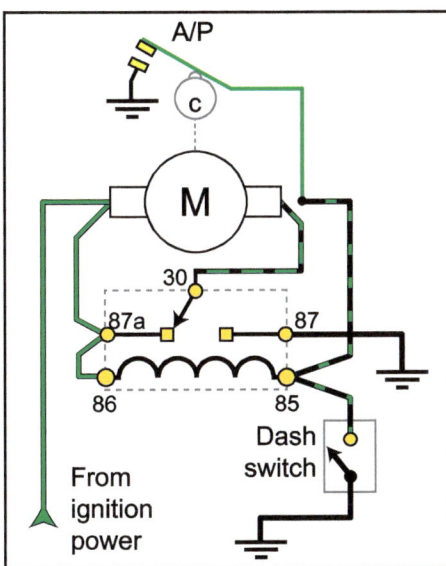

Figure 15.11. Circuit for regenerative-braking modification to the pre-1967 wiper system.

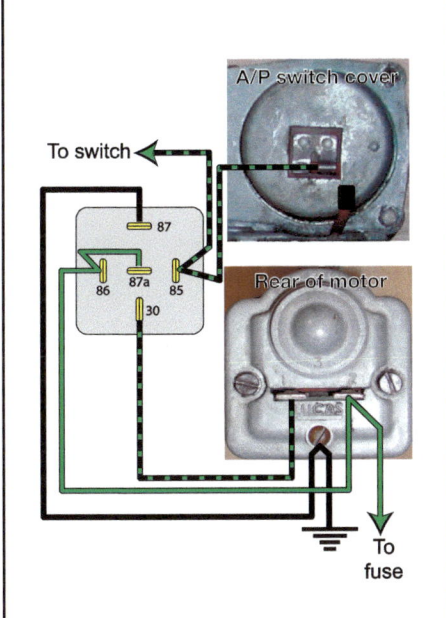

Figure 15.12. Layout for regenerative-braking modification to the pre-1967 wiper system.

motor can continue to turn as long as A/P remains closed.

When the wiper reaches its parked position A/P opens, and with the dash switch also open, the relay becomes de-energized. The connection between relay terminals 30 and 87 is broken, removing the earth path for the motor and that between terminal 30 and 87a is made, shorting the motor out and causing regenerative braking again.

Figure 15.12 shows the same circuit in a more practical layout format. Note that the original wire from the A/P switch to the motor has been cut and capped off.

1968 and later wiper circuit

The circuit diagram for the later wiper circuit is shown in Figure 15.13. Current flows from the battery to on a heavy cable that is anchored at the starter motor solenoid (4). From there a brown (N) wire takes the current to the fuse block (19), another anchor point, and from there to the ignition switch.

In the circuit shown in Figure 15.13, the ignition switch (not shown) has an auxiliary position between off and ignition that can be used to power the wiper circuit, as well as the heater blower motor and radio (if fitted) without having the ignition system energized too. The auxiliary terminal on the ignition switch is powered both in the auxiliary and ignition-run positions.

A white/green (WG) wire takes the current from the ignition switch, through an in-line fuse (67a) and to the wiper motor and its switch on a green/pink (GK) wire. Cars without an accessory position on the ignition switch provide power to the wiper circuit directly from the fuse block via a green (G) wire, described as the alternative power source in Figure 15.13. The wiper motor switch may be a dedicated toggle device (36) or part of the combined wipe/wash/overdrive stalk switch (118) mounted on the steering column.

With the wiper switch in the off position (O) shown in Figure 15.13, the wiper has stopped with no power applied and with the A/P switch completing a circuit that shorts the motor out causing regenerative braking.

With the toggle switch in the normal-speed (N) position as per the left hand image in Figure 15.14, power from the green/pink (or green wire if applicable) can pass through the switch to a red/light-green (RLG) wire and to the normal-speed brush of the motor. Similarly, with the switch in the high-speed (H) position, the current will travel on a blue/light-green (ULG) wire to the high-speed brush.

If the driver moves the wiper switch to the off position but the wipers have not reached the park position, the A/P switch will provide power from the green/pink wire (or green wire if applicable) to a brown/light-green (NLG) wire that will supply current to the

30 becomes connected to power terminal 87. Now ignition power can flow through the motor, the relay and to earth, so completing the circuit and causing the motor to turn.

As the motor turns, so the cam (c) also turns, closing the auto-park switch (A/P). A second path to earth is now provided for the relay coil so that even when the dash switch is opened, the

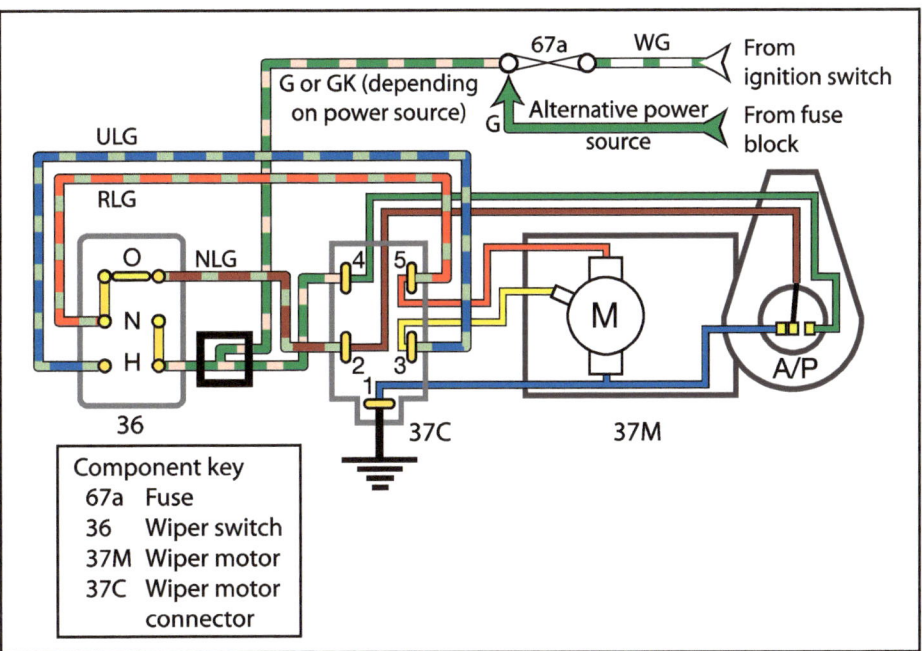

Figure 15.13. Late wiper system circuit diagram with toggle switch control.

MGB ELECTRICAL SYSTEMS – THE ESSENTIAL MANUAL

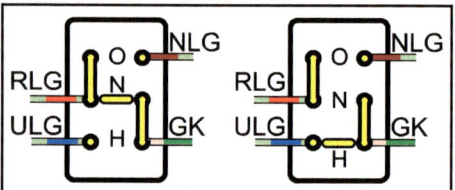

Figure 15.14. Wiper switch normal and high speed positions.

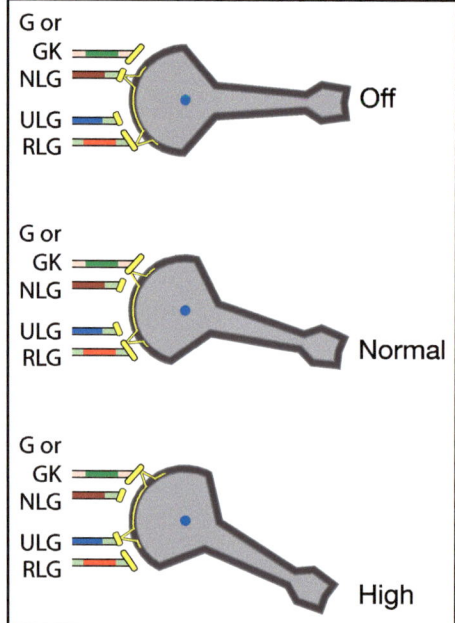

Figure 15.15. Column mounted wiper switch action.

Rather than a toggle switch to operate the wipers, many cars have a column-mounted switch that also has a washer function on an end push and an overdrive control that works with a push-pull action.

The column switch's electrical functionality is identical to the toggle switch in that it makes the same electrical connections to the circuit components in the O, N and H positions, however, because the switch rotates, its action is somewhat different.

Figure 15.15 shows the switch in the off (O), normal-speed (N) and high-speed (H) positions.

Referring to both Figures 15.13 and 15.15, in the O position, the switch bridges between the red/light-green (RLG) and brown/light-green (NLG) wires. There is no power connected to the motor and the motor is shorted out, indicating that when it last stopped, regenerative braking was applied.

In the N position, the switch bridges between the green (G) or green/pink (GK) wire, depending on how the car is wired, and the red/light-green wire (RLG), so providing power to the normal-speed motor brush.

In the H position, the switch bridges between the green or green/pink wire, depending on how the car is wired, and the blue/light-green wire (ULG), so providing power to the high-speed motor brush.

Later auto-park mechanism

The action of the A/P switch is illustrated in detail in Figures 15.16 to 15.19. To simplify the circuits, the high-speed brush, which is not used for auto-parking, is not shown.

In Figure 15.16, the driver has closed the switch and the motor (M) begins to turn.

Figure 15.17 shows the motor turning and with it the cam (C), causing the auto park switch (A/P) to change state but not, however, change the current flow in any way.

When the driver opens the wiper switch, but the park position is not yet reached, as in Figure 15.18, the motor continues to run as current continues to pass through the A/P switch.

In Figure 15.19, when the driver's switch is off and the auto-park position is reached, the A/P switch changes state, disconnecting the power but shorting the motor out, regenerative braking causing it to stop abruptly.

LATER WIPER MOTOR

Cars from 1968 use a permanent magnet, 5-pole armature brush wiper motor located, like the early motor, under the dash on the extreme right side. It is easily distinguished from the earlier motor by its circular and the somewhat larger motor housing required to contain the permanent magnets, see Figure 15.20.

If buying a used motor it may be necessary to remove the four screws retaining the crank cover to identify it and compare it to that being replaced. The wiper blade sweep arc depends on the distance of the crank pin to the centre of the crank wheel and the resulting arc in degrees is usually stamped on the wheel. The angle required for a particular car will vary

motor's normal-speed brush until the A/P switch changes state, whereupon it shorts the motor again and brakes the wiper motion.

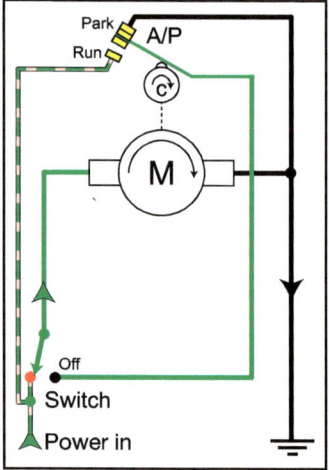

Figure 15.16. The driver closes the switch.

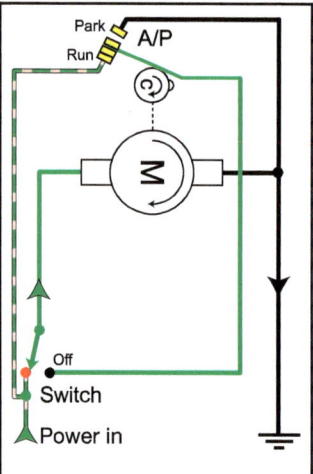

Figure 15.17. The motor begins to turn.

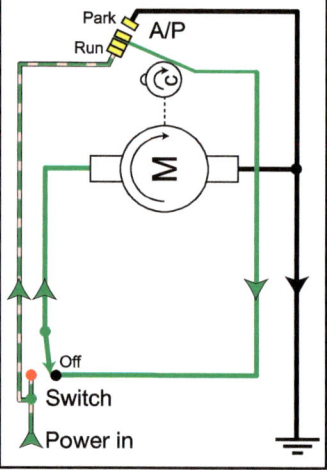

Figure 15.18. The driver opens the switch.

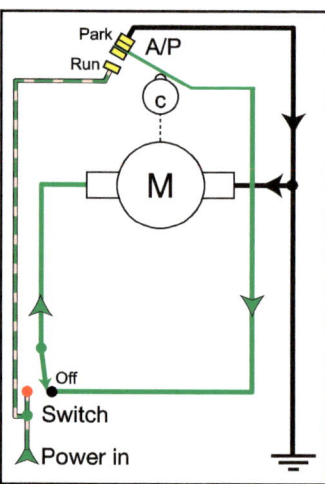

Figure 15.19. The A/P switch short-circuits the motor.

WIPERS & WASHERS

depending on various factors including the number of blades, the territory to which is was sold and whether it is a roadster or GT.

The crank position you find on removing the cover will usually, but not always, indicate to which side the wiper auto-parked when last switched off. Look also for an arrow, often stamped on the crank cover, that indicates the park direction. Figure 15.21 shows a motor that parks to the left and is for left-hand drive cars.

The crank wheel can be removed to exchange it for one with a more suitable wiper arc or to change the park direction. Look at where the crank wheel shaft passes through the body and locate the C clip. On some motors the end of the shaft is slotted and looks like a screw head, but this was just a locating feature to aid manufacture. Remove the C clip and the thrust washer below it so that the metal crank wheel can be lifted out of the wiper body separating it from the plastic gear wheel. Care must be taken when easing them apart because the plastic will almost certainly have become brittle over the years. They need only be separated a small amount in order to un-key the plastic and metal wheels from one another. The metal wheel can then be rotated and re-keyed 180° from the original orientation relative to the plastic wheel so that the auto-park position is reversed.

If the crank angle of a replacement motor is different from that originally in the car, the metal wheels will have to be removed completely and exchanged.

The regenerative braking system means that no adjustment, other than a 180° park position reversal described above, is necessary.

The auto-park (A/P) switch, Figure 15.22, is combined with the wiper motor input connector. It simply clips onto the back of the motor, and a raised section on the nylon gear wheel acts as a cam and presses the switch button inward when the park position is reached.

Figure 15.23 shows the wiper motor connections.

The brush card (Figure 15.24) commutator and armature (Figure 15.25) can be easily accessed for inspection by removing the two screws at the end of the motor housing. Only do this on a clean workbench because the very strong permanent magnets inside the cylindrical housing will easily attract any ferrous debris. Invert the housing onto clean paper to stop any foreign matter getting into it.

Brushes are easily released. Like the early motor, in the event that replacements are unobtainable, they can be fabricated from similar sized brushes obtainable from a motor repair shop. Note the odd shape and position of the high-speed brush connected to the yellow wire. It is extra narrow so that it can never bridge two armature segments at the same time as the other two brushes.

Inspect the commutator for wear and have it skimmed if it has any narrowing or scoring where the brushes run. The armature shaft is on a worm gear and twists out of the

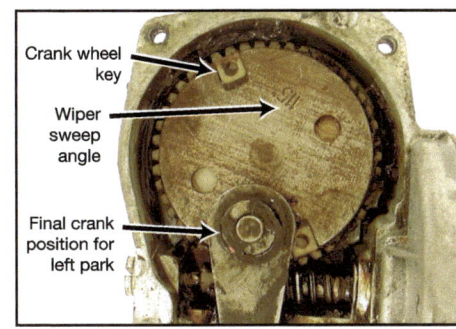

Figure 15.21. Late wiper crank wheel.

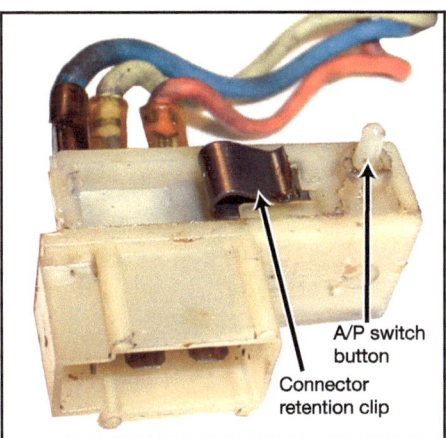

Figure 15.22. Late wiper combined connector and auto-park switch.

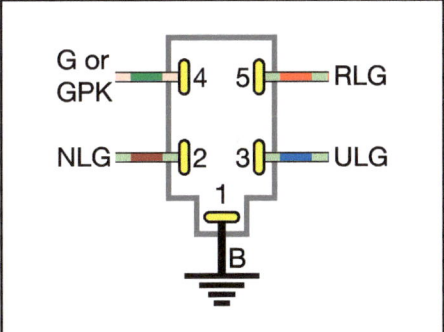

Figure 15.23. Late wiper motor harness connector viewed from wiring side.
Terminal #1 – Earth.
Terminal #2 – A/P power output.
Terminal #3 – High-speed brush.
Terminal #4 – Motor and A/P power input.
Terminal #5 – Normal speed brush.

nylon gear wheel very easily. The tricky part is reassembly. The three brushes must be spread in order to insert the commutator between them. Hold the commutator in place with a thin bladed screwdriver when bringing the housing over the armature, as it tends to want to jump towards the magnets and out from between the brushes.

Figure 15.20. The 2-speed wiper motor on the right is easily distinguished from the earlier single speed type on the left by the round body used to contain the permanent magnets.

MGB ELECTRICAL SYSTEMS – THE ESSENTIAL MANUAL

Figure 15.24. Late wiper brush card.

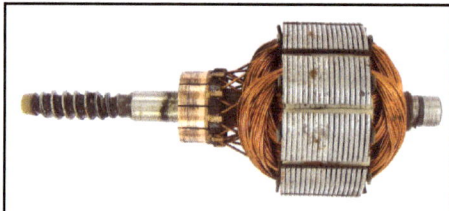

Figure 15.25. Late wiper commutator and armature.

Figure 15.26. Windscreen washer motor.

WINDSCREEN WASHER

A windscreen washer motor was fitted from to some export cars from 1968 and to domestic vehicles from about 1974. Many of the problems associated with it are due to water blockage in the pipes, water filter and jets. Debris can also accumulate in the impeller. It can be accessed by removing the two screws, cover plate and gasket at the front of the motor.

If it is necessary to remove old tubing from the motor, it is better to do so by cutting it off just beyond the spigots and then slitting the remaining short lengths to release them. This action is necessary because the plastic tubing will have hardened over time and formed over the spigots so tightly that it takes less force to break the spigots than pull off the tubing.

The motor must be connected in the correct polarity, so look for the + and – indicators next to the input terminals The motor is low side switched and is powered from a green wire. A light-green/black wire takes the current to earth via the washer switch.

When the switch is closed, a circuit tester should reveal power to the green wire but none at the now earthed light-green/black wire.

If the impeller is worn or the motor inoperative, repair is not usually possible.

Very inexpensive generic motors, supplied with all new tubing can be purchased from auto accessory stores that can replace .damaged motors or add the power wash facility to cars with manual pumps.

WIPERS & WASHERS

WIPER AND WASHER FAULT-FINDING

Symptom	Possible causes	Action
Motor does not operate.	Fuse failure.	Check for failure of other components on the same fuse (e.g. turn signals and brake lamps). Some late cars have a dedicated in-line fuse. Check in-line fuse near fuse block that has a green/pink and a white wire attached.
	Motor or switch failure. (Early motor)	Jumper terminal #1 of motor to earth. If motor operates then check connections to switch and switch operation. If motor does not operate, inspect brushes. Change brushes or motor as necessary.
	Switch failure. (Late motor)	Remove connector at wiper motor. Connect earthed wire to terminal 1. Connect a live power wire alternately to terminals 3 and 5. If motor operates then check connections to switch and switch operation. If motor does not operate, inspect brushes. Change brushes or motor as necessary.
Auto-park does not work (early type).	Auto park switch contacts bent.	Open crank case and inspect moving contact (Figure 15.9) or fixed contact (Figure 15.10) and bend to adjust if necessary.
Auto-park does not work (late type).	Auto park switch broken or incorrectly located.	Un-clip combined auto-park switch and connector from motor casing. Manually operate switch as motor turns. Pressing button on switch (Figure 15.22) should stop the motor. If motor stops, check integrity of the nylon cam via aperture in housing. Reinstall switch making sure it locates properly. Replace switch if necessary.
	Wiring fault.	Check integrity of green or green/pink wire to wiper connector terminal #4.
Washer does not work and makes no sound.	Motor or switch failure.	With switch operated motor should be felt to attempt to move and get warm. With switch operated, check power at green input wire. If none, check wiring back to fuse block. Check power at light-green/black output wire. If circuit tester glows or voltmeter indicates any voltage present, check switch operation.

Table 15.1. Windscreen wiper and washer fault-finding chart.

Chapter 16
Fuel pump

The fuel pump is an electro-hydraulic system. Non-electrical aspects are discussed here for elimination purposes only and, unless trivial, will not be analysed in detail.

LOCATION

Probably the biggest problem with the SU fuel pump as used on the MGB/C, especially early cars, is its location, in front of the right rear wheel where, should the sealing fail, its sensitive electrical toggle contacts may be exposed to moisture and consequent oxidization.

The fuel pump shown in Figure 16.1 is typical of those found on a regularly used car. Note the corrosion of the bracket fasteners that can make what should be a simple removal operation quite difficult.

Some attempt was made to shield the sensitive electrical end of the pump by having it project into the left side battery well. However, as Figure 16.2 illustrates, the effort was only partly successful, water and dirt still finding its way to the rear cover. From 1974 the pump was relocated so that the rear of the pump is in the boot with a rubber seal around it. It also has a metal cover over the rear assembly to protect it from damage that might be caused by movement of the contents of the boot.

Figure 16.3 shows an installation on a 1980-LE model. The radio suppression capacitor (also known as a condenser) was a standard fitment. Its purpose is to prevent electrical interference travelling down the electrical harness to the radio, if fitted, where it would be heard as a clicking noise.

Figure 16.1. A typical pre-1974 fuel pump installation.

Figure 16.2. Another view of the pre-1974 fuel pump installation.

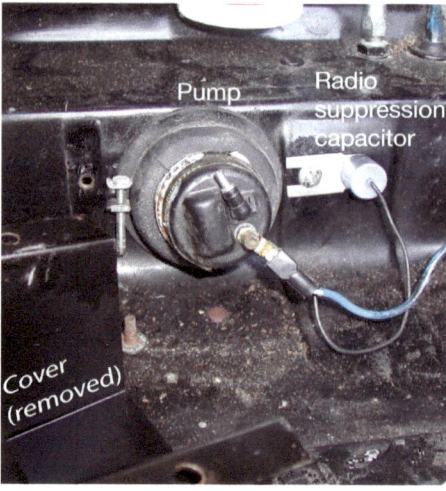

Figure 16.3. A post 1974 fuel pump installation with the cover removed.

FUEL PUMP

FUEL PUMP ELECTRICAL CIRCUIT

The electrical supply to the pump is so simple as not to require a dedicated circuit diagram. However, it is shown as part of Figure 13.5.

Drivers are used to hearing the pump click when the ignition key is turned. Each click is a cycle of the pump diaphragm and, if the engine is not started, it will only continue until the float chamber fills. If the car has been standing some time since it was last started, the pump may need several seconds to replace the fuel that has evaporated from the float chamber(s). Continuous clicking may be an indication of a faulty pump diaphragm or valve or a carburettor float needle that is not blocking the fuel off when its float chamber is full. It may also indicate a fuel leak elsewhere. Any continuous operation of the pump when the engine is not running should be investigated immediately. Look for fuel dripping from a carburettor bowl from where it can fall on the hot exhaust manifold and become a fire hazard.

North American cars, built from mid 1974, have a fuel shut off inertia switch like that in Figure 16.4, in series with the pump and connected with a white wire on both its input and output. It is located under the extreme left of the under-dash area. In the event of any high shock to the vehicle, as could happen in a collision, the switch will break the circuit to the fuel pump. It is reset by depressing the button located on the end.

FUEL PUMP IDENTIFICATION

Several versions of the fuel pump were used over the life of the MGB or were supplied as replacement items. Each has an identification plate located as per Figure 16.5. However, the plate is not visible when the pump is in the car and often needs cleaning before it can be read. From the electrical point of view, there were three major types.

- Non-polarity sensitive pumps with capacitor arc snubbing. These have part numbers starting HP or AUF. The rear cover has a flat profile like that in Figure 16.2
- Polarity sensitive pumps with TVS diode arc snubbing. These have part numbers:
AZX 1318. positive earth.
AZX 1307. negative earth but replacements made after 2011 are dual polarity.

Figure 16.5. Part number location.

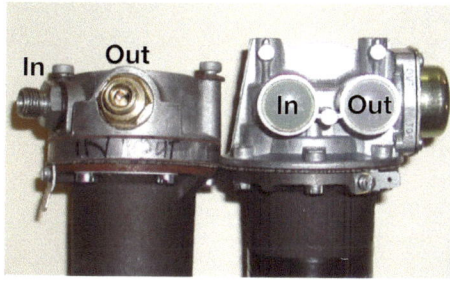

Figure 16.6. Early pump (left) and later pump (right).

Figure 16.7. Electronic pumps have an additional identification plate.

They are most easily distinguished by the bump in the rear cap required to accommodate the diode as per the pump in Figure 16.3.

Positive earth pumps have red tape for sealing the join between the end cover and the pump body.

Negative earth pumps have black tape.

- Electronic contact-less type. These newer pumps have an additional identification plate with the word "electronic" stamped on it (see Figure 16.7).

FUEL PUMP OPERATION

All pumps have a solenoid consisting of an armature that moves under the influence of a magnetic field produced when a coil is electrically energized. The forward motion of the armature rod also causes the pump diaphragm to move and fuel to be sucked into a chamber at the far end. Once the forward stroke is completed, the circuit opens and the rod, which is spring loaded and no longer under any electromagnetic force, tries to return to its original position and in doing so pumps fuel out to the carburettors; valve action ensuring fuel can only flow from the tank and to the fuel line. However, should the float chambers in the carburettors be full, the needle valves in them will close and result in a back pressure, preventing the diaphragm and the rod from returning, and so the contacts remain open until fuel is required. By pumping under spring pressure, when the needle valve in a carburettor float chamber blocks the fuel pumping action, the pump is not trying to continuously operate under any electrical power.

The non-electronic pumps have electrical contacts that alternately energize and de-energize the coil. As described in respect to ignition systems on page 87, any coil in which current is flowing and that becomes suddenly disconnected will produce a high voltage that arcs across the gap

Figure 16.4. Fuel cut-off inertia switch.

MGB ELECTRICAL SYSTEMS – THE ESSENTIAL MANUAL

between the contacts and in doing so damages them. Some kind of device is required across the contacts to 'snub' the arc. SU used a capacitor in early models and a special diode in later versions.

The over-centre spring mechanism that operates the contact points ensures that they flip either open or closed with no possible hovering between the two states. In addition to the toggle action, the sophisticated points mechanism also ensures that the points slide across one another as they close, so providing a cleaning action.

In much the same way as electronic ignition system operate a coil to produce a spark, electronic pumps use semiconductors to switch a coil too, although in this case the purpose is to produce mechanical motion. Similar advantages can also be claimed for the use of electronic switching in the fuel pump as for an ignition system, in that there are no contacts to be damaged or require adjustment and hence reliability is much improved.

Capacitor snubbed pump

Figure 16.8 shows a schematic representation of the capacitor snubbed pump.

There are two pairs of contacts in each pump giving a degree of redundancy and sharing the load so that contact life is lengthened. When the armature moves forward on the pump stroke it operates a mechanism that causes the contacts to close. Current can then pass through the solenoid coil, resulting in a magnetic field building up around it. The field causes the armature to reverse direction, re-compressing the spring and operating the pump diaphragm, which sucks fuel into a chamber. On completion of the stroke, the contacts open, and the magnetic field collapses.

The collapsing magnetic field causes a reverse polarity, high-voltage to form across the separating contacts or points. The voltage rises so rapidly that it can jump across the points before they have any significant gap between them. Once established, the jumping spark, called an arc, can sustain itself even as the gap between the points increases. If, however, the high voltage can be delayed, or snubbed, for a brief period until such time as the contacts have separated some reasonable distance, the gap will be too great for the spark to jump and the arcing will be non existent or at least minimal.

A capacitor C placed, in parallel with the points, absorbs the initial energy that would have formed the spark. The capacitor can only do its job for a very brief period, but that is sufficient time for the points to separate enough so that the voltage produced can no longer jump the gap.

If a high rate of contact erosion occurs on this type of pump then the capacitor may need changing. A suitable replacement would be any axial leaded 0.47µF, 220V or greater value, metallized film capacitor. Such a device should have dimensions of about 0.3in (8mm) diameter × 0.3in (20mm) long and fit in the space vacated by the original.

TVS diode snubbed pumps

A TVS or transient suppression diode, sometimes called an avalanche diode, is described in Appendix 2. In brief, it conducts electricity when a certain voltage is reached.

The circuits for diode snubbed pumps, shown in Figures 16.10 and 16.11, as well as the pump operation itself, are identical to that for the capacitor snubbed pump type except that the voltage – which again is in reverse polarity to that energizing the coil – is allowed to build up to about 30V; not a sufficient voltage to cause any real arcing at the contacts. Above that voltage, the diode conducts and consumes the energy that would otherwise cause an arc. Note that

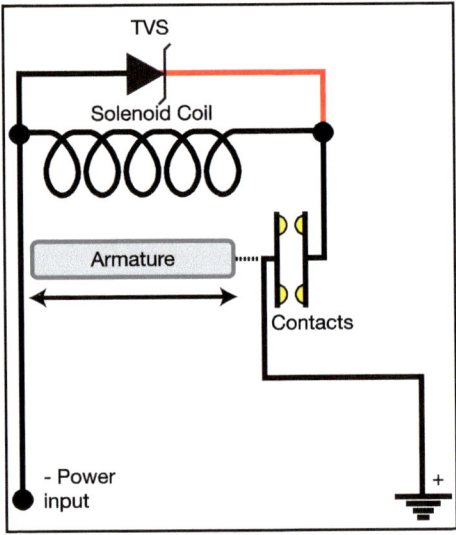

Figure 16.10. Schematic of the positive earth TVS diode snubbed pump.

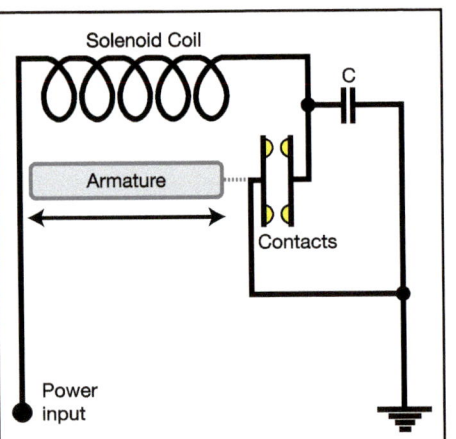

Figure 16.8. Schematic of the capacitor snubbed pump.

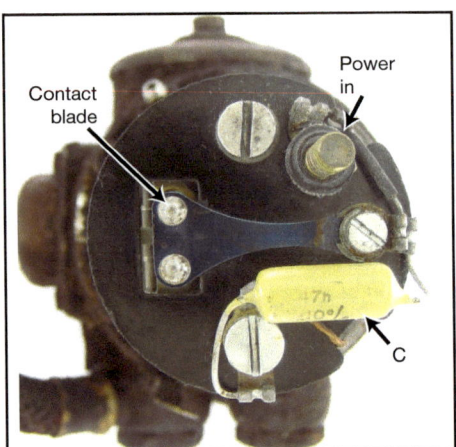

Figure 16.9. The electrical components of the capacitor snubbed pump.

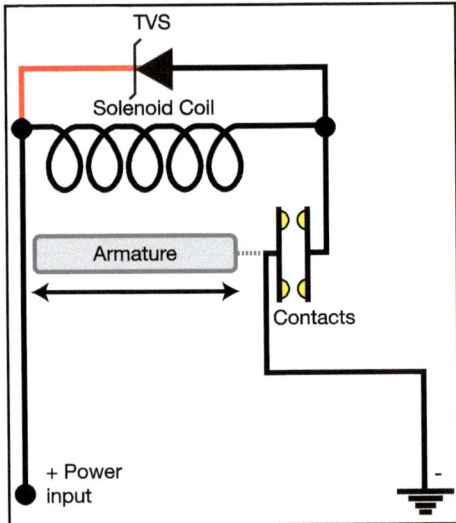

Figure 16.11. Schematic of the negative earth TVS diode snubbed pump.

FUEL PUMP

the diodes are connected in opposite directions for positive and negative earth cars. Although the diodes used for the different polarity cars are actually identical, the diode colour coding depicted in the diagrams and on the diodes themselves is important. Should the diode be connected the wrong way round it will short across the battery and burn itself out. See also fuel pump polarity reversal later in this chapter.

Fuel pump service

Access to the interior is gained by removing the sealing tape, the terminal cover cap (often long gone) and the nut that retains the power input contact, star washer and the cover itself. There is an O-ring on the power input terminal, see Figure 16.9. It should be inspected and replaced if it can no longer form a good seal.

With the cover off, test the toggle action of the lower contact rocker assembly. As shown in Figure 16.12, a screwdriver can be used to rock the cradle up and down. This action will also move the armature and the diaphragm will be heard moving. Watch the contact movement to see that it snaps from the open to close positions without sticking and that there is a wiping action across the top contact.

If you have to change the diode or contact set, then the power input screw will have to be further dismantled. There are so many parts on this screw, and its assembly is so critical to the sealing to the cap, that this operation needs care and attention. Remove the rubber sealing ring. Before undoing the nut, measure the distance from the top of the nut to the plastic base. Note the measurement then remove the nut. Take off the spring washer and remove the diode terminal ring, see Figure 16.13.

When removing the other diode

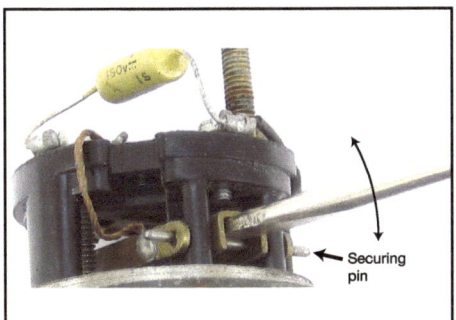

Figure 16.12. A screwdriver can be used to check the contact toggle operation.

Figure 16.13. The electrical components of the TVS diode snubbed pump.

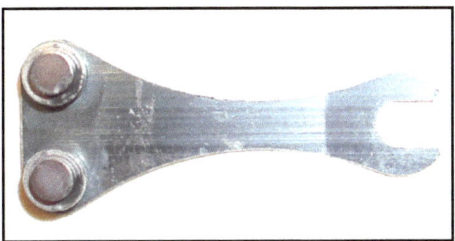

Figure 16.14. The upper contact blade.

wire, the contact blade fixing screw will have to be loosened, but not removed, the terminal being a slide-in fork. However, be aware that the contact blade, Figure 16.14, will become misaligned, so it's a good time to remove it – it simply slips out – and inspect the contact points, see Figure 16.14. If any damage is minimal the points may be lightly abraded with fine sandpaper, otherwise renew them as part of a full contact set.

With the contact blade removed, the bottom contacts can be inspected for wear or damage too.

If an original diode is not available, then any TVS or avalanche diode with a reverse standoff voltage (V_R) of about 30V and a peak pulse current of about 20A will work fine. It may be hard to get a radial leaded device, one with both connection leads coming from the same side of the body, but an axial leaded product, with wires coming from each end can be used instead.

If it is necessary to change or re-finish the bottom contacts, they can be accessed by removing the two screws that secure the plastic pedestal so that it may be pivoted back as shown in Figure 16.15. The pump illustrated had been stored in the car boot as a

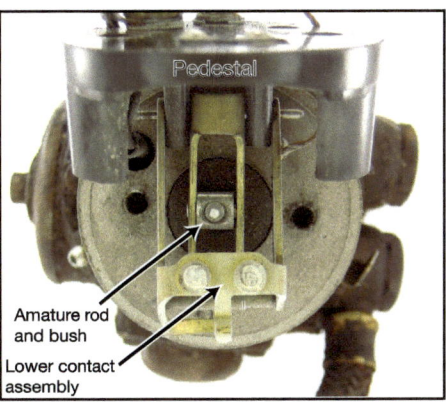

Figure 16.15. With the pedestal tilted back, the lower contacts can be accessed.

spare but when called upon to replace another pump it would not operate. The points had become dull and oxidized through lack of use; a common cause of pump failure after prolonged inactivity.

Should it be decided to replace the contact set, the securing pin will have to be removed and the rocker assembly unscrewed from the armature rod. Count the number of threads of the armature rod that can be seen above the rocker pivot bush. Use this count as a starting point when the new assembly is fitted. If the screwdriver test does not toggle the assembly, adjustments may be necessary. It is easy to do this if the bottom of the pump is also disassembled, allowing the diaphragm to be rotated rather than the rocker assembly.

On reassembly, don't forget to reattach the rocker earthing strap.

Whether the contact points

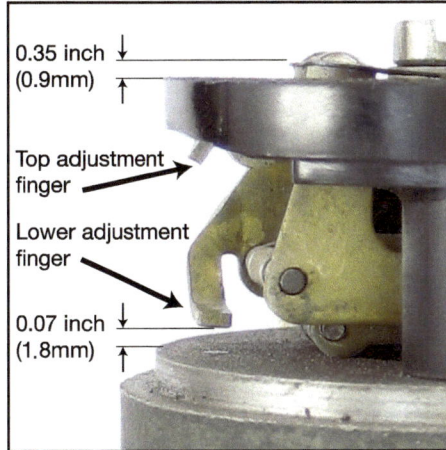

Figure 16.16. The upper and lower contacts require adjustment to the dimensions shown.

have been replaced or not, it is worth checking and if necessary adjusting them. Figure 16.16 shows the SU recommended dimensions for the protrusion of the upper contact blade above the pedestal as well as the gap between the bottom finger and base. Both dimensions are adjusted by slight bending of the relevant finger.

Some older pumps will be found to have a roller instead of a lower adjustment finger. In this case there is no adjustment for the top contact, its gap being set by a rib moulded into the pedestal. The lower gap should be 0.030in (0.8mm). Adjustment is by slight bending of the tip of the blade carrying the upper contact.

If the interior nut on the power input terminal and its associated components have been reassembled to the original order and dimensions, then when the rear cap is fitted, it should compress the O-ring seal correctly without the cap being distorted or leaving a gap between it and the pump body. Clean the exterior of the cap and body with methylated spirit (denatured alcohol) and apply wide PVC adhesive tape of the correct colour across the join between them. If the original tape is in good condition it may be reused.

Electronic pumps, Figure 16.17, have no contact points to wear and so require no electrical maintenance. Electrical failure will probably require complete replacement of the pump. Whereas the contacts in conventional pumps turn the solenoid on and off by mechanical interaction with the solenoid rod, the electronic pump uses a power transistor to do the switching and a special semiconductor called a Hall effect device to detect the position of the solenoid rod and in turn instruct the power transistor when to energise the solenoid.

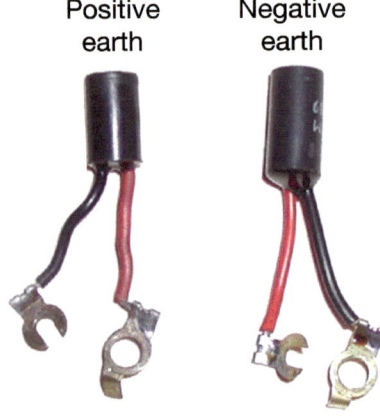

Figure 16.18. The positive and negative earth TVS diodes are identical apart from the way the terminals are connected.

Fuel pump polarity reversal

Most pumps with the prefix AZX and electronic pumps require some modification if the vehicle polarity is changed. However, from 2011, replacement AZ 1307 pumps were fitted with a Metal Oxide Varistor (MOV) instead of a TVS diode. MOVs operate bi-directionally, and so the pump is now polarity insensitive.

The usual advice when changing the polarity of a pump from positive to negative earth is to buy the correct diode. In fact, the diodes, Figure 16.18, are identical, only the terminals need be swapped so that when the diode is reinstalled, the red and black wires connect the opposite way round.
- On positive earth cars:
black goes to the power input
red goes to the contact blade fixing screw.
- On negative earth cars:
red goes to the power input
black goes to the contact blade fixing screw.

You can also replace the TVS diode with an MOV as Burlen-SU have now done. The part number is 7D101K but any 7mm, 100V break-over MOV will work equally well.

No other changes are required but it has been found that mechanical pumps that have been converted from one polarity to the other often fail after a short time. The reason is that the contact points, which have been subject to pitting and piling (see page 104), do not lend themselves to undergoing the effects of reversing the

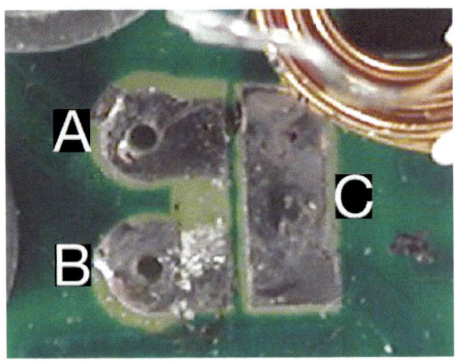

Figure 16.19. The sequence of procedures for changing an electronic fuel pump polarity from positive to negative earth.

current that they carry. As a result, it is prudent to fit new contact points when changing the pump polarity.

Electronic pumps can also be changed in polarity but the procedure does require some light electronic soldering. If you feel the task is beyond your skill or tool set, then take these instructions and the disassembled pump to an electronic or computer equipment repair shop and ask them if they will do the work. The cost should be minimal, the procedure taking less than 10 minutes.

Locate the area on the circuit board shown in Figure 16.19. Reference to the picture of the complete circuit board in Figure 16.17 should help. Changing a pump from

Figure 16.17. The circuit board of an electronic pump.

FUEL PUMP

positive to negative earth will be the most common requirement, but should a negative to positive ground conversion be required, simply reverse this procedure.

The top picture shows the positive earth circuit board. Note the wire going to the lower circuit pad from the coil.

In the centre illustration, the solder link between pad A and C has been removed and the wire from the coil to pad B has been unsoldered. Removing the solder may be difficult without special tools such as a custom solder pump or a copper braid that wicks up the solder. Use a continuity checker to ensure that the small gap between A and C is clear of solder and that there is no longer an electrical connection. Running a sharp blade between the two solder pads can also help.

In the bottom picture the wire from the coil has been moved to contact A and a new solder link made from B to C. The conversion is complete and the cover can be reinstalled and re-taped to the pump body.

Breather pipes

All pumps have a body vent, see Figure 16.20, which is required in order to allow the diaphragm to move back into the main body without the interference that would be caused by compressing air in that area. It should have a 5/32in (4mm) internal diameter plastic tube attached and taken to a clean area, like the boot. The tube should be secured and its end turned downward.

When a new pump is exchanged for an early type, you are confronted with an end cap vent that was not on the pump being replaced. The question of what to do with it is not an easy one to answer.

To seal or not to seal? It would be ideal if the pump could be hermetically sealed so that absolutely no moisture could enter. That is not possible with a pump with a plastic cap and adhesive tape sealing, all plastics being slightly vapour porous. That means that as a result of leakage from the active end of the pump, or changing atmospheric pressure due to weather or just driving up a hill, the electrical end of the pump will breathe and inhale some moisture. If moisture enters, and the pump has any degree of sealing, it will not easily remove itself and will have a detrimental effect on the contact points. SU evidently did not consider this an issue

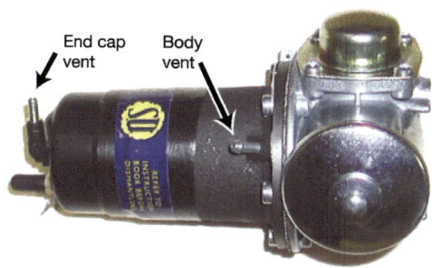

Figure 16.20. The vent holes on a later SU fuel pump.

on the early pump and provided no vent. Following SU's logic the rear vent could be sealed off with a material like silicone caulk.

The other view is: if the area cannot be totally sealed then let it breathe freely into a clean atmosphere, where it can vent out any moisture with the help of the normal heating that occurs when the pump is operated. Using this argument, the rear cap vent should have a pipe attached and terminated in the same way as the body vent.

Note: the most recent SU replacement pumps have no end cap vent. Further, the author has observed some very detrimental effects to the circuit boards of electronic pumps with vented end caps.

INSTALLING AN AFTERMARKET FUEL PUMP

Owners of late MGB/Cs with a fuel pump installation like that in Figure 16.3 are strongly encouraged to replace any faulty pump with an SU electronic unit. MG understood the hazards of bringing the fuel pipes into the boot area and chose not to do so. The installation should be a relatively easy direct swap of one pump for the other.

It can be understood why owners of older cars are tempted to use an aftermarket or an SU electronic pump mounted in the boot; after spending good money on a shiny new product, why expose it to wet and dirt in the original location under the car? However, any plan to bring the fuel pipes into the boot needs to be carefully considered. Leakage of fuel in this area can result in an explosive mixture with the air in the boot of a roadster or under the floorboard area of a GT.

Figure 16.21 shows a typical installation. The installer has taken the trouble to put non-chafing rubber

Figure 16.21. A typical aftermarket pump installation in an MGB-GT.

grommets where the fuel pipes come through the body metal, but they are otherwise unprotected. Close inspection of these pipes show that something, possibly tools stored under the floorboard of this GT, has caused some damage to the left hand pipe.

If you choose to install a pump in the boot, make sure the pipes used are of the highest quality material designed for carrying fuel and that they have braided armour protection. Fit grommets as in Figure 16.21 where the pipes penetrate the body metal. Check the tightness of the hose clamps after the pipes have had a few days to bed in.

Consider putting a shut-off valve in the input fuel line when fitting any new pump. It will avoid having a sleeve full of fuel every time you want to do any work on the system. Mounting a pump on a rubber pad is also a good idea, as a noisy pump can turn the boot floor into a drum that will amplify the sound. It is also highly recommended that a simple cover be fabricated to add extra protection to the installation.

Don't be tempted to buy a bigger pump than you need. The SU models could pump about 30 gallons (36 gallons US, 136 litres) per hour at some 3psi (0.2bars). At high speed, even the MGB-GT V8 will consume fuel at only one tenth of that rate, and any higher pressure than 4.5psi (0.3bars) is both unnecessary and possibly problematic because it may push fuel past the float chamber valves, causing flooding. If you belong to an MG club, it is worth polling other members on what pumps they have found available in your territory that are quiet, reliable and affordable.

FUEL PUMP FAULT-FINDING

Symptom	Possible causes	Action
Pump does not operate.	Inertia switch tripped (post 1974 US).	See page 167.
	Contact points require service.	See page 169.
	Power input or earth wire detached.	Check that the earth wire is attached to the main body of the pump. Use a circuit tester to erify that battery voltage is present on the rear terminal of pump. (Ignition must be switched on).
	Blocked fuel output line.	Clear line of obstruction.
	Float chamber needle valves sticking or dirty.	Service carburettor(s).
Pump clicks but does not pump.	Fuel filter blocked. Pump diaphragm damaged. Valves blocked or stuck. Blocked fuel input line.	Service non-electrical part of pump.
Pump works then stops.	Fuel cap vent blocked causing the pump to pull a partial vacuum in the fuel tank.	Remove fuel cap. If a hissing noise is heard, and/or if pump works without the cap, then the cap vent is blocked and requires clearing or replacement.
Noisy pump.	Leaky pipe unions between the tank and pump or loose screws on the pump causing air to enter.	Disconnect the fuel pipe at the forward carburettor and use a vessel to collect fuel as pump operates. Look for bubbles and if present, tighten unions and pump screws.

Table 16.1. Fuel pump fault-finding chart.

Chapter 17
Horn

HORN CONSTRUCTION

The horn is basically an electromagnet that operates an electrical contact and a diaphragm. In that illustrated in Figure 17.1, one horn terminal is earthed by means of the fixing bolt. When the power terminal is energized current can flow through the coil winding, to the fixed contact, and from there via the moving contact to the case earth. The current that flows in the coil produces a magnetic field in the core, attracting the armature toward it, but in doing so, a step on the armature pushes the moving contact away from the fixed contact. Current stops flowing and the armature, no longer with any magnetic attraction to the core, moves back to its rest position, again allowing the contacts to connect and the coil to re-energize. The cycle is repeated, the armature moving toward then away from the core very rapidly. The diaphragm, being attached to the armature, moves too, creating air pressure waves which we hear as the note of the horn. If, for example, the cycle occurs 440 times in one second, also written as 440Hz, it would sound the note of middle C, that being that note's frequency.

The actual note played can be adjusted with a screw, normally retained with a lock nut, which moves the contacts closer or further apart. The horn is designed to produce optimal output at frequencies in the order of 400Hz to 500Hz. After years of service, the diaphragm can become weak due to relaxation and corrosion and the contacts dirty and worn. The result is that the frequency changes to be outside the optimum range and the loudness of the horn diminishes.

Figure 17.1 shows a horn with a single contact, the earth connection being made through the metal body. As will be seen in some of the circuit diagrams, other horns were earthed via the horn push switch.

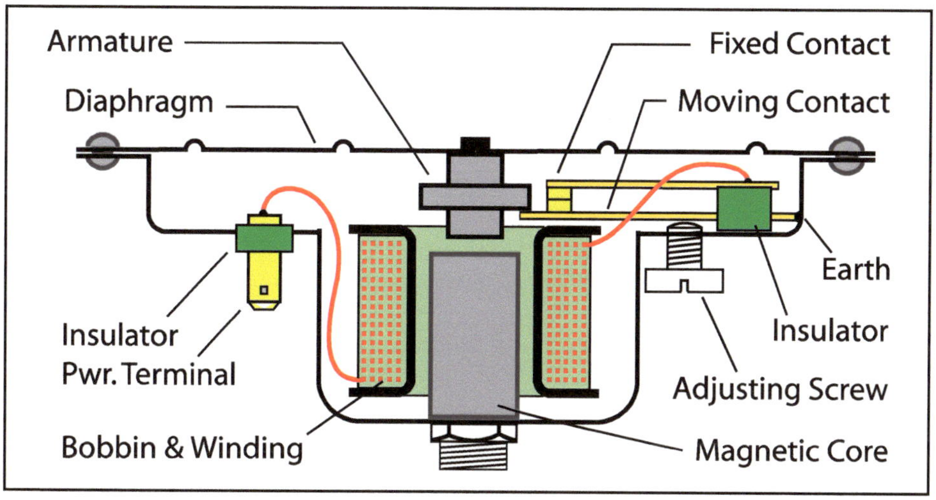

Horn identification

Figure 17.2 shows a horn taken from a pre-1975 MGB. Its condition is typical, its location behind the grille exposing it to dirt and weather. The horn can be identified as the original type because

Figure 17.1. Principal horn components.

173

MGB ELECTRICAL SYSTEMS – THE ESSENTIAL MANUAL

Figure 17.2. A typical pre-1975 horn. The adjustment screw is arrowed.

it has two sets of terminals. Post 1977 horns are earthed via the casing and have a single terminal.

HORN CIRCUIT – PRE-1977

Figure 17.3 shows the horn circuit for pre-1975 cars. Strictly speaking the drawing depicts pre-1968 wiring. In cars built after 1968 there is no separate control box (2) to which the brown power wires are anchored and from 1971 onward the fuse block (19) carries four fuses, like that in Figure 17.6.

Current flows from the batteries via the anchor points of the starter solenoid (4) and control box (2) to the fuse block (19). From the fuse block, a purple (P) wire takes power to both horns (23). When the horn switch (24) is pressed, current can flow through the horns, out on purple/black (PB) wires and to earth via the switch.

From 1962 until 1967, the horn push switch was located in the centre

Figure 17.4. The pre-1968 horn brush contact (black arrow) and slip ring (red arrow).

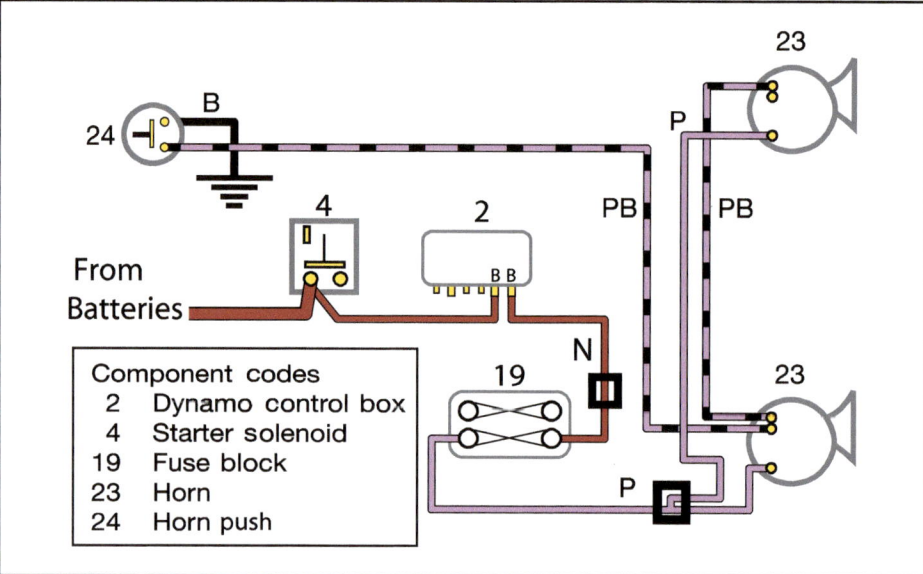

Figure 17.3. The pre-1977 horn circuit.

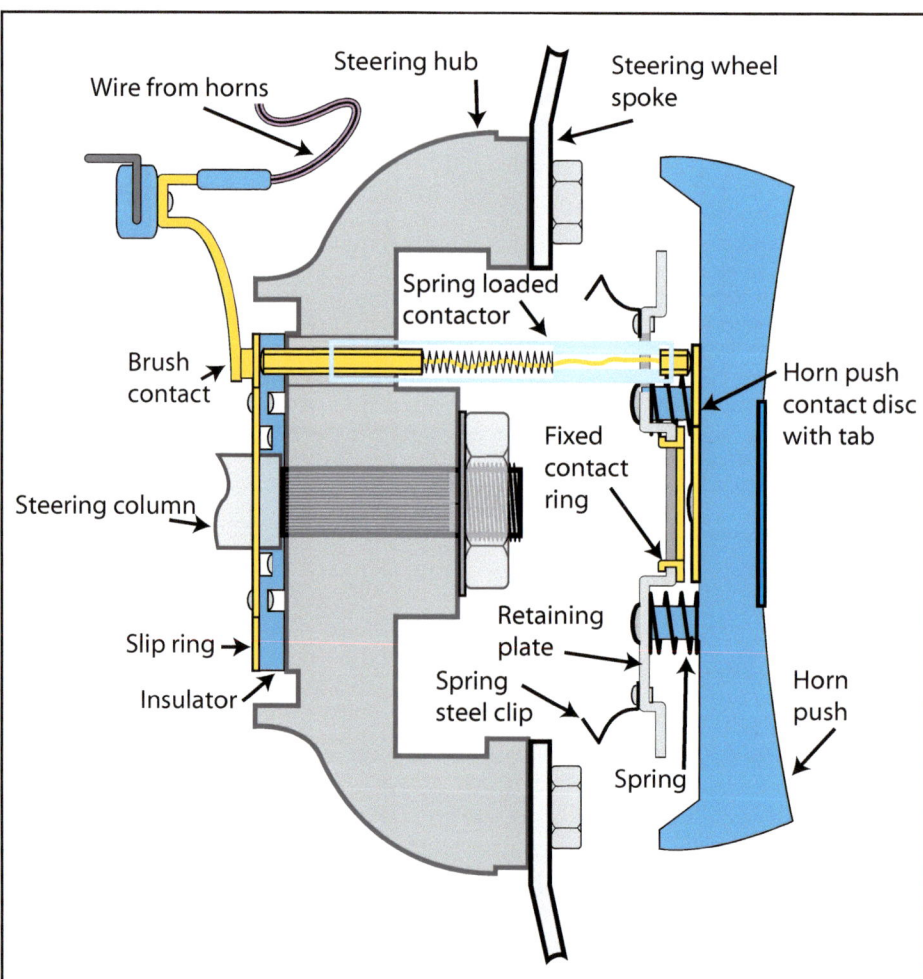

Figure 17.5. The 1971 to 1977 horn push was a complex design that included a large number of fault prone pressure contacts.

HORN

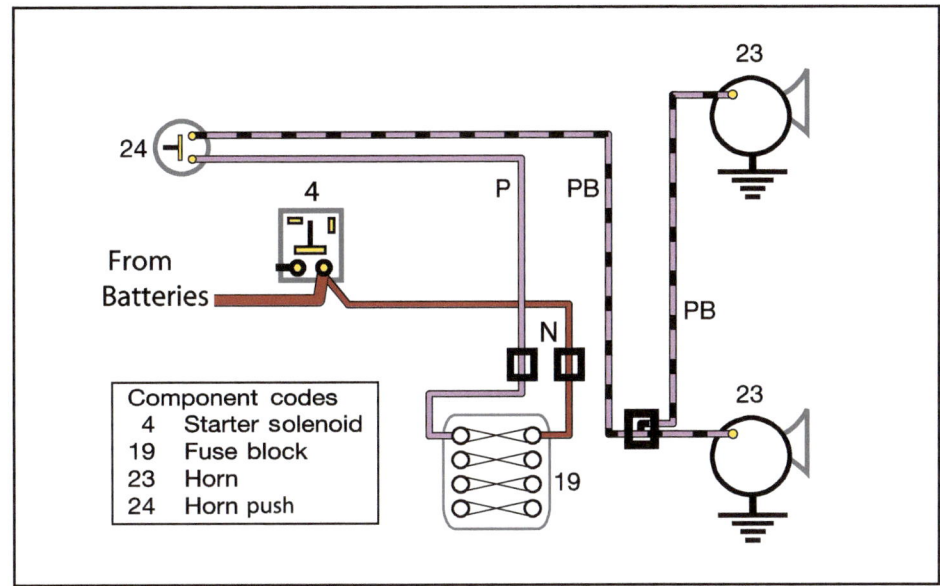

Figure 17.6. The 1977 and later horn circuit.

HORN CIRCUIT FROM 1975

From 1975 on the horn was changed to one with a single external terminal, the other connection being made through the horn body to earth. Having earth connections already at the horns themselves, the horn push switch had now to provide a power feed to them rather than an earth return.

Figure 17.6 shows the later car's horn circuit. Current flows from the batteries (3) via the anchor point of the starter solenoid to the fuse block (19). From there a purple (P) wire takes power to the horn push switch (24). When the horn switch is pressed, current can flow to the horns on a purple/black (PB) wire, through them and to earth.

HORN VOLUME

The horn in Figure 17.2 was one of a pair that exhibited poor volume. The author works in the automotive industry and was able to have them examined at the laboratories of the largest horn producing company in the world. This company can tune horns in a special chamber while using instruments to determine the optimum loudness. If there are two horns, they can be tuned to different frequencies to give a harmonious dual-tone. The horns that operated so poorly were, simply by tuning, brought back to a sound output level comparable to that of new ones.

Without the luxury of a special laboratory, tuning can be difficult. The problem is that the horns need to be operated for several seconds at a time, so the procedure needs to be performed where it will not cause a nuisance and with the use of ear protection by the person doing the tuning. That person also needs to be able to exercise some judgement about the sound output level and, to a lesser extent, the frequency.

Tune one horn at a time, only sounding both when checking that they work well as a dual-tone pair. The horns should not be operated for more than 30 seconds at a time, after which a one minute cool down period should be allowed; they are not designed for continuous operation and can burn-out if driven for too long. Use the adjustment screw to find the best sound output. As the screw is turned from one extreme of its range to the other, you should find that the volume will rise, plateau and then fall. The plateau should be found to be broad enough to allow each horn

of the steering wheel. This required a method of making an electrical connection to the rotating hub. To achieve this a brush contact, part of the turn signal switch, makes electrical contact to a slip ring that is connected to the horn switch, see Figure 17.4. The earth connection from the switch relies on continuity between the steering inner shaft and the metal components with which it is in contact such as the outer shaft and the steering rack.

From 1967 to 1970, the horn switch was re-located to the end of the multi-function switch that also operates the turn signals and headlamp beams.

In 1971, the horn push was moved back to the centre boss of the steering wheel. This again meant that a slip ring had to be incorporated in order to take the electrical current from the fixed electrical feed to the moving wheel boss. The resulting design seems over-complex and incorporates several pressure contacts, most of which are vulnerable to poor connection, thus making the system quite unreliable.

Figure 17.5 shows the principle of operation. Note it is not a scale engineering drawing, some components having been reoriented so as to be more visible. Current from the horns travels on a purple/black wire and terminates at a brush. The fixed spring copper alloy brush contacts a moving slip ring attached to the rear of the aluminium steering wheel hub, but electrically separated from it by a plastic insulator disc. A hole in the insulator and another, aligned with it in the steering hub, accept a spring loaded contactor. This device, incorrectly described as a brush in most parts catalogues, is a plastic tube that carries two brass contacts that are joined together by a flexible wire and pushed apart by a spring. This arrangement allows it to continuously carry current as its length changes due to the horn push being depressed. At the horn push end, the contactor touches a tab extending from a disc attached directly behind the horn push.

The horn push assembly snaps into, and is retained in, the steering hub by three spring steel clips, which are riveted to a retaining plate. The plate has a large hole in the middle into which is pressed a copper ring. The plate also retains the horn push and contact disc, which are held off from it by three springs. Once snapped into the steering hub the plate is effectively fixed and the horn push can be moved toward it by compressing the springs. When this happens an electrical connection is made between the horn push's contact disc and the retaining plate's contact ring.

In this way current flows from the horns via a wire to the brush, slip ring, spring loaded contactor, the horn push disc, the contact ring, the retaining plate, the steel spring clips, the steering hub and, with luck, eventually to earth by means of the steering column bearings and rack.

MGB ELECTRICAL SYSTEMS – THE ESSENTIAL MANUAL

within a pair to be tuned to noticeably different frequencies and to produce an acceptable dual-tone

Any loud knocking noise occurring during tuning is due to the armature hitting the magnetic core and should be avoided if possible.

IMPROVING THE HORN CIRCUIT

The complete horn circuit is rather long and so has a significant wire resistance. The contact resistance of the horn switch and the slip ring, if fitted, can further lead to poor horn performance.

Adding a relay in the circuit to operate the horn and having the push switch circuit only operate the relay coil can result in louder and more reliable horn performance.

Each horn will, if given a good electrical supply, consume about 4A. If there is 0.5Ω of resistance in the circuit then the voltage will drop by:

2horns × 4A × 0.5Ω = 4V.

That is very significant considering the supply voltage is only between 12V and 14V. A relay coil will only require the horn switch circuit to provide 0.2A and will operate its contacts down to 7.2V. That means that with a 12V battery, the switch circuit could drop as much as 4.8V and the relay would still operate. At a current of 0.2A the circuit will still work even when the resistance is as much as:

4.8V ÷ 0.2A = 24Ω.

A high resistance connection of this order would, therefore, not inhibit the horn operation. Operating the horns by use of the relay contacts and from a much shorter power feed will reduce the possibility of any significant voltage drop and noticeably enhance their performance.

You can learn more about relays and their selection by consulting Appendix 1. If the relay you purchase has a centre terminal numbered 87a, then simply leave it unconnected. The terminal marked here as number 30 may be labelled 30/51 on some brands of relay. Try to mount the relay close

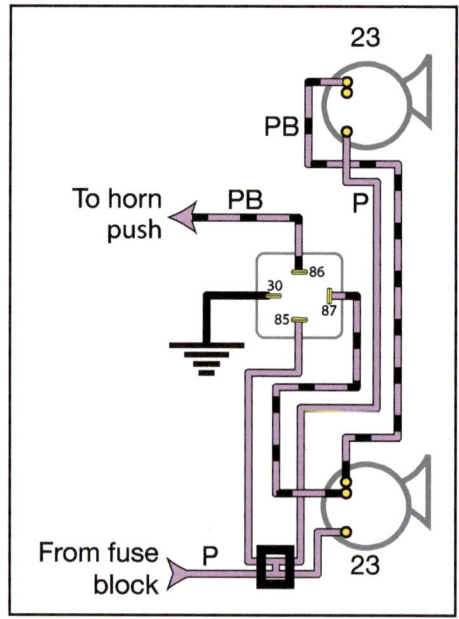

Figure 17.7. Using a relay in the pre 1977 horn circuit.

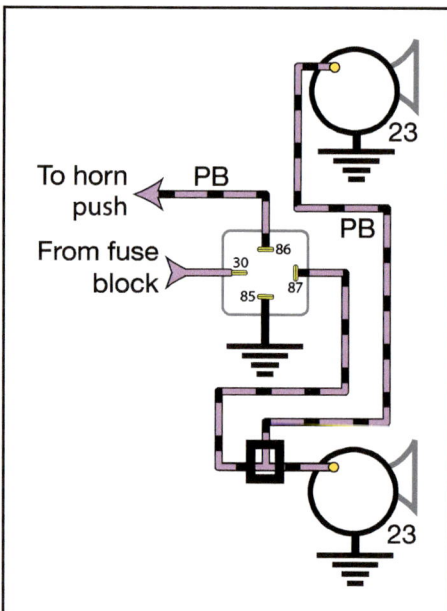

Figure 17.8. Using a relay in the 1977 and later horn circuit.

to the right horn and connect it to the harness at the right front of the vehicle.

Using a relay in the early horn circuit

Figure 17.7 shows a portion of Figure 17.3 in which a relay has been interposed in the purple/black (PB) line back to the horn push switch. An additional wire has been taken from the bullet connectors that terminate the purple (P) wires and has been connected to terminal 85 of the relay.

When the horn switch is closed, the relay coil is energized as current flows from the purple circuit, through the relay coil, via the purple/black wire and through the switch to earth. With the coil energized terminals 30 and 87 of the relay are switched together so that current flows from the purple circuit, through the horns, via a short section of the purple/black circuit to the relay and through it on a short link wire to earth.

If the additional wire from the bullet connector to the relay and the wire from the relay to earth are kept short and are 16AWG (1.5mm²) or 14AWG (2.5mm²), then the circuit resistance will be minimized to the benefit of the horns' performance.

Using a relay in the late horn circuit

Figure 17.8 shows a portion of Figure 17.6 in which a relay has be interposed in the purple/black (PB) line back to the horn push switch. An additional wire has been taken from the fuse block to terminal 30 of the relay.

When the horn switch is closed, the relay coil is energized as current flows from the switch on the purple/black circuit, through the relay coil, and to earth via the wire connected to terminal 85. With the coil energized, terminals 30 and 87 of the relay are switched together so that current flows from the purple (P) circuit, through the relay, through the horns and to earth.

If the additional wire from the fuse block to the relay and the wire from the relay to earth are kept short and are 16AWG (1.5mm²) or 14AWG (2.5mm²) then the circuit resistance will be minimized to the benefit of the horns' performance.

www.velocebooks.com/www.veloce.co.uk
All books in print • New books • Special offers • Gift Vouchers

HORN

HORN FAULT-FINDING

Symptom	Possible causes	Action
Horns do not operate.	Fuse or fuse clip failure.	Use a circuit tester to check for presence of power on the fuse terminal connected to a purple wire. If there is no power there check fuse or clean clip as per page 43.
	Horn push circuit failure (pre 1977).	Use a spare piece of wire to make a connection between a good earth point and the right hand horn terminal on to which a purple/black wire is connected. If horn sounds then use a circuit tester to check for presence of power at the purple/black wire and slip ring (if fitted, see Figures 17.4 and 17.5) inside the steering column cowl half shells. Tester light should extinguish when the horn push is pressed. If not, repair or change switch. If horn does not sound, use a circuit tester to check for presence of power at the right hand horn terminal that carries a purple wire.
	Horn push circuit failure (post 1977).	Use a spare piece of wire to make a connection between a brown wire at the fuse block and the right hand horn terminal. If horn sounds then use a piece of wire to jumper between a brown wire under the dash (or switch the ignition on and jumper to a white wire) and the purple/black connection to the multi-function switch. If horn sounds again then change the horn push.
One horn does not operate.	Wiring disconnect (left hand horn only).	Check wiring between right and left horns.
	Horn failure.	Check the resistance of the suspect horn. It should be 2Ω to 3Ω. If high, turn adjustment screw, in an attempt to clean the horn contacts. If to no avail, change horn.
Horn performance is weak or intermittent.	Horn failure.	Try to tune horns as per this chapter.
	Horn push or slip ring/brush failure (pre 1977).	Clean switch and brush contacts. Re-tention brush finger.
	Horn push failure (post 1977).	Change switch.
	High resistance switch.	Consider adding relays as per this chapter.

Table 17.1. Horn fault-finding chart.

Chapter 18
Cooling & heating fans

ELECTRIC COOLING FAN

The electric radiator cooling fan was only installed in 4-cylinder cars from 1977 until the end of production in 1980 but there were nonetheless several variations.

Cars were fitted with either one or two fans depending on the territory to which they were shipped. The wiring changed too. An in-line fuse was initially installed in the fan circuit but it tended to nuisance blow in double fan installations. This occurs because, unlike the mechanical fan, the electric type is a 'pusher' device situated in front of the radiator where it can still be in a cold air stream even though the thermostat is calling for cooling of the hot engine. The cold grease in the motor often makes it stall for a short period or labour when spinning up, during which time it draws a high current of a magnitude of about twice the normal running current. A fuse, which is a very fast acting device and ideal for protecting against short-circuits, can blow during the time it takes the motor to warm up and get up to full speed. Adding the next higher rated fuse doesn't help either; it requires too much current to blow in the event of a permanent fault. To solve this problem a Type 1 circuit breaker, see page 46, was substituted, often by the dealership, for the fuse as shown in Figures 18.1 and 18.2. This device is much slower to act and is ideal for motor protection.

A stalled motor may draw two or three times its normal running current and eventually burn itself out. The circuit breaker will pulse on and off, retrying to start the fan but only supplying an average of about half the stall current, not enough to burn the motor out but sufficient to warm it so that the grease becomes less viscous.

One problem with using a single over-current protection device on a two-fan installation is that if one motor causes the circuit to open, then both

Figure 18.1. A circuit breaker substituted for the cooling fan in-line fuse is located just to the front of and below the fuse block.

Figure 18.2. A new 12V, 20A circuit breaker; the same rating as that in Figure 18.1.

fans stop. Replacing the single 20A circuit breaker with two separate 10A devices provides some redundancy in the event of motor fan failure.

The action of the thermostat or a circuit breaker that cycles on and off can make a fan start unexpectedly. To prevent injury to anyone working on the car, make certain a guard is fitted like that in the original installation of Figure 18.3.

Thermostat

The thermostat, Figures 18.3 to 18.5, closes the circuit at about 180°F (82°C) and operates the fan. It reopens and breaks the circuit to the fan

COOLING & HEATING FANS

Figure 18.3. The thermostat location in the 4-cylinder MGB.

Figure 18.4. The thermostat location in the MGB-GT V8.

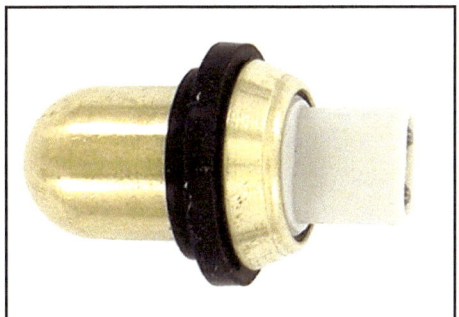

Figure 18.5. The radiator fan thermostat used from .1977 to 1979. A slightly shorter version was used in 1980 cars.

when its temperature drops to about 165°F (74°C). The thermostat proved unreliable when required to directly switch the high fan current, especially on 2-fan installations. To improve the circuit, a relay was fitted to some cars to do the heavy current switching, leaving the thermostat to switch only the ¼ amp or so of relay coil current.

Radiator fan circuits

Figure 18.6 shows the circuit for the first MG to have an electric radiator fan, the MGB-GT V8.

Current flows from the battery on a large cross section area cable to the starter motor/solenoid (5), which is used as a securing point. There it connects to a thinner brown (N) wire that goes to the fuse block (19).

At the fuse block another brown wire takes current to the ignition switch (38). When the ignition switch is on, current can flow from it on a white (W) wire and back to the fuse block. There a fuse connects to a green wire that provides power to the cooling fan relay (174) that differs a little from the standard 6RA device described in page 82, in that it has a combined C2 and W2 terminal. If the thermostat is calling for cooling, its contacts close and relay contact W1 becomes earthed. The energized relay closes and current can flow to the fan motors.

With other accessories running, there is rather too much current flowing on the green circuit when the fans are operating too. As a result, nuisance fuse failures may occur. The problem can be overcome by routing the green wire from the fan relay via a circuit breaker, like that in Figure 18.2, to the white circuit at the fuse block instead.

The 4-cylinder MGB was fitted with electric fans from 1977 until the end of production.

The circuit is shown in Figure 18.7. Current flows from the battery on a large cross section area cable to the starter motor/solenoid (5), which is used as a securing point. There it connects to a thinner brown (N) wire that goes to the fuse block (19). At the fuse block another brown wire takes current to the ignition switch (38). When the ignition switch is on, current can flow from it to the 86 coil connection on the ignition relay (42). The relay becomes energized and the resulting electromagnetic force pulls the contacts connected to 30 and 87 together allowing current to flow from the always live brown circuit to a white/brown wire (WN) that goes back to the fuse block.

Adding relays to the fan circuit

As stated previously, fan thermostat failures are common because its contacts are not really robust enough for the high fan current. If a failure of the thermostat occurs, it will require replacement. Most 4-cylinder MGB installations did not have a dedicated fan relay. When installing the new thermostat, if relay is not already installed, it is worthwhile adding one.

Although the circuit in Figure 18.7 includes a relay, the thermostat still has to do all the work of switching the fan(s) on and off. Figure 18.8 provides a suggested method of adding a fan relay too. The power output wire from the thermostat has been cut and a new wire added at the output from the

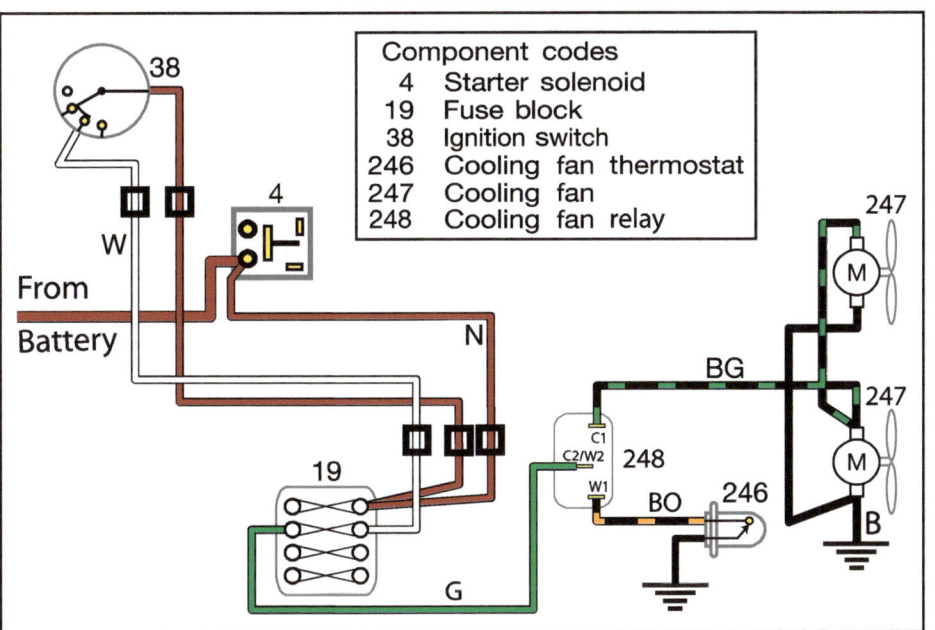

Figure 18.6. MGB-GT V8 cooling fan circuit.

MGB ELECTRICAL SYSTEMS – THE ESSENTIAL MANUAL

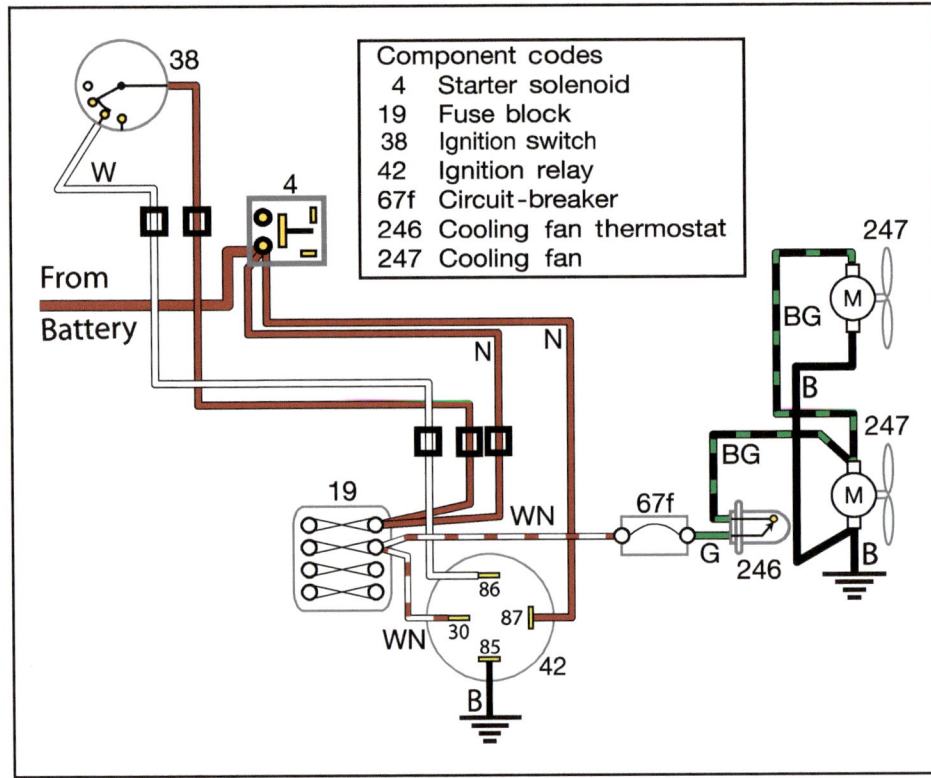

Figure 18.7. The radiator fan circuit 4-cylinder MGBs.

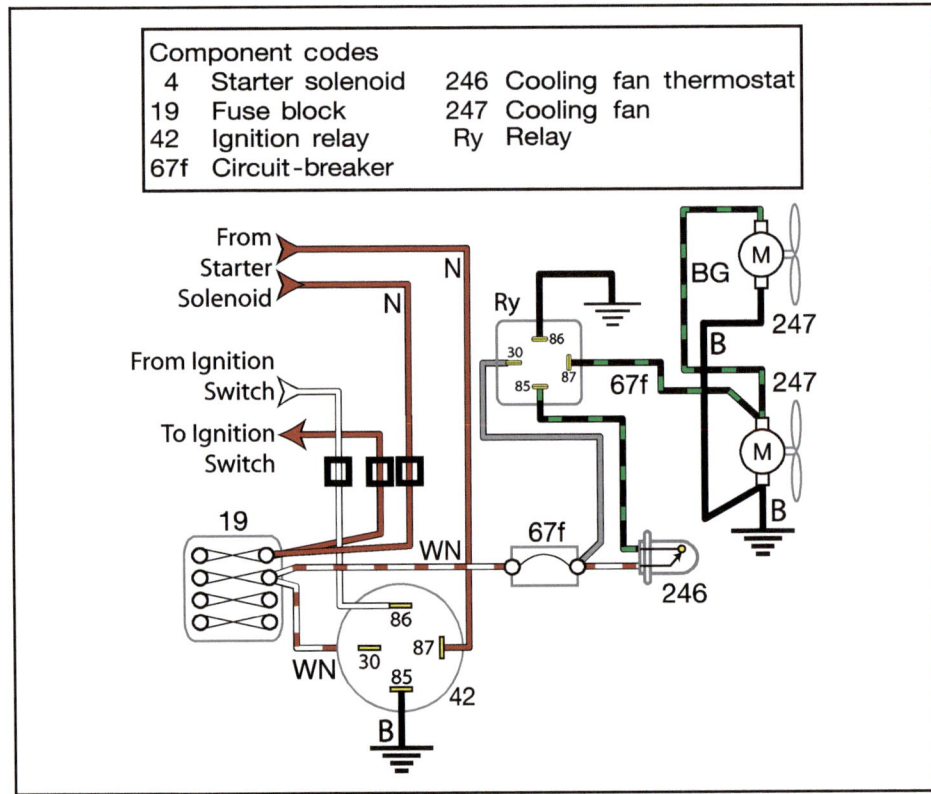

Figure 18.8. The radiator fan circuit in Figure 18.7 with an additional relay.

circuit-breaker that goes from it to the power input terminal 30 of the relay. The now free black/green (BG) power wire to the fans is connected to the output power terminal 87 of the relay. The free wire from the thermostat is connected to one of the relay coil terminals 85 or 86, the other relay coil terminal joining to earth.

In operation, when the ignition switch (38) is on, the white/brown (WN) output power wire from the ignition relay (42) becomes powered. When the radiator temperature reaches a level at which the thermostat (246) closes, current can flow through it and energize the fan relay (Ry) coil. The relay power contacts 30 and 87 then connect together, and in doing so, supply current to the fan motors (247).

The relay can usually be positioned on the radiator shroud close to the thermostat in such a way as to make the existing wires reach. An ISO relay, like that shown in Figure A1.2 of Appendix 1, can be installed using a panel screw. It is easy to make the earth connection by simply using a short pigtail wire to a ring terminal and serrated washer (see page 15) secured under the same screw.

The current switching and carrying capability of an ISO relay is far above the demands of the fans and it will last indefinitely, as should the now lightly loaded thermostat.

AFTER-MARKET COOLING FANS

A number of after-market fans are available that may be used to replace an existing electric fan or the mechanical fan fitted to earlier cars. It is estimated that a mechanical fan can require up to 3 horsepower to drive it. An electric fan can save fuel because the engine warms up quicker and it consumes only about 0.5 horsepower; the extra efficiency coming from its ability to run at much higher speeds.

Selection of a brand depends very much on what is available in a given territory. Look for a complete kit with a 10 inch (250mm) pusher fan with a throughput of at least 600cfm ($17m^3/m$). Note that this rating is for a fan operating in free air, once attached to the vehicle radiator the restriction caused by the radiator core and fins will reduce the flow by about 20% and even more if the radiator is partially blocked with debris; so hose it clean before fitting the fan. If replacing a mechanical fan, an adjustable thermostat will also

COOLING & HEATING FANS

Figure 18.9. The typical aftermarket radiator fan installation.

Figure 18.10. The heater motor.

be needed. In all probability such a thermostat will not require the radiator to be drilled, instead a probe is pushed between the cooling fins that surround the water tubes or surface mounted as close to the radiator as possible. Before fitting the fan, make a note of the reading on the dash temperature gauge that is considered normal for that car. Start by having any adjustable fan thermostat at its lowest setting and make adjustments from there. The fan should come on before the gauge reaches the normal running temperature because there will be some delay before it can bring the water temperature in the engine block down.

HEATER FAN

The heater fan changed little during the life of the car, the only major variation being the optional availability of a two speed motor.

The motors are not easily opened so any service is best left to a specialist workshop. Refer to the chapter on windscreen wipers for information about similar single and two speed motors.

The circuit is so simple as not to warrant its own diagram yet at the same time it did vary over the life of the car.

In the early car the motor switch is fed via the green wire from the fuse block. When in the on position, the switch provides power to the motor on a green/brown wire. The other motor wire simply goes to earth.

On later cars, with an accessory position on the ignition switch, the fan in connected to the same 67a fuse as the two-speed wiper (see Figure 15.13). The green/pink wire from that fuse then supplies power to the heater fan switch. When in the on position, the switch provides power to the motor on a green/yellow wire. Again, the other motor wire simply goes to earth.

Those cars with two-speed heater motors have a second terminal on the switch. The switch either powers the normal-speed motor brush via a green/brown or the high-speed brush via a green/yellow wire.

CARBURETTOR COOLING FAN

Late production MGCs destined for North America had a small fan fitted to the left side radiator skirt for the purpose of preventing fuel boiling in the carburettors. The boiling is often referred to as percolation because it can sometimes be evidenced, before it causes running problems, and after the car stops running, by the sound it makes, which is not unlike coffee brewing.

Figure 18.11, shows the MGC circuit.

Earlier MGCs and V6 & V8 conversions may also benefit from adding a fan to cool the carburettor(s). However, it's worthwhile first trying the simplest solution, which is (providing it does not interfere with carburettor spacing under the bonnet) to add a thicker gasket between the carburettor and the inlet manifold from which

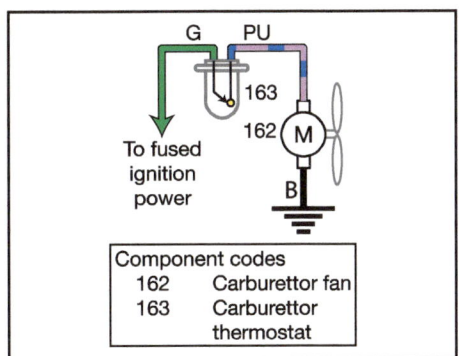

Figure 18.11. The MGC carburettor cooling fan circuit.

most of the heat probably comes. Commercial versions of these are available for some carburettors and can easily be copied. They are generally cut from 5/16in (8mm) medium density fibreboard (MDF) coated and sealed with high temperature paint. An extension arm can be added to carry a thermostat (should it be needed after all) in a similar manner to the manifold heater in Figure 19.2.

Most petrol blends boil at around 225°F (107°C), which is close enough to that of water to be able to use the same thermostat as is used in the MGB cooling system (Figure 18.5). Suitable fans are easy to come by, virtually all desktop computers are cooled by a small 12V fan. If the air requires ducting to the carburettors, then 4in (100mm) hose used for the MGA air intake to the heater and carburettors can be used as can that used to duct hot air from a laundry dryer.

AIR-CONDITIONING (A/C)

A Jaguar/Rover/Triumph air-conditioning system was available for the rubber-bumper MGB, which had plenty of room behind the grille to install a condenser that displaced the left-hand pusher-fan, a puller-fan being mounted instead behind the radiator.

The system works by action of two general principles of physics:
1. When fluid changes from a liquid to a vapour, it requires energy to do so. It gets it by drawing heat energy from its surroundings. This is the reason why a solvent that evaporates at skin temperature feels cold as it turns to a vapour. The energy remains latent in the vapour and is given up again as heat when it turns back to a liquid.
2. The boiling point of a fluid changes with pressure. This means that a liquid close to its boiling temperature can be vaporised simply by reducing the pressure. Similarly, a vapour close to its condensation temperature can be liquidised by increasing the pressure.

Certain fluids exhibit these characteristics more significantly and at temperatures and pressures more convenient for use in A/C systems than others. These are generally called refrigerants.

The fluid is contained in a sealed closed-loop system that consists of a number of components illustrated in Figure 18.12.

181

MGB ELECTRICAL SYSTEMS – THE ESSENTIAL MANUAL

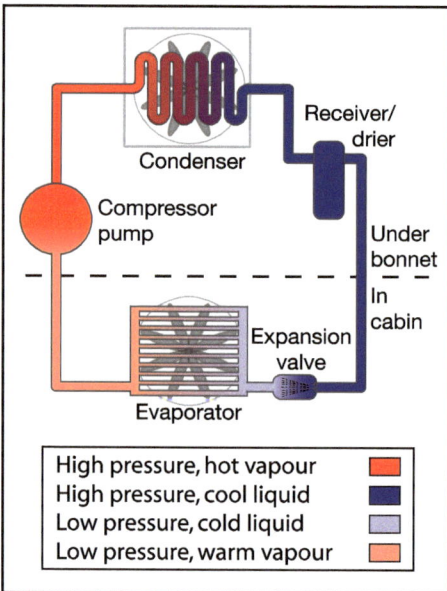

Figure 18.12. Air-conditioning refrigerant circuit.

A A fan-belt driven pump compresses the vapour, which is laden with heat absorbed in the cabin. The compressor has an electrically operated clutch that has to be energized before it will pump.

B The compressor moves the vapour to a condenser radiator, placed in the cool air-stream in front of the standard radiator. The compressed vapour gives up its latent heat to the air-flow and turns to a liquid in the condenser.

C The liquid moves on to a receiver/drier that contains a desiccant to remove any moisture or particles.

D The liquid moves to an expansion valve, which is a dividing component between the high and low pressure sections of the loop; the compressor being the other. It contains an expansion valve that sprays the liquid into the low-pressure section.

E As the liquid moves to the low-pressure part of the loop, it again evaporates into a vapour in the in-cabin radiator-like evaporator, absorbing heat energy from the air around it. For improved efficiency, a blower fan behind the evaporator moves cabin air through it. The vaporised and the now warmer refrigerant vapour is moved on to the compressor/pump and the cycle restarts.

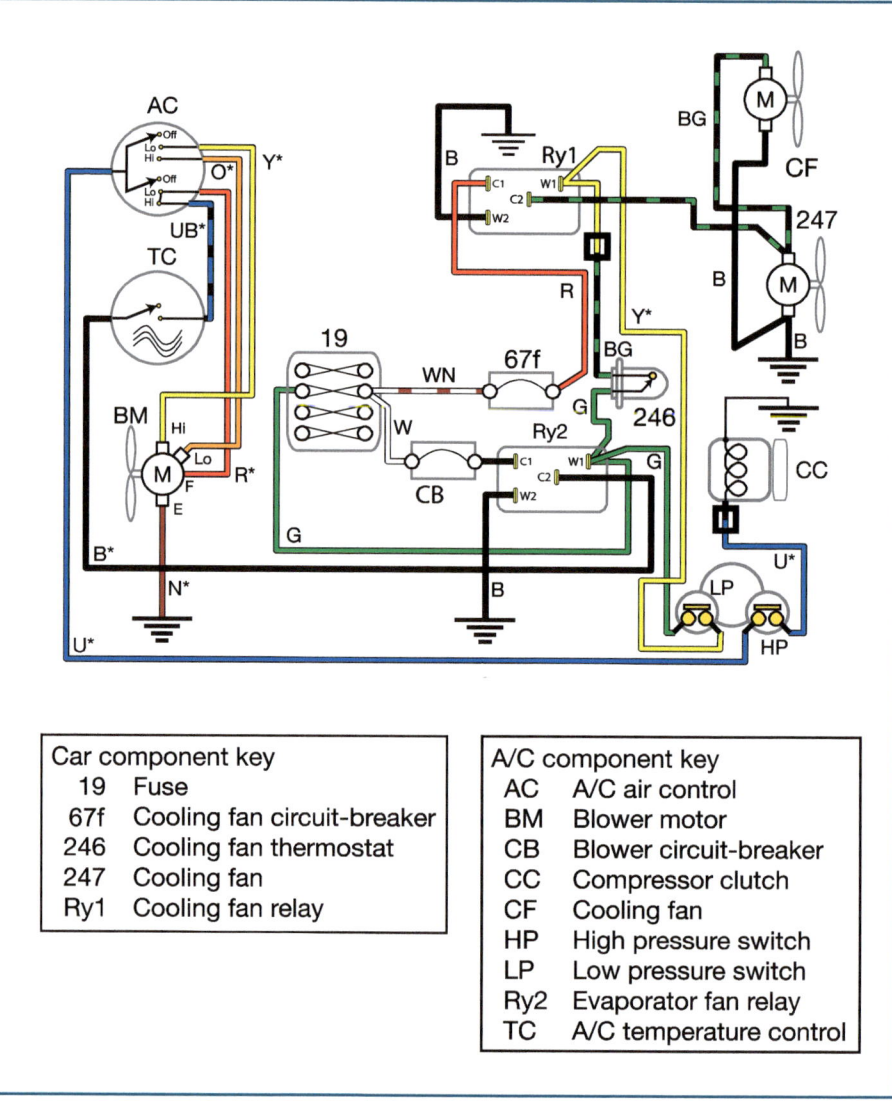

Figure 18.13. The air-conditioning circuit.

Electrical circuit

The A/C circuit in Figure 18.13 is an extension of that in Figure 18.7.

The radiator and condenser cooling fans (247 & CF) will switch on only when the ignition powers the green circuit (G) and when relay (Ry1) is energized, either by closing of the radiator thermostat (246) or when the low pressure switch (LP) mounted on the receiver/drier detects that the A/C system is operating because the gas is being pumped down to low pressure.

The A/C relay (Ry2) is energized when the ignition is on. The compressor clutch (CC) can be driven from it only when the driver's air control (AC) is in either the Lo or Hi positions, the driver's variable thermostat control (TC) calls for cooling and the high pressure switch mounted on the receiver/drier is closed because the pressure is not already at maximum.

The air-control (AC) delivers power to the blower-motor (BM) field (F) and to either the Lo or Hi speed brushes.

Chapter 19
Miscellaneous systems

There are a number of systems that are not mentioned elsewhere and that require brief discussion.

THE SEQUENTIAL SEAT BELT SYSTEM

This system is intended to warn the driver in the event that the seat belt is not latched when it also detects the presence of a driver and/or passenger, the door is closed, the key is in and the car is in gear. In order to do so a module looks at the status of a number of connections and switches. When necessary it lights a dash warning lamp and/or runs a buzzer. Because it needs inputs from so many devices including door, key, gear and seat pressure sensor as well as the seat belt buckle connectors, it is extremely unreliable and has been disconnected by most owners of cars to which is was fitted. The author knows of nobody who has managed to get the system working reliably for any significant time and so refers anyone wishing to attempt it to the excellent description of the system in *The Complete Original MGB* published by Robert Bentley.

FITTING A RADIO

Most of the wiring required for a radio should be found behind the centre console. A circuit tester is helpful in identifying wires that are required to be powered all the time, that are powered only when the key is in the accessory and ignition positions (or ignition alone) or when the lights are on.

The standard colours used by car radio manufacturers and the MGB/C wires to which they should be attached are listed in Table 19.1. Where a choice of car wire colours is suggested they are listed in preferred order. That order is determined in some cases by whether the wire is fused. Most car radios include in-line fuses in the connecting wires, so having a vehicle fuse in circuit is not always necessary.

Other wires will be needed to connect the audio equipment to the speakers and aerial (antenna).

If the car has a battery disconnect switch and the radio to be installed has a station memory, CD track memory or a clock function, see page 56 for a method of maintaining these when the switch is off.

HEATED BACKLIGHT

The MGB/C GT, was offered with an optional heater in the rear window, also known as the backlight, to defrost and demist it. This is a large area heater which consists of several electrical conductors printed on the rear glass. The resistance of the material causes it to heat when a current passes through it. This is one of the largest continuous loads in the vehicle, drawing some 20A. Two variations of the circuit are shown in Figure 19.1. That in diagram A has no relay so the high current has to be routed through the switch, which is usually found in the centre console. A relay was fitted to some late cars, shown in diagram B, to allow the wiring to more directly route to the heater and

Function	Car wire	Radio wire
Always live	Purple or brown	Yellow
Live with key on	White/green or white or green	Red
Earth	Black	Black
Dim display at night	Blue or red or red/white	Orange
Power aerial	None	Blue

Table 19.1. Car radio connection guide.

MGB ELECTRICAL SYSTEMS – THE ESSENTIAL MANUAL

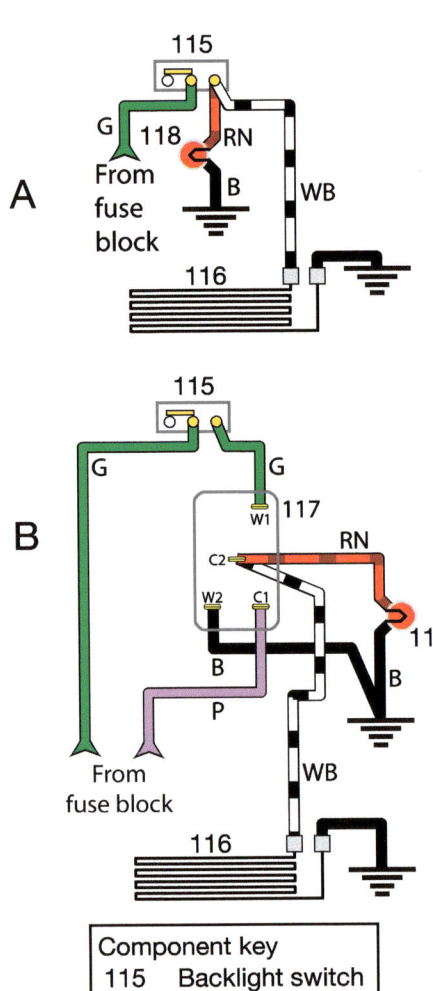

Figure 19.1. Heated backlight circuits

Component key	
115	Backlight switch
116	Heated backlight
117	Backlight relay
118	Indicator lamp

The most common problems occur because the 30 degree rake of the rear door results in the inside of the window or the electrical connections coming in contact with an object placed inside the rear hatch. Repair may be possible from a specialist automotive glass company. The problem is a common one and most automotive accessory stores sell a special repair kit. The grid needs to be cleaned with methylated spirit (denatured alcohol) for a short distance either side of the break, the glass masked off with tape and the conductive paint applied in the slot between the tapes. Remove the tape before the paint fully hardens

MANIFOLD HEATER

Some late cars having Zenith-Stromberg carburettors and sold to cold climates were fitted with heaters to prevent icing in the inlet manifold (header). The heater consumes a lot of power, about 100W, but only switches on for a short time until a thermostat senses that the manifold temperature is above 32°F (0°C). Power is sourced from the white/brown (WN) output wire of the ignition relay, see Figure 11.9.

There were two styles used, the most common is shown in Figure 19.2.

The resistance of the heater should be about 1.5Ω and the value can be checked by measuring between vehicle earth — or should the heater be out of the vehicle, the heater coil earth connection indicated by the red arrow — and the case of the thermostat indicated by the black arrow. If the paint on the thermostat is fully intact, then a small scratch will have to be made in order to make the measurement. In practice, the heater wire is very robust and is unlikely to fail.

The second form of heater can be identified by the rectangular thermostat housing as shown in Figure 19.3.

Figure 19.2. The more common shape of manifold heater.

Figure 19.3. A rectangular form of thermostat was fitted to some manifold heaters.

Any failure of the heater will most likely be caused by contact damage in the thermostat. It may be checked by removing the heater assembly from the car and placing it in a freezer for a few minutes, after which time it should be possible to measure a low resistance between the power terminal and the heater earth connection. As the assembly warms up and its temperature rises above freezing, an audible click should be heard as the thermostat opens and a resistance measurement should now indicate open circuit.

to put less stress on the switch. It is highly recommended that a relay be fitted to any backlight heater that heater that does not already incorporate one.

Appendix 1
Relays

RELAY OPERATION

A relay is a special form of electromagnetic switch. Figure A1.1 shows a basic relay with both normally open and normally closed contacts. A low magnitude current is passed through a coil which is wound on a bobbin installed over a magnetic core, such as iron. The resulting magnetic force in the core attracts an armature toward it. The armature carries a moving contact that then connects to the normally open contact and disconnects from the normally closed one. The internal contacts can carry much more current than is used to switch them. Thus a low current can control a much larger one.

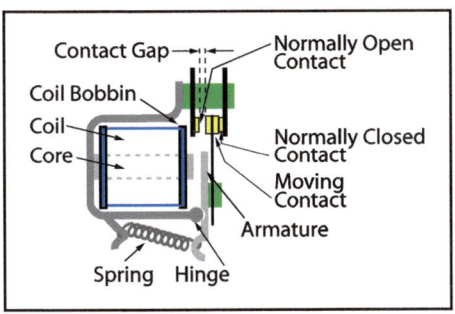

Figure A1.1. A fundamental relay mechanism.

AUTOMOTIVE RELAYS

In MGBs, relays are used to drive the starter motor solenoid, ignition system and sometimes the rear backlight heater and cooling fan when fitted. The original Lucas relays used in MGBs had lower resistance coils than relays made today and so they required more current to drive them. That can sometimes cause a problem, see page 95. Further information regarding the relays originally fitted to MGBs can be found in pages 81, 82 and 95.

An automotive relay usually has four or five terminals, two of which, labelled 85 and 86, are used to drive the coil while the others connect and disconnect either two or three contacts.

The relay terminals are usually numbered according to German specification DIN72552 as follows:
85   Coil earth (but see below).
86   Coil power (but see below).
30   Common contact.
87   Normally open (NO) contact.
In addition on 5-terminal relays only:
87a Normally closed (NC) contact.

While, strictly speaking, contact 85 should always join to earth and contact 86 should be powered, in practice they can be connected either way around and for the purposes of simplifying circuit diagrams, this has been done in some of the circuits shown in this book.

When only two of the power terminals are being used such as 30 and 87 or 30 and 87a, these connections can also be swapped if it makes wiring simpler.

Other modules may look similar

Figure A1.2. A standard automotive relay.

to relays but have different numbers. Those most likely to be encountered are turn signal modules with numbers:
49   Input power.
49a Output to lamps.
5   Pilot lamp

The most commonly available relays are the full International Standards Organization (specifications ISO 7880 and 7588) size relays shown in Figure A1.2, which are also known as minis and as ice cube relays, owing to their approximate 1 inch (25 mm) cubic size. Common brands and types are Tyco Electronics (formerly Potter & Brumfield) type V4F and Omron type GHJN. They are available with and without fixing brackets.

Where a bracket is fitted, there appears to be no convention as to its position relative to the terminals. Always mount relays with the contacts pointing downward. They do not have to be precisely vertical but this general attitude prevents water build-up between contacts or its ingress into an unsealed relay.

ISO relays are usually rated at 30 Amps but in fact, because this is specified at the maximum under-bonnet temperature found in modern cars of 275°F (135°C), in the cooler temperatures found in MGBs they have greater current capability. Manufacturers state that their versions of this relay have continuous ratings of 40 Amps at 185°F (85°C) and 35 Amps at 257°F (125°C) with an allowable 3 second peak in-rush of 120A and a current interrupt capability of 60A for the NO contacts.

The normally closed (NC) contact 87a, where fitted, is less used and often has a lower current carrying capability (nominally 20A) compared to the NO contact.

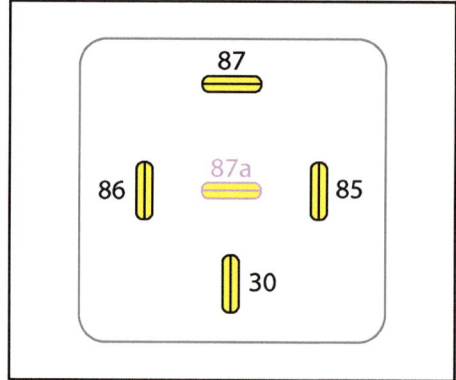

Figure A1.3. The relay terminal layout.

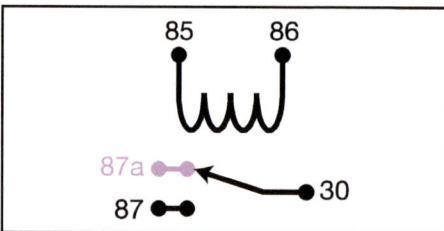

Figure A1.4. The ISO relay internal circuit.

4-terminal relays are often listed as SPST-NO (single pole, single throw-normally open) or as 1-Form A.

5-terminal relays are listed as SPDT (single pole, double throw) or 1-Form C. They can always be used instead of a 4-terminal, but the reverse is not true.

Figure A1.3 shows the base view and terminal layout. Terminal 87a, which connects to the NC contact, will not be present on a 4-terminal device. Each terminal is 1/8 inch (6.35mm) wide and 7/16 inch (11mm) long. The internal circuit can be seen in Figure A1.4. Some relays have a resistor placed across the coil.

Just like the ignition coil, the relay coil is capable of producing high voltage spikes when suddenly disconnected and the resistor's purpose is to damp these down or 'snub' them, indeed it is often referred to in relay catalogues as a snubber resistor. It is unlikely that a relay will be in such close proximity to anything electronic that it can cause any damage in an MGB, so a snubber resistor is not essential, but if included in the relay, it will certainly do no harm either.

The contact arrangements for the original relays are shown on pages 82 and 95. The internal circuit for the circular relay is like that of the ISO relay shown in Figure A1.4, with the exceptions that there is never an 87a contact and the terminal shown as 30 is often marked 30/51.

Coil resistance

The full ISO relay has a coil resistance of about 90Ω so that at 12V it draws approximately 0.13A. By contrast, the rectangular relay originally fitted to early MGBs has a coil resistance of 35Ω, consuming some 0.34A at 12V, while the circular relay used in later cars has a resistance of 50Ω, so that at 12V it uses draws about 0.24A. There are smaller relays than the ISO available with even higher resistance coils. Manufacturers increase the coil resistance so as to reduce its power consumption because that results in less internal heating, which allows the contacts to carry more current. In the MGB, the ability of a modern relay to operate at a lower coil current can be a disadvantage, making it more susceptible to being inadvertently operated by a sneak current, see pages 26 and 94.

Appendix 2
Diodes

RECTIFIER DIODES

A small number of diodes can be found in MGB/Cs, they are used in the alternator, in the handbrake warning light circuit and in some fuel pumps. In order to understand their operation it is useful to use a hydraulic analogy.

Figure A2.1 shows a section of pipe with two areas A and C separated by a flap valve B. When the pressure at A is somewhat greater than that at C, the valve will be forced open and fluid can flow from A to C.

In Figure A2.2, the pressure differential has been reversed so that the area of the pipe C is now at a higher pressure than that at A. Now the flap valve B is tightly shut and no current can flow.

A diode is rather like a electrical version of such a valve, allowing electrical current to flow in one direction only.

Figure A2.3 shows the electrical symbol for a rectifier diode — that is a diode used to convert alternating current (ac) to direct current (dc). When the anode, always represented by a triangle, is more positive than the cathode, represented by the bar, the current 'I' can flow from the anode to the cathode.

If, as in Figure A2.4, the polarity is reversed, so that the cathode is more positive than the anode, the diode blocks current flow.

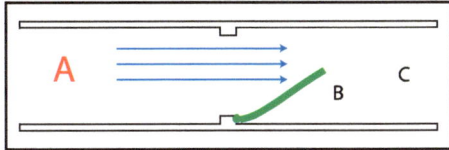

Figure A2.1. A hydraulic valve can pass current from the high pressure side A to the low pressure side C by moving flap valve B.

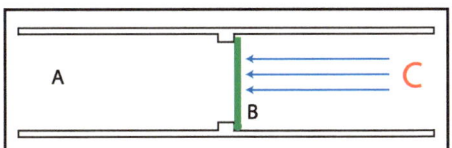

Figure A2.2. When the area C is at a higher pressure than A, the flap valve B blocks flow.

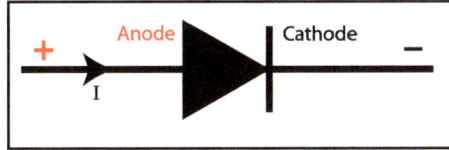

Figure A2.3. A diode works in a similar way to the hydraulic valve. When the voltage is more positive at the anode, current can flow.

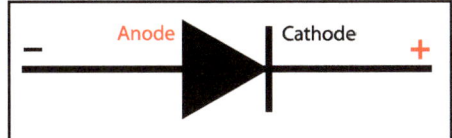

Figure A2.4. With the voltage reversed so that the cathode is the more positive, no current flows.

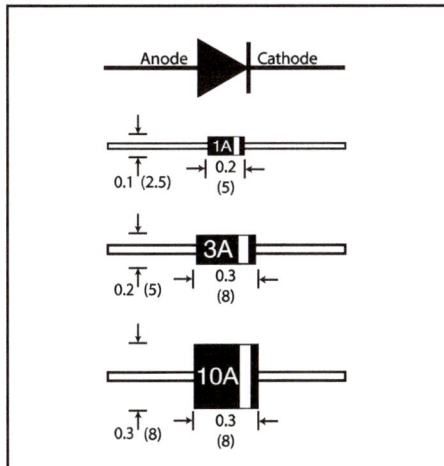

Figure A2.5. The electrical symbol for a rectifier diode (top) and the comparative sizes of three real diodes, Dimensions in inches and (mm).

While the electrical symbol uses a bar to represent the cathode, on a real diode it is indicated by a ring at one end as shown in Figure A2.5.

Note that in Figure A2.1, the flap valve and its seat restrict the flow to some extent so that there will be a pressure drop across it. The electrical diode also restricts current flow somewhat such that there is always some voltage (electrical pressure) drop, or loss, across it. In the case of the most common diodes, those made from silicon, the drop is about 0.6V -0.7V. This is not an insignificant amount. Should a current of 10A be flowing, power will be generated in the diode as heat; the value of which would be:

$$0.6V \times 10A = 6W.$$

If the diode is not large enough or is insufficiently thermally connected to something else, it may gain heat faster than it can lose it, heating more and more until it destroys itself. For that reason, one of the most important diode selection parameters is the current rating.

OVER-VOLTAGE DIODES

Referring again to Figure A2.2, it is obvious that the flap valve can only block so much pressure and if that at C is continuously increased, a point will be reached when the valve will be forced open and reverse current will avalanche over the valve. It is, however, easy to envisage a device that, with some restriction to the maximum reverse flow, could repeatedly break down under reverse pressure without permanent damage; indeed, such items are common and are known as pressure-relief or safety valves.

Electrical diodes can only take so much electrical pressure too and will also break-down if the reverse voltage is raised too high. Just like the hydraulic valve, so long as some restriction in the form of a resistor is placed in the circuit to limit the maximum reverse current and/or the time that current is allowed to flow is limited, then the diode can pass the reverse current repeatedly and without permanent damage. Diodes are often operated like this, under reverse polarity (or bias) so that they act rather like pressure relief valves, shunting current away in the event that the circuit voltage rises to a higher than predetermined level. Such diodes are variously known as zener diodes, silicon avalanche diodes (SADs), transorbs and transient voltage suppressor

Figure A2.6. The electrical symbol for a diode used to protect against over-voltage.

(TVS) diodes. They can be recognized in circuit diagrams by the modified symbol shown in Figure A2.6. TVS diodes are used in some fuel pumps (see page 168) while some alternators have a zener diode in them to protect the voltage regulator from damage due to high transient voltages. Indeed, the alternator voltage regulator incorporates a zener diode to set the maximum charge voltage.

SELECTING AND USING DIODES

Ordinary silicon rectifier diodes used in the projects in this book are very inexpensive; several can be bought for the price of a hamburger. The common diodes, which are available from several manufacturers and many sales sources, are listed in Table A2.1 and the typical sizes are illustrated in Figure A2.5.

Although the maximum constant voltage that will ever be found in any MGB/C is less than 16V, the charging and ignition systems can generate some short high-voltage spikes. For that reason it is not recommended that rectifier diodes with a voltage rating of less than 50V are used. Higher voltage diodes may cost a fraction more and can be used without affecting circuit operation.

Higher current diodes may be needed for some applications. They are harder to find in the consumer market. Look for part numbers such as 6A05 through 6A19 for 6A devices and 10A01 through 10A04 for 10A devices, both series from Diodes Inc. Maplin in the UK and other distributors elsewhere offer 6A diodes under part number P600. Any diode with a current rating larger than 10A is likely to be in a format that requires it to be bolted to a heat sink.

Diodes can be connected in parallel with one another to increase the total current rating. Because of the difficulty of getting heat away from diodes in a bundle, derate them to about 80% of the total current so that, for example, five 1A diodes equate to:

$$80\% \text{ of } 5 \times 1A = 4A$$

Figure A2.7 is a representation of three diodes joined in parallel and soldered together. When forming the

Type	Current	Voltage
1N4001	1A	50V
1N4002	1A	100V
1N4003	1A	200V
1N4004	1A	400V
1N5400	3A	50V
1N5401	3A	100V
1N5402	3A	200V
1N5403	3A	400V

Table A2.1. Some generic low current diodes part numbers and parameters.

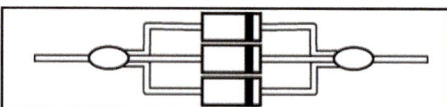

Figure A2.7. Diodes can be soldered in parallel with one another to arrive at a higher current rating.

wire leads of a diode, or any other electrical component, try not to bend them too closely to the device body, otherwise a leakage path for moisture or some internal damage might result.

A convenient method of installing a 1N4002 equivalent diode is as a plug-in mini-fuse (see page 45) style device that can fit into an in-line fuse holder like that illustrated in Figure 7.10. This type of diode, illustrated in Figure A2.8, is made by Littelfuse, Inc. and sold under part number 240113. If can be purchased at Ford spares departments where it is known as the A/C clutch relay diode, in which application it is always located in the under-bonnet power distribution box.

Note the arrowed protrusion close to the anode, designed to prevent reverse insertion into its dedicated cavity in a fuse block. This safety feature will not work when it is plugged into an ordinary fuse holder, so care must be taken to orientate it correctly.

Figure A2.8. A plug-in diode.

ALSO FROM VELOCE PUBLISHING –

Available again after a long absence! Covers all aspects of improving these classic cars for today's road conditions, and for higher performance.

ISBN: 978-1-84584-187-4
Paperback • 25x20.7cm • £40* UK/$70* USA • 224 pages • 494 colour pictures

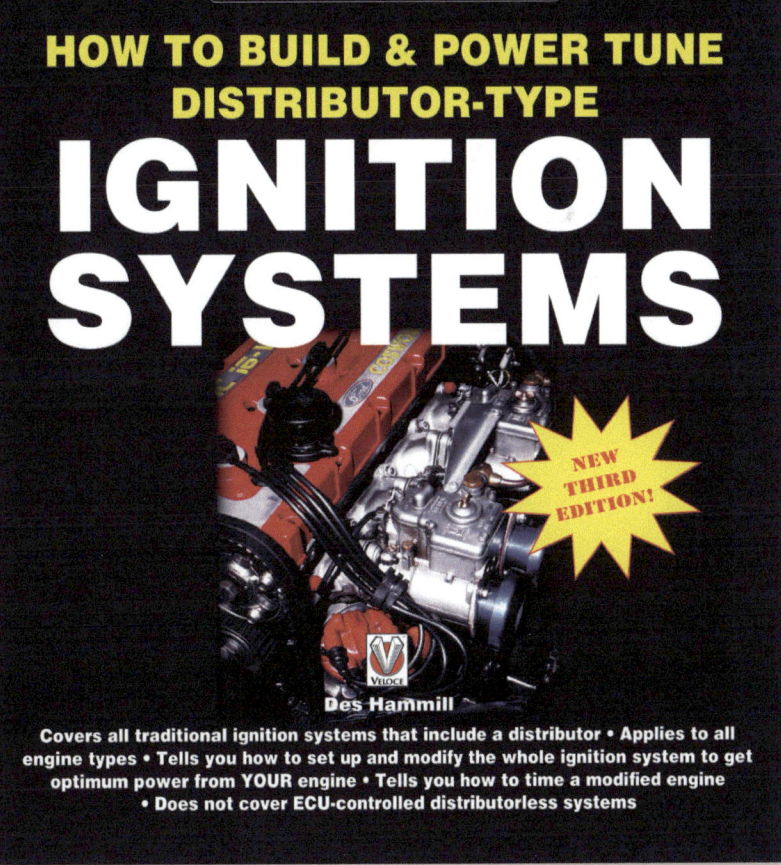

How to build an excellent ignition system and optimise the ignition timing of any high-performance engine. Applies to four-stroke engines with distributor-type ignition systems (including electronic ignition modules). Does not cover engines controlled by ECUs.

ISBN: 978-1-84584-186-7
Paperback • 25x20.7cm • £16.99* UK/$33.95* USA • 80 pages • 98 colour and b&w pictures

For more info on Veloce titles, visit our website at www.veloce.co.uk • email: info@veloce.co.uk • Tel: +44(0)1305 260068
* prices subject to change, p&p extra

ALSO FROM VELOCE PUBLISHING –

All you need to know about getting maximum performance for road and track from the MGB 4-cylinder B-Series engine.

ISBN: 978-1-84584615-2
Paperback • 25x20.7cm • £27.50* UK/$44.95* USA • 144 pages • 100 pictures

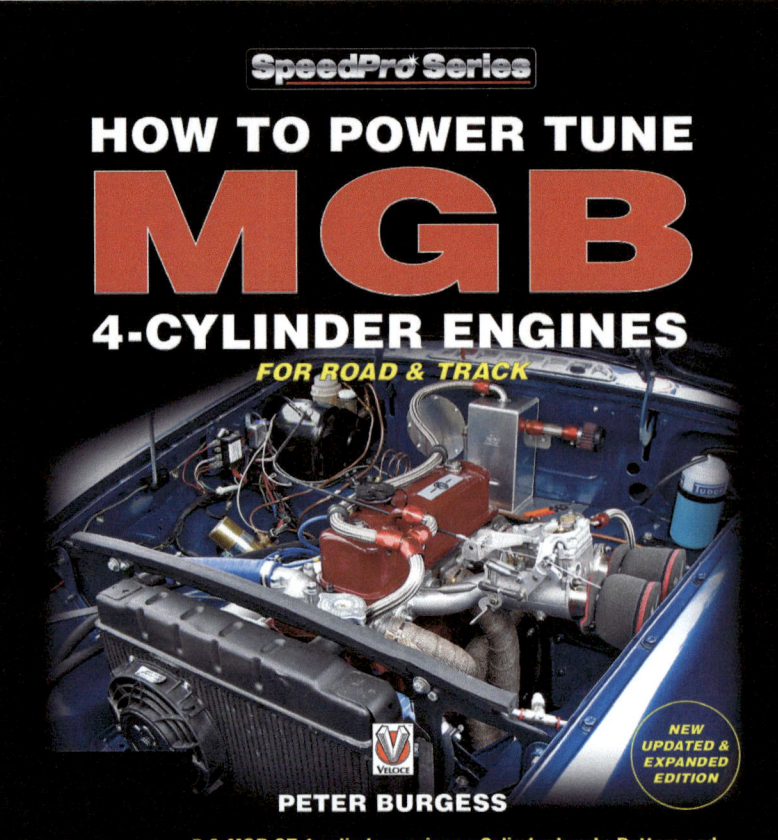

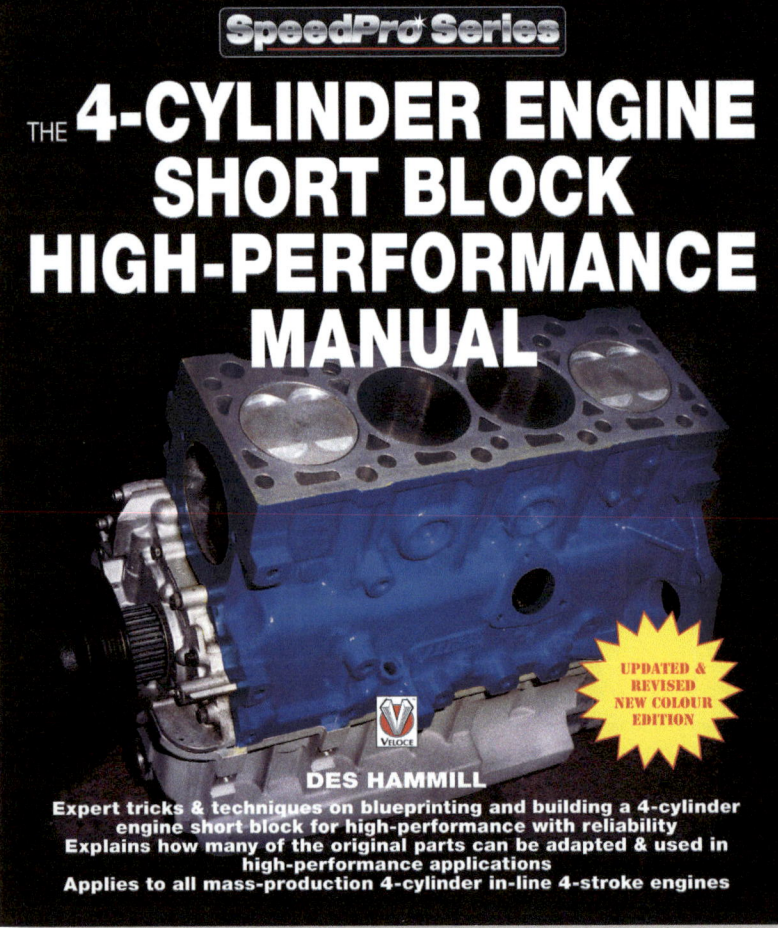

Blueprint the short block of a 4-cylinder, four-stroke engine for maximum performance & reliability, without wasting money! Gives guidance on choosing bearings, crank, cylinder block, con-rods, pistons, camshaft, balancing, expert check-build procedures, and much more.

ISBN: 978-1-845844-14-1
Paperback • 25x20.7cm • £17.99* UK/$32.95* USA • 112 pages • 195 colour pictures

For more info on Veloce titles, visit our website at www.veloce.co.uk • email: info@veloce.co.uk • Tel: +44(0)1305 260068
* prices subject to change, p&p extra

190

Index

Acid burns 9
Ah 48
Air conditioning 181
Alternator 65
    brushes 68
    fault-finding 75
    regulator 69
    service 67
    testing 67
Ammeter 157
Amp – defined 18
Anti run-on 27, 109
Automatic transmission 135, 141

Ballast resistor 95, 96
Battery 48
    charging 49
    discharge 50
    disconnect switch 54
    dual to single conversion 52
    electrolyte 51
    failure 54
    fault-finding 56
    group size 49, 53
    problems 50
    ratings 48
    safety 9
    temperature effects 50
    testing and maintenance 51
    under-bonnet location 54
Brake lamps 129
    balance warning 131
    switch 130

CCA 48
Centrifugal ignition advance 99
Charging system 57
Circuit breaker 46, 178
Circuit tester 11
Clock 10, 56, 157
Component codes 38
Connectors 13
    blade 13
        crimping 14
    bullet 13
        soldering 13
    earthing 15
    IDC 16
Contact-breaker 103, 104
Control box 62
    adjustment 64
Cooling & heating fans 178
    aftermarket 180
    carburettor 181
    circuit breaker 178
    thermostat 178
Corrosion 20
Courtesy lamps 133

Daytime running lamps 115, 122
Diodes 187
    over-voltage 188
    rectifier 187
    selection 188
Dip beam switch 120
Distributor 97
    25D 97

45D 98
35D 99
    advance mechanisms 99
    capacitor 87, 98
    CEI 93, 98
    condenser 87, 98
    contact-breaker 102, 103, 104
    clamp 102
    drive gear 105
    drive orientation 102, 105
    dwell angle 102
    OPUS 93, 99
Distributor points 102, 103, 104
    rotor arm 98
Dynamo 59
    alternator – conversion to 72
    armature 61
    brushes 61
    control box 62
    fault-finding 65
    field coils 61
    service 60
    testing 59

Electric cooling fan 177
Earth strap 28
Electric shock 9
Electrical theory 18
Electrical units 18
Electronic ignition 88
Emergency repairs 22

Filament lamps 115

Fire 10
Flasher 125
    hazard 125
    module 125
Fuel pump 166
    adjustment 169
    aftermarket 171
    capacitor 168
    contacts 169
    diode 168, 170
    electronic 167, 170
    fault-finding 172
    identification 167
    operation 167
Fuel pump polarity 170
    venting 171
Fuse 42
    block 45
    holders 45
    line 43
    rating 41
    selecting value 44
    technology 41
    types 45
Fusing architecture 41

Gauges 144
    moving iron 144
    thermal 145
    voltage regulator 145

Halogen bulbs 120
Handbrake warning lamp 131
Harness 29, 30
    tape 16
Hazard flashers 125
Headlamps 121
    beam alignment 121
    daytime running 115, 122
    halogen 121
    relays 122
Heat burns 9
Heat shrink tubing 17
Heated backlight 184
Heater fan 181
Horn 173
    circuit – improving 174
    construction 173
    fault-finding 177
    volume 175

Ignition 86
    advance mechanisms 99
    ballast resistor 95
    coil 94, 96
    contact-breaker 103, 104
    conventional 86
    distributor 97
    dwell angle 102, 103, 104
    electronic 88
    fault-finding 113
    firing order 106
    relay 93
    rotor arm 98
    spark polarity 111
    sparkplugs 109
    timing 106
    wires 111
Ignition switch 25, 112
Inhibitor switch 141
Instrumentation 144
    ammeter 157
Instrumentation circuit 149
    clock 157
    fault-finding 150
    gauges 144
    senders 147
    tachometer 151
    voltage regulator 145
    voltmeter 157

Jump starting 52
Jumper wires 13

Lamps 115
    back-up 135
    brake 129
    brightness 114
    courtesy 133
    daytime running 115, 122
    dip switch 120
    earthing – improving 132
    filament 115
    halogen 120
    hazard flasher 125
    headlamps 121
    LED 117
    reversing 135, 141
    side markers 118, 120
    stop 129
    turn-signal 125
    voltage – effect of 116
Light bulb chart 136
Lighting 115
    fault-finding 136
    switches 119

Manifold heater 184
Motor and generators 57
Multimeter 12

Ohm – defined 18
Overdrive 137
    circuit 137, 139
    flip-on/off circuit 142
    problems 139
    switches 139
    warning lamp 143

Parking brake warning lamp 131
Positive to negative conversion 72
PTC 47, 56, 147

Radiator fan circuit 178, 179
    adding relays 178
Radio 56, 183
Relays 82, 93, 185
Reversing lamps 135
    switch 135, 140, 141
Rotor arm 98

Safety 9
Screwdrivers 11
Sealed beam units 25, 121
Senders 147
    fuel 147
    oil pressure 148
    temperature 148
Sequential seatbelt system 183
Sneak currents 26, 94
Spark polarity 111
Sparkplugs 109
    gap 110
    heat range 109
Speedometer 156
    calibration 156
    operation 156
Starter 77
    circuit 79
    fault-finding 85
    inhibitor switch 135
    motor 83
    relay 82
    remote switch 85
    solenoid 79
    system 76
Stop lamps 129
Stop/turn signals – improving 133

Tachometer 151
    calibration 155
    fault-finding 156
Tape – insulating 16
Thermostat – radiator fan 177
Timing light 108
Tools 11
Toxic gas 10
Turn signals 125
    audible 129

Vacuum ignition advance 101
Volt – defined 18
Voltage regulator 62, 69, 145
Voltmeter 10, 157

Watt – defined 18
Windscreen washer 164
Wiper and washer fault-finding 163
Wiper motor 156, 161
Wipers and washers 158
    auto park 159, 160, 162
    fault-finding 165
    motor – single speed 159
    motor – two speed 162
Wire 12, 40
    colours 29, 31
    handling 12
    harness 29, 30
    joining 15, 25
    protection 16
    sizes 40
Wires & components 29